The Routledge International Handbook of Forensic Intelligence and Criminology

Despite a shared focus on crime and its 'extended family', forensic scientists and criminologists tend to work in isolation rather than sharing the data, methods and knowledge that will broaden the understanding of the criminal phenomenon and its related subjects.

Bringing together perspectives from international experts, this book explores the intersection between criminology and forensic science and considers how knowledge from both fields can contribute to a better understanding of crime and offer new directions in theory and methodology.

This handbook is divided into three parts:

- Part I explores the epistemological and historical components of criminology and forensic science, focusing on their scientific and social origins.
- Part II considers how collaboration between these disciplines can bring about a better understanding of the organizations and institutions that react to crime, including the court, intelligence, prevention, crime scene investigation and policing.
- Part III discusses the phenomena and actors that produce crime, including a reflection on the methodological issues, challenges and rewards regarding the sharing of these two disciplines.

The objective of this handbook is to stimulate a 'new' interdisciplinary take on the study of crime, to show how both forensic and criminological theories and knowledge can be combined to analyse crime problems and to open new methodological perspectives. It will be essential reading for students and researchers engaged with forensic science, criminology, criminal behaviour, criminal investigation, crime analysis and criminal justice.

Quentin Rossy is Assistant Professor at the École des sciences criminelles Université de Lausanne, Switzerland.

David Décary-Hétu is Assistant Professor at the École de criminologie Université de Montréal, Canada.

Olivier Delémont is Full Professor at the École des sciences criminelles Université de Lausanne, Switzerland.

Massimiliano Mulone is Associate Professor at the École de criminologie Université de Montréal, Canada.

The Routledge International Handbook of Forensic Intelligence and Criminology

Edited by Quentin Rossy, David Décary-Hétu, Olivier Delémont and Massimiliano Mulone

Routledge
Taylor & Francis Group
LONDON AND NEW YORK

First published 2018
by Routledge
2 Park Square, Milton Park, Abingdon, Oxon OX14 4RN

and by Routledge
52 Vanderbilt Avenue, New York, NY 10017

First issued in paperback 2020

Routledge is an imprint of the Taylor & Francis Group, an informa business

The cover picture was made by Rodolphe Archibald Reiss (1875–1929, founder of the school of Lausanne), near 1911, when he was teaching in St-Petersburg and Moscow. This board was used to train police officers to understand what should be observed during a control to identify specific burglars known as "Ceiling drillers". Indeed, in the early years of the 20th century, some offenders went upstairs of the targeted premises, made a small hole in the floor, inserted the umbrella and opened it, they could then enlarge the hole (the debris fell down in the umbrella) and finally they used the ladder to go down to commit the theft. The Russian inscription on the board is "The physical evidences collected at the scene of the crime".

British Library Cataloguing-in-Publication Data
A catalogue record for this book is available from the British Library

Library of Congress Cataloging-in-Publication Data
Names: Rossy, Quentin, editor.
Title: The Routledge international handbook of forensic intelligence and criminology / edited by Quentin Rossy, [and three others].
Description: Abingdon, Oxon ; NewYork, NY : Routledge, 2018. |
Series: Routledge international handbooks | Includes bibliographical references and index.
Identifiers: LCCN 2017029096| ISBN 9781138688216 (hardback) |
ISBN 9781315541945 (ebook)
Subjects: LCSH: Forensic sciences. | Criminology.
Classification: LCC HV8073 . R7265 2018 | DDC 363.25—dc23
LC record available at https://lccn.loc.gov/2017029096

ISBN 13: 978-0-367-58100-8 (pbk)
ISBN 13: 978-1-138-68821-6 (hbk)

Typeset in Bembo
by Keystroke, Neville Lodge, Tettenhall, Wolverhampton

Contents

Figures

Tables

Contributors

Simon Baechler holds a PhD in forensic science from the Université de Lausanne, Switzerland. He is deputy chief of the forensic science unit with the Police neuchâteloise, Switzerland. Since 2009, he has investigated various crime scenes and cases, ranging from property crimes to arsons and homicides. He is the chair of the Western Switzerland fraudulent documents working group. Baechler also works part time as the continuing professional education coordinator of the École des sciences criminelles, Université de Lausanne. He is an associate professor at the Université de Québec in Trois-Rivières, Canada, as well as an associate researcher with the Forensic Research Group there. His research and training activities are mainly focused on forensic intelligence and crime analysis, the profiling of false travel and identity documents in the investigation of organized crime groups, and the use of images to support investigation and intelligence efforts. Baechler has published several scientific papers in international journals and has led workshops in different countries on these subjects.

Frederic Been holds a PhD in forensic science from the École des sciences criminelles at the Université de Lausanne, Switzerland. His research focused on evaluating the added value of wastewater analysis as a complementary tool to monitor illicit drug use at the population level. This work consisted in developing instrumental methods for the analysis of wastewater samples and implementing interpretive frameworks, with particular emphasis on triangulating environmental and epidemiological (e.g., surveys, population statistics) data through various modelling approaches. He also designed sampling campaigns and the online measurement of water quality parameters. After completing his PhD, Been was appointed by the Swiss Federal Office of Public Health to plan a nationwide sampling scheme to monitor the use of illicit and prescription drugs via wastewater analysis. Since February 2016 he has been working as a postdoctoral researcher at the Toxicological Centre of the University of Antwerp. His current research focuses on extending the use of wastewater analysis to monitor human health (i.e., exposure to carcinogens and environmental contaminants).

Lisa Benaglia is a PhD student at the École des sciences criminelles of the Université de Lausanne. In 2013, she received her Master's degree in forensic science from this institution, more specifically in chemical criminalistics. She is currently using wastewater analysis as a tool to better understand the dynamics of illicit drugs consumption in specific environments, such as festivals and prisons.

Sonja Bitzer completed a PhD in forensic science at the École des sciences criminelles at the Université de Lausanne, Switzerland, in 2017. Her topic was the use and utility of traces in investigation and the inherent triaging decision involved. Currently, she is working on a postdoctoral project at the National Institute of Criminalistics and Criminology (NICC/INCC) in Brussels, Belgium. In this project, the role of the forensic advisers of the NICC/INCC is formalized in order to assess their contribution to judicial cases, the factors leading to their involvement and their influence on the use of forensic science. This project is funded by the Swiss National Science Foundation. Her main interests are in the definition and understanding of forensic science in different countries, its integration and its use and the evaluation of its effectiveness in the criminal justice process and the general security context.

Rémi Boivin is associate professor at the École de criminologie of the Université de Montréal. He also serves as deputy director of the Centre international de criminologie comparée. His work on crime analysis and police intervention has been published in the *Journal of Quantitative Criminology*, *Journal of Research in Crime and Delinquency* and *Journal of Experimental Criminology*. He has collaborated on joint publications on fake identity documents and drug trafficking as objects of interest to both forensic science and criminology. He recently started a research project on body-worn cameras as an innovative tool generating traces of police interventions.

Stefano Caneppele (PhD) is associate professor at the École des sciences criminelles, Université de Lausanne. Currently, he teaches courses on research methods in criminology, and criminal analysis, economic crime, security governance and terrorism. Until December 2015, he was associate professor at the Catholic University of Milan, Italy, and coordinator of the Master in Security Policies. Since 2002, he has been involved in more than 30 European and national projects on several topics (organized crime, trafficking in firearms, illicit trafficking in tobacco products, terrorism, corruption in public procurement). His research interests include crime prevention, organized crime, economic crime and private/public security.

Christophe Champod received his MSc and PhD, both in forensic science, from the Université de Lausanne, in 1990 and 1995 respectively. From 1999 to 2003, he led the Interpretation Research Group of the Forensic Science Service (UK), before taking a full professorship position at the École des sciences criminelles of the Université de Lausanne. He is in charge of education and research on identification methods and serves as an expert witness in these areas. He is also operational manager of the ISO/SEC 17025 accredited forensic laboratory of the ESC. He serves on the steering committee of the International Fingerprint Research Group (IFRG), is a past member of SWGFAST (Scientific Working Group on Friction Analysis, Study and Technology) and, since 2014, has been an invited member of the Friction Ridge subcommittee (part of the Physics and Pattern Evidence Scientific Area Committee) of the Organization for Scientific Area Committees (OSAC). In 2015, he received the Distinguished ENFSI (European Network of Forensic Science) Scientist Award for his contribution to forensic science. His research is devoted to the inferential aspects associated with forensic identification techniques. The value to be attached to fingerprint evidence is at the core of his interests.

Simon A. Cole is professor of Criminology, Law and Society and director of the Newkirk Center for Science and Society at the University of California, Irvine. He received his PhD in Science and Technology Studies from Cornell University. Dr Cole is the author of *Suspect Identities: A History of Fingerprinting and Criminal Identification* (Harvard University Press, 2001), which was awarded the 2003 Rachel Carson Prize by the Society for Social Studies of Science, and *Truth Machine: The Contentious History of DNA Fingerprinting* (University of Chicago Press, 2008, with Michael Lynch, Ruth McNally and Kathleen Jordan). He is co-editor of the journal *Theoretical Criminology*.

Frank Crispino graduated with a PhD in forensic science from the École des sciences criminelles at the Université de Lausanne, Switzerland, and joined the academy in 2012 after 27 years in the French Gendarmerie. Having served for six years in the forensic lab of the Institut de recherche criminelle de la gendarmerie nationale, he built from scratch counterterrorist forensic capacities in the West Bank and Gaza Strip from 1999 to 2002 under the umbrella of the European Union Special Adviser's Office on Counterterrorism in the West Bank and the Gaza Strip. A graduate of the French War College, he also commanded two criminal investigation departments (organized crime and terrorism) in France and was deputy head of the Antiterrorist Bureau at the General Headquarter of the French Gendarmerie in Paris. He concluded his military career as representative of the Division General in charge of the Pôle judiciaire de la gendarmerie nationale—Forensic and Intelligence Hub of the French Gendarmerie—in order to launch a new forensic academic curriculum at l'Université du Québec à Trois-Rivières (UQTR). Professor Crispino is author or co-author of two books, six book chapters and more than forty peer-reviewed articles. He is the director of the Forensic Research Group at the UQTR and a regular researcher at the Centre international de criminologie comparée.

Maurice Cusson is professor emeritus of the École de criminologie at the Université de Montréal and a researcher at the Centre international de criminologie comparée. He is the author of several books: *Why delinquency?*; *Le contrôle social du crime*; *La Délinquance, une vie choisie*; and *L'Art de la sécurité*, *Les Homicides: criminologie historique de la violence et de la non-violence*. He co-edited the publication of the *Traité de sécurité intérieure* and the *Traité des violences criminelles*.

Cândido da Agra is full professor at the Universidade do Porto. He has an MSc and a PhD from the University of Louvain. Da Agra is the founder of the School of Criminology—Faculty of Law at the university and served as its dean for several years. Currently, he develops and coordinates research projects on epistemology and history of criminology and forensic science, philosophy of law, research methodologies and social control systems. Internationally, he is a member of the Scientific Board of the Groupe européen de recherches sur les normativités. Since 1991, he has collaborated with the Université de Montréal, and he is a research fellow and administrator of the International Society of Criminology at the Centre international de criminologie comparée. He serves on the board of scientific journals such as *Déviance et Société*; *Drogues, Santé et Société*; and *Revue internationale de criminologie et de police technique et scientifique*. In 2014, he received the international Beaumont-Tocqueville prize, awarded by the Association internationale des criminologues de langue française. He is the president of the Portuguese Society of Criminology (SPC) and of the International Association of Portuguese Speaking Countries Criminologists (AICLP).

David Décary-Hétu has a PhD in criminology from the Université de Montréal. He worked as a senior scientist at the École des sciences criminelles of the Université de Lausanne before assuming his current position as an assistant professor at the École de criminologie of the Université de Montréal. His thesis focused on the impact of the Internet on crime as well as on how offenders have adapted to the virtual environment. Décary-Hétu has since continued his research on online illicit markets and is now particularly interested in cryptomarkets, 2nd generation online illicit markets. He has developed the DATACRYPTO tool to collect large amounts of information on cryptomarket participants. His research goals are to better understand the structure of markets and the actors who participate in them as well as to understand their performance in the context of online illicit markets. The results of his research, funded by both the provincial and federal governments, have been published in journals such as the *Journal of Research* *in Crime and Delinquency*, have been presented at numerous conferences and have been disseminated to a wide audience in a number of interviews with the media.

Jan De Kinder worked as a postdoctoral researcher in the field of solid state physics and spectroscopy after obtaining his PhD in science in 1992. In 1996, he was tasked to develop the area of crime scene ballistics/firearms identification at the National Institute of Forensic Science and Criminology. In 2001, he became the head of the Ballistics Section. Since July 2006, De Kinder has been the director-general of the National Institute of Forensic Science and Criminology, a Belgian Federal Scientific Institute. During his career, he has made numerous contributions to scientific journals and serves on a number of scientific committees of international meetings and panels. He was the chair of the European Network of Forensic Science Institutes (ENFSI) from 2009 to 2011, as well as of the International Forensic Strategic Alliance (IFSA) in the periods 2007–2008 and 2009–2010. In May 2014, he was re-elected as the ENFSI chairman-designate and has served as this organization's chair since May 2015.

Olivier Delémont is a professor in forensic science at the École des sciences criminelles of the Université de Lausanne, Switzerland. Between 2003 and 2011, he was employed part-time in the forensic unit of a Swiss state police, where he worked in operational forensic activities. Since his appointment as a professor at the Université de Lausanne in 2005, he has conducted research at regional, national and international levels in relation to several areas of expertise, and in particular crime scene investigation, fire investigation and chemical criminalistics. His research activities and interests cover a wide range of domains in forensic science, and he defines himself as a generalist in his field.

Sabine De Moor holds a master's degree in criminology (Ghent University, 2004), a master's degree in communication studies: media studies (University of Antwerp, 2005) and has done postgraduate work in management and communication (HoGent, 2006). De Moor worked as a researcher at the University of Antwerp and as panel manager and data analyst at iMinds-imec, a Flemish digital research centre, where she conducted quantitative research on diverse topics. She is currently doing a PhD on the strategic implications of forensic DNA databases. Data from the Belgian national DNA database and police recorded crime data are used to evaluate the usefulness of forensic DNA data for criminological research.

Pierre Esseiva is professor at the École des sciences criminelles of the Université de Lausanne. He has an active research and teaching programme with a focus on illicit drugs analysis and especially on the extraction of profiles from street samples in order to highlight connections between seizures and as a way to decipher the structure of criminal organizations. He has also developed expertise in the domain of wastewater-based epidemiology through the combination of the available data related to the illicit drug domain. He has been a member of the Drug Working Group (DWG) of the European Network of Forensic Science Institutes (ENFSI) since its creation in 2003. He has also participated in European projects dedicated to illicit drug profiling, such as the European Drug Profiling System (EDPS), which seeks to harmonize drug profiling and drug intelligence, and CHAMP (Collaborative Harmonization of Methods for Profiling of Amphetamine Type Stimulants), dealing with the development of a harmonized profiling analytical approach. He is also part of the project SCORE (Sewage Analysis CORe group Europe), bringing together experts from relevant disciplines interested in the application and development of wastewater analysis for evaluating lifestyle, health and exposure at the community level.

Francis Fortin is assistant professor at the Université de Montréal and researcher at the Centre international de criminologie comparée of that university. His research focuses on cybercrime, criminal intelligence, data mining and forensic analysis. His publications include scientific papers and one book on cyberpedophiles and another on cybercrime. He has also worked in the field of criminal investigations and intelligence for 15 years.

James French is a teaching fellow at the Department of Security and Crime Science at University College London, where he has been based since he completed his PhD at UCL in 2013. He teaches undergraduate and postgraduate students and, as part of the interdisciplinary UCL Centre for the Forensic Sciences, he is involved in a number of research projects in various fields of forensic science. His principle research interests include trace physical evidence, evidence dynamics and the interpretation of forensic evidence, particularly the use of Bayesian Networks for reasoning about forensic evidence. A major area of interest is the use of gunshot residue (GSR) in forensic investigations, and French's experimental work on the secondary and tertiary transfer of GSR has considered the implications of these dynamics for the investigation of firearms offences.

Jean-Pierre Guay is a professor with the Université de Montréal École de criminologie and a senior researcher at the Institut Philippe-Pinel de Montréal. He holds a PhD in criminology from the Université de Montréal, and completed two years of postdoctoral studies at the Department of Psychology, Brandeis University, in Massachusetts. His research focuses mainly on measuring criminal phenomena, including the risk of re-offending, psychopathy and membership in street gangs. He has been teaching evaluative research, statistics and risk assessment issues at the Université de Montréal École de criminologie since 1999.

Manon Jendly is associate professor in the École des sciences criminelles at the Université de Lausanne, Switzerland. Her research interests include crime prevention, prison and probation. She is currently involved in an evaluation of probation practices in the French part of Switzerland; an international project on health interventions in prison together with colleagues in Canada, France and Belgium; and a cross-comparative study on criminal justice professions in Switzerland and Belgium. Her work aims to develop a more comprehensive and sustainable approach to social reactions to crime.

Patrick P.J.M.H. Jeuniaux was a researcher at the National Institute of Forensic Science and Criminology (NICC/INCC), in Brussels, Belgium. At the NICC, he focused on the analysis of databases (e.g., forensic DNA databases, judicial expenses records and law-enforcement databases). He holds a BA and an MA in psychology (UCL, Belgium, 1999), a degree in statistics (UCL, 2000), a degree in artificial intelligence (KU Leuven, Belgium, 2004) and a PhD in psycholinguistics (University of Memphis, US, 2009). Before entering the NICC/INCC, he conducted research in the areas of pedagogy, psychology and computational linguistics at UCL, KU Leuven, the University of Memphis and Université Laval (Québec, Canada). He now works at University of Pisa, Italy.

Roberta Julian (PhD) is an associate professor in the School of Social Sciences and director of the Tasmanian Institute of Law Enforcement Studies (TILES) at the University of Tasmania, Australia, where she teaches and conducts research in policing and criminology. Over the past decade, she has developed an innovative programme of social science research in the field of forensic studies/forensic criminology that has attracted postgraduate students from Australia and overseas. Since 2002, she has been chief investigator on various projects examining knowledge and awareness of forensic science by criminal justice actors and the social processes that underpin the use of forensic evidence in criminal investigations. More recently, she was the lead CI on an Australian Research Council Linkage Project with the Victoria Police, the Australian Federal Police (AFP) and the National Institute of Forensic Science (NIFS) that examined the effectiveness of forensic science in the criminal justice system. Julian is president of the Tasmanian branch of the Australian and New Zealand Forensic Science Society (ANZFSS), a member of the Board of Studies of the Australian Institute of Police Management (AIPM), a regional representative for the Australian Institute of Professional Intelligence Officers (AIPIO) and a past president of The Australian Sociological Association (TASA).

Paul Knepper is professor of criminology in the Department of Law and Justice at Central Washington University and visiting professor of criminology at the University of Lausanne. He is the author of *Writing the History of Crime* (Bloomsbury, 2016) and editor, along with Anja Johansen, of *The Oxford Handbook of the History of Crime and Criminal Justice* (Oxford University Press, 2016). Recent work combining forensic science and criminology includes a chapter entitled 'Theorising a Forensic Model of Crime Prevention', in Danielle Reynalds and Benoit Leclerc, eds., *Criminology at the Edge: The Future of Rational Choice for Crime Prevention* (Routledge, in press).

Benoit Leclerc is associate professor of criminology and criminal justice at Griffith University, Brisbane, Australia. His research interests include the application and development of crime script analysis for purposes of situational prevention, including the prevention of sexual offending. He is the lead investigator of 'What Works, What Doesn't, and What Is Promising for Preventing Sexual Violence and Abuse: The Effectiveness of Situational Prevention', a project funded by the Australian Research Council.

Pierre Margot fell early into the cauldron of forensic science by obtaining a combined degree in forensic science and criminology at the Université de Lausanne in 1974. A short spell in the UK attracted him to pursue an MSc followed by a PhD in forensic science at Strathclyde University in Glasgow. Postdoctoral research led him from Salt Lake City (US) in forensic toxicology at the Center for Human Toxicology (University of Utah), to the Federal Institute of Technology (EPFL) in Lausanne (research in chromatography) and to the Australian National University in Canberra to pursue research and development in dactyloscopy. He is the fourth professor to occupy the first academic chair in forensic science, created in 1909 at the Université de Lausanne. One of his major contributions is a research centre where over 60 PhD theses have been completed in the last 20 years. The centre is committed to the further development of this discipline as a key actor of forensic intelligence, investigative science and the provision of solid and measurable evidence in court. His group has published over 220 peer-reviewed papers in forensic science within the last 10 years. Margot's contributions to forensic science are internationally acclaimed, with major awards such as the Douglas M. Lucas Medal of the American Academy of Forensic Sciences, a doctorate honoris causa from the Université de Québec in Trois-Rivières (Canada), and accession to the French-speaking pantheon of criminalistics, ENFSI (European Network of Forensic Science) Contributor Award. Margot is associate editor of *Forensic Science International*, the major scientific journal in forensic science.

Carlo Morselli is a professor at the École de criminologie, Université de Montréal, and director of the Centre international de criminologie comparée (ICCC/CICC). His research focuses on criminal networks and organized crime, with recent studies aimed specifically at illegal firearms markets, collusion in the construction industry and denunciation. In 2011, he was awarded the Outstanding Publication Award from the International Association for the Study of Organized Crime for his book *Inside Criminal Networks* (Springer, 2009). He is also the author and co-editor of *Contacts, Opportunities, and Criminal Enterprise* (University of Toronto Press, 2005), *Crime and Networks* (Routledge, 2014), *Les réseaux criminels* (Presses de l'Université de Montréal, 2016), and a series of articles that have been published in *Criminology*; *Journal of Research in Crime and Delinquency*; *Critical Criminology*; *Crime, Law, and Social Change*; and *Social Networks*. Since 2011, he has served as the editor-in-chief for the journal *Global Crime*.

Massimiliano Mulone is associate professor at the École de criminologie, Université de Montréal, and a researcher at the Centre international de criminologie comparée. Working in the field of policing and security studies, his main research investigates the commodification of security—how policing and security are progressively being transformed from a collective to a private good—and its consequences on the governance of security. The private security industry, the commercialization of police services, public–private security partnerships, the dynamics of security consumption and private military companies' apparatus are among his objects of inquiry. Other topics of interest include the policing of protest and the control of police deviance.

Glenn Porter is an associate professor in criminology at University New England (Australia). His previous academic and professional experience includes head of Creative Arts and Media at James Cook University, head of program of the Bachelor of Science (Forensic Science) degree at the Western Sydney University and a forensic photographer with the Australian Federal Police. Porter studied photography at the Sydney Institute of Technology and his postgraduate qualifications include a Graduate Diploma in Science from the University of Sydney, a Master of Applied Science (Photography) from RMIT University and a PhD in communication arts from Western Sydney University. Porter has been awarded the Accredited Senior Imaging Scientist (ASIS) distinction, Fellow of the Royal Photographic Society (FRPS) and Research Fellow of The Cairns Institute. Porter has worked for more than two decades within forensic criminology as a practitioner, academic and researcher. His current research interests include how images are considered and form forensic evidence within the criminal justice system. Porter's evidence has been heard or presented in various courts and jurisdictions, including the District and Supreme Courts of NSW, Coroners Court of NSW, NSW Court of Criminal Appeal, High Court of Australia and the United Nations Human Rights Council.

Bertrand Renard has been a researcher in the Department of Criminology of the NICC/INCC since 1997. He has research expertise on organized crime, use of information and databases, technologies in criminal investigation, judicial expertise, in particular with forensic DNA, and management in criminal justice. He obtained his PhD in criminology (2008) at Université catholique de Louvain (UCL, Belgium) and wrote a dissertation entitled 'What Does DNA Make Justice Do—Translational Sociology of the Identification by Genetic Analysis in Penal Justice'. Since 2009, Renard has been a visiting professor at the Faculty of Law and Criminology at UCL. He is an associate-member of the Centre of Interdisciplinary Research on Deviation and Penalty (CRID&P–UCL). He is the coordinator of the Be-Gen project and oversees the first work package (WP1) in which the operational implications of forensic DNA in Belgium will be assessed.

Olivier Ribaux is a full professor of forensic intelligence at the École des sciences criminelles, Université de Lausanne, Switzerland, and since 2014, has been the school's director. Previously, he was employed at a Swiss canton's police department as a crime analyst. His task was to develop and implement a methodology for linking crimes that cross Swiss jurisdictions. He then joined the university to conduct research on the contribution of forensic science to intelligence-led policing. His studies range from the formalization of methods to the development of computerized tools, mostly for the analysis of repetitive crimes. He trains students, law enforcement officers and magistrates in crime analysis and forensic intelligence. He is the author of many peer-reviewed scientific publications, book chapters, and a book on forensic intelligence, *Police scientifique. Le renseignement par la trace.*

Luc Robert is a researcher at the National Institute of Forensic Science and Criminology (NICC/INCC), Brussels, Belgium. His research interests are imprisonment, prisoner release, recidivism and, more recently, criminal careers.

Quentin Rossy, professor in crime analysis, is the respondent for the master's program in Traceology and Crime Analysis at the Université de Lausanne, which is a shared program with the École de criminologie of the Université de Montréal. He is a former crime analyst with the Police neuchâteloise (Switzerland), where he developed the shared platform currently in use by the crime intelligence units of seven Swiss police departments to detect and analyse serial crimes. As a criminal intelligence analyst, he has been involved in national and international investigations related to serial and organized crime. He developed many CPD-type programmes in crime analysis, criminal intelligence analysis and forensic intelligence for law enforcement officers, intelligence analysts and magistrates in Switzerland and in Europe. His research interests include the contribution of forensic science to crime analysis, the use of visualization methods in crime analysis and the role of Internet traces to monitor and analyse online crimes.

Claude Roux migrated to Australia in 1996 after completing his undergraduate and PhD studies in forensic science at the Université de Lausanne, Switzerland. Roux has been pivotal to the development of forensic science in his adopted country over the past 21 years by developing and leading the first undergraduate degree and PhD programme in forensic science. He is currently professor of forensic science and director of the Centre for Forensic Science at the University of Technology Sydney (UTS). His professional motivation has been largely driven by his vision of forensic science as a distinctive academic and holistic research-based discipline. Throughout his career, Roux has published over 160 refereed papers, 25 book chapters and a large number of conference presentations. He is a member of the editorial board of six scientific journals and of a number of working and advisory groups. He was president of the Australian and New Zealand Forensic Science Society (ANZFSS) from 2010 to 2016. He is the current vice-president of the Australian Academy of Forensic Sciences and a fellow of the Royal Society of New South Wales. Between 2014 and 2016, he also served on the Scientific Advisory Board of the International Criminal Court, The Haag, the Netherlands.

Caroline Stappers earned her bachelor's degree (2012) and master's degree (2013) in criminology from the Katholieke Universiteit (KU) Leuven. Since 2014, she has been working as a junior researcher at the National Institute of Forensic Science and Criminology (NICC/INCC) in Belgium. Her focus of interest is police and judicial investigation. She is involved in a research project examining the operational, strategic and political implications of forensic DNA in criminal cases. She is working toward the completion of her PhD and is also an affiliated junior researcher at the KU Leuven, where she studies the effectiveness and efficiency of the use of forensic DNA in Belgium.

Nick Tilley is a professor within UCL's Jill Dando Institute of Security and Crime Science. He is also an adjunct professor in the Griffith Criminology Institute, Brisbane and emeritus professor of sociology at Nottingham Trent University. His long-term research interests concern policing, crime prevention, programme evaluation methodology, and the use of science to inform improvements in policy and practice. Recent projects relate to the international drop in crime rate, what works in crime reduction and the prevention of youth-related sexual abuse and violence. He was awarded an OBE for services to policing and crime reduction in the Queen's Birthday Honours in 2005 and elected a Fellow of the Academy of the Social Sciences (FAcSS) in 2009.

Vanessa Vanvooren holds a PhD in biomedical sciences. She was hired by the National Institute of Forensic Science and Criminology (NICC/INCC) as an expert at the Belgian National DNA database in 2004, and was the custodian of the database beginning in 2006. Vanvooren was responsible for handling requests made by magistrates to the database and the reporting of the results. From 2006, she was involved in the process of making Belgium Prüm operational for forensic DNA and in drafting new legislation on DNA. She also directed organizational and computer-based innovations of the management of the database. Since 2016, she has been the manager of the biology unit at the NICC/INCC. Vanessa is a member of the European Network of Forensic Science Institutes (ENFSI) working group.

Joëlle Vuille is privat-docent at the Faculty of Law of the University of Neuchâtel (Switzerland), where she teaches evaluation of evidence. She holds a Master's degree in Swiss law and a PhD in criminology from the Université de Lausanne (Switzerland) and spent two years as a post-doctoral researcher at the University of California, Irvine. She has written articles, book sections and scientific reports in the fields of admissibility of scientific evidence and its evaluation by the courts, and the use of probabilities in the judicial context. She regularly gives conferences and short talks on these topics in academic settings and at national and international institutions (Council of Europe, Interpol, European Network of Forensic Science Institutes, École Nationale de la Magistrature). She is currently conducting a research project funded by the Swiss National Science Foundation to investigate the contribution of flawed scientific evidence to miscarriages of justice in Europe.

Frank Zobel is a sociologist and public health researcher. He is currently deputy director at Addiction Switzerland, the largest centre for substance use epidemiology in the country. His former positions were with the European Monitoring Centre for Drugs and Drug Addiction in Lisbon, as policy analyst and coordinator of the European Drug Report and, with the University Institute of Social and Preventive Medicine in Lausanne, as external evaluator of the Swiss drug strategy. His current research includes the structure and size of the drug market, international models for the regulation of cannabis markets and the implementation of the Swiss law on narcotics. Zobel is also a member of the national advisory board for addiction issues in Switzerland and of the scientific board of the French Monitoring Centre for Drugs and Drug Addiction (OFDT).

Acknowledgements

This collection is the result of an international collaborative process. We would like to thank all of the contributors for their leading research, for accepting the challenge to formalize relationships between forensic science and criminology and thus opening innovative perspectives, for having taken time to join us in this venture, and for their prompt and kind attention to the editorial process. We are especially grateful for the wonderful support and assistance given by Kate Merriman in copy editing all the chapters. We also thank all the staff at Keystroke for the second copy editing. The editors and authors acknowledge the permission granted by several copyright holders for the reproductions and extracts of already published materials. At Routledge, we thank Thomas Sutton for giving us the opportunity to publish this handbook, Hannah Catterall for her patience, assistance and commitment to the book, and all individuals who have worked behind the scenes to produce this book. We also thank the International Relations Offices of the Universities of Lausanne and Montreal for their support to promote student and staff exchanges as well as many joint research projects such as this handbook. Finally, we thank Olivier Ribaux, a trailblazer for the development of research and practices that combine forensic science and criminology, particularly through the field of forensic intelligence. Thank you for your support, your work and the opportunity to carry out this collaborative work.

Introduction

Massimiliano Mulone, Quentin Rossy, David Décary-Hétu and Olivier Delémont

The initiative to draw up and publish a *Handbook of Forensic Intelligence and Criminology* emerged in the early 2010s as a natural continuation of the collaboration between the two institutions to which the editors belong, the École de criminologie de l'Université de Montréal (Canada) and the École des sciences criminelles de l'Université de Lausanne (Switzerland).[1] The handbook seeks to address an important weakness in the study of crime and the responses to crime—the lack of knowledge sharing between forensic scientists and criminologists. Even though both groups are working on a similar object—crime and its 'extended family' (the criminals, the victims, policing and the penal system)—they tend to shut themselves into the silos of their disciplines. This handbook is based on the premise that a pooling of forensic and criminological data, methods and knowledge will broaden our understanding of the criminal phenomenon and its related objects. This premise itself is based on the many joint publications, conferences, courses and seminars and research studies that we have worked on either as forensic scientists or criminologists. This handbook, which compiles contributions from around the world, represents both a compendium and the next step of our reflections. Our objective is to stimulate a 'new' interdisciplinary take on the study of crime, to show how both forensic and criminological theories and knowledge can be combined to analyse crime problems and to open new methodological perspectives. Actually, this is not a completely original convergence, but a new wave of what used to be a reality in the historical development of these disciplines. This handbook covers the use of forensic specimens, as elementary data, to better understand criminal activities, litigations or security problems. It also addresses the exploitation of traces in policing and criminal justice, and, conversely, the crucial contribution of criminological theories and methods to informing, guiding and evaluating crime scene investigation and forensic scientists' practices.

A first observation is that both disciplines are concomitantly engaged in epistemological debates about their identity and scientific foundations. In a very narrow, almost etymological way, we can define criminology as the study of crime, but its scope is usually much wider and encompasses many forms of social harms and approaches to mitigate them. Everything that is linked to the notion of crime can fall under the 'criminology' umbrella, which explains why criminologists come from very diverse backgrounds (psychology, sociology, law, political science, history, anthropology, etc.) and why there is no consensus on its definition and position within the scientific system. Criminology produces knowledge about the dynamics surrounding crime, criminals and victims, as well as about the institutions that react to crime and criminals. Similar questions have emerged within forensic science, which is usually understood as the analysis of traces (biological specimens containing DNA, fingermarks, etc., as well as digital traces) left by a criminal activity. It encompasses the use of natural science (biology, chemistry, physics, etc.) and computer science to detect, collect and analyse traces to assist criminal inquiry and inform court decisions. Forensic scientists usually work closely (at least more closely than criminologists) with policing and judicial actors, as they play a specific and significant role in the production and evaluation of evidence. Some refer to this discipline through the multiple technical perspectives that may be involved to support the criminal system and detect crimes and thus name it 'forensics' or 'forensic sciences', denying the status of a science per se. If it is often perceived as more applied and oriented toward technique than is criminology, it also relies on core principles and generates fundamental knowledge about crime and its related topics—their dynamics, structures and culture. Contributors to this handbook thus have agreed to refer to this discipline as 'forensic science' (i.e., without the 's'). That being said, and as we noted earlier, the knowledge produced by the two disciplines is rarely shared, since forensic scientists and criminologists usually don't interact with each other.

Why is that so? We can find several reasons to explain the relative indifference between criminology and forensic science, and the general lack of knowledge sharing over the years. First, although they share common objects of study, they don't have exactly the same goals, and thus they adopt diverse perspectives. Forensic knowledge is primarily produced to help actors within the penal system do their job; criminology has a less focused scope, aiming at bringing a better understanding and explanation of crime and its related actors and institutions. And because they have different objectives, most of the time they don't have the same research questions. Second, and this is the most significant point, they stand on different bedrocks: 'soft' social and human science for criminology and 'hard' natural and computer science for forensic science. As a consequence, they don't publish in the same journals and don't intervene in the same conferences. They, in fact, don't always speak the same 'language', to a point that it can sometimes be difficult to even understand some of their respective scientific publications. Fundamentally, they differ on the epistemological ground on which they stand.

But if these—significant—differences can explain why the scientists in the two disciplines do not communicate often with each other, there are no arguments against such communication. On the contrary, by producing a large amount of varied information on similar (policing or criminal) activities, by having different takes on the same topics, by examining their object through diverse disciplines, they can be seen to complement one another; and we strongly believe that a joining of forces can have a positive impact on both criminology and forensic science.

To strengthen our argument, let's take an example: the study of crime networks that are typically involved in drug trafficking, and more precisely, the mapping of such networks. The criminologist who tries to understand how drug trafficking is organized will usually rely on criminal investigation data, court proceedings and, if possible, interviews with members of the network. By doing so, the criminologist will be able to identify the individuals that constitute the network, the links between them and, sometimes, the nature of these links. *In fine*, the criminologist may be able to produce a map of the criminal network and, through network analysis methods, will bring some understanding of the dynamics of drug trafficking, of how such groups are organized and, more broadly, of how they function. The forensic scientist can also rely on police data, but being more often involved in the analysis of drug seizures (most notably, to identify the nature of the product that has been seized), the forensic scientist is able, through physical and chemical profiling, to connect different seizures and to reconstruct another schema of the criminal network behind drug trafficking based on the information conveyed by the raw material that is trafficked. Thus, the forensic scientist, like the criminologist, is able to decipher information in terms of individuals, events or places, and to link them in order to compose a possible map of the criminal organization(s) involved in the traffic, as well as making observations on its (their) inner dynamics. But the two maps (the criminological and the forensic), because they are based on different data, provide more often than not different images of the criminal network. And this dissonance is the reason why sharing this complementary knowledge is important. First, the mixing of both maps may reveal a more accurate, more valid and/or more complete picture of the reality, and a more robust understanding of the actual criminal network. Our mutual knowledge of this criminal activity (or whatever topic we're jointly studying) will then be strengthened. Second, the differences in themselves are worthy of scientific inquiry and could help us better understand the object of study as well as some of the limits of each approach. For example, they can highlight the eventual bias that could be associated with police surveillance, or more broadly how a specific data collection method can shape our observations. They can even help us better understand how the strategies adopted by a police organization to fight drug trafficking can influence the output of its investigation.

This simple, and quickly presented, example shows why combining criminology and forensic science is a promising step forward. And this is the aim of the handbook: to help where the worlds of criminology and forensic science collide. To do so, we have organized the handbook into three parts. The first—'Criminology and forensic science: historical developments and epistemological perspectives'—explores the epistemological and historical components of criminology and forensic science, with a particular look at their scientific and social origins, how they can and/or could interact, and/or have interacted so far. Indeed, before getting to more specific and concrete problems, it is necessary to consider the founding principles of criminology and forensic science, to have a thorough look at what they share and what they do not share, where they can find common ground and where they cannot, and what they can talk about together. The section opens perspectives on the potential for a problem-solving oriented, collaborative approach to contribute to broader debates on crimes and social harms. The second part of the handbook, titled 'Forensic practices and crime regulation', is devoted to the study of how the combining of these disciplines can bring about a better understanding of the organizations and institutions that react to crime. A significant part concerns the judicial process, but the section goes well beyond the court, exploring intelligence, prevention, crime scene investigation and, more broadly, policing. The discussions are twofold. How can forensic science broaden its contributions beyond its traditional role in trials? And how can criminology support the whole forensic process through the provision of relevant and actionable knowledge about crime and criminals and adequate methodologies? But also, how can criminology shed light on forensic science as a discipline and thus critically evaluate its contributions and efficiency? Finally, the third part—'Forensic science and crime analysis'—focuses on crime itself, the phenomenon and the actors that produce it. Looking, for instance, at cybercrime and crime trajectories (and how a twofold approach can broaden our understanding of these topics), this section develops an in-depth reflection on methodological issues regarding the sharing of the two disciplines, and the challenges and rewards that can be found in between.

We hope that this handbook will convince readers of the benefits of developing the interdisciplinary take advocated here on the study of crime and its extended family. And, by doing so, we hope that it will inspire future research initiatives in building new bridges between criminology and forensic science.

Note

1 School of Criminology of the University of Montreal (Canada) and School of Criminal Justice of the University of Lausanne (Switzerland).

Part I

Criminology and forensic science

Historical developments and epistemological perspectives

1

Twin sciences?

The history of forensic science and criminology

Paul Knepper

Introduction

According to recent accounts of the history of criminology, the prison played an important role in the development of that science. This idea originated in the work of French philosopher-historian Michel Foucault, who proposed that the nineteenth-century conception of the modern prison contained the knowledge of surveillance and control. From Foucault's perspective, the attempts to define the criminal led to fabrication of a 'science' of 'the other' (Becker and Wetzell 2006; Wetzell 2000; Simon 2006). Foucault's perspective has been developed for Britain by David Garland, who portrays the prison as a laboratory from which new knowledge of criminality can develop (Garland 1985a, 1985b). The British tradition of scientific thinking about criminals, Garland proposes, was situated in an institutional framework that had the support of the prison establishment and the prestige of medicine behind it.

In this essay, I suggest a different institutional origin for criminology and a different kind of laboratory at work: the forensic laboratory. My account has been motivated by re-evaluation of the contribution of Hans Gross. The history of criminology inspired by Foucault dismissed Gross as a marginal figure. a judge who produced a textbook summarizing techniques for scientific analysis of debris at crime scenes. But as recent accounts of his work have demonstrated, Gross was concerned with a more evocative project at the centre of criminology: reconstruction of past events from traces available in the present (Valier 1998; Vyleta 2006; Burney and Pemberton 2011).

In other words, the history of criminology has been braided with that of forensic science: frayed in recent years, but tied together at the start. We can see this in Britain where developments in Europe initiated the study of forensic jurisprudence in the early nineteenth century and the popularity of American sociology in the twentieth century shaped the development of criminology. Specifically, we will examine developments at several British universities—Edinburgh, Cambridge and Sheffield—during three periods. The first is the period of common origins in the decades before the First World War (1885–1914). Owing to the work of Lombroso, criminology emerged from forensic medicine as a science of criminology. Second is the period of divergence during the interwar period (1919–1939). Forensic science and criminology split from one another between the wars owing to the 'sociological turn' in criminology. And third, the period of separate sciences (1945–1980). Since the Second World War, criminology and forensic science have pursued different disciplines, so much so that it is difficult to imagine that they were once united in a common effort to understand criminal behaviour.

Common Origins, 1881–1914

Traditionally, the history of criminology begins with Cesare Beccaria's *Dei Delitti e Delle Pene* (1764). The Enlightenment view of human nature brought a new understanding of crime and punishment. Beirne (1993) shows how Beccaria's views contained a 'positivist' view of humanity, which meant that behaviour could be systematically observed, predicted and manipulated. He charts the development of positivist study of crime from Beccaria, through the statistical reasoning of Adolphe Quetelet, A.M. Guerry and Gabriel Tarde, to Charles Goring's *The English Convict* (1913).

But there was another figure important to what would become known as criminology. Mathieu Orfila did not propose a theory of crime in the abstract, but a knowledge developed from the study of individual criminal acts. He studied chemistry at Valencia and Barcelona before arriving in Paris in 1807 to pursue medicine. After completing his degree, he set up a laboratory and gave demonstrations in forensic chemistry to overseas visitors. By 1819, when he became professor of chemistry and natural philosophy in the medical faculty at the University of Paris, he had worked out tests for common poisons. Rather than trying to detect poisons in soup, wine and vomit, which had thwarted scientists at the time, Orfila realized that poisons accumulate in body organs and suggested examinations of liver, spleen and kidneys as well as blood. His book, *Secours à donner aux personnes empoisonnées ou asphyxiées, suivis des moyens propres à reconnaître les poisons et les vins frelatés et à distinguer la mort réelle de la mort apparente* (1818), appeared in several editions and translations, including English (Bertomeu-Sánchez and Nieto-Galan 2006).

Orfila's work reached Scotland where forensic medicine got an early start at universities. The first chair of medical jurisprudence was established in 1803 at Edinburgh with Andrew Duncan. The subject was already well established at Edinburgh's medical school in 1822 when Robert Christison was appointed professor. Christison had been a student of Orfila and developed toxicology. In murder trials involving poison, chemical tests often proved decisive, although the tests commonly used by doctors to detect poisons were not reliable. Christison knew that although poisons could be found in the body, this didn't necessarily reveal the cause of death. He also knew that it was difficult to prove that a crime had been committed if no poison had been found in the body. He set aside some common tests and replaced them with more conclusive and simpler tests (Colely 1998, 144–145). It was at Edinburgh that Arthur Conan Doyle, a medical student in the 1870s, found inspiration for his literary creation, Sherlock Holmes. In a speech he gave in 1929, Conan Doyle named Henry Littlejohn and Joseph Bell as important influences. Littlejohn lectured at the medical school and served as police surgeon. Bell held an outpatient surgery at the Royal Infirmary and assisted Littlejohn in cases involving medical jurisprudence (O'Brien 2013, 12–14).

Scottish universities did not take an interest in medical jurisprudence because they recognized the value of forensic medicine in detecting crime. Rather, they were interested in 'medical police' or public hygiene. Medical jurisprudence developed from state medicine, or 'legal medicine' as it was known in France and Italy. The idea came from Germany where 'state medicine' meant attention to the overall health of the population, ranging from disposal of dead bodies to disinfection of prostitutes (Crowther and White 1988, 7). But the needs of courts pulled doctors into the role of 'forensic detective', and Scotland's chairs earned reputations from appearing in court for criminal cases. John Glaister's widely read book *Medical Jurisprudence* (1902) combines forensic medicine, in the sense of public health, and criminal detection. Glaister served as police surgeon for the city of Glasgow and lectured at the hospital; he was appointed professor of forensic medicine and public health at the University of Glasgow in 1898.

In the late nineteenth century, the ambition to develop a science of criminal behaviour emerged around the figure of Cesare Lombroso. Born in 1836 at Verona, Lombroso studied medicine and in 1859 volunteered to serve as a military surgeon. He worked as professor of psychiatry at Pavia and director of an asylum at Pesaro. In 1876, he became chair of forensic medicine and public hygiene at the University of Turin. At his request, the university agreed to separate forensic medicine from public hygiene. Lombroso believed his contributions would be made in public hygiene, having had some success with locating the source of pellagra (Villa 2013, 8).

In 1876, Lombroso published *L'uomo delinquente*, the work that would make him famous. He combined ingredients of forensic medicine, psychiatry and phrenology with an understanding of evolutionary development to produce the recipe for the 'criminal type of human being'. Lombroso theorized that some criminals embodied an arrested state of evolution. The 'atavistic' or 'degenerate' criminal reproduced the features of an earlier stage of human development; atavism could be read from the persistence of 'stigmata', such as shape of the skull, tattoos and left-handedness. Lombroso said the idea had first occurred to him while working as a military surgeon in Calabria in the 1860s. While conducting autopsies, he began to notice physical differences between 'evil' soldiers and their 'honest' colleagues. The theory came together in 1871 while Lombroso was examining the body of Villela, a notorious bandit. Lombroso referred to his new scientific view of criminal behaviour as criminal anthropology, the science of the criminal species of human being. From the beginning, it was clear that the criminal type was a false lead, but criminal anthropology provided a common language for medical jurisprudence and emerging social sciences (Gatti and Verde 2012).

To promote his theory of criminality, Lombroso organized the congresses of criminal anthropology. From 1885 until the First World War, lawyers, doctors, judges and others convened every four years or so to discuss scientific approaches to crime and its treatment. The congresses brought together figures that studied the criminal body and social milieu in the criminological sense, but also those studying the body and crime scene evidence. The participants at the second congress of criminal anthropology at Paris in 1889 included a number who had experience of giving evidence in criminal cases. Paul Brouardel was professor of forensic medicine at the University of Paris; he was particularly concerned with food safety, alcoholism and venereal disease. Paul-Louis Ladame, privat-docent of the University of Geneva, taught neurology, psychiatry and criminal anthropology. Alexandru Sutzu, originally from Greece, lectured on mental pathology and legal medicine at the University of Bucharest. Alexandre Lacassagne held the chair of legal medicine at Lyon, where he specialized in toxicology. During the course of the congress, Alphonse Bertillon provided a tour of his anthropometric laboratory (Wilson 1891, 673). Although others used anthropometric techniques to explore Lombroso's theory, Bertillon did not. He aimed to aid the police in identification of suspects and recidivists, and cautioned against reading signs of criminality into the measurements.

The way the story has been told, the congresses involved the clash between rival Italian and French schools of criminology. The Italians, led by Lombroso, insisted on the reality of the atavistic criminal type. The French, led by Léonce Manouvrier, countered with the importance of environment (Nye 1976). But what we miss from this narrative is the importance of forensic science to the study of criminology. The congresses reveal the way in which the scientific study of crime, as it emerged in the late nineteenth century, included multiple theories and methods. It included criminology, as Paul Topinard defined it in 1889, in which statistical analysis of trends, correlations and distributions was used, but also *kriminalistik*, as Hans Gross defined it—the knowledge from material evidence and crime scene analysis built up from experience of individual cases. These were not rival schools or national traditions, but understandings maintained and practised by the same individuals.

Lacassagne has been remembered for stressing the importance of social milieu in explaining criminal behaviour. The criminal, he said, could be compared to a microbe that propagated only under certain conditions (Nye 1976). But he pursued both criminological science and forensic science. At the Rome congress of criminal anthropology in 1885, Lacassagne displayed maps and charts showing correlations of crime rates with season, alcohol consumption and grain prices. Like Lombroso, he had been a military doctor and built a collection of tattoo designs. He saw these not as revealing biological tendencies, but as aspects of a criminal subculture. Lacassagne was, for all his sociological thinking, an accomplished forensic scientist. He devised new forensic techniques, such as estimating the time of death from the rate of decay and using rifling to match a spent bullet to a gun. In the case of Joseph Vacher, a serial murderer who stalked rural France in the 1890s, Lacassagne demonstrated the value of reconstruction of the event from evidence at the crime scene. Why Vacher embarked on a series of murders may have been irrational, but there was a rational aspect to how he committed them. Each murder had been accomplished in the same circumstances, carried out in the same way, and revealed an identical operating procedure (Starr 2011, 46, 127, 207).

Like Lacassagne, Rodolphe Reiss pursued criminology and criminalistics. Reiss, who earned a doctorate in chemistry, founded the Institute of Forensic Science (*police scientifique*) at Lausanne in 1909. He contributed to 685 cases between 1904 and 1919 including work on crime scenes, documents, explosive devices and forged notes. At the same time, Reiss stressed the importance of leaving the laboratory to study criminality in situ. In his *Manuel de police scientifique* (1911), he explained that to understand professional criminals, such as the Apaches of Paris, it was necessary to enter the criminal underworld, to talk to them in their own language, to study their work and the tools they used. On visits to Paris, he collected information and made numerous photographs of cafés, bars, hotels and hovels inhabited by Apaches; he wanted to learn their specialization, recruitment methods and information-gathering techniques; the places where they met for leisure and to drink alcohol; their fashion style, tools and instruments, and tattoos (Montani 2014).

Britain did not participate in the congresses until 1896 when the Home Office sent Major Arthur Griffiths to the fourth congress at Geneva. Griffiths styled his report an assessment of the 'science of criminal anthropology'. He focused on the reception accorded Lombroso's theories, especially on the arguments of those who rejected his claims. The consensus of opinion was that crime did not originate in anatomical anomalies, yet Lombroso persisted in his belief in the existence of a criminal type. Griffiths did, however, comment on the wide range of topics examined by the participants, from growth of new forms of crime to classification of prisoners. He encountered a significant number of 'medico-legalists' at the congress, including Hans Gross, with whom he had several conversations (Griffiths 1896, 11). A few years later, the Medico-Legal Society was formed to promote medical jurisprudence in London medical schools. William J. Collins, the first president, gave an inaugural address on the history of forensic medicine from ancient times and urged the University of London to implement greater academic training in forensic medicine (Collins 1945).

Divergence, 1920s–1930s

In 1928, the Rockefeller Foundation of New York published a survey of facilities for medico-legal research and training worldwide. Most of the descriptions have to do with physical facilities, architecture and equipment in order to illustrate the range of activities carried out in the service of the courts. Only a few of the reports mention criminology. Raimundo de Castro described plans for an ambitious Institute of Legal Medicine at the University of Havana. In 1925, he had visited institutes of legal medicine across Europe and understood the importance of criminology. The new institute would provide a course in criminology for magistrates and judges, and instruction in police science for prison doctors and staff of penitentiaries (Rockefeller Foundation 1928, 27–39). Knud Sand, professor of legal medicine at the University of Copenhagen, mentioned the importance of building up the 'vast subject of criminology' initiated by Lombroso. Sand proposed Gross's criminal psychology as an essential 'forensic principle' (Rockefeller Foundation 1928, 353).

Nevertheless, most of the reports included photographs of criminal museums—Berlin, Cracow, Geneva, Lund, Lyon, Prague and Vienna to name a few. The museums reflect the institutional context from which criminology had emerged. By 1907, the medical buildings at Glasgow contained a new forensic laboratory along with a library and a museum. The museum contained murder weapons, bullets, casts of footprints, pieces of fractured skulls, drawings and illustrations. The museum had been formed from Glaister's personal collection. It was not designed to illustrate the natural history of the 'criminal type' but knowledge of criminal behaviour acquired on a case-by-case basis (Crowther and White 1988, 32–33). Looking back from the twenty-first century, the role of the crime museum is less obvious because historical accounts have emphasized the prison, but also because criminology diverged from forensic science in the decades between the wars.

For authorities at the Home Office, the Rockefeller survey represented something of an embarrassment. The Rockefeller survey contained descriptions of institutes across Europe. Austria and Poland had well-established institutes; Germany, France and Italy had multiple medico-legal facilities; and Denmark and Switzerland had opened new institutes. Scotland had its institutes, but England had nothing to report (Rockefeller Foundation 1928). Arthur Dixon was assistant under-secretary of state in charge of the Home Office police department and amateur microscopist. When the Rockefeller survey appeared, Dixon wrote a memorandum on police training in which he suggested the need for instruction in physiology, chemistry and medico-legal problems. 'The application of science to detective purposes is a branch of police work in which this country is definitely backward', Dixon told the Home Secretary. 'Very useful work has been done in a few forces, but this has been a matter of local and individual enterprise' (quoted in Ambage and Clark 1994, 298).

There were several police-based forensic initiatives underway in England during the 1920s, including the forensic laboratory at Sheffield. Percy Sillitoe became chief constable at Sheffield in 1926; he later served as Glasgow chief constable and head of MI5 security service. Sillitoe said that he could see the value of medical expertise in the scientific detection of crime, but rejected the 'monopoly' over forensic science maintained by celebrity criminalists such as Bernard Spilsbury (Burney and Pemberton 2011). He appointed a full-time police surgeon as the initial step in acquiring in-house capabilities. James M. Webster took the job, and within a few years, Sheffield's 'little police laboratory' carried out tests of fibres and wood, analysis of blood and other body stains, investigation of scratches revealing forcible entry and examination of counterfeit coins and notes. The Sheffield laboratory took another step when it became linked, through Webster, to the University of Sheffield. Webster became lecturer in toxicology and forensic medicine in 1929 and won access to more extensive laboratory equipment and medical expertise (Sillitoe 1955, 70–73).

Dixon consulted with several people, including Sillitoe, about the possibilities for applying science to police work. When in 1931 he released his plan for establishment of forensic science in England, much of it was drawn from Sheffield's experience (Sillitoe 1955, 72). Dixon proposed that: (1) police should receive instruction in scientific techniques; (2) police forces should be equipped with technical apparatus to stimulate interest; (3) regional laboratories should be staffed with scientists and provided with a full range of laboratory equipment; (4) the Home Office should create a national laboratory to serve as a clearing house for information, to coordinate research and to house a library and a museum; and (5) arrangements should be made in which local police could call on scientific and medical expertise. The new regional laboratories should be located in university towns where consultants could be found (Ambage and Clark 1994, 299).

In 1931, Hugh Trenchard took over as commissioner of the Metropolitan Police. A distinguished aviator of the First World War, he had been marshal of the Royal Air Force before joining the police service. He decided that a forensic science laboratory should be set up at Hendon, in north London, alongside his new Metropolitan Police College. Trenchard failed to lure one of the chairs of medical jurisprudence from Scotland to serve as director, but he did manage to get Edinburgh pathologist James Davidson and opened the new Metropolitan Police Laboratory in 1935. The Advisory Committee on the Scientific Investigation of Crime, which had been created to oversee development of the Hendon laboratory, noted the following year that the facility would 'follow naturally upon an increasing realisation of its value as part of the crime-fighting machinery'. The committee, however, lost interest in Trenchard's laboratory and encouraged plans for a national medico-legal laboratory, to be established with the expertise of staff at the University of London (Ambage and Clark 1994).

These developments meant that 'forensic science', as distinct from 'forensic medicine', emerged in Britain. Dixon's plan for regional laboratories established an institutional platform and encouraged a professional organization for the application of forensic examinations involving chemistry, biology and physics to criminal cases. Within the next ten years, regional laboratories opened at Nottingham, Birmingham, Cardiff, Bristol and Preston. At this time, the split between forensic science and criminology became clear. In London, the Medico-Legal Society changed the name of its journal from *Transactions of the Medico-Legal Society* to *Medico-Legal and Criminological Review*. In other words, two disciplines with a common interest rather than a single criminal science.

This split was due to 'the sociological turn' in criminology. In Britain, the reasons why can be found in a 1932 address by Alexander Paterson, the prison commissioner, to the London Medico-Legal Society. Paterson argued for a chair in criminology to be established at Oxford University. The criminologist's tasks would be: (1) to investigate the causes of crime along the lines of Lacassagne's social milieu, not Lombroso's criminal anthropology; (2) to examine the means employed in the detection of an offender, such as modus operandi; (3) to systematize and clarify the field of penal law; and (4) to identify the proper treatment of the criminal. Given his emphasis on criminal law, he suggested the chair would need to be filled by a lawyer. But it is also clear from his comments that he regarded criminology as a sociological enterprise. In unravelling the causes of crime—heredity, housing, education and unemployment, mental and physical defect—'the sociologist will hand the criminologist his first clue' (Paterson 1931–1932, 184).

In responding to questions at the end of his talk, Paterson revealed that he had taken his idea of a criminologist from the American model, specifically, Edwin Sutherland (Paterson 1931–1932, 200). Paterson likely met Sutherland two years earlier. When crime rates fell after the First World War, contrary to expectation, the Home Office accelerated the pace of closing local prisons. The story of 'England's empty prisons' reached the Bureau of Social Hygiene in the United States, and the bureau decided to send a top criminologist to investigate. Edwin Sutherland had earned a national reputation with the publication of his book *Criminology* (1924); he worked in the Department of Sociology at the University of Minnesota and came to work for the Bureau of Social Hygiene for about a year before joining the University of Chicago. Sutherland arrived in England in June 1930. He met his research assistant, who had gathered statistical information, and began sifting through it. Sutherland also met with representatives from the Home Office and the

Howard League. He toured penal institutions at Wormwood Scrubs, Wakefield and Borstal, and prepared a report on English prisons for the Bureau (Knepper 2015).

Separate Sciences, 1945–1980

In 1951, Sir Sydney Smith urged the Medico-Legal Society to establish an Institute of Forensic Medicine and Criminology. Smith had been appointed to the chair of legal medicine at Edinburgh University in 1927 and had worked in Cairo as director of its medico-legal institute. He reviewed trends in police statistics to show that crime remained a significant social problem and chided the society for not doing enough to promote the study of criminology. The institute he envisioned would possess all the technology available for the study of forensic science that had been developed and would include biochemical, biological and physics departments. It would also have capabilities for research into criminology and penology with working ties to departments of law (Smith 1951, 64). An institute did appear in the 1950s, but it did not include forensic science.

In 1959, the Institute of Criminology opened at Cambridge University. The Home Secretary, R.A. 'Rab' Butler, believed the penal system needed a radical reappraisal and only a modest programme of research at universities. There were only a few researchers, scattered across universities, attempting to tackle difficult problems with extremely limited resources. He encouraged the formation of a research institute that would be independent of the Home Office and discussed several options with the Howard League. Butler wanted an institute that would offer postgraduate courses, carry out research and establish contacts with professionals in criminal justice. Cambridge University had a Department of Criminal Science led by Leon Radzinowicz and took some interest in plans for establishing an institute. When Butler secured funding from the Isaac Wolfson Trust, Cambridge moved ahead. Radzinowicz became the first Wolfson professor and director of the Institute of Criminology (Butler 1974).

Leon Radzinowicz had emigrated from Poland to Britain in 1938. Poland had a tradition of legal medicine led by Jagiellonian University in Cracow. Leon Wachholz, the chair of forensic medicine, devised a popular test for detecting carbon monoxide in blood. He lectured in the Faculty of Medicine and the Department of Law (Glazek and Piekoszewski 2002). Radzinowicz completed a doctor of law degree at Cracow, so he could hardly have missed Wachholz. But he brought nothing of forensic science with him. In 1960, Radzinowicz did preside over the British Academy of Forensic Sciences. In his presidential address, he described criminal law, criminology and forensic science as 'three basic groups of disciplines concerned with the problem of crime and punishment' (Radzinowicz 1960, 7). While they differed in methods and objectives, they did 'supplement each other in many vital matters' and shared an awareness 'of their common fundamental object' (Radzinowicz 1960, 7). He acknowledged the 'magnificent tradition' of forensic science established at Edinburgh, but could not think of any ways in which forensic scientists and criminologists might actually collaborate.

When in April 1961 Radzinowicz spoke to the Medico-Legal Society, he acknowledged the 'genuine and sustained interest ... in the broad field of criminology' demonstrated by the society for more than 50 years. He also explained that the development of criminological studies at Cambridge would have nothing to do with medico-legal studies. The research programme, supported by a grant from the Home Office, reflected the interest in criminal behaviour and criminal justice administration. There were six projects underway: attendance centre orders, robbery in London, offenders and employees, crimes of violence against the person, honesty in the careers of persistent thieves and psychopathic traits of offenders in preventive detention. Four long-term projects had been established: social side effects of a conviction, family development study, the economic costs of crime and the state of crime in England and Wales (Radzinowicz 1961).

Beginning in 1964, the Cambridge Institute hosted national conferences in criminology every two years. The conferences, which took place in Cambridge, were meant to serve as a 'national catalyst' for criminology. But in 1968, at the third Cambridge criminology conference, a group of sociologists broke away to form a rival forum. Originally convened several times a year in cities across the United Kingdom, the National Deviancy Congress attracted wide support. Drawing on American sociology, the participants brought subcultural theory, and labelling and interactionist approaches, to the study of the British response to crime. Although the original framework for the symposia had disintegrated by 1980, it had been a time of rapid expansion in the 'sociology of deviance' (Downes 1988).

By this time, criminology and forensic science were very much separate sciences. This can be seen in developments at Sheffield. When Webster left Sheffield in 1937 for Birmingham (to direct one of the new Home Office forensic science laboratories), Gilbert Forbes became police surgeon and lectured at the university. In 1948, the university set up a Department of Forensic Medicine with Forbes as director. Although the department operated out of the basement of a church building that had been acquired by the university, it had responsibility for all forensic services throughout the city. Doctors, solicitors, police and private citizens relied on the basement laboratory for everything from routine autopsies to murder inquiries. When Forbes left Sheffield (to take the Regius Chair of Forensic Medicine at Glasgow), he was replaced by Alan Usher (Usher 1970).

Usher, who had completed his medical degree at Durham, arrived in 1960. He began as deputy police surgeon of the Sheffield City Police and lecturer in forensic pathology in the Department of Forensic Medicine. He specialized in analysis of blood, hair and fibre and performed up to a thousand routine autopsies each year. Usher contributed to a national campaign by forensic pathologists for improved facilities and organizational resources. The *Observer Magazine* ran a story in 1973 on 'Crime Doctors—A Dying Profession' with Usher on the cover. There were too few forensic pathologists to devote needed attention to murder cases. 'Someday soon', said Home Office pathologist Bernard Knight, 'the police are going to end up stranded alone with a body left in a muddy field' (*Observer Magazine* 1973). Usher also campaigned for improved facilities at the university and, following a visit to Ghent, decided to pursue a medico-legal centre. The university and local authority approved of his plan and jointly supported the establishment of the Sheffield Medico-Legal Centre in 1977. It was the first effort in Britain to bring a public mortuary, coroner's court, police surgeons' suites and university department of forensic pathology under one roof (Cozens 1978).

In the 1960s, the Sheffield University administration identified criminology as a 'growth point' subject and established the first lectureship. In 1968, Anthony E. Bottoms became the first lecturer in criminology at Sheffield. He taught an undergraduate course on criminal law and criminology and initiated the research concerning crime and urban social structures. He also led the Sheffield Criminology Group, which developed plans for a research centre. The group won approval for their plans, and in 1976, the Centre for Criminological Studies opened with Bottoms as director. It was the third of its kind at a British university; Edinburgh opened a centre in 1974 (Croft 1983). The Sheffield criminologists chose 'criminological studies' to avoid copying the Cambridge model and to advertise their sociological orientation. Staff lectured in the Master of Arts programme in criminological studies and pursued research projects concerning the defendant's view of the legal system, juvenile justice and social work ideology, and measuring serious crime (Sheffield University 1976). In 1984, Bottoms left Sheffield to become the Wolfson Professor of Criminology and director of the Institute of Criminology at Cambridge, the role that had been held by Radzinowicz.

The Centre for Criminological Studies invited Professor Nils Christie of the University of Oslo to give the foundation lecture at the inaugural event. The choice of Christie registered the radical strain of criminology initiated by the National Deviancy Congress. 'When the Norwegian sociologist Nils Christie, a leading criminologist and abolitionist, was invited to receive an honorary degree from the University of Sheffield and open its Centre of Criminology, he began his speech by saying that our proper role should be to close, not to open, such centres' (Cohen 1988, 5). Four years later, the centre was renamed the Centre for Criminological and Socio-Legal Studies, a configuration meant to support 'criminologists, penologists, public lawyers, sociologists of law and experts in research methodology'. It was a big umbrella, but not big enough to include collaboration with staff at the Medico-Legal Centre on nearby Watery Street.

Conclusions

Criminology and forensic science live separate lives today, but they were born twins. The scientific study of crime emerged in the late nineteenth century, an amalgamation of forensic medicine and emerging social sciences. Lombroso and Lacassagne, celebrated for championing rival schools of criminology, both came from forensic medicine. One legacy of this common origin is the criminal museum. During the 1920s, police-based forensic science emerged. Police departments opened forensic science laboratories and the Home Office organized a regional system combining police and university expertise. But the sociological turn in criminology brought about a split with forensic science. When Paterson encouraged the Medico-Legal Society to lobby for a chair in criminology, he had the American model in mind. Sociology, not forensic science, became the paradigm.

Following the Second World War, criminology and forensic science represented separate sciences. Although Sydney Smith dreamed of a national institute that combined the two, England established a criminological institute along the lines Paterson had suggested. The Institute of Criminology at Cambridge University, directed by Leon Radzinowicz, left out forensic research altogether. At Sheffield University, the split can be seen in 1976 when the new Medico-Legal Centre opened, and the following year, the Centre for Criminological and Socio-Legal Research. Both interested in crime, neither interested in the other. It raises an important question about what might have been. What would the study of crime look like now if criminologists and forensic scientists had remained part of a shared method of inquiry?

References

Ambage, N., and M. Clark. 1994. 'Unbuilt Bloomsbury: Medico-Legal Institutes and Forensic Science Laboratories in England between the Wars'. In M. Clark and C. Crawford, eds., *Legal Medicine in History*, 293–313. Cambridge: Cambridge University Press.

Becker, P., and R. Wetzell. 2006. *Criminals and Their Scientists: The History of Criminology in International Perspective*. Cambridge: Cambridge University Press.

Beirne, P. 1993. *Inventing Criminology: Essays on the Rise of 'Homo Criminalis'*. Albany, NY: State University of New York Press.

Bertomeu-Sánchez, J., and A. Nieto-Galan, eds. 2006. *Chemistry, Medicine and Crime: Mateu J.B. Orfila and His Times*. Sagamore Beach, MA: Science History Publications.

Burney, I., and N. Pemberton. 2011. 'Bruised Witness: Bernard Spilsbury and the Performance of Early Twentieth-Century English Forensic Pathology'. *Medical History* 55(1): 41–60.

Burney, I., and N. Pemberton. 2013. 'Making Space for Criminalistics: Hans Gross and *fin-de-siècle* CSI Studies'. *History and Philosophy of Biological and Medical Sciences* 44(1): 16–25.

Butler, R.A. 1974. 'The Foundation of the Institute of Criminology at Cambridge'. In R. Hood, ed., *Crime, Criminology and Public Policy: Essays in Honour of Sir Leon Radzinowicz*, 1–10. London: Heinemann.

Cohen, S. 1988. *Against Criminology*. New Brunswick, NJ: Transaction Books.

Coley, N. (1998) 'Forensic Chemistry in 19th-Century Britain'. *Endeavour* 22(4): 143–147.

Collins, W.J. 1945. 'Early Days of the Medico-Legal Society'. *Medico-Legal and Criminological Review* 13(4): 201–202.
Cozens, R.W. 1978. 'The Sheffield Medico-Legal Centre'. *Police Journal* 51(3): 243–250.
Croft, J. 1983. 'Criminological Research in Great Britain, with a Note on the Council of Europe'. *Crime and Justice* 5: 265–280.
Crowther, M.A., and B. White. 1988. *On Soul and Conscience: The Medical Expert and Crime*. Aberdeen: Aberdeen University Press.
Downes, D. 1988. 'The Sociology of Crime and Social Control in Britain 1960–1987'. *British Journal of Criminology* 28(2): 45–57.
Foucault, M. 1978. 'About the Concept of the "Dangerous Individual" in 19th-Century Legal Psychiatry'. *International Journal of Law and Psychiatry* 1(1): 1–18.
Garland, D. 1985a. *Punishment and Welfare*. Aldershot: Gower.
Garland, D. 1985b. 'The Criminal and His Science: A Critical Account of the Formation of Criminology at the End of the Nineteenth Century'. *British Journal of Criminology* 25(2): 109–137.
Garland, D. 1988. 'British Criminology before 1935'. *British Journal of Criminology* 28(2): 1–17.
Gatti, U., and A. Verde. 2012. 'Cesare Lombroso: Methodological Ambiguities and Brilliant Intuitions'. *International Journal of Law and Psychiatry* 35(1): 19–26.
Glazek, A., and W. Piekoszewski. 2002. 'Forensic Sciences in Cracow'. *Problems of Forensic Sciences* 50: 138–145.
Griffiths, A. 1896. *Report to the Secretary of State for the Home Department on the Proceedings of the Fourth Congress of Criminal Anthropology Held at Geneva*. London: HMSO.
Harrison, L. 1931. 'German Institute for Police Science and Criminology'. Rockefeller Archives, BSH Collection, Series 4, Box 19, Folder 713.
Horn, D. 2003. *The Criminal Body: Lombroso and the Anatomy of Deviance*. London: Routledge.
Knepper, P. 2015. 'Falling Crime Rates: What Happened Then'. *Theoretical Criminology* 19(1): 59–76.
Mannheim, H. 1960. *Pioneers in Criminology*. London: Stevenson.
Montani, I. 2014. 'Accounts of the "Underworld": Rodolphe Archibald Reiss (1875–1929) of the University of Lausanne'. Paper presented at the 14th Annual Conference of the European Society of Criminology, 10–13 September, Prague.
Nye, R. 1976. 'Heredity or Milieu: The Foundations of Modern European Criminological Theory'. *Isis* 67(3): 334–355.
O'Brien, J. 2013. *The Scientific Sherlock Holmes: Cracking the Case with Science and Forensics*. Oxford: Oxford University Press.
Observer Magazine. 1973. 'Crime doctors—A Dying Profession'. 28 October 1973, 22–29.
Paterson, A. 1931–1932. 'Should the Criminologist Be Encouraged?' *Transactions of the Medico-Legal Society* 26(1): 180–200.
Radzinowicz, L. 1960. 'Criminal Law, Criminology and Forensic Science'. *Medicine, Science and the Law* 1(1): 7–15.
Radzinowicz, L. 1961. *The Study of Criminology in Cambridge*. Cambridge: Institute of Criminology.
Radzinowicz, L. 1988. *The Cambridge Institute of Criminology: Its Background and Scope*. London: HMSO.
Rockefeller Foundation. 1928. *Methods and Problems of Legal Education: Institutes of Legal Medicine* (Ninth Series). New York: Division of Medical Education.
Sheffield University. 1976. 'Opening of the Centre for Criminological Studies'. News release in file marked 'Centre for Criminological and Socio-Legal Studies'. University Archives, Western Bank Library, University of Sheffield.
Simon, J. 2006. 'Positively Punitive: How the Inventor of Scientific Criminology Who Died at the Beginning of the Twentieth Century Continues to Haunt American Crime Control at the Beginning of the Twenty-First'. *Texas Law Review* 84: 2135–2172.
Sillitoe, P. 1955. *Cloak Without Dagger*. London: Cassell.
Smith, S. 1951. 'The Medico-Legal Institute and the Problem of Crime'. *Medico-Legal Journal* 19(2): 57–64.
Starr, D. 2011. *The Killer of Little Shepherds: The Case of the French Ripper and the Birth of Forensic Science*. London: Simon and Schuster.
Usher, A. 1970. 'Forensic Medicine—The Sheffield Pattern'. *Medicine, Science and the Law* 10(4): 243–247.
Valier, C. 1998. 'True Crime Stories: Scientific Methods of Criminal Investigation, Criminology, and Historiography'. *British Journal of Criminology* 38(1): 88–105.

Villa, R. 2013. 'Lombroso and His School: From Anthropology to Medicine'. In P. Knepper and P.J. Ystehede, eds., *The Cesare Lombroso Handbook*, 8–29. London: Routledge.

Vyleta, D. 2006. 'Was Early Twentieth-Century Criminology a Science of the "Other"? A Re-evaluation of Austro-German Criminological Debates'. *Cultural and Social History* 3(4): 406–423.

Walls, H.J. 1976. 'The Forensic Science Service in Great Britain: A Short History'. *Journal of the Forensic Science Society* 16(4): 273–278.

Wetzell, R. 2000. *Inventing the Criminal: A History of German Criminology, 1880–1945*. Chapel Hill: University of North Carolina Press.

Wilson, T. 1891. 'Criminal Anthropology: A Report on the Second International Congress of Criminal Anthropology'. Annual Report of the Board of Regents of the Smithsonian Institution, 617–686. Washington, DC: Government Printing Office.

2

Criminology and forensic science as a *Unitas Multiplex*

An epistemological approach

Cândido da Agra

Epistemological analysis

Epistemology, the theory of knowledge, is a vast field. From the spiritualist epistemology of Thomas Aquinas to current naturalistic perspectives, through Kant's transcendental idealism, we find a multitude of perspectives on the foundations and the construction of knowledge and science. Within such diversity, which instruments of analysis should I use? As in previous analyses, I seek to bring together elements from the Anglo-Saxon logicist tradition and the French historicist tradition.

Criminology and forensic sciences as archaeological territories

In this section, I briefly summarize my application of the archaeological method, conceived in Foucault's philosophy of knowledge, to criminology and forensic sciences. This method is systematized in the book *L'Archéologie du savoir* (1969). In this presentation, I follow the terminology used in the English translation (Foucault 1972).

My archaeological description of criminology and forensic science, supported by the Foucauldian concept of *archaeological territories*, leads to the following questions: Are criminology and forensic sciences mere *discursive practices*, mere 'knowledge' (*savoir*)? Are they sciences? Are they formal sciences? In their current state, criminology and forensic science discourses show diverse, and even opposite, levels. We can observe different *thresholds*.

From the second half and toward the end of the nineteenth century, different practices, discourses and notions emerged around science, crime, police, security and justice. In this period, these disciplines still did not possess well-defined boundaries. They coexisted in a criminological-forensic territory called 'criminal disciplines'. A willingness to apply the scientific method emerged progressively in these disciplines. What was the purpose of this movement? As stated by Ferry, one of the founders of Italian Positivist Criminology, the use of the 'positive method' is fruitful compared to the useless abstractions and obscurities of legal dogmatics, whose discourse arises exclusively from an abstract logic (H. Ferri in Altavila 1982, 15). We may say that at this time criminological and forensic practices had reached the *threshold of positivity*. This level is characterized by stress on the use of objective knowledge to support practices and judicial and political decisions. The production of truth in the field of justice through the use of empirical methods led to the emergence of several new practices, such as the creation of 'identification bureaus'. Many countries saw the co-existence in the same institution of identification practices, criminal anthropology and even judiciary and criminal psychology.

This diffused knowledge became more defined during the first decades of the twentieth century. Criminology became 'knowledge' with an epistemological status. Why was this? For the first time, several groups of articulated statements emerged, seeking to be validated by the norms of coherence and empiricism. For the first time, criminology had models, critiques and verifications. The model of the School of Criminal Anthropology was questioned not only for theoretical but also for empirical reasons. The acknowledgement of methodological and conceptual mistakes led to the development of other orientations and perspectives. Other factors contributed to the emergence of criminology as knowledge: criminology was constituted into an academic and administrative institution; the first international conferences were held; and the first scientific society, the International Society of Criminology (1938), was created in Europe.

Regarding the forensic sciences, we can observe new emergences that went beyond legal medicine in countries such as Germany, Austria and Switzerland. Debuyst's detailed analysis (1998) of German psychology and psychiatry between 1850 and 1920 illustrates how forensic and criminological knowledge became differentiated during this period. For example, under the influence of the Austrian judge Hans Gross, criminal psychology drifted toward judiciary psychology and criminalistics. The creation of the Criminalistics Institute at the University of Graz in 1912 represents the shift toward an orientation in which the truth is sought more in the traces left behind by the criminal than in the biopsychological, moral or social characteristics of the criminal him or herself. At the same time, 'laboratories' and 'experts' on forensic sciences were created. The creation of a first scientific community was signalled by two events: the establishment of the Académie Internationale de Criminalistique en Lausanne in 1929 and of the American Academy of Forensic Science in 1948.

During the same historical period, this movement of internal differentiation within the criminal disciplines was reinforced by a movement of external differentiation, which was inherent to science in general. I am speaking about the first attempts of dual categorization of knowledge and science, which emerged at the end of the nineteenth and beginning of the twentieth centuries: the sciences of nature—the sciences of culture (Du Bois-Reymond); ideographic approaches—nomothetic approaches (Windelbrand); sciences of the knowledge of causal laws—sciences of the comprehension of human nature (Dilthey); and sciences of a generalizing character—sciences of an individualizing character (Richert). The two movements of differentiation (internal and external) contributed to a progressive delimitation of the boundaries between criminology and forensic sciences. The criminological-forensic territory was divided into two autonomous territories. The first leaned toward the formal, natural and bio-psychological sciences; the second leaned toward the socio-psychological, social and juridical sciences. Each of these territories was seeking a status of autonomous knowledge, embodied in its own corpus of knowledge and practices. An indicator of this division was the introduction of psychology into crime and justice. This separation was consecrated in the Cologne Congress of Criminal Anthropology (1911). Ferri concludes the argument on this matter as follows: 'criminal psychology is the study of the criminal as the performer of the offence, paying attention to his ways of feeling, thinking, wanting and acting. On the other hand, the judiciary psychology is the scientific study of those who participate in justice administration, that is, the criminal as the accused, the judge, the victim, the denouncer, the defender and, above all, the witnesses' (translated from Ferri 1911; in Debuyst 1998, 458).

We must say that by the end of the nineteenth and the first decades of the twentieth century, criminology and forensic science in Europe had crossed the threshold of *epistemologization*.

In a third historical period, between the end of the Second World War and the 1980s, criminology and the forensic sciences became ambivalent, hesitant and contradictory. We can observe a movement that I will call an epistemic 'big bang' of criminological disciplines.

Opposite tendencies emerged in criminology—on the one hand, sociological criminology and, critical criminology; on the other, etiological criminology, psychologic criminology and clinical criminology. This movement of internal differentiation and specialization was also discernible in the laboratorial forensic sciences. But as P. Margot observes, 'when laboratories were created in the 1950s, they were usually not combined with pattern-type marks but built separately and in different law enforcement sectors' (Margot 2011, 798–799).

But we can also observe a stagnation: both criminology and the forensic sciences entered a sort of epistemological lethargy that closed off access to the *threshold of scientificity*. A true scientific criminology was not established; a true forensic science was not established. Why? We would need a more profound historical-epistemological analysis than space allows here to answer this question. I would merely refer to two major epistemological obstacles. Until the end of the 1950s, criminology in Europe was colonized by medical-psychological influence, penal law and moralism; after that, during the 1960s and the 1970s, it was colonized by sociologism and political ideology. Forensic science was colonized by an alliance between law and medicine. Neither law nor medicine is a true science. Much less scientific is a police organization whose practical knowledge is overdetermined by justice.

Thus, could we say that the so-called 'criminal sciences', namely criminology and forensic sciences, are false? Largely, yes. Nevertheless, from the 1980s, a will for scientific autonomy was reborn, a will to establish criminology and forensic sciences as real *scientific domains*.

By describing these levels and situating them in history, I am not claiming that there has been an evolution in criminology and in forensic sciences as a whole. Let's just say that the criminological and forensic territories are built by four large unities or discontinuous formations: discursive practices, knowledge, *epistemologization* and *scientificity*. Currently, we have a *system of dispersion* that goes from the misuse of the words 'criminology' and 'forensic sciences' to define a disorganized mixture of ideology, moralism, psychologism, technicism, utilitarianism, etc., to a very narrow fringe of scientific criminology and forensic science. Therefore, it is not clear what establishes criminology's and forensic sciences' identity. Their unity is a relative concept. Beneath the apparent unity, claimed by the word, there are several and even opposite levels of criminological and forensic discourse.

Criminology and forensic science as scientific domains

The need for a paradigm shift

During the last 30 to 40 years, many have talked about the need for a *paradigm shift*. This discourse is accompanied by a desire to transform criminology and forensic sciences into true sciences. In line with and supported by G. Bachelard's epistemology, many criminologists and forensic scientists seek an 'epistemological cut'. They intend to identify and remove the 'epistemological obstacles' that block the path to a wider scientific rationality. So, we should ask the following: What is the scientific paradigm today? How do criminology and the forensic sciences behave within the contemporary scientific paradigm?

(a) In answer to the first question, we have witnessed a paradigm shift in science in general. Based on the work of many philosophers of science—T. Khun, M. Serres, M. Foucault, I. Prigogine among others—I have concluded that the paradigm of science is systemic, informational and communicational (Agra 1986). Today, knowledge and science form a vast dynamic system whose subsystems are linked and communicate with and influence each other. Science's functioning, contrary to the positivist hierarchical system, is similar to a communication network system. In this sense, scientific disciplines and their actors function as nodes within a network.

(b) Regarding the second question, let's see how criminology and forensic sciences adapt themselves to the new paradigm of science.

As for the perception of the object of criminology as a system, M. Cusson outlines a first synthesis (1998). The author uses the metaphor of the solar system to define the object of criminology. Around the crime gravitate the main actors of the criminal drama: delinquents and victims; beyond that, social controls and their experts (police, judges, security experts); and, beyond that, the criminal environment (accomplices, etc.). Finally, there are the proximal and distal causes of crime. Criminology embraces everything that concerns crime. It brings to convergence the delinquent, victim, environment, social controls and explicative factors toward the same point: the crime (Cusson 1998, 2–3).

Regarding explanation schemes, after the 1980s the project of scientific criminology has been revived. New approaches and concepts have emerged, such as 'gene–environmental interaction', 'evolutionary perspectives' and 'nature–nurture interplay'.

Concerning theoretical strategies, we can list several directions highlighting changes and transformations. After an epistemological turn into specialized criminologies, a desire for integration arose in the late 1960s and early 1970s led by Wolfgang and Ferracuti. The idea of an 'integrative criminology' became a central issue in the criminological agenda. The epistemic transformation of the 1980s intensified the discourse on the unity, or synthesis, of criminology. The 15th Annual Conference of the European Society of Criminology was devoted to this theme under the concept of *unitas multiplex* (Agra 2015a; Agra 2015b).

The same concern exists regarding forensic sciences. I find the desire for a new paradigm in the criticism of Margot and O. Ribaux.

The allegory developed by P. Margot (2011, 800) to describe the current state of forensic sciences has wide epistemological resonance. 'Forensic science', he says, 'is like a hospital serviced by clerics and nurses for most of the activities, and brain surgeons and cardiologists for highly specialized areas of medicine, but with no medical doctor in the middle'. The author defends the idea of forensic sciences without the 's', that is, an autonomous scientific discipline. A culture of research in forensic sciences does not exist outside a true scientific science, the *forensic science*.

The pioneering work of O. Ribaux (2014) represents a profound development of this epistemological position that claims a new paradigm. Supported not only by texts on the theory and methodology of science, but also by examples of forensic practice, the author argues critically against the absence of abstraction and against anthropomorphism. At the same time, he specifies the coordinates for training and research in a true forensic science, one that has a method and relies on the idea of a system.

According to what was mentioned in (a) and (b), we conclude that there exists, among thinkers from different territories, the same goal of system, synthesis and unification.

The conditions for a new paradigm

I understand these concerns and tendencies in criminology and forensic sciences under three epistemological theses.

Thesis 1: We have to conduct an *epistemological cut* (as in G. Bachelard) not only with *naif* practices devoid of critical thinking but also with dependence on other disciplines, such as legal medicine, law, psychology and sociology.

Thesis 2: We need a *new paradigm*, a wide structure of thinking (as in T. Kuhn), *that corrects the structural mistakes* (as in K. Popper) of pseudo-scientific criminology and forensic sciences. To the dispersion of practices, theories and movements that characterizes the pre-scientific stage, a wide and flexible system of critical thinking on the criminal phenomenon, conceived as a system, must follow.

Thesis 3: We need a criminological and a forensic synthesis, perceived as a structure of integration. The truth about crime, the criminal and criminality is not only in its constitutive elements but also in the *system* itself.

The history of science is the history of contradictions and a clash between movements and opposed perspectives: elementarism vs totalism; reductionism vs holism; singularity vs generality. I believe that currently we have reached a willingness for a synthesis of opposites: I see it in the paradigm of *complex systems,* whose ontology is more informational and communicational than natural. The reconstruction of criminology and the forensic sciences forces the abandonment of classical oppositions and their reconfiguration into large structures of dynamic integration: elements and totalities; singular events and general patterns; individuals and populations. How can this be done? We have now reached the process and operation naturally inherent to scientific reasoning: method.

Methodological synthesis: truth and method

Critical thinking has a way of pursuing truth: the scientific method.

Methodology and epistemology seek an answer to the same problem: What is science? How is it done? How should research be conducted? How can evidence be obtained? How do we decide what is true and what is false?

Nomothetic methods

The practice of scientific research takes place in two moments. In a first moment, problems are apprehended, questions are posed, theories and models are elaborated and hypotheses are raised. In a second moment, scientific ideas are tested using external criteria. There are several criteria. In the nomologic sciences, observation and experiment constitute the main criteria.

Observation

Observation is a procedure central to all empirical knowledge. It works inside a bipartite system: a system that observes and a system (object) that is observed. Both systems are placed in an environment, that is, the circumstances of the observation. The phenomena or the facts are a result of the interaction between the two systems. The natural order of the observation process is: the fact, the observation and the observation datum (M. Bunge 2005, 175). The concrete objects of observation are things, processes, phenomena or events. In reality, we do not observe the objects entirely; we observe some of their traits. There are several meanings of observation, from the common sense to the philosophical. For our purpose, we are interested in its sense in science. I follow Bunge's perspective: 'observation proper can be characterized as purposeful and enlightened perception' (181). This perspective is highlighted because it involves a cluster of knowledge and a means of observation. According to Bunge, direct observation, or inference, comprises several stages, of which I emphasize two that are the most relevant for the process: interpretation and description. Interpretation is the recognition of the object or trait that is captured by perception, placing it in a broad outline. This is the stage of preliminary interpretation.

This stage is, somehow, an identification of the thing, the event, etc., that is observed. Description is a series of propositions that has data as a correspondent: 'every proposition in it is a *datum*'. The description uses a language whose terms designate theoretical or empirical concepts. The set of data described, with more or less technical terms, constitutes the material for a new level of interpretation: the theoretical interpretation—'a deeper and more detailed interpretation than the one contrived by observer' (183–184).

Experiment

Observation requires experiment. The experiment is the moment for testing the theoretically supported conjectures conceived by scientists to explain the phenomena. The testing of conjectures has an aim: to verify, confirm and perform the falsifiability test (K. Popper 1945). In one word: justification. Observation is the first stage of the experimental method, as designed by C. Bernard in the 1860s. By the end of the nineteenth and beginning of the twentieth century, the experimental method spread from natural sciences and experimental medicine to social sciences, through psychological sciences and education. By the 1920s, there was great enthusiasm for the application of experiment in the study of behaviour, namely Thorndike's behaviourism. This enthusiasm was extended to research on education, especially through the work of McCall. Also in this period, Fischer introduced innovations. His contribution was essential to the development of the randomization technique. After this wave of enthusiasm came a wave of pessimism. D.T. Campbell talks about 'disillusionment with experimentation in education'. This last author, assuming an 'evolutionary perspective on cumulative wisdom and science' (Campbell and Stanley 1963), resurrected this tradition, but with significant innovations, such as 'quasi-experimental designs'. This technique allows the use of experiments not only for 'research in teaching' but also for every social science. However, the experimental method did not return to social science until the 1980s. Experimental social psychology is one of the disciplines that has developed it the most extensively (e.g., Tajfel 1978).

Ideographic methods

After the Second World War, holistic and qualitative methods experienced a meaningful evolution, from biological sciences to social sciences.

As an example, the first experimental psychology was followed by psychoanalysis, the gestalt theory and phenomenology. In the social sciences, there emerged a multiplicity of methodologies dispersed between 'methodological holism' and 'methodological individualism', field observation and structural analysis. Ethnography, as conceived by W.F. Whyte, is an example of direct observation. Under the influence of H. Garfinkel, ethnomethodology was founded in the mid-1960s, creating a rupture with the 'orthodox consensus'. During the 1920s and 1930s, the Chicago School of Sociology was fruitful in ideographic methods, such as 'life-history'. Classic authors of this approach, well known in criminology, are I. Thomas, F. Znaniecki and C. Stanley.

What was the reason for this methodological dualism? What can explain these fluctuations in scientific methods? What are the reasons for the controversy between nomothetic and ideographic methods? In my view, these are a result of the complex interaction between two quite different thinking operations: explanation and understanding.

Explanation

Scientific explanation is a very complex cognitive operation. Philosophy of knowledge, epistemology and methodology have developed abundant and profound research on it for at least a century. From the classic work of E. Meyerson (1921) to current thought, we are far from finding a consensus. In a first synthesis, I have differentiated and characterized three types of explanation: causal, structural and procedural (Agra 2002). I will now complete that synthesis with what I present next.

According to N. Abbagnano (2010), theories of method distinguish two essential techniques for explanation, or techniques for answering the 'why' question: causal explanation techniques and conditional explanation techniques.

(a) Causal explanation comprises two types of causality: deductibility and uniformity. The first type calls for deduction. Explanation through deduction was used not only in metaphysics but also in science and positivism, namely logical positivism. This last epistemological perspective distinguishes two elements in explanation: the *explanandum* (the statement that describes the phenomenon that must be explained); and the *explanans* (the set of true statements brought to explain the phenomenon that contains general laws). The *explanans* must contain empirical content capable of being tested through experiments and observation. And what is causality defined as uniformity? It is the consistency of the relation between phenomena, the covariance between the different elements that constitute a situation, a fact, an event. It is the causal law that is established not by a logic-deductive reasoning but rather through a process of empirical confirmation. The proper evidence for this causality is uniform interaction. Which is the feature common to both types of causality? Both recognize the existence of causal links that allow precise predictions. Causality has a non-fallible and generalized character.

(b) The conditional explanation technique denies this feature to the explicative scheme. That is, the nomologic-deductive model is complemented by the statistic-inductive model. Explicative knowledge is part of descriptive knowledge. Science does not explain only through theory but also through the system, which is composed by the fact, the context and the theory. This is a pragmatic and constructive approach that reduces explanation to the status of likely probability.

(c) Unlike causal explanation, conditional explanation is open to another operation of thought: understanding.

Understanding

I present three considerations on this matter.

(a) The term 'understanding', defined as a method for knowledge, was conceived within historical analytical philosophy and hermeneutics to serve the interpretation of historical facts, things, or particular and singular events, most of all those related to human nature, society and culture. By the end of the nineteenth century and the beginning of the twentieth, understanding was established, namely though the thinking of Dilthey, as a method that separates hermeneutic sciences (sciences of spirit and history) and the formal and natural sciences. General laws, causality, nomologic-deductive and stochastic-inductive models would not be useful in the process of producing knowledge about society, human nature and history. Here, signification prevails over causality, hermeneutic interpretation over scientific explanation.

(b) Phenomenology and hermeneutic philosophy are the articulating knot of the theories of understanding. In the complex debate about understanding, we should highlight three authors: (1) M. Weber, who argues that historical phenomena are characterized by a particular and singular nexus, and not by general laws. They depend on a specific causality; (2) Heidegger, who defends an understanding applied not only to events, history or human nature, but also to things; and (3) H. Gadamer, who defines understanding as a game between a broad scheme and a specific case. To understand is to apply a general law to a concrete situation.[1] This is an operation of thought that creates innovative knowledge.

(c) It is not clear that understanding is opposed to explaining. There are epistemological perspectives (like the ones presented in b), which establish connections between explanation and understanding (even if they are complex).

Between methodological monism and epistemological anarchy

Through considering the thought of the greatest philosophers of knowledge and epistemology, it is obvious that, although they are different, the two methods—causal explanation and understanding—are not mutually exclusive. Because of space limitations, this reflection on method has not been undertaken with the desired epistemological and methodological depth.

During the 1970s the so-called movement of 'methodological pluralism' was born and expanded within the social sciences. What was the main idea behind this movement? There is not only one style of sociological research, but several. Some have called it 'epistemological anomie' in order to reflect the perceived need to abandon the rules of method, and above all the rules of positivist methodologic orthodoxy, functionalism and empiricism. Feyerabend has radicalized and legitimated this movement, arguing that in the sciences of nature as well there is not one research style, but several. *Against Method* is a work of epistemological anarchy.

Is there a way out of this chaos? The theories of scientific method have oscillated between two sides. If we take a look at the history of science we find, on one side, a methodological monism that generalizes the nomologic model and the formal and logical techniques to all knowledge domains. On the other side, we find a hypercritical model that stands for the abolition of rules, theory and method. The complexity of the problems that science should solve calls for a concertation between the different operations of reasoning and scientific methods. In fact, that concertation, even though in an undifferentiated manner, already exists in our spontaneous way of thinking and seeking the truth: What? Why? How? When? What for? Science, being a general method of critical thinking, has merely differentiated and theorized those questions. A pragmatic vision forces us to integrate the several methods that scientific practice has dispersed. Thus, I shall say: explanation requires understanding; quantitative requires qualitative; nomologic requires ideographic. We need a methodological pragmatism that is capable of removing the epistemological obstacle that impedes the establishment of a true science of human behaviour.

What meaning shall I give to the term 'pragmatism'? I found the concept of 'pragmatism' in the North American pragmatic philosophy that emerged at the end of the nineteenth century and was developed by several authors throughout the twentieth century. Pragmatic philosophers stand for 'more useful descriptions of the world and of ourselves' through 'reconciliation of science and value'. One of America's leading philosophers, John Dewey, stressed the importance of linking theories to action and to practical problem solving.

The method and the truth of human behaviour

Biological behaviourism, ethology, psychoanalysis, phenomenology and social behaviourism (e.g., symbolic interactionism) are failed attempts to explain and understand human behaviour. Why? Because they do not have a pragmatic definition of human being. What is the pragmatic definition of human being? John Dewey stressed the unity of nature and values in the human being. Both 'work together'. I would say that a pragmatic definition of human being, such as the one conceived by Dewey a century ago, inspired by Darwin and Hegel, is the most appropriate for a new behavioural science. But is there not still a true science of behaviour?

Let's hear recent statements from Boston University philosopher L. McIntyre. 'Why don't we have a true science of human behaviour today?' asks the author. 'The primary reason … is that we fear the threat that such science might pose for our … political beliefs about human autonomy, environmental determinism, race, class, and gender. In short, I believe that … the primary barrier to a science of human behaviour is ideological. Political ideology is today doing to social science what religious ideology did to natural science in the first Dark Ages' (McIntyre 2006, xviii).

I present three major conditions for this science.

(a) At the conceptual contents level, the vocation of the new science is to overcome the nature–culture dualism.

(b) At the methodological level, it is essential to abandon the methodological dualism that places in opposite sites nomothetic and ideographic methods; explanation and understanding; causality and signification. A true science of human behaviour should adopt an *evolutionary epistemology*, whose origins are found in the North American pragmatic philosophy of the end of the nineteenth century, and in its revitalization in the 1980s. This broad methodology should incorporate proximal or equivalent methodologies, like *naturalized epistemology* (W.V.O. Quine [1969] 1997). In fact, the 'continuity between natural and social scientific methodology' was supported by K. Popper (1945) seven decades ago. Today several authors, among them Cartwright and McIntyre, support it.

(c) At the social and cultural level, this new science should contribute to clarifying the problems faced by humanity today. The new science must clarify, above all, the problems whose origins lie in human behaviour, such as terrorism, corruption, economic crime and so on.

Can criminology and forensic science become a *unitas multiplex*?[2]

The epistemological status of criminology and forensic science forces them to link nature and value, facts and norms, behaviour and subjectivity, and ethology and ethics. These two disciplines, which have a common study object—the criminal phenomenon— have a central role in the articulation of natural and social sciences. A *unitas multiplex* of both disciplines has a singular role and perhaps a leading one as an *epistemological catalyst*.

Regarding criminology, L. McIntyre says, 'criminology, after all, might seem to be one of the best hopes for a true social science' (2006, 5). So, I shall say that the current vocation of criminology and forensic science is to assure hope in building a new science of human behaviour in the near future. Under what conditions?

The criminological-forensic territory

Crime has a juridical definition enshrined in the criminal codes. The *Forum*[3] is the institutional structure where law is applied and justice is made. That is, our disciplines are applied knowledge. Their work frame is defined by norms and their use. So, criminology and forensic science include a normative dimension. But they include, as well, a dimension of knowledge and scientific status: criminology and forensic sciences include a dimension of the sciences of facts and events of nature. The territory of our disciplines is vast: it goes from law and justice to mathematics, passing by way of physics, chemistry, biology, neurosciences, psychologic sciences … It brings together normative matrixes and scientific methods.

Methods and techniques

FORENSIC SCIENCE

The research of the forensic generalist asks questions similar to those asked by any other scientist: the *what* of crime; the *who* of crime; the *how* of crime (understanding). In order to answer these questions, the forensic generalist uses reasoning techniques quite similar to those used either in hermeneutic sciences (understanding) or in nomothetic sciences (explanation and observation).

(a) The hermeneutic method

In a conference that took place in Vienna in 1906, the founder of psychoanalysis, S. Freud, stated that the police detective and the psychoanalyst use the same method for seeking the truth. However, there is one difference: the patient does not know his or her truth; the criminal knows it very well. More recently, some authors place medicine and natural sciences as models for police investigation (O. Ribaux 2014, 182–183). What is the nature of a method that is able to inspire such distinct areas as psychoanalysis, clinical medicine, historical natural sciences and the scientific police? It is about the process of demonstration, truth construction, through the art of bringing together a multiplicity of signs, symptoms, indexes, traits (either visible or occult and underlying) and signification. The understanding of singularities and specific cases is the privileged method of the hermeneutic approach.

(b) The nomothetic method

Similar to the astronomer who develops several hypotheses about the spotlight that he observes in space, the forensic generalist develops conjectures from the crime scene. As she is obtaining information, she is selecting those hypotheses during a process in which the 'indiciary logic' (O. Ribaux) creates evidence through deductive and inductive reasoning techniques. She tests the hypotheses that grant her a major truth 'capital', using experiment and observation. The forensic generalist always reasons under an 'as if' logic: as if she was a psychoanalyst, a linguist, an archaeologist, an astronomer, a logician and a mathematician.

CRIMINOLOGY

(a) Ideographic criminology

I place in this category two traditions: the clinical criminology of a phenomenological orientation from the Louvain School (E. Degreff and C. Debuyst) and the criminology of a biographic orientation from the Chicago School. Both traditions are more focused on the understanding of the meaning of delinquent behaviour than on its explanation. I place here as well the ethno-criminology that uses participant and naturalistic observation in order to understand not so much the causes but, primarily, the processes. Recently, since the 1990s, new expressions of this ideographic criminology have emerged, such as 'existential criminology', 'narrative criminology', 'criminology of the deviant trajectories' and 'transcultural criminology'.

(b) Nomothetic criminology

In contrast to ideographic criminology, nomothetic criminology focuses more on explaining than on understanding. The search for causes and initial conditions for criminal behaviour constitutes the main axis of this criminology. Behavioural prediction is one of its main goals. I place here the tradition initiated by the studies of Glueck, work that was interrupted for about 40 years; I place here the tradition influenced by Hirschi's work. It is a fact that during the last 40 years, a tradition has been reborn that follows more the model of formal sciences (mathematics and statistics) and the natural sciences than social and human sciences. Examples are the studies of 'actuarial criminology', 'experimental criminology', 'developmental criminology' and 'quantitative criminology'. Similar to the forensic generalist, the criminologist works according to an 'as if' logic—sometimes as if he were an existentialist philosopher, a clinical psychologist, an anthropologist; other times as if he were a statistician, a physician and a biologist.

Conclusion

Can criminology and forensic science become a *unitas multiplex*? I shall say yes for six reasons.

They have the same study object: the criminal phenomenon. They have the same historical and epistemological matrix. They adapt to current epistemological shifts. In their territories, different scientific methods and techniques intersect. They have the same vocation: the scientific clarifying of crime and the investigation of criminal and security policies. They face the same challenge in the future: to function as catalysts in the construction of a true science of human behaviour. However, this possibility relies on two conditions:

(a) that forensic sciences become a true autonomous science; and
(b) that criminology becomes an integrative criminology.

Each should stop being a system of dispersion in order to establish a true theoretical and empirical system. In this way, we will have the conditions for a true communication between the two territories.

Acknowledgements

I wish to thank Gilda Santos and Pedro Almeida from the School of Criminology for their assistance in translating this text.

Notes

1 The judicial hermeneutic is an example of this game. As stated by the great German philosopher, the jurist defines the sense of the law based on a concrete case and because of this concrete judicial case (Gadamer 1978).
2 *Unitas multiplex* is a paradoxical concept. It articulates opposite notions: unity and diversity; the homogeneous and the heterogeneous. Angyal created the concept in 1941 in order to capture the complexity of the concept of 'system'. Forty years later, E. Morin redesigned this notion through the concept of 'complex organized unit'. The concept is useful to deconstruct the idea of substantial unit, of inseparability, of indivisibility. It also illustrates the complex relationship between the parts and the whole, between the object and its components.
3 *Forum* is a Latin word that signifies either a public square of an ancient Roman city, a centre of judicial and business affairs or a place of assembly for the people.

References

Abbagnano, N. 2010. *Diccionario de Filosofía*. Mexico: Fondo de Cultura Economica.
Agra, C. 1986. *Science, maladie mentale et dispositifs de l'enfance: du paradigme biologique au paradigme systémique*. Lisboa: Instituto Nacional de Investigação Científica.
Agra, C. 2002. 'The Complex Structures, Processes and Meanings of the Drug/Crime Relationship'. In S. Brochu, C. Agra and M.-M. Cousineau, eds., *Drugs and Crime Deviant Pathways*, 9–32. Burlington, VT: Ashgate.
Agra, C. 2015/a. 'Criminology and the Portuguese Experience of Crime: An Epistemological and Historical Approach'. *Newsletter of the European Society of Criminology: Criminology in Europe* 14: 4–11.
Agra, C. 2015/b. 'Criminology at the University of Porto: A "Unitas Multiplex"'. *Newsletter of the European Society of Criminology: Criminology in Europe* 14: 12–16.
Altavilla, E. 1982. *Psicologia Judiciária*, vol. 1, 3rd ed. Coimbra: Arménio Amado.
Bunge, M. 2005. *Philosophy of Science*, vol. 2. 3rd printing, rev. ed. New Brunswick, NJ: Transaction Publishers.
Campbell, D., and J. Stanley. 1963. *Experimental and Quasi-Experimental Design for Research*. Boston, MA: Houghton Mifflin Company.

Cusson, M. 1998. *Criminologie actuelle*. Paris: Les Presses Universitaires de France.

Debuyst, C. 1998. 'Les différents courants psychiatriques et psychologiques en rapport avec les savoirs criminologiques'. In C. Debuyst, F. Digneffe and A. Pires, eds., *Histoire des savoirs sur le crime et la peine*, vol. 2, *La rationalité pénale et la naissance de la criminologie*, 449–532. Brussels: De Boeck Université.

Foucault, M. 1969. *L'Archéologie du savoir*. Paris: Gallimard.

Foucault, M. 1972. *The Archaeology of Knowledge*. New York: Pantheon Books.

Gadamer, H. 1976. *Vérité et méthode. Les grandes lignes d'une herméneutique philosophique*. Paris: Ed. du Seuil.

Gouinlock, J. 1994. *The Moral Writings of John Dewey*. New York: Prometheus Books.

Margot, P. 2011. 'Commentary on the Need for a Research Culture in the Forensic Sciences'. *UCLA Law Review* 58(3): 795–801.

McIntyre, L. 2006. *Dark Ages: The Case for a Science of Human Behavior*. Cambridge, MA: Bradford/MIT Press.

Meyerson, E. 1921. *De l'explication dans les sciences*. Payot.

Popper, K. 1945. *The Poverty of Historicism*. London: Routledge & Kegan Paul.

Popper, K. 1968. *The Logic of Scientific Discovery*. London: Hutchinson & Co.

Quine, W.V.O. 1997. 'Epistemology Naturalized'. In H. Kornblith, ed., *Naturalizing Epistemology*, 15–33. Cambridge, MA: MIT Press.

Ribaux, O. 2014. *Police scientifique: Le renseignement par la trace*. Lausanne: Presses polytechniques et universitaires romandes.

Tajfel, H. 1978. *Differentiation between Social Groups: Studies in the Social Psychology of Intergroup Relations*. London: Academic Press.

3

Traceology, the bedrock of forensic science and its associated semantics

Pierre Margot

In the twentieth century, forensic science evolved from a method of investigation (Gross 1893) into a technological identification process focused on evidence in a legal procedure (Robertson et al. 2014). The high identification power obtained with fingermarks, tool marks, etc., and more recently with DNA, has fed technological developments focused on the identification capacities offered by chemistry, biology, or physics, with little or no relation to the object of study—the remnants or vestiges[1] left by criminals while committing their crimes. This has reached a point where extreme technological developments are highly controlled to safeguard and ensure the quality of analysis of specific items without any, or hardly any, consideration of the object itself. This has led to the creation of specialized and skilled laboratories akin to service factories, able to deliver analytical results to their clients: highly controlled deliverables but of questionable value. These developments have also resulted in an economic disaster—for example, the recent closure (in 2012) of the Forensic Science Service in the UK—and the turmoil of forensic science in the US with ongoing reviews that followed the scathing National Research Council Report (National Academy of Sciences 2009) after serious mistakes were identified. This crisis is further compounded today with the lack of consideration of electronic trace information (phones, computers, surveillance cameras, GPS, cyberspace) as it relates to other forensic science data.

A simple example should illustrate and help demonstrate the difficult scientific questions fundamental to forensic science, those due to the very nature of its object: the trace, clue of an event that needs to be understood, the identities of its participants, their contribution to the event, etc.

Example

A fight breaks out on a dance floor. One participant to the fight breaks a wine glass and uses the broken glass in his hand to cut the throat of his opponent. Realizing the potential consequences, this participant runs out of the dance club and flees in the direction of an underground station. An individual is stopped and arrested after traditional police investigation. This person denies having been at the dance despite fitting witness descriptions, and a recording by surveillance cameras apparently showing him run into the underground station. His clothing is collected, a fragment of broken glass is found in the wound of the deceased and a couple of glass fragments are recovered from the dance floor.

Brought to the laboratory, two small pieces of broken glass are found during the search of the clothing of the man under arrest. Laboratories can provide glass analyses which may go from simple density and refractive index (RI) measurements to multi-element qualitative and quantitative analyses (such as ICP–MS). Multi-element analytical research has focused on the analysis of windows, bottles, drinking glasses, windbreakers, showing the internal variation of composition of various items, the variation between types of items, sometimes even focusing on differentiating production batches, etc. This is all done using sampling, i.e., selecting a given number of fragments from a source to delimit the spread of values for a given (identified) source. This process is valuable in determining the discrimination power of the method applied and documenting the diversity in production of a given item but has little relation to the problem at hand. The trace items found on the floor and on the clothing are not identified as standard source materials. It is not even sure that they are glass fragments, and if they are, the analyst does not know whether these fragments are representative of their source or not, since they were not selected and they represent only a vestige (what is left from an event, i.e., they are not formally 'samples').

Taking a general approach, it is first determined that all fragments are pieces of glass: they are all apparently colourless and transparent. Using the refractive index measurements, they may fit the broad category of glass used for making drinking glasses (not bottle or window or spectacle). Refining the analyses, it now appears that the RI differs between the fragments in the wound, the fragments recovered from the floor and the fragments in the garments. One obvious conclusion is that they are not from the same source! This conclusion, however, may be utterly misleading since a drinking glass may be made of one generic type of glass whose composition may vary for the drinking bowl, the stem and the base. Three pieces of broken glass may be from a single source but differ in their composition! The analytical response is correct, but the forensic conclusion would be wrong if it is decided that the broken pieces are not from the same source. On the other hand, some valuable forensic science research starting in the 1970s (Pearson et al. 1971) has been relegated to the past by laboratories and is ignored most of the times. This research involved population studies looking at clothing to see the likelihood of finding glass fragments in a population of garments, what happens when you break glass, what is happening to glass transferred during the action, etc. These studies have shown that the chance (or risk) of finding glass fragments on clothing in a general population is not unusual but that transferred glass during an event is not persistent and falls rapidly off the clothing with activity. In the example, finding glass on the clothing is therefore relevant since there was glass broken. It has value because the source has material features typically found in drinking glass. Going any further has little relevance since the difference in composition cannot be explained by a difference in source but solely by the lack of homogeneity arising from the manufacture of the drinking glasses in that scenario, and in general. Studying the activity (with time and space or location, pictures taken by witnesses with their mobile phones, surveillance cameras, activation of communication points, etc.) combined with the glass findings in such a scenario is much more relevant than determining a multi-element composition of a fragment whose source and sampling is not controlled. The logic applied in most forensic science laboratories does not follow this path, and most scientists are uncomfortable with this situation since it is out of control of their technical skills.

This example is simple and almost a caricature. It concerns a closed set, a single crime with a limited number of participants but with significant and difficult forensic questions that are not approached by the current discussions on forensic science worldwide.

Linkage blindness

Looking at the wider sociological picture, Egger studied the reasons for failures in criminal investigation. He identified many factors, but one was found to dominate all others, which he coined 'linkage blindness' (Egger 1984). Linkage blindness is the incapacity to link crimes committed by the same criminal or group of criminals, crimes that are linked in nature but that investigations have failed to link. Linkage blindness accounts for a large number of these failures in criminal investigation since a great number of crimes are committed by a small number of criminals (habitual/professional/organized/terrorism) with a high recidivist rate. Diminishing this linkage blindness has been key to the developments of various databases—collecting modus operandi; data collection on crimes, on victims, etc.—for example, databases such as VICAP—violent crime apprehension programme—in the US or ViCLAS—violent crime linkage analysis system—in Canada (Collins et al. 1998). But this approach has failed to afford the expected successes because of its subjective and highly administrative nature. Forensic science, maintaining its focus on analytical technology rather than on the problem to be solved, was unable to propose a solution. It was only with the advent of DNA, its high individualizing capacity as well as its presentation as a sequence of digits to express the profiles that computers handle perfectly, that it was soon apparent that DNA traces on various crime scenes were connecting the crimes, whereas the criminal was not in the database or in the frame of the investigation (Kind 1987). One essential feature with DNA is that, in principle, all cells from the source share an identical DNA profile. Nevertheless, all efforts remained on the discrimination power and identifying strength of DNA by multiplying research into more loci, rather than exploiting the connecting power of even partial profiles. Looking for connections, it is necessary to move away from the highly selective to a much lower level of distinction to be able to group what is similar (which allows linkage) from what is different (which allows dissociation).

Research starting in the 1990s looked at highly repetitive crimes, volume crimes such as burglaries, by collecting files of solved linked cases. It was found that most files contained indications that material evidence had been collected but was rarely, if ever, used for investigative purposes, but usually only retrospectively, after a person was arrested, to demonstrate the extent of the crimes (Ribaux, Taroni et al. 1995). The investigative strength of material evidence was lost. Since then, research and practice have demonstrated the power and strength of such material evidence in describing criminal phenomena and reducing linkage blindness in a great variety of crimes from burglaries to terrorism, doping, counterfeiting, etc. (Ribaux and Margot 1999; Walsh et al. 2002; Ribaux, Baylon et al. 2010a; Ribaux, Baylon et al. 2010b; Rossy et al. 2013; Morelato et al. 2014; Baechler et al. 2015). The study of material left or modified by criminals while committing their crimes, or taken with them from the scenes of their crimes, got back on its original tracks, which it should not have left. Electronic information is further nourishing this capacity of linkage but with an explosion in the volume of information that needs to be searched, measured, compared, connected, etc. The study and understanding of the meaning of traces as a whole is therefore fundamental to forensic science. Indeed, the Berlin school, created in the 1920s, maintained teaching, research and development in the use of traces for investigation in direct line with the 'Kriminalistik' of Gross (1893). The name it gave for the major defining course in forensic science was 'traceology', which we now adopt.

Trace and traceology

The word 'trace' comes from Latin (*tractus*) and the old French to mean the path someone or something takes; since the fourteenth century, it has been extended to mean the vestige or mark of a presence, an existence or an action of someone or something in a location or space that did not belong to that space initially (Margot 2014).

The fact that it is a vestige or a remnant indicates that it is affected by the asymmetry of time (we cannot use the rewind button), and it is determined by the past. Cleland argues (Cleland

2002) that there is an over-determination of the past; it tells something of the past that is not haphazard. This means, also, that it may not be representative of its original state, but most of the time it has a retrodictive capacity sufficient to allow a reasonable explanation of a common cause as highlighted by Cleland (Cleland 2001; Cleland 2013) because it exists! This material existence is independent from its potential meaning unlike a discourse or a written statement, which incorporates an author's meaning. It allows detection, measurements, classification and comparison using a scientific methodology. The information content of this vestige may be sufficient to identify its source (such as with DNA, fingermarks, toolmarks, etc.), to specify the 'presence' or 'existence' of 'someone' or 'something', but it also gives information related to space (where and how—orientation, action, electronic connection, images) and time ('initially' or when, succession, sequence, communication, etc.) to describe the overall activity that created the trace. Since it is not possible to go back in time, we can only construct a model that is descriptive of a given crime scenario, supported by what is observed. This is not a general model, but a specific retrodictive model that can only be probabilistic in nature.

In the majority of cases, the quality of the vestige is such that it is incomplete, imperfect and degraded by time passing, and these losses increase uncertainty or may support only approximations about the past event. These approximations need to be revised as new or complementary information becomes available. This may be unsettling for scientists focused on the precision and accuracy of measurements.

The definition of 'trace' as used here is clearly divergent from a recent usage that has come from chemistry, where a trace is a very small quantity, near the detection limits of technologies, and often described as an impurity or imperfection in a product or process. This comes from the development of chemistry in the nineteenth century and a definition given by Faraday in 1807 (according to the English Oxford Dictionary). The perception of the trace is here negative; it is considered an undesirable factor, whereas in forensic science, the trace is the fundamental and positive vector of the information. A trace is a vector of knowledge and is capable of being questioned depending on the scenarios that are proposed, since it is the result of an activity under investigation that needs to be understood or demonstrated. Looking at the literature, toxicologists often refer to 'impurities' when trying to link illicit drug seizures. They may be impurities for the producer of the illicit drug, but they are the essential trace for forensic science. This contrasting view emphasizes the essential difference in perspectives (Lociciro et al. 2007).

It must be emphasized that the role of traceology is not to determine cause but to give an indication of how the trace findings measure when different versions of causes are given. Mathematical models help give dimensions on how likely are the traces observed, given various propositions about the crime and how it was committed. A whole research field studies this type of interpretation based on Bayes theorem (Aitken and Taroni 2004). This approach is intellectually satisfying and helps with both understanding the reasoning processes involved in retrodiction and the development of tools for forensic expert systems integrated to databases (Neumann et al. 2012; Taroni et al. 2014).

Unfortunately, this end product has little value if the relevance of the traces detected is faulty since the environment is full of traces from the 'normal' uses and activities that contaminate scenes of investigation. They constitute a background noise (Hazard 2014) and this is why heuristics should be developed to target the searches toward known trace transfer with a rich potential (point of entry, object not at its usual place, point of contact observed by a surveillance camera, etc.) or to situations that are such that they fit a crime model (see Delémont et al., 'The practice of crime scene examination in an intelligence-based perspective', chapter 8, in this volume). Specific traces may also be targeted (even of poor quality) if a phenomenon (serial crime) has been detected and is known to be ongoing. The focus can be directed toward specific traces identified in earlier cases of the series (Girod et al. 2008).

Further, if no precautions are taken, the scenes of investigation may be further polluted by careless handling of scenes (carelessness may also be detected by surveillance cameras!).

The trace exists, whether detected or not, and will remain without meaning unless detected. Its presence and its detection is a first indication of relevance and may lead to the detection of further traces that will help develop an understanding of the crime and its circumstances. From a hazy picture, each relevant finding unveils contours with more or less acuity and may, in certain cases, offer a clear picture with information of maximum quality. The whole range of information will therefore go from a simple clue to a full probative story line.

Understanding this grey scale offered by trace findings, and how they can feed the other processes (investigation, intelligence, prevention, court proceedings, etc.), is what forensic science is about. Traces constitute a sign language and forensic science develops the methods and the grammar to understand the meaning of these signs with their ambiguities, confusions and strengths. Combining findings, analyzing them as a logical puzzle where pieces only fit in certain combinations, belong to the overall forensic science process as a problem-solving quest. It starts from a territory full of unknown elements, and where forensic science should start its quest (not in the laboratory) and as contours become clearer, full laboratory analyses may become necessary to resolve ambiguities.

This argumentation makes apparent that technological analytical developments, although important in their detection and measurement capabilities, remain blind if they are not applied within a developed logical framework and a well-understood investigative methodology: the Kriminalistik of Gross (Gross 1893).

Forensic science and its object: the semantics of the trace and its context

Unfortunately, language and semantics used within the profession have been led astray, by practice and/or under the influence of primarily chemistry, but also biology, physics, mathematics, etc. The language used thus needs clarification because it underlies fundamental misunderstandings and raises fundamental issues relevant to forensic science and its role.

The first confusion is between 'findings' and 'evidence'. Forensic scientists should not use the latter despite the courts' claim that 'expert witnesses are giving evidence'. Forensic scientists are highlighting traces they have found and their information content. Given certain propositions, they may highlight their likelihood, supporting one or other propositions. The courts will receive these findings and decide if they help in their understanding of the issues they have to judge. Findings become evidence if they help in any measure to decide on the issue and the causality of a given case. This subtle distinction clarifies the situation and that the scientist cannot take the role of the judge. Evidence concerns the issue and means used to reach a verdict, only if they are found relevant and informative for the judge.

A second confusion appears with 'sample'. In science, a sample has a definite and narrow meaning in that it is part of a whole selected to be representative of this whole. Sampling gives an indication of the range of values typical for an item. The selection process is an essential element of the representativeness. A trace is never 'selected' because it is representative, but it is taken because it is present and, apparently, relevant. It may be, more often than not, representative of its source, but this is only an assumption that cannot be made without logical information supporting it. The example given in the introduction with the glass fragments highlights this misuse: by saying 'we analyzed the glass samples collected from the clothing,' the inference is that they are representative of their source (which they are not!); therefore, if they differ in their physics (RI) or chemistry, we should exclude that they come from the same source as the fragment in the wound. It is proposed that 'specimen' is a more correct word since a specimen is a part of a whole but expresses the fact that it is a 'one off' element, without indication about a selection or representativeness. But other words can be used like 'item' and 'collected trace'. Using 'sample' in this case is not only wrong and misleading, but shows a fundamental misunderstanding in the way the trace is created. It is true that some traces, like DNA, do share the same profile as their source since all living cells contain an identical DNA (with few exceptions), but the trace that contains DNA may be partially degraded and will therefore be only partially representative of its source. This is where scientific knowledge and interpretation come in.

A third confusion concerns the term 'print' as in 'fingerprint', 'shoe print', etc. The term 'finger print' or 'fingerprint' was used by Galton (Galton 1892) to designate the pattern made by papillary ridges on the skin of the surface of hands, fingers and feet that were 'printed' to register habitual criminals in order to be able to identify them again after a later arrest. The perception that it could be used to identify a source through its finger traces left at scenes of investigation was a separate, fundamental change in perspective proposed by Faulds (Faulds 1880). It became the embodiment of what could be used to identify with alleged certainty. It was therefore coined by biologists (DNA fingerprinting, virus, bacteria, plant ... fingerprinting), by chemists (looking at the fingerprint region of an IR spectrum), by forensic scientists (voiceprint) and even by computer scientists (website or server fingerprinting) to indicate the highly selective nature of a technique, of a feature or of a method. A single term should apply to all those: a 'profile' that emerges from the analyses. A bibliographic database search for 'fingerprint' will deliver thousands of papers that have nothing to do with the ridge features of the skin, or forensic science for that matter. But the confusion is not only created outside the field; within forensic science some have started to designate without distinction the pattern (the pattern made by ridges), the reproduction of the pattern for databases or comparison (the print of this pattern—the true fingerprint) and the traces left unknowingly while touching an object (the trace made by the pattern—the fingermark), making the object quite confusing at times. In the UK, the distinction is provided by the 'fingerprint' for the reference print and 'fingermark' for the trace: 'the fingermark which, generally, implies a lesser quality impression that includes latent, partial, distorted, reversed (tonally or laterally), or superimposed impressions' (Champod et al. 2016).

Kind and colleagues (Kind et al. 1979) already showed, as far back as 1978 in Wichita, that the diversity of vocabulary used was very confusing because a single word could be used to describe different concepts, whereas different words could be used to apply to one single concept. Although they did not make a distinction between samples and specimens (see above), they found 21 different terms to designate samples (i.e., reference material). These authors did not go very far, but stopped at defining three specific concepts:

(1) 'samples with known association with crime', which they call the 'crime sample': this may be paint from a door where a burglar used a tool, the soil from the garden where a body was found, etc.—that is, samples representative of the environment with which the criminal has had contact (paint on a tool or soil on car mat are traces that can be compared with these samples);
(2) 'samples with suspected association with crime' for which they offer the name of 'questioned sample'. This definition does not make clear whether it is a sample, but it is apparent from the context that these are the specimens—trace material that may be compared to the crime samples of (1);

(3) 'samples from reference collection' or 'reference samples': these constitute the accumulated events, as they say, in the statistical sense, that compose the collection of data.

This initial attempt at defining what was perceived to be highly confusing was not pursued, but occasional questions arise in the literature. They also failed to note some very important distinctions among reference samples, and indeed their 'crime sample' is a form of reference in itself, perhaps the most relevant.

References can cover many relevant concepts for forensic science, less so in other disciplines:

i) The controls which are of three types: the blanks, the positive and the negative controls:

   a. Blanks are usually crime samples taken to document background information. This process was used, as far as we know, for the first time in forensic science by Orfila, considered the founder of forensic toxicology with his treatise on poisons (Orfila 1814), who took soil from the environment of an exhumed body suspected to have been poisoned by arsenic (in the Lafarge case in 1840). The presence of arsenic in the body could not be explained by diffusion from the environment since it was devoid of arsenic. The arsenic found in the body must have been ingested and the allegation of poisoning could be decided upon by the court. These are important controls in forensic toxicology and fire investigation.
   b. Positive controls are samples known to contain the type of materials for which the analyses are done. They should show positive indications of the expected results. This demonstrates that the technique/method works as it should. This type of control was systematically seen on the same reaction plates in serology, testing for blood groups, or species where wells were arranged, one with a blank control (saline extraction of background), a well with human blood group A, a well with human blood group B and a well with blood group O. Antibodies were tested to see that they reacted with their correct antigen. Antibody anti-A should be reacting with A and only A.
   c. Negative controls. In the example under b., in testing antibody anti-A, there should be no reaction with samples of blood group B or O. These are the negative controls. The absence of reaction with the blank control corresponds to a., above.

ii) The standards
The standards are certified materials/measures against which a specimen is tested. Standard organizations provide or validate these standards, which may be used to build a reference collection that may be shared and against which methods and techniques are calibrated. This allows for comparisons on a larger scale, across borders and jurisdictions.

iii) Population collections
These are collections that are built on the basis of samples of a relevant population and help determine frequency or rarity of some features relevant to the interpretation of some findings.

It is apparent that these distinctions may be made when questions are raised in court or after reading reports, but they should be part of the overall discipline because they demonstrate a deep understanding of the role of forensic science and traceology.

Another dimension requiring clarification or emphasis (already mentioned earlier in this chapter) is the distinction between contamination and pollution. Any investigation scene is contaminated. Contamination cannot be avoided and one may say that relevance is the essential factor distinguishing the clue-giving trace from the background that constitutes the history of the investigation scene. There is an illusion that contamination can be avoided by careful handling of the scene (overalls, gloves, masks, etc.). These measures are useful and necessary to avoid introducing further, unwanted elements to the scene. The fact of being conscious of this risk justifies the use of a terminology that is essentially negative, like pollution, something that investigative teams know that they should avoid, whereas background and relevant traces belong to the fundamental baggage of forensic scientists.

Finally, a problem that was almost unknown 30 or 40 years ago is now becoming extremely demanding and needs attention: the distinction between an original and a copy. With current electronic developments, the distinction between the original of a document and a copy (mail, letter, contract, image) may be very difficult to make. Indeed, the signal used to produce one document is identical for a second copy of the same document, a third, fourth, etc., and this may need massive investigation into metadata of huge quantities of electronic events or actions. The change of dimensions and the critical issue about chain of custody become even more pressing. This is an issue essential in electronic investigations and, unfortunately, has received too little attention so far, but changes are rapid, and this observation may be obsolete when this chapter is published!

Conclusion

Forensic science has a specific object of analysis, the trace left as witness of an event that needs to be investigated and understood. This vector is a rich support for information whose reading may be very complex and obtained through multiple and various dimensions. The complexity makes its approach a permanent research problem whose solution is never known; it may be alleged, supposed and expected, but the ground truth remains past and largely not accessible. Science, using logic and analyses, is capable of providing rich information of value to investigators, to researchers of crime and to courts. Because of its materiality, the trace can be questioned, measured and analyzed in different ways without uncontrollable variations in its dimensions unlike other less robust information such as that produced by witnesses. The difficulty is not only scientific since the trace's status often remains accessory to more valued human investigation in traditional policing, and in many instances single pieces of particular interest in a given inquiry are afforded the poor recognition. Science has a role to play, but that role needs to be defined and based in science and not on scientists as providers of certified and accredited tests. Scientists trained in the discipline also need to understand that the language used in their endeavours underscores the problems they tackle and covers essential concepts unique to the discipline, at least to some extent. This chapter highlights some of these conceptual difficulties mostly ignored or misunderstood by scientists working in forensic science but who are specialists of their trade, be it chemistry, physics, biology or computer science. Their discipline is useful and rich, but there is a large gap to bridge before these disciplines offer their full potential in the study of crimes and their signs. Forensic science has been in crisis around the world during the last twenty years for lack of will or understanding, and the limited research dedicated to the scientific and relevant questions. Calls were published that focused on relevant research and the problem-solving paradigm (Margot 2011; Margot 2011b; De Forest 2001) but current initiatives in many countries continue to focus attention on technologies, standards and regulatory measures rather than on science. This is a wake-up call.

Note

1 The distinction between remnants and vestiges is subtle and shows a gradation, the remnant being a residue or a small remaining part that may not be visible, whereas the vestige is usually a visible sign of something. They are used synonymously in this chapter.

References

Aitken, C.G.G., and F. Taroni. 2004. *Statistics and the Evaluation of Evidence for Forensic Scientists*. Chichester, UK: John Wiley & Sons.

Baechler, S., M. Morelato, O. Ribaux, A. Beavis, M. Tahtouh, K.P. Kirkbride, P. Esseiva, P. Margot and C. Roux. 2015. 'Forensic Intelligence Framework. Part II: Study of the Main Generic Building Blocks and Challenges through the Examples of Illicit Drugs and False Identity Documents Monitoring'. *Forensic Science International* 250(May): 44–52.

Champod, C., C. Lennard, P. Margot and M. Stoilovic. 2016. *Fingerprints and Other Skin Ridge Impressions*. Boca Raton, FL: CRC Press.

Cleland, C.E. 2001. 'Historical Science, Experimental Science, and the Scientific Method'. *Geology* 29(11): 987–990.

Cleland, C.E. 2002. 'Methodological and Epistemic Differences between Historical Science and Experiemntal Science'. *Philosophy of Science* 69: 474–496.

Cleland, C.E. 2013. 'Common Cause Explanation and the Search for a Smoking Gun'. *Geological Society of America Special Papers* 502: 1–9.

Collins, P.I., G.F. Johnson, A. Choy, K.T. Davidson and R.E. MacKay. 1998. 'Advances in Violent Crime Analysis and Law Enforcement: The Canadian Violent Crime Linkage Analysis System'. *Journal of Government Information* 25(3): 277–284.

De Forest, P.R. 2001. 'What Is Trace Evidence?' In B. Caddy, ed., *Forensic Examination of Glass and Paint: Analysis and Interpretation*, 1–25. London, UK: Taylor and Francis.

Egger, S.A. 1984. 'A Working Definition of Serial Murder and the Reduction of Linkage Blindness'. *Journal of Police Science and Administration* 12(3): 348–355.

Faulds, H. 1880. 'On the Skin-Furrows of the Hand'. *Nature* 22: 605.

Galton, F. 1892. *Finger Prints*. London: Macmillian and Company.

Girod, A., C. Champod and O. Ribaux. 2008. *Traces de souliers*. Lausanne: Presses polytechniques et universitaires romandes.

Gross, H. 1893. *Handbuch für Untersuchungsrichter als System der Kriminalistik*. Graz: Leuschnen und Lubensky.

Hazard, D. 2014. 'La pertinence en science forensique'. PhD diss., Université de Lausanne.

Kind, S.S. 1987. *The Scientific Investigation of Crime*. Harrogate: Forensic Science Services Ltd.

Kind, S.S., R. Wigmore, P.H. Whitehead and D.X. Loxley. 1979. 'Terminology in Forensic Science'. *Journal of the Forensic Science Society* 19(3): 189–191.

Lociciro, S., P. Hayoz, P. Esseiva, L. Dujourdy, F. Besacier and P. Margot. 2007. 'Cocaine Profiling for Strategic Intelligence Purposes: A Cross-Border Project between France and Switzerland. Part I. Optimisation and Harmonisation of the Profiling Method'. *Forensic Science International* 167(2–3): 220–228.

Margot, P. 2011. 'Forensic Science on Trial—What Is the Law of the Land?' *Australian Journal of Forensic Sciences* 43(2–3): 83–97.

Margot, P. 2011b. 'Commentary on *The Need for a Research Culture in the Forensic Sciences*'. *UCLA Law Review* 58: 795–801.

Margot, P. 2014. 'Traçologie: la trace, vecteur fondamental de la police scientifique'. *Revue internationale de criminologie et de police technique et scientifique* 67(1): 72–97.

Morelato, M., S. Baechler, O. Ribaux, A. Beavis, M. Tahtouh, P. Kirkbride, C. Roux and P. Margot. 2014. 'Forensic Intelligence Framework. Part I: Induction of a Transversal Model by Comparing Illicit Drugs and False Identity Documents Monitoring'. *Forensic Science International* 236(March): 181–190.

National Academy of Sciences. 2009. *Strengthening Forensic Science in the United Sates: A Path Forward*. Washington, DC: National Academies Press.

Neumann, C., I.W. Evett and J. Skerrett. 2012. 'Quantifying the Weight of Evidence from a Forensic Fingerprint Comparison: A New Paradigm'. *Journal of the Royal Statistical Society. Series A (Statistical Society)* 175(2): 371–415.

Orfila, M.J.B. 1814. *Le traité des poisons*. Paris: Crochard.
Pearson, E.F., R.W. May and M.G.D. Dabbs. 1971. 'Glass and Paint Fragments Found in Men's Outer Clothing—A Report of a Survey'. *Journal of Forensic Sciences* 16(2): 283–302.
Ribaux, O., A. Baylon, C. Roux, O. Delémont, E. Lock, C. Zingg and P. Margot. 2010a. 'Intelligence-Led Crime Scene Processing. Part I: Forensic Intelligence'. *Forensic Science International* 195(1–3): 10–16.
Ribaux, O., A. Baylon, E. Lock, O. Delémont, C. Roux, C. Zingg and P. Margot. 2010b. 'Intelligence-Led Crime Scene Processing. Part II: Intelligence and Crime Scene Examination'. *Forensic Science International* 199(1–3): 63–71.
Ribaux, O., and P. Margot. 1999. 'Inference Structures for Crime Analysis and Intelligence: The Example of Burglary Using Forensic Science Data'. *Forensic Science International* 100(3): 193–210.
Ribaux, O., F. Taroni and P. Margot. 1995. 'La recherche et la gestion des liens dans l'investigation criminelle: une étape vers l'exploitation systématique des données de police'. *Revue internationale de criminologie et de police technique* 48: 229–242.
Robertson, B., G.A. Vignaux and C. Berger. 2014. *Interpreting Evidence—Evaluating Forensic Science in the Courtroom*. Chichester, UK: John Wiley & Sons Inc.
Rossy, Q., S. Ioset, D. Dessimoz and O. Ribaux. 2013. 'Integrating Forensic Information in a Crime Intelligence Database'. *Forensic Science International* 230(1–3): 137–146.
Taroni, F., A. Biedermann, S. Bozza, P. Garbolino and C. Aitken. 2014. *Bayesian Networks for Probabilistic Inference and Decision Analysis in Forensic Science*. Chichester, UK: John Wiley & Sons.
Walsh, S.J., C. Roux, A. Ross, O. Ribaux and J.S. Buckleton. 2002. 'Forensic DNA Profiling: Beyond Identification'. *Law Enforcement Forum* 2(3): 13–21.

4

A method that combines criminology and forensic science

Considering the case of antiterrorism

Maurice Cusson

Is there an approach common to forensic science and criminology, a method focused on the problems and solutions rather than on laboratory techniques or statistical models? How could criminologists and forensic scientists work together to study crime problems and propose solutions? More specifically, how could they join forces to pose the problem of terrorism inspired by jihadist movements, help to identify terrorist cells, and prevent attacks? These are the questions this chapter tries to answer.

A method that answers these questions exists. It was gradually developed by authors who conceived policing in terms of problem-solving, situational prevention and forensic science contribution (Goldstein 1990; Clarke 1995; Clarke and Eck 2003; Cusson 2010; Cusson et al. 2007; Ribaux 2014). However, with regard to terrorism, the problem-solving method requires modifications because terrorist attacks are rare events, terrorists are difficult to detect and their attacks are unpredictable.

The chapter is divided into five parts. This structure aims at situating a theoretical framework that can clarify the combined value of criminology and forensic science in the area of antiterrorism.

The first part is a short presentation of problem oriented policing;
The second answers the question: what is the specific contribution of criminologists and forensic scientists to the analysis of crime problems?
The third presents a brief autopsy of a terrorist attack;
The fourth lists the conditions for the success of a terrorist attack;
The last part analyses the tactics of antiterrorism.

Problem oriented policing

'A problem is a recurring set of related harmful events in a community that members of the public expect the police to address. This definition draws attention to six elements that define a problem: Communities; Harm; Expectation; Events; Recurring; Similarity' (Clarke and Eck 2003, 15). Gravity appears as an obvious criterion of a problem. A serious crime spreads fear and arouses the desire for revenge. A problem analysis should lead to a solution. Crime analysts cannot simply accumulate data; it is also their duty to put forward possible solutions. This assumes that they are knowledgable about effective measures and those that are not (Clarke and Eck 2003).

Sometimes solving a problem boils down to identifying one suspect and arresting him. The steps that follow are the main responsibility of the justice system. But in many cases, this is not enough. It has indeed been known for centuries—since at least the birth of modern policing in Paris in 1667—that police work is not only about serving justice; it is also about prevention. In Paris in the seventeenth century, one of the first decisions by the *lieutenant de police* had to do with street lighting: a preventive measure.

Basically, a crime problem analysis can be broken down into six steps (Ribaux 2014; Cusson and Ribaux 2015).

1. *The detection.* Some problems are obvious by their gravity or the extent of the damage. The frequency or the recurrence of similar crimes is detected by a crime analyst or a crime scene investigator. Sometimes crime mapping locates a hot spot of crime. By its very nature, a terrorist attack cannot escape attention: to induce the state of terror, such attacks need to be perceived and recognized by a maximum number of persons. Its impact relies on the publicity it can achieve.
2. *A preliminary position of the problem.* A first draft of the problem is outlined, possibly by interviewing a few patrol officers, detectives or crime scene investigators aware of the problem; or reading some journalists' articles describing jihadist terrorist attacks.
3. *Literature review and formulating of initial hypotheses.* Through a literature review, knowledge is gained about the outlines of the problem and its foreseeable solutions. In the case under discussion here, the literature on terrorist attacks and solutions adopted elsewhere were specifically highlighted. A more precise definition of the problem is then stated.
4. *Data collection and testing of hypotheses.* Hypotheses about the problem and possible solutions dictate the choice of data collection and analysis: traces, observations made at the crime scene, databases, reports of intelligence service.
5. *The meeting.* The crime analyst, the intelligence agent, the forensic specialist and the investigator meet. Everyone shares her findings, explanations and solutions. The assumptions contradicted by the facts are rejected. Promising solutions are retained.
6. *A report* describes the problem and its frequency and offers some solutions to solve the problem.

The specific contribution of criminologists and of forensic scientists: traces and words

One way to distinguish the contribution of criminologists from that of forensic scientists is to argue that the nature of the information used by the first category is expressed in *words*, while the latter examines the *traces* of criminal acts. A *trace* is what is left unintentionally by the criminal on the crime scene or what he carries on himself, like the blood of the victim on his shirt (Locard 1920). It is a sign of the criminal's activities as well as a sign of something that is present where it should not have been. It can be traced back to its source (the criminal), or can inform on an action, in order to reconstruct, understand, explain, prove or link events (Margot 2014; Delémont et al. 2014). In his reflections of the practice of forensic science, Ribaux (2014) recognizes a multiplicity of basic functions to traces. The information conveyed by traces may, for instance, be used to:

- Determine the *source* of the trace: those fingermarks have been produced by this particular individual.
- Identify the *nature and profile* of the source: these traces of paint on the scene of an accident are those of a car of such make and model.

- *Link* two crimes together: the same DNA profiles are found on the premises of two different crime scenes, unveiling the repetitive activity of the offender.
- *Link* a criminal to a victim: the profile of the rapist is extracted from a biological trace found on the victim.
- *Locate* a criminal or the place where a mobile phone call comes from.
- *Reconstruct* events: broken objects, injuries to the forearm of the victim and blood stains widely distributed are indications that the murder was preceded by a fight.

If the forensic scientist focuses on the traces, the criminologist focuses on *words*: the statements of the victims, testimonies, confessions, telephone calls, the hearsay of police informants and alarms of whistleblowers. They are true or false. They are credible when they are corroborated by several eyewitnesses or traces. The non-exhaustive list below gives an idea of the origins of words that provide information about crime problems.

- phone calls to the police;
- statements by the victim;
- testimonies;
- denunciations;
- accounts of police informants;
- interception of telephone conversations;
- recording of conversations with hidden microphones;
- emails and other Internet communications; and
- responses to victimization surveys and questionnaires.

All these sources allow the police to be aware that a crime was committed, how it took place, the relationship between the criminal and her victim, the motive and the premeditation.

The autopsy of a terrorist attack

When focusing on terrorism, the problem-solving approach requires modifications to be adapted to this category of criminal activity. Since major terrorist attacks are very rare, quantitative analysis is difficult or impossible. An alternative approach could be to conduct an *autopsy* of a number of attacks perpetrated in a recent past. An autopsy describes and narrates the sequence of events of a terrorist attack beginning with the first step up to the last stage, which could be the arrest or the killing of the terrorists. What happened before, during and after the crisis are noted, as well as the 'successes' and 'failures' not only of the police but also of the terrorists. This approach leads to the discovery of the importance of the conditions of a successful terrorist attack and thus to the formulation of relevant solutions.

As an example, the following autopsy highlights the steps of the terrorist attack that occurred in 2016 in Grand-Bassam in Ivory Coast. It is grounded on the information flow that was published online during the course of the event.[1]

- On Sunday, 13 March 2016, between 12:30 and 1:00 pm, on the beach in Grand-Bassam near Abidjan, the first shooting sounds are heard: six men shouting 'Allah Akbar' strafed the tourist crowd on the beach.
- The terrorists are affiliated with AQIM: the organization will later claim this operation.
- The members of the commando use Kalashnikovs and, according to some witnesses, grenades.

- They came to the beach by taxi or by 4x4.
- The sites targeted by the attack are a beach and three/four hotels crowded with Ivorians and Frenchmen. The places are not well secured.
- The counterattack by Ivorian security forces is launched between 1:15 and 2:00 pm by Special Forces.
- Total number of deaths: 14 or 15 civilians, 3 soldiers and 2 or 3 terrorists (the others managed to escape).
- The investigations following the events discover that the terrorists were mostly Malians. A number of Malians related to the attack are then arrested in Mali and Port-Bouet, a suburb of Abidjan (Ivory Coast).

It should be noted that the intention of this kind of autopsy is not generalization, but the description of a single event. The purpose is to draw from this event the lessons that will eventually serve to correct the mistakes of the past.

The conditions for the success of a terrorist attack

Based on this summary description, it is possible to list some conditions that made this bloody attack a success: (1) a site (beach and hotels) offering a good target for terrorists: visible, busy, frequented by tourists and poorly defended; (2) a group of terrorists; (3) journeys from Mali to Ivory Coast (to convey assailants and weapons); and (4) weapons: assault rifles and grenades.

From the perspective of a terrorist, the degree of success of an attack can be measured by the number of victims killed and by the media coverage of the event. Thus, deciphering the conditions for the success of a terrorist attack reveals with some certainty the targets of efficient antiterrorism actions: targets toward which the police and intelligence services can direct their actions to make this crime impossible.

Now, bringing together what is known about a number of terrorist attacks that occurred in Europe and Africa over the past years, it is possible to pinpoint nine conditions for successful terrorist attacks (Marret 2002; Mickolus and Simmons 2014; Pape 2005).

(1) *At least one terrorist.* The contemporary terrorist can be defined as a clandestine *warrior* driven by political, ideological or religious claims (e.g., the commitment to jihad). He is not fighting on the battlefield but in cities, attacking poorly defended targets. He does not wear a uniform. Clearly, the terrorists can be described as *extremists*. They are willing to risk their lives to achieve their goal. In the case of extremists inspired by jihadist movement, they are often poorly integrated in a society in which, they believe, injustice reigns. Their fanaticism results from a process of radicalization—sometimes fast—under the influence of friends or relatives. Some dream of obtaining the palm of martyrdom. Their beliefs justify holy war and, therefore, the act of killing 'crusaders'. However, the strength of their convictions does not mean they are unanalterable.

Such terrorists are not very different from the common *criminals* well known to criminologists. They think they are above the law, of all laws, making them capable of committing a variety of crimes. In addition, there is the absence of inhibition when the time comes to kill. The majority of the terrorists recently active in France and Belgium had criminal backgrounds including robberies and burglaries. Therefore, preventive and repressive strategies to fight general crime could also apply to terrorists (on the characteristics of terrorists, see Atran 2016; Bauer and Soullez 2014; Bronner 2009; Chaliand 2002, 2004,

2002; Clarke and Newman 2006; Ducol 2015; Guidère 2015; Kepel 2015; Leman-Langlois and Brodeur 2005; Leman-Langlois 2007; Marret 2002; Martin 2013; Merari 2002; Pape 2005; Sageman 2008).

(2) *Vulnerable sites exposed to a surprise attack.* The terrorists did not attack any individual target. Terrorists choose sites and buildings that house the enemies they hate: Jews, Christians, police officers, blasphemers, journalists, Americans, tourists, politicians. The most frequently attacked sites are visible, well known, iconic, busy and poorly protected.

(3) *A small group and a network involving several terrorists in contact with each other.* The most devastating terrorist attacks were carried out in bands of extremists who were part of a wider network of individuals in communication with one another. Interception of communications between potential terrorists, despite encryption of communication, and dismantling their cells will eliminate another condition of a successful attack.

(4) *A safe haven and a base of operations.* Investigations triggered by the attacks in Paris in 2015 and Brussels in 2016 have discovered that a surprising number of terrorists were living in Molenbeek, Belgium (Fraihi 2016; Lamfalussy and Martin 2017). Terrorist organizations need bases of operations in which members feel safe. Outside of European territory, important safe havens in which terrorist apprentices receive training in combat techniques are located in Iraq, Afghanistan, Pakistan and Northern Mali (Mobley 2012).

(5) *Eluding detection.* Terrorists are doomed to failure, perhaps even death, if they fail to outwit the vigilance of police and citizens. They may have the use of a false passport to travel. They must purchase a weapon only from somebody who will remain silent. They need to talk to their accomplices far from eavesdroppers and only to very reliable people (Mobley 2012).

(6) *Escaping surveillance.* Any group that enters the police radar should redouble precaution because it will be spied on, wiretapped, recorded, interrogated and infiltrated. Its new members will have to be vetted, their background checked. The group must use coded language or secured/crypted means of communication. Its leaders must partition the network in sealed cells. Any group that fails to escape police surveillance will eventually be dismantled (Mobley 2012).

(7) *Weapons, ammunition, explosives.* If the objective is to kill many people, the attack may involve the use of automatic weapons, abundant ammunition and sometimes explosives. Additional funds may thus be required to buy weapons and explosives, to travel, to purchase false passports, etc. Thus, measures aimed at cutting off terrorist funds or preventing them from acquiring and possessing weapons, firearms and explosives could remove this condition.

(8) *Training and shooting practice.* The terrorists who managed to kill several people knew how to fight and shoot. Terrorists must therefore train somewhere (in Syria, Pakistan or Mali, in the case of jihadists, or perhaps be in local facilities), and have a shooting range at their disposal. In their camps, major terrorist organizations such as Al Qaeda and the Islamic State offer their recruits sessions during which they deepen religious concepts, policy and strategy that justify jihad. They are introduced to particular fighting techniques. Without indoctrination and training, another condition of a successful terrorist attack falls.

(9) *Operation planning and coordination.* The attack must be prepared: building a team, assigning tasks, getting weapons and explosives, casing the target of the attack. If the plotters are not in communication, they cannot adequately prepare for the attack.

Reasoning deductively from this list, antiterrorism actions should be directed toward conditions that favour the launching of an attack. Properly targeted actions can have significant impact on the disruption of successful terrorist attacks.

Table 4.1 Possible actions grounding a defensive antiterrorism strategy targeting 'success' conditions of terrorism attack

Actions		*Targets*
1	Detect	terrorists eluding detection
2	Interrogate and infiltrate	terrorists escaping surveillance
3	Fighting back	terrorist attack
4	Dismantling	cells and sanctuary
5	Intercepting	communications
6	Protecting	exposed site
7	Disarming	weapons and explosives
8	Maintaining a distance	mobility and proximity

Antiterrorism operations targeting the conditions of a successful attack

This section discusses the basis of a defensive antiterrorist strategy targeting the conditions for the success of a terrorist attack. Table 4.1 presents a schematic overview of possible measures that are explained in the following paragraphs.

(1) *Detect.* This is to identify cells and potential terrorists. The difficulty is that terrorists are rare in most countries. It's like finding a needle in a haystack. In the US and Canada, some terrorist cells planning an attack were identified and reported by private citizens (neighbours or merchants), by police during routine traffic control, by double agents, by moderate Muslims who feared and hated the fanatics and by the intelligence services monitoring the Internet (Mobley 2012). Warnings sent by the intelligence service of another country also play a significant role in the detection of terrorist cells present in the country receiving the information.

(2) *Interrogate and infiltrate.* A first detection of a terrorist suspect leads the police and intelligence services to search databases to find existing information on the individual. Based on this search, they may decide to arrest and interrogate the suspect or to infiltrate the group to which he belongs (Mobley 2012).

(3) *Interception of communications.* To coordinate their actions, terrorists phone, exchange emails and messages and communicate on social networks. The interception of these communications, and the analysis of their content and metadata, may detect suspects, help to locate them and force them to limit their exchanges, which will hinder the development of their networks.

(4) *Dismantling.* Once a suspected terrorist or network is detected and located, a Special Forces group can be dispatched. One of the mistakes made by some intelligence services is to continue monitoring for too long, for months, even years, in order to accumulate more information and evidence or because the political authorities are reluctant to launch a raid. Past examples have shown that sometimes such procrastination is costly: the terrorist group managed to be faster and attacked despite the surveillance, killing many people (Burdan 1990, Ouellet 2009).

(5) *Fighting back.* If terrorists attack, the Special Forces counterattack usually in two steps: first, they arrive without delay and kill or arrest the terrorists. Afterward, in the following weeks, the police uncover accomplices and launch a series of raids, destroying the network. Thus, after the recent bombings in Paris and Brussels, traces left at the scene of the crimes, including cellular phones and DNA, enabled services to find and arrest many terrorists.

The operation described above target the terrorists themselves. Other targets of antiterrorism may be anticipated, starting with the places targeted by the terrorists and needing protection. This kind of antiterrorism is a matter of situational crime prevention (Clarke and Newman 2006).

(6) *Protect.* Buildings and other sites that are likely to be exposed to an attack may be made less vulnerable (or at least to appear less vulnerable): they are surrounded by physical, technological and human protection walls, armoured doors, alarms, CCTV, metal and explosives detectors, X-ray, access control, security gates, baggage searches and armed guards (CNPP 2007; Garcia 2008).

(7) *Disarm.* To achieve this aim, it is not enough to pass laws on gun control. More proactive actions must be undertaken: guns found on a suspect or in her house have to be confiscated by the police, gun trafficking networks must be dismantled and screening of baggage and trans-border parcels by customs officers must be reinforced (Blais et al. 2013).

(8) *Maintaining a distance between the terrorists and their target.* It is possible to prevent a terrorist group having access to the place it wants to attack by border controls, no-fly lists and access controls (Wilkinson 1986; Clarke and Newman 2006).

Conclusion

This chapter has presented the elements of a method that would combine criminology and forensic science in solving a crime problem as difficult and complex as terrorism of jihadist inspiration. In the spirit of problem-solving policing, it starts with gathering the necessary information to develop a solution that is mainly preventive. The data to be gathered are in the form of material and digital traces (collected and analysed by forensic scientists) and also of verbal or written exchanges (which criminologists are trained to analyse). The forensic scientists, criminologists and also police officers, especially investigators, gather their information, analyse and deduce a solution. Then comes the moment when this information has to be shared with the entire group of police, criminologists and forensic scientists. The assumptions of each are discussed. Solutions should be not only repressive but mainly preventive. This prevention will take many forms: e.g., the dismantling of the cell preparing for an attack or the interception of communications to disrupt the exchange of information between the potential perpetrators. It is also important to identify targets that may be attacked by jihadists and to protect them carefully. If terrorists cannot get their hands on weapons and explosives, they will be hard pressed to carry out devastating attacks. Arms control is therefore indicated. All of these operations require that criminologists, forensic scientists and police officers work together on traces and words for analysis, synthesis and looking for solutions.

Note

1 Internet source: www.abidjan.net (13 March 2016).

References

Atran, S. 'L'État islamique est une révolution'. 2016. *Le Nouvel Observateur monde*. http://linkis.com/nouvelobs.com/x3GRz.

Bauer, A., and C. Soullez. 2014. *Le Terrorisme pour les nuls*. Paris: Éditions First.

Blais, É. I. Linteau and M.-P. Gagné. 'Le contrôle des armes à feu, les homicides et les violences armées'. 2013. In M. Cusson, J. Proulx, S. Guay and F. Cortoni, eds., *Traité des violences criminelles*, 651–672. Montréal: Hurtubise.

Bronner, G. *La Pensée extrême*. 2009. Paris: Denoël.

Burdan, D. 1990. *DST: Neuf ans à la division antiterroriste*. Paris: Robert Laffont.

Chaliand, G., ed. 2002. *Les stratégies du terrorisme*. 2nd ed. Paris: Desclée De Brouwer.

Chaliand, G. 2002. *L'arme du terrorisme*. Paris: Audibert.

Chaliand, G. 2004. *Histoire du terrorisme*. Paris: Bayard.

Clarke, R.V. 1995. *Situational Crime Prevention*. In M. Tonry and D.P. Farrington, eds., *Crime and Justice: A Review of Research*. Vol. 19, *Building a Safer Society: Strategic Approaches to Crime Prevention*, 91–150. Chicago: University of Chicago Press.

Clarke, R.V., and J. Eck. 2003. *Become a Problem-Solving Crime Analyst*. London: Jill Dando Institute of Crime Science.

Clarke, R.V., and G.R. Newman. 2006. *Outsmarting the Terrorists*. Westport, CT: Praeger Security International.

CNPP (Centre national de prévention et de protection). 2007. *Traité pratique de sûreté malveillance*. Saint-Marcel: CNDP entreprise.

Cusson, M. 2010. *L'Art de la sécurité, les enseignements de l'histoire et de la criminologie*. Montréal: Hurtubise.

Cusson, M., B. Dupont and F. Lemieux, eds. 2007. *Traité de sécurité intérieure*. Montréal: Hurtubise HMH and Lausanne: Presses Polytechnique et universitaires romande (coédition 2008).

Cusson, M., and O. Ribaux. 2015. 'Vers une méthode commune à la police scientifique et à la criminologie'. *Revue internationale de criminologie et de police technique et scientifique*, 68(3): 266–284.

Delémont, O., P. Esseiva, F. Béen and L. Benaglia. 2014. 'La police scientifique au-delà de ses frontières actuelles. La perspective de nouvelles connaissances'. *Revue internationale de criminologie et de police technique et scientifique* 67(3): 283–304.

Ducol, B. 2015. 'Devenir jihadistes à l'ère numérique'. PhD diss., Université Laval.

Fraihi, I. 2016. *En immersion à Molenbeek*. Paris: Éditions de la Différence.

Garcia, M.L. 2008. *The Design and Evaluation of Physical Protection Systems*. Amsterdam: Elsevier Butterwert-Heinemann.

Goldstein, H. 1990. *Problem-Oriented Policing*. New York: McGraw-Hill.

Grove, W.M., D.H. Zald, B.S. Lebow, B.E. Snitz and C. Nelson. 2000. 'Clinical versus Mechanical Prediction: A Meta-Analysis'. *Psychological Assessment* 12(1): 19–30.

Guidère, M. 2015. *Terreur, la nouvelle ère*. Paris: Autrement.

Kepel, G. 2015. *Terreur dans l'Hexagone*. Paris: Gallimard.

Lamfalussy, C., and J.P. Martin. 2017. *Molenbeek-sur-djihad*. Paris: Éditions Grasset.

Leman-Langlois, S. 2007. 'Le terrorisme et la lutte contre le terrorisme'. In M. Cusson, B. Dupont and F. Lemieux, eds., *Traité de sécurité intérieure*, 199–222. Montréal: Hurtubise HMH.

Leman-Langlois, S., and J.-P. Brodeur. 2005. 'Terrorism Old and New'. *Police Practice and Research* 6(2): 121–140.

Locard, E. 1920. *L'enquête criminelle et les méthodes scientifiques*. Paris: Flammarion.

Margot, P. 2014. 'Traçologie: la trace, vecteur fondamental de la police scientifique'. *Revue internationale de criminologie et de police technique et scientifique* 67(1): 72–97.

Marret, J.-L. *Techniques du terrorisme*. 2002. 2nd ed. Paris: Presses Universitaires de France.

Martin, C. 2013. *Understanding Terrorism*. Los Angeles. Sage.

Merari, A. 2002. 'Du terrorisme comme stratégie d'insurrection'. In G. Chaliand, ed., *Les stratégies du terrorisme*, 73–112. 2nd ed. Paris: Desclée De Brouwer.

Mickolus, E.F., and S. Simmons. 2014. *The 50 Worst Terrorist Attacks*. Santa Barbara, CA: Praeger.

Mobley, B.W. 2012. *Terrorism and Counter-Intelligence*. New York: Columbia University Press.

Ouellet, G. 2009. 'Les causes célèbres'. In S. Leman-Langlois and J.-P. Brodeur, eds., *Terrorisme et antiterrorisme au Canada*, 72–102. Montréal: Presses de l'Université de Montréal.

Pape, R. 2005. *Dying to Win: The Logic of Suicide Terrorism*. New York: Random.

Ribaux, O. 2014. *Police scientifique. Le renseignement par la trace*. Lausanne: Presses polytechniques et universitaires romandes.

Sageman, M. 2008. *Leaderless Jihad*. Philadelphia: University of Pennsylvania Press.

Wilkinson, P. 1986. *Terrorism and the Liberal State*. London: Macmillan.

5

A rendezvous between forensic science and criminology

Toward a public forensic criminology?

Roberta Julian and Manon Jendly

Drawing on recent critical debates on the concept of public '-ologies', this chapter discusses the potential and pitfalls of what could be considered an emerging 'public forensic criminology'. First, we discuss why and how a social and a natural science might be interested in participating in a broader public discussion about crime and justice that takes them beyond the boundaries of the academy. In doing so, we discuss what 'going public' means, what is at stake and what might be the role of forensic science and criminology in bridging the gaps between scientific productions, civil demands, policy discourses and professional experiences related to criminality. Then we describe the characteristics of the growing public 'knowledge' of these disciplines, before critically examining how a dialogue between them could contribute to a better understanding of crime-related events. While providing an empirical account of this attempt, we finally outline broader issues facing public forensic criminology and advocate for reflexivity, pluralism and an engagement with human rights along the way.

Introduction

There are several recurring debates in social science, one of which addresses the relationship between knowledge and public action with a view toward (social) justice (Wacquant 2011). Criminology and forensic science appear to be connected disciplines. They share a common interest in crime and social reaction to crime, which infiltrates numerous controversial discussions among various 'publics' (Sanders and Eisler 2014). They share several paradigms, methodologies and systematic problem-oriented approaches. They have in common epistemological and utilitarian debates and a quest for clarifying their identity and enhancing their legitimacy in a competitive world (Haggerty 2004). They are regularly misrepresented and their scientific bases and methodological approaches often poorly understood beyond academia (Cole 2013). Some authors argue that they can support and strengthen each other and should be urged to develop an interdisciplinary dialogue (Ribaux et al. 2015; Julian and Kelty 2012). Is this dialogue feasible beyond scientific discourses, particularly in a context saturated with crime talk (Chancer and McLaughlin 2007)? Should criminology and forensic science participate in a broader public discussion about what they can 'bring to the world'? Should they engage in a process that leads them far beyond the boundaries of the academy and the criminal justice system? This contribution explores the pitfalls and opportunities of going public: What could it mean? And what are the issues? We reactivate this old 'going public' debate in terms of a new place for these disciplines to meet. We map out their common concerns, interests and controversies over opportunities to share knowledge about crime and crime control with a broader audience. We touch on their capacity to address critical issues raised by crime control policies and practices. Ultimately, we analyse what could be their pathway to the creation of a broad interdisciplinary epistemic community that could lead to a better understanding of crime.

What does 'public' or 'going public' mean?

The concept of public '-ologies' has been hotly debated since the 1980s (Nickel 2010). There is no single definition on which all '-ists' (e.g., sociologists, criminologists, anthropologists, political scientists) agree. Generally, the term refers to any discipline that aims to communicate and engage with a wider audience than academia only. Indirectly, it leads to a general interrogation about the role, value and impact of a discipline within society at large. In sociology, these questions go back to 1988 with Herbert J. Gans' presidential address to the American Sociological Association. For Gans (1989), public sociologists are those who can easily share complex ideas, are open-minded in terms of sociological interests and keen to address public matters.

Following Gans, there have been many calls for academics to 'go public', meaning embarking on a process of sharing science with diverse audiences outside their 'ivory tower' and eventually influencing popular representations and policy decisions on diverse phenomena (Clawson et al. 2007; Griffin et al. 2016). In fact, the idea of the 'public' requires critical reflection on the diversity of audiences potentially interested in specific topics and the purpose of sharing knowledge with them. 'Publics' are plural and vary across time and space: they can be governmental bodies, political leaders, practitioners, stakeholders, students, the media and the citizens. They can be local or global, oppressed or powerful, passive or active. Publics evolve in a rapid, connected physical and digital environment. If publics are multiple, likewise, there can be many reasons to go public: to influence policy and social action, inspire political agendas, (re)shape professional practices, support project allocations, educate people and influence their representations of facts and/or values. For some authors, these assumptions are questionable, e.g., because they are ambiguous, arrogant, normative and/or politically (if not ideologically) engaged (Tittle 2004; Wacquant 2011). For others, in contrast, these mantras are important because science bears a responsibility to address the 'hot topics' society faces (Currie 2007; Blomberg et al. 2013). One way or another, the matter of public debate is relevant to any science and is significant for three main reasons:

- it explores the tensions between science, power and governance;
- it lies at the very heart of knowledge production and consumption; and
- it reveals the dilemmas anyone can face in a career, whatever this career may be, between independence, involvement, competing interests and loyalty to oneself and others.

From 'public sociology' to 'public criminology' to 'public forensic criminology'

Among the calls for social science to go public, the most famous probably comes from the sociologist Michael Burawoy. Whereas Gans calls for a sociological discourse that renders knowledge easy to understand, Burawoy focuses on the discipline of sociology itself (Nickel 2010). In his 2004 American Society of Sociology presidential address, Burawoy (2005, 6ff) elaborates a division of labour among sociologists, suggesting there are four ways of doing sociology: professional, policy, critical and public. 'Public sociology' directly addresses the relationships between academic sociology and diverse audiences and pursues the idea of reframing cultural images of social facts by disseminating academic sociology's work widely and in an accessible way. At the same time, the goal of public sociology is to enrich public policy and public debates on contemporary moral and political issues. Mapping the discussions on the topic among sociologists reveals many controversies,[1] to such an extent that Burawoy (2009) himself refers to these as 'The Public Sociology Wars'. Much of the criticism deals with the division of labour and, more generally, the rejection of an academic sociology being seized by politics (Calhoun 2005; Braithwaite 2005; Wacquant 2011). It is also argued that this division of labour could lead to different academic statuses ranging from the 'theorist' to the 'researcher' and the 'activist', which might contribute in turn to atomizing the field from the inside (Matthews 2009).

Such debates are not totally new to criminology either, at least in the Anglo-Saxon world (Uggen and Inderbitzin 2010). On the contrary, controversies about the role of criminology beyond academia, its relationships with crime policies and practices and its influence on social control have mobilized many criminologists (Chancer and McLaughlin 2007). Numerous presidential addresses at the American Society of Criminology have dealt with this topic. In 1998, Zahn's presidential address argues for criminology to be public-oriented and to contribute to 'just communities'. In 1990, Petersilia urges more practitioner-academic collaborations to enhance 'policy impact' (Petersilia 1991). In 2009, Clear sees *the* moment for criminologists to engage 'in building a broad and forward-looking evidentiary base for fundamental innovation in justice policy' (Clear 2010, 1). In 2014, Belknap emphasizes 'criminologists' responsibility to advocate for social and legal justice' (Belknap 2015, 1). On the other side of the Atlantic, beginning in 2000 in Great Britain, Garland and Sparks call for British criminologists to take part in the public crime-debate in rapid-flow, globalized and ultra-connected worlds. The same year, Carrabine et al. (2000, 208) insist on the political nature of crime and as such, urge criminologists to engage in the dissemination of critical evidence to enlighten the 'ordinary public' and promote 'social justice and human rights'. In 2010, Loader and Sparks (2010a) published one of the most thorough but controversial standpoints on public criminology. Their work advocates for criminologists to 'go public' in order to 'make a difference' (Carrier 2014, 89) and for 'public criminology' to contribute to 'better politics of crime and its regulation' (Loader and Sparks 2010a, 117; Loader and Sparks 2011). Here also, many criticisms were raised against public criminology, ranging from the emptiness of a new 'branding', its 'messianic' and ideological approach, its 'political desirability', its 'naive belief' that politics can be influenced, its condescension toward supposedly 'ignorant citizens' and finally its normative apprehension of what is 'good' and 'bad' with crime control, justice and social rights (Carrier 2014).

The emergence of what could be called a 'public forensic criminology' took a less explicit path. It is not so much that there were clear calls for forensic science to go public; rather, in practice, contemporary debates in forensic science began to involve wider publics beyond academics and the forensic science community. Within the context of a strengthening neoliberalism in the Global North, these debates were stimulated by questions regarding the impact of forensic science on the wider criminal justice system and related calls for the accountability of state-allocated funding. Criticisms of forensic science also began to emerge in the wake of analyses of wrongful convictions identifying forensic errors as significant contributors to unjust outcomes (Saks and Koehler 2005; Garrett and Neufeld 2009). At the same time, the 'CSI effect' led to increased expectations of forensic science from the general public, including but not limited to television audiences and juries (Cole and Dioso-Villa 2007; Dioso-Villa 2015). Research on the CSI effect also stressed the misrepresentations of forensic science that were predominant in the CSI-type television programmes and the subsequent misunderstandings held by 'the public' with regard to the capacities and capabilities of forensic science. As a consequence, forensic scientists have been urged to become more engaged in public discussions in order to defend the discipline from its critics (Donnelly 2012; Black and Nic Daeid 2015). In these debates in the public sphere, it is possible to identify the emergence of a public forensic criminology in the early 2000s.

Key debates in public criminology and forensic science

So, what does this emergent public forensic criminology look like? What 'conversations' have been taking place between forensic scientists in the academy, forensic science practitioners and diverse publics? Who are these publics and in what ways are they engaged in various dialogues about forensic science? We have identified eight key conversations and/or debates about forensic science that have occurred with audiences beyond the forensic science community. The first four conversations are those in which forensic scientists are currently heavily engaged; the boundaries of these conversations have broadened to include non-forensic scientists as they begin to address issues related to the role of forensic science beyond the laboratory and into the wider criminal justice system. In the latter four, we identify key debates in 'public criminology' and show how the interests and concerns of forensic scientists are increasingly infiltrating these.

Key conversations in forensic science

Public conversation on the role of forensic science in the criminal justice system

Central to this 'conversation' is the question: Given the increased reliance on forensic science in police investigations and criminal trials, should other actors in the criminal justice system have some knowledge of forensic science? If so, what knowledge should they have? In 2000, the publication of the Home Office's report *Under the Microscope* (Blakey 2000) was significant in raising the idea that in order for forensic science to make a positive contribution to criminal justice outcomes, other actors in the criminal justice system should have an awareness of forensic science. No longer was the discourse on forensic science limited to technological improvements driven by the 'science' per se. The publication of this report prompted interest from a much wider range of publics, including other academics, researchers and criminal justice practitioners. In the United States, Fradella et al. (2007) published a significant article recommending tertiary education in the field of 'forensic studies'. This was distinguished from forensic science, in that 'forensic studies programs are uniquely tailored to the needs of criminal justice professionals, to help them understand the nature of criminal evidence and appreciate how forensic methods may aid in the quest for justice' (Fradella et al. 2007, 264). Here we see an explicit call for knowledge of forensic science to extend systematically beyond the forensic science community.

Public conversation on the effectiveness of forensic science in the criminal justice system

Seeing forensic science as one part of a larger criminal justice system has been fundamental to conversations about its effectiveness (Ludwig and Fraser 2014). Rather than measuring the 'success' or 'value' of forensic science in terms of laboratory outcomes (e.g., identifications), conversations that included wider publics led to questions about the impact of forensic science on criminal justice outcomes further downstream, such as arrests and convictions. In the United States (Peterson et al. 2010, 2012) and Australia (Briody 2004; Briody and Prenzler 2005), researchers conducted quantitative case processing studies to measure the impact of forensic evidence, Houck and colleagues (2009) launched the FORESIGHT program that enabled crime laboratory managers to measure efficiencies in the laboratory, and national grants were awarded for projects examining the effectiveness of forensic science in the criminal justice system (Petersen et al. 2010; Julian et al. 2011). In the UK, debates emerged about the effectiveness of the DNA expansion programme that extended conversations about forensic science beyond the criminal justice system and into the parliament (McCartney 2006). In Europe, Ribaux and colleagues (Ribaux 2006; Ribaux et al. 2010a) discussed the potential for a forensic intelligence model to enhance the effectiveness of forensic science for police, and in the US, the UK and Europe, alternative models of forensic service provision were mooted (Cook et al. 1998; Thompson 2011; Ribaux 2010b; Lawless and Williams 2010). Thus, conversations about the effectiveness of forensic science necessarily involved new publics: the police; parliamentarians; academic researchers in economics, social science and forensic science; and criminologists. At the same time, this public concern has clearly impacted forensic science academics by informing research that critically examines, and redefines, the meaning of 'utility' prior to evaluating its impact (Bitzer 2016).

Public conversation on human factors and the underpinning science

Questions about the scientific validity of many of the forensic science disciplines lie at the heart of the National Academy of Science Report (the NAS Report) that sent ripples throughout the international forensic science community when it was released in 2009. Concerns over the scientific underpinnings of many of the forensic disciplines had been expressed previously (e.g., Cole 1999), but the audience for the NAS Report was broader than the forensic science community; it included members of the judiciary and the legal fraternity, social scientists, psychological and behavioural scientists and other actors in the criminal justice system. Concerns over the impact of 'human factors' in the interpretation of forensic evidence (especially those based on pattern recognition and comparison techniques) were also raised. An important debate arose between critics who reacted by questioning the need for forensic scientists to be exposed to contextual information (Dror et al. 2006) and those forensic scientists who argued that 'context is everything' (Margot 2011).

Public conversation on the relationship between forensic science and the law

Alongside these emerging conversations about the role and effectiveness of forensic science in the criminal justice system has been an ongoing conversation among socio-legal scholars about the tensions between forensic science and the law (Lynch and McNally 2003; Jasanoff 2004; Edmond 2013; Vuille 2013; Roberts 2015). While in the past these conversations have tended to take place between socio-legal scholars in the academy, and been directed toward the judiciary and the legal fraternity, more recently these scholars have redirected their critique toward forensic scientists (Martire et al. 2013; Edmond 2015; Edmond et al. 2016). Additionally, communication between forensic scientists and fact-finders has been an ongoing concern (McQuistin-Surrett and Saks 2008) that, more recently, has been extended to examining communication between other actors in the criminal justice system (Howes et al. 2013; Kelty et al. 2012).

Key debates in public criminology

Engaging in debates about the value of forensic science in the criminal justice system necessarily exposes forensic scientists to key debates in public criminology. These revolve around four main controversial statements. They address issues that range from a culture of expertise on one hand, to a culture of contestability on the other (Nickel 2010).

Public criminology to dictate what works to the 'outside world'

For some authors, criminology suffers from a lack of influence on policy development, practitioner applications and public opinions on crime, victimization and insecurity. To counteract its poor policy and societal relevance (Loader and Sparks 2010a), some authors advocate for an 'evidence-based criminology' they believe can inspire and sustain 'better' politics and practices on crime and crime control (Cullen 2005; Clear 2010; Sherman 2009; Uggen and Inderbitzin 2010; Goldson and Hughes 2010). In their 'fight for the truth' as Turner (2013) puts it, they argue that criminology produces sufficient knowledge about what works in crime reduction for decision-makers to use (Currie 2007). However, this approach also raises critical questions. How arrogant is it to believe that criminology has a monopoly on knowledge of crime and that it can inspire decision-makers in a 'good' way? What is a 'better' politic of crime and crime control? Who is stating it? 'Truth', 'Better', 'Relevance' are shaped by prevailing powers at stake in a given context (Hallsworth and Lea 2012, 193). Problems of methods, government funding and partisan research are also cited here to critique the rise of an 'administrative criminology' that is more market- than evidence-led (Haggerty 2004; Matthews 2009).

Forensic science has been drawn into this debate in public criminology through the claim that forensic data is under-used in establishing the evidence base for crime control and crime prevention strategies. As Ross et al. note, 'Traditionally, the primary focus of forensic science is evidentiary and the product is expert evidence or evidence of fact for the courts. However, forensic science can play other roles including the provision of information, which can influence the focus of investigations and the production of intelligence *aimed at crime disruption and crime prevention*. For forensic science to be most effective, it should be engaged in each of these roles' (Ross et al. 2015, 6; emphasis added).

These authors, and others, argue that forensic data has the potential to enhance intelligence-led policing through the provision of valuable information for decision-makers at strategic, operational and tactical levels (Ribaux 2006; Aepli et al. 2011; Ribaux and Talbot Wright 2014). For example, De Ceuster et al. (2012) discuss and evaluate the costs and benefits of creating a European database of ballistics traces in terms of its potential impact on crime. Thus, the concept of 'forensic intelligence' extends the role of forensic science—and its potential benefits—to earlier stages of the criminal justice system. A necessary corollary is that forensic scientists begin to address a wider range of criminal justice practitioners than those traditionally focused on the courts.

Public criminology to 'cool down the heat' about crime and crime control

There have also been several calls for criminology to go public in order to soothe down the 'moral panics' regarding crime and the 'tough on crime' political discourses (Ruggiero 2012). From this perspective, the media are regularly shown 'to influence public policy through the opinion pages of newspaper, TV, and radio' (Skolnick 1995,12). They are also urged to collaborate with criminologists (or the other way around) to frame crime-related stories in a way likely to educate people (Barak 1988; Uggen and Inderbitzin 2010; Groombridge 2007; Rowe 2012). The belief is that criminologists are the 'experts' in matters dealing with crime and insecurity and as such, they should actively participate in changing public fears and inaccurate perceptions on these topics. Nevertheless, critics of this option, referred to as 'newsmaking criminology', highlight the over-importance it places on the public's apparent (mis)perceptions.

Critics also raise concerns about the discursive strategies used by 'experts', some of them more motivated by their own agendas, rather then trying to educate anyone—what Crépault names a 'partisan pedagogy' (Crépault 2016). Eventually, once knowledge enters the public realm, it is very difficult if not impossible to control the way it is going to be transformed and understood, no matter how this knowledge is delivered (Rock 2014).

Similar issues have arisen with respect to the role of forensic scientists in educating the public about the 'reality' of forensic science. Debates about the CSI effect revolve around concerns that forensic science-themed police dramas (such as the *CSI* franchise) contaminate the public with 'distorted' scientific knowledge and information (Shelton et al. 2006; Shelton 2008; Cole 2013, 3). The media have played an important role in constructing the CSI effect as a social problem and have continued to sustain this perspective despite a rigorous debate about its existence among social scientists and media researchers (Cole 2013). This has generated explicit calls for forensic scientists to become more engaged in such public debates (Donnelly 2012). While forensic science has been the object of this debate, its protagonists have predominantly been non-forensic scientists. The benefits and pitfalls of such engagement with the media are manifold and yet to be fully explored in light of changing media portrayals of new forensic technologies and the possibility that the CSI effect is a 'generational effect' (Clifford and White 2017).

Public criminology to inspire the next generation of professionals and decision-makers

The popularity of criminology among students is such that for some authors, public criminology should be first and foremost a question of 'teaching criminology' (Chancer and McLaughlin 2007; Uggen and Inderbitzin 2010). Voices emerge for criminology programs that enhance students' cautiousness on crime topics, rigorous thinking and curiosity on public matters. Others call for applied programmes that educate future professionals and decision-makers to reform criminal justice agencies from the inside. One way or another, any lecturer in criminology inevitably plays a public role while serving his or her teaching mission (Hamilton 2013). The competitive situation is such, however, that crime-related disciplines represent a huge market (Calhoun 2005). Because they need to survive, higher education institutions, both private and public, are likely to engage more in the marketing of their programme than in the 'enlightenment' of their students. As some of their promotional packages suggest, academic courses are progressively becoming the scene of their poor marketing allegories, in the quest for a new 'crime expert' that does not exist, except in movies. There is also an ambivalence about the idea of teaching more and more students and at the same time ignoring the consequences of this (over)production.

We see a parallel process in forensic science: there has been a growth in tertiary education programmes internationally since the early 2000s. Interest in, and demand for, such programmes is symptomatic of an increased public awareness of forensic science, in part stimulated by increased media attention. Given the financial imperatives among increasingly market-driven universities, it is not surprising to see this demand being met by the (over)supply of forensic science courses. This has led to concerns about the quality of educational programmes, the differential benefits of education versus training, the relative strengths and weaknesses of generic science programs versus specialized forensic programs (Roux and Robertson 2009) and, more recently, calls for the development of innovative educational programmes in the area of forensic intelligence (Crispino et al. 2015). At the same time, questions have been raised about the ethics of enrolling large numbers of students in forensic science programmes when there are limited employment prospects for forensic science professionals (Roux and Robertson 2009). This has led universities to market their forensic science graduates to employers outside the traditional forensic science laboratories; for example, the pharmaceutical industry, occupational health and safety and science education (Roux and Robertson 2009). Calls for education in forensic science have also come from academics teaching students in criminology (Fradella et al. 2007) and law (Cassella and McCartney 2011) who have argued for the benefits of forensic science knowledge among a broad range of criminal justice practitioners. These educational debates have extended knowledge and awareness of forensic science to more diverse audiences, including educators and employers beyond traditional forensic science laboratories.

Public criminology as a means to participate in social action and activism

Here lies the idea that criminology should also 'be driven by a desire to improve responses to injustices' (Belknap 2015, 1) and that criminologists should 'engage in social and/or legal justice at individual, organizational and/or policy levels, which goes beyond typical research, teaching and service' (ibid, 5). A lot of work has already been done from this perspective (e.g., studies dealing with race, gender, class or citizenship) including the development of a closer collaboration with the marginalized, as in 'narrative criminology' and 'convict criminology', for instance. Thus, 'activist criminology' refers to a certain kind of proximity with our field of inquiry and a quest for changing the world. In this approach, public criminology is envisaged as a commitment to social criticism (Ruggiero 2012) and means to address 'what is public in public criminology?' (Piché 2015, 160). Nevertheless, this ambition is also subject to controversies, essentially because it blurs the frontiers between 'true science' and advocacy, hard data and life experiences, scholars and 'outsiders' and objectivity and subjectivities.

Similar debates have emerged in forensic science. What is the role of forensic science in relation to broader issues of criminal and social justice? Should the forensic scientist have a disinterested role in the criminal justice system as an objective scientist? Is there, or should there be, an 'activist forensic criminology'? In other words, what are the ethical and moral responsibilities of forensic scientists? Donnelly, for example, urges forensic scientists, as criminal justice practitioners, to become more engaged in wider debates about human rights. In her view 'there is an inherent tension between the notion of "value free scientific method" and the conflicting dictates of government freedoms whilst being increasingly reliant upon forensic science in the detection, prevention and prosecution of criminality … [F]orensic practitioners must actively engage with societal concerns. We cannot be simple onlookers in this debate' (2012, 93).

This heralds an emerging debate in a public forensic criminology. Do forensic scientists identify as engaged criminal justice practitioners or as objective scientists? If the former, do they see themselves as contributing to a neoliberal 'law and order' agenda of more policing, a growing prison population and greater exclusion in a security-driven world, or do they see themselves as supporting a human rights agenda with a focus on social justice and greater tolerance of difference (Lawless 2016)?

Engaging in the public debates: beyond labels, one posture?

While discussing the public issues regarding the discipline, the role of their ambassadors—the criminologists themselves—is also inevitably addressed. Loader and Sparks (2010a, 30ff) identify various ideal typical modes of criminological engagement, together with their associated (public) figures. These figures refer to a variety of labels, e.g., the 'scientific expert', the 'policy adviser' or the 'activist', and their famous but non-consensual figure of the 'democratic underlabourer' who has 'a commitment both to generating and disseminating knowledge and to a more deliberative politics of big public questions such as the future of punishment and crime control'

(Loader and Sparks 2010b, 779). These figures have also led to many criticisms (Carrier 2014). One is that most criminologists do not bear one role only, but several, and that their boundaries are not mutually exclusive.

If this typological attempt is not satisfactory, first and foremost because it gives a fragmented and utilitarian impression of diverse camps, it has at least the merit of raising our vigilance about what sense we give to our daily activities, what we want to stand for and under which conditions (Rock 2014). Bourdieu and Wacquant (1992) would refer here to reflexivity, Loader and Sparks (2010a, 2010b) to pluralism and Turner (2013) to diplomacy, drawn from Latour's figure of the diplomat. Regardless of the label, the significance is to encourage any one of us, natural and/or social scientists, to reflect on our own position and contribution to the world around us. It is only at the heart of such introspection that an interdisciplinary dialogue might enrich the debate.

Forensic scientists, criminologists, socio-legal scholars, psychologists, educators and criminal justice practitioners are increasingly engaging in various sites in which this dialogue is taking place. This is evident in the editorials of journals such as *The Australian Journal of Forensic Sciences*, the growth of new journals (e.g., *Forensic Science Policy and Management*), the publication of books that extend the conversation beyond the science itself (e.g., Strom and Hickman 2015, *Forensic Science and the Administration of Justice*) and the National Institute of Justice's program of Social Science Research on Forensic Science launched in 2004. It is equally evident in the growing popularity of the Science and Justice stream in international conferences such as those held by the Australian and New Zealand Forensic Science Society (Found 2015), the discussion of forensic science and justice at the Royal Society Meeting in the UK in 2015 and, even more recently, the addition of forensic criminology as a theme in forensic science conferences (e.g., Forensic Science—Criminalistics Research, 2016) and criminology conferences (e.g., ANZSOC 2016). It is in such spaces that we can begin to see an emergent public forensic criminology in which forensic science knowledge and understanding is brought to bear on criminal justice issues as well as moral, ethical and social issues that lie beyond the boundaries of the crime laboratory.

Discussion: Issues surrounding a public rendezvous between forensic science and criminology

The public debate offers another insight into the opportunity for forensic science and criminology to construct a broad interdisciplinary epistemic community to address crime phenomena. Both disciplines share concerns in a world of rapid social, political, cultural and economic change. Whereas criminology offers a social science insight to these transformations and their consequences on our everyday lives, forensic science provides methods, models and cases that help to understand the physical and virtual issues at stake. To paraphrase Mills (1959/2000), a 'criminological imagination' would certainly benefit from being stimulated by other disciplines; one of them is forensic science. From the other perspective, forensic science would certainly be invigorated by integrating sociologically based studies of crime and crime control. Eventually, both probably stand to benefit from what is at stake beyond academia, laboratories, crime scenes and the criminal justice system.

Nevertheless, the path toward a public rendezvous between forensic science and criminology contains a number of challenges. Any representation and discourse on crime, the criminals and the victims, insecurity, risk and surveillance is historically, socially, politically, culturally and digitally situated. Thus, contextualizing the setting and timing of the reception of knowledge, both in the natural and social sciences, is crucial. Knowledge is used and transformed differently with respect to each society's social structure, culture, law and policy-making process, as well as governmental attributes and the nature of the judicial system (inquisitorial/adversarial). Thinking about crime and crime control requires a 360° analysis of the State, the institutions, the multidimensional aspects of civil society and their relationships, at the local, national and international levels (Matthews 2009). Moreover, the overwhelming mass of knowledge production on crime and crime control, in both disciplines, essentially comes from the Global North. It is Anglo-Saxon oriented, Western self-centred, and neo-liberal driven, while a cultural pluralism, in terms of standpoints, structures, cultures and languages would be a source of enrichment and better mutual comprehension (Melossi 2000; Calhoun 2005; Haggerty 2004).

The overall debate regarding the opportunity of any science to go public also deals with power: (mis)power to suggest, influence and dispose. Relations of power (e.g., political, economic and cultural) always mediate knowledge production and consumption. This is evident in the complex ways in which criminological research has influenced politics in areas such as capital punishment (Radelet and Borg 2000), and the controversial implementation of the 'broken windows' theory as it morphed into 'zero tolerance' policing in New York City (Herbert 2009). Brodeur (2004, 154) warned us in 2004 about an expertise that 'no longer serves an emancipatory interest in the field of criminal justice, [but] is essentially used to pursue security, viewed as a set of limitations imposed upon the freedom of others'. It is clear that our disciplines might contribute to this kind of 'security'. Appadurai's reflections on public culture, understood as a 'rubric for collectively thinking about aspects of modern life now thought about separately' offers a pathway for new (public) spaces of sharing, confronting and contesting knowledge and experiences on crime and its control. In Appadurai and Breckenridge's words (1988, 6) this would be an 'arena where other types, forms and domains of culture are encountering, interrogating, and contesting each other in new and unexpected ways'.

Because we have much to learn from other experiential and intellectual resources, criminology and forensic science are due to interact not only together but also with other sources of debates in the interpretation of crime and responses to it (Young 2004; Zedner 2007; Doyle and Moore 2011). It seems useful to embrace a diversity of perspectives and to encourage pluralism in terms of methodology, paradigms and attitudes, including curiosity for the 'outside world' and other disciplines such as ethics, human rights and philosophy. Reflexivity is an essential aspect of this project as we try to make sense of what we do, why, with whom, under which conditions and with what outcomes, both tangible and symbolic. Eventually then, and following Christie (2011, 708), we might be in a position to try functioning as 'readers and translators' who share the quest of any human being to know oneself and understand humanity better.

Conclusion

We have identified the existence of numerous conversations about the relationship between forensic science and the criminal justice system that have occurred among an ever-increasing number of publics. We see in these conversations a move away from 'good' forensic science as a goal in itself toward viewing forensic science as an integral component of a criminal justice system that has a broader goal of achieving (social) justice. Thus, a rendezvous between forensic science and criminology has the potential to contribute to broader debates on social, moral and human rights issues. However, this growing dialogue has not yet crystallized into a clear set of debates, suggesting that there is not yet a fully developed public forensic criminology.

We suggest that there are potential benefits to building and strengthening an epistemic community beyond forensic science while strengthening the diverse roles played by forensic scientists as scientific experts, policy advisers or activists. However, as with any social movement, there are also pitfalls and challenges in following a path toward a public conversation in which the voices of forensic scientists and others can be heard. That path will be complex, but it could lead to a more holistic approach to addressing crime and, ultimately, a fruitful set of debates that contributes to a more socially just society.

Note

1 Access to the literature informing these controversies may be found at http://sociologicalimagination.org/resources/public-sociology-bibliography, compiled by Albert Tzeng © (accessed 10 December 2016).

References

Aepli, P., O. Ribaux and E. Summerfield. 2011. *Decision Making in Policing: Operations and Management*. Lausanne: EPFL Press.

Appadurai, A., and C.A. Breckenridge. 1988. 'Why Public Culture?' *Public Culture* 1(1): 5–9.

Barak, G. 1988. 'Newsmaking Criminology: Reflections on the Media, Intellectuals, and Crime'. *Justice Quarterly* 5(4): 565–587.

Belknap, J. 2015. 'Activist Criminology: Criminologists' Responsibility to Advocate for Social and Legal Justice'. The 2014 American Society of Criminology Presidential Address. *Criminology* 53(1): 1–22.

Bitzer, S. 2016. 'Utility of the Clue: Formalisation of the Decision to Analyse a Trace and Insights into the Evaluation of the Investigative Contribution of Forensic Science'. PhD diss., University of Lausanne, Switzerland.

Black, S., and N. Nic Daeid. 2015. 'Time to Think Differently: Catalysing a Paradigm Shift in Forensic Science'. *Philosophical Transactions of the Royal Society* B, 370(1674): 1–4.

Blakey, D. 2000. *Under the Microscope: Thematic Inspection Report on Scientific and Technical Support*. London: Her Majesty's Inspectorate of Constabulary.

Blomberg, T.G., J. Mestre and K. Mann. 2013. 'Seeking Causality in a World of Contingency: Criminology, Research, and Public Policy'. *Criminology & Public Policy* 12(4): 571–584.

Bourdieu, P., and L. Wacquant. 1992. *An Invitation to Reflexive Sociology*. Chicago: University of Chicago Press.

Braithwaite, J. 2005. 'For Public Social Science'. *British Journal of Sociology* 56(3): 345–353.

Briody, M. 2004. 'The Effects of DNA Evidence on Homicide Cases in Court'. *Australian and New Zealand Journal of Criminology* 37(2): 231–253.

Briody, M., and T. Prenzler. 2005. 'D.N.A. Databases and Property Crime: A False Promise?' *Australian Journal of Forensic Sciences* 37(2): 73–86.

Brodeur, J.-P. 2004. 'Expertise not Wanted: The Case of the Criminal Law'. In E. Kurz-Milcke and G. Gigerenzer, eds., *Experts in Science and Society*, 123–158. New York: Kluwer Academic Publishers.

Burawoy, M. 2005. 'For Public Sociology'. The American Sociological Association 2004 Presidential Address. *American Sociological Review* 70(1): 4–28.

Burawoy, M. 2009. 'The Public Sociology Wars'. In V. Jeffries, ed., *Handbook of Public Sociology*, 449–473. Lanham, MD: Rowman & Littlefield Publishers.

Calhoun, C. 2005. 'The Promise of Public Sociology'. *British Journal of Sociology* 56(3): 355–363.

Carrabine, E., L. Maggy and N. South. 2000. 'Social Wrongs and Human Rights in Late Modern Britain: Social Exclusion, Crime Control, and Prospects for a Public Criminology'. *Social Justice* 27(2): 193–211.

Carrier, N. 2014. 'On Some Limits and Paradoxes of Academic Orations on Public Criminology'. *Radical Criminology* 4(Autumn): 85–114.

Cassella, J., and C. McCartney. 2011. 'Lowering the Drawbridges: Legal and Forensic Science Education for the 21st Century'. *Forensic Science Policy and Management: An International Journal* 2(2): 81–93.

Chancer, L., and E. McLaughlin. 2007. 'Public Criminologies: Diverse Perspectives on Academia and Policy'. *Theoretical Criminology* 11(2): 155–173.

Christie, N. 2011. 'Reflections from the Periphery. A Symposium of Reviews of Public Criminology?' *British Journal of Criminology* 51(4): 707–710.

Clawson, D., R. Zussman, J. Misra, N. Gerstel, R. Stokes, D.L. Anderton and M. Burawoy. 2007. *Public Sociology: Fifteen Eminent Sociologists Debate Politics and the Profession in the Twenty-First Century*. Berkeley: University of California Press.

Clear, T.R. 2010. 'Policy and Evidence: The Challenge to the American Society of Criminology'. The American Society of Criminology 2009 Presidential Address. *Criminology* 48(1): 1–25.

Clifford, K., and R. White. 2017. *Media and Crime: Content, Context and Consequence*. Melbourne: Oxford University Press.
Cole, S. 1999. 'What Counts for Identity? The Historical Origins of the Methodology of Latent Fingerprint Identification'. *Science in Context* 12(1): 139–172.
Cole, S. 2013. 'A Surfeit of Science: The "CSI Effect" and the Media Appropriation of the Public Understanding of Science'. *Public Understanding of Science* 24(2): 130–146.
Cole, S., and R. Dioso-Villa. 2007. 'CSI and Its Effects: Media, Juries, and the Burden of Proof'. *New England Law Review* 41(3): 435–469.
Cook, R., I.W. Evett, G. Jackson, P. Jones and J.A. Lambert. 1998. 'A Model for Case Assessment and Interpretation'. *Science and Justice* 38(3): 151–156.
Crépault, D. 2016. 'The Rise of Partisan Pedagogy: How Stakeholders Outside of the Academy Are Answering the Call to Public Criminology'. *British Journal of Criminology*, advance online publication, 12 March 2016, 1–19. https://doi.org/10.1093/bjc/azw034.
Crispino, F., Q. Rossy, O. Ribaux and C. Roux. 2015. 'Education and Training in Forensic Intelligence: A New Challenge'. *Australian Journal of Forensic Sciences* 47(1): 49–60.
Cullen, F.T. 2005. 'The Twelve People Who Saved Rehabilitation: How the Science of Criminology Made a Difference'. *Criminology* 43(1): 1–42.
Currie, E. 2007. 'Against Marginality: Arguments for a Public Criminology'. *Theoretical Criminology* 11(2): 175–190.
De Ceuster, J., R. Hermsen, M. Mastaglio and R. Nennstiel. 2012. 'A Discussion on the Usefulness of a Shared European Ballistic Image Database'. *Science & Justice* 52(4): 237–242.
Dioso-Villa, R. 2015. 'Is There Evidence of a "CSI Effect"?' In K.J. Strom and M.J. Hickman, eds, *Forensic Science and the Administration of Justice*, 21–41. Los Angeles: Sage.
Donnelly, S. 2012. 'Forensic Science in a Human Rights Framework'. *Australian Journal of Forensic Sciences* 44(1): 93–103.
Doyle, A., and D. Moore. 2011. 'Questions for a New Generation of Criminologists'. In A. Doyle and D. Moore, eds, *Critical Criminology in Canada: New Voices, New Directions*, 1–24. Vancouver: UBC Press.
Dror, I.E., D. Charlton and A.E. Peron. 2006. 'Contextual Information Renders Experts Vulnerable to Making Erroneous Identifications'. *Forensic Science International* 156(1): 74–78.
Edmond, G. 2013. '(Ad)ministering Justice: Expert Evidence and the Professional Responsibilities of Prosecutors'. *University of New South Wales Law Journal* 36(3): 931–937.
Edmond, G. 2015. 'What Lawyers Should Know about the Forensic "Sciences"'. *Adelaide Law Review* 37(1): 33–99.
Edmond, G., B. Found, K. Martire, K. Ballantyne, D. Hamer, R. Searston, M. Thompson, E. Cunliffe ... and A. Roberts. 2016. 'Model Forensic Science'. *Australian Journal of Forensic Sciences* 48(5): 496–537.
Found, B. 2015. 'Deciphering the Human Condition: The Rise of Cognitive Forensics'. *Australian Journal of Forensic Sciences* 47(4): 386–401.
Fradella, H., S. Owen and T. Burke. 2007. 'Building Bridges between Criminal Justice and the Forensic Sciences to Create Forensic Studies Programs'. *Journal of Criminal Justice Education* 18(2): 261–282.
Gans, H.J. 1989. 'Sociology in America. The Discipline and the Public'. The American Sociological Association 1988 Presidential Address. *American Sociological Review* 54(1): 1–16.
Garland, D., and R. Sparks. 2000. 'Criminology, Social Theory and the Challenge of Our Times'. *British Journal of Criminology* 40(2): 189–204.
Garrett, B.L., and P.J. Neufeld. 2009. 'Invalid Forensic Science Testimony and Wrongful Convictions'. *Virginia Law Review* 95(1): 1–97.
Goldson, B., and G. Hughes. 2010. 'Sociological Criminology and Youth Justice: Comparative Policy Analysis and Academic Intervention'. *Criminology & Criminal Justice* 10(2): 211–230.
Griffin, T., A. Pason, F. Wiecko and B. Brace. 2016. 'Comparing Criminologists' Views on Crime and Justice Issues with Those of the General Public'. *Criminal Justice Policy Review*, advance online publication, 25 March 2016, 1–21. DOI: 10.1177/0887403416638412.
Groombridge, N. 2007. 'Criminologists Say ... : An Analysis of UK National Press Coverage of Criminology and Criminologists and a Contribution to the Debate on "Public Criminology"'. *The Howard Journal* 46(5): 459–475.
Haggerty, K.D. 2004. 'Displaced Expertise: Three Constraints on the Policy Relevance of Criminological Thought'. *Theoretical Criminology* 8(2): 211–231.
Hallsworth, S., and J. Lea. 2012. 'Reconnecting the King with His Head: The Fall and Resurrection of the State in Criminological Theory'. *Crime, Media, Culture* 8(2): 185–195.

Hamilton, C. 2013. 'Towards a Pedagogy of Public Criminology'. *Enhancing Learning in the Social Sciences* 5(2): 20–31.
Herbert, S. 2009. 'Broken Windows Theory'. In A. Wakefield and J. Fleming, eds., *The Sage Dictionary of Policing*, 12–14. Los Angeles: Sage.
Houck, M.M., R.A. Riley, P.J. Speaker and T.S. Witt. 2009. 'FORESIGHT: A Business Approach to Improving Forensic Science Services'. *Forensic Science Policy and Management: An International Journal* 1(2): 85–95.
Howes, L.M., P.K. Kirkbride, S.F. Kelty, R. Julian and N. Kemp. 2013. 'Forensic Scientists' Conclusions: How Readable Are They for Non-Scientist Report-Users?' *Forensic Science International* 231(1–3): 102–112.
Jasanoff, S., ed. 2004. *States of Knowledge: The Co-Production of Science and Social Order*. London: Routledge.
Julian, R., and S. Kelty. 2012. 'Introduction. Forensic Science and Justice: From Crime Scene to Court and Beyond'. *Current Issues in Criminal Justice* 24(1): 1–6.
Julian, R., S. Kelty, C. Roux, P. Woodman, J. Robertson, A. Davey, R. Hayes, P. Margot, A. Ross, H. Sibly and R. White. 2011. 'What Is the Value of Forensic Science? An Overview of the Effectiveness of Forensic Science in the Australian Criminal Justice System Project'. *Australian Journal of Forensic Sciences* 43(4): 217–229.
Kelty, S., R. Julian and A. Ross. 2012. 'Dismantling the Justice Silos: Avoiding the Pitfalls and Reaping the Benefits of Information-Sharing between Forensic Science, Medicine and Law'. *Forensic Science International* 230(1–3): 8–15.
Lawless, C. 2016. *Forensic Science: A Sociological Introduction*. Oxon, New York: Routledge.
Lawless, C., and R. Williams. 2010. 'Helping with Inquiries, or Helping with Profit? The Trials and Tribulations of a Technology of Forensic Reasoning'. *Social Studies of Science* 40(5): 731–755.
Loader I., and R. Sparks. 2010a. *Public Criminology?* London: Routledge.
Loader, I., and R. Sparks. 2010b. 'What Is to Be Done with Public Criminology?' *Criminology & Public Policy* 9(4): 771–781.
Loader, I., and R. Sparks. 2011. 'Criminology's Public Roles: A Drama in Six Acts'. In M. Bosworth and C. Hoyle, eds, *What Is Criminology?* 17–34. Oxford: Oxford University Press.
Ludwig, A., and J. Fraser. 2014. 'Effective Use of Forensic Science in Volume Crime Investigations: Identifying Recurring Themes in the Literature'. *Science and Justice* 54(1): 81–88.
Lynch, M., and R. McNally. 2003. '"Science", "Common Sense", and DNA Evidence: A Legal Controversy about the Public Understanding of Science'. *Public Understanding of Science* 12(1): 81–103.
Margot, P. 2011. 'Forensic Science on Trial—What Is the Law of the Land?' *Australian Journal of Forensic Science* 43(2–3): 89–103.
Martire, K.A., R.I. Kemp and B.R. Newell. 2013. 'The Psychology of Interpreting Expert Evaluative Opinions'. *Australian Journal of Forensic Sciences* 45(3): 305–314.
Matthews, R. 2009. 'Beyond "So What?" Criminology: Rediscovering Realism'. *Theoretical Criminology* 13(3): 341–362.
McCartney, C. 2006. 'The DNA Expansion Programme and Criminal Investigation'. *British Journal of Criminology* 46(2): 175–192.
McQuistin-Surrett, D., and M.J. Saks. 2008. 'Communicating Opinion Evidence in the Forensic Identification Sciences: Accuracy and Impact'. *Hastings Law Journal* 59(5): 1159–1190.
Melossi, D. 2000. 'Changing Representations of the Criminal'. *British Journal of Criminology* 40(2): 296–320.
Mills, C.W. 1959/2000. *The Sociological Imagination*. New York: Oxford University Press.
Nickel, P.M. 2010. 'Public Sociology and the Public Turn in the Social Sciences'. *Sociology Compass* 4(9): 694–704.
Petersilia, J. 1991. 'Policy Relevance and the Future of Criminology'. The American Society of Criminology 1990 Presidential Address. *Criminology* 29(1): 1–15.
Peterson, J.L., M.J. Hickman, K.J. Strom and D.J. Johnson. 2012. 'Effect of Forensic Evidence on Criminal Justice Case Processing'. *Journal of Forensic Sciences* 58(1): 78–90.
Peterson, J.L., I. Sommers, D. Baskin and D.J. Johnson. 2010. *Role and Impact of Forensic Evidence in the Criminal Justice Process*. Washington, DC: National Institute of Justice.
Piché, J. 2015. 'Playing the "Treasury Card" to Contest Prison Expansion: Lessons from a Public Criminology Campaign'. *Social Justice* 41(3): 145–167.
Radelet, M.L., and M.J. Borg. 2000. 'The Changing Nature of Death Penalty Debates'. *Annual Review of Sociology* 26: 43–61.

Ribaux, O. 2006. 'The Contribution of Forensic Science to Crime Analysis and Investigation: Forensic Intelligence'. *Forensic Science International* 156(2–3): 171–181.

Ribaux O., A. Baylon, C. Roux, O. Delémont, E. Lock, C. Zingg and P. Margot. 2010a. 'Intelligence-Led Crime Scene Processing. Part I: Forensic Intelligence'. *Forensic Science International* 195(1–3): 10–16.

Ribaux, O., A. Baylon, E. Lock, O. Delémont, C. Roux, C. Zingg and P. Margot. 2010b. 'Intelligence-Led Crime Scene Processing. Part II: Intelligence and Crime Scene Examination'. *Forensic Science International* 199(1–3): 63–71.

Ribaux, O., F. Crispino, O. Delémont, and C. Roux. 2015. 'The Progressive Opening of Forensic Science toward Criminological Concern'. *Security Journal*, advance online publication, 2 November 2015, 1–18. doi:10.1057/sj.2015.29.

Ribaux, O., and B. Talbot Wright. 2014. 'Expanding Forensic Science through Forensic Intelligence'. *Science & Justice* 54(6): 494–501.

Roberts, P. 2015. 'Paradigms of Forensic Science and Legal Process: A Critical Diagnosis'. *Philosophical Transactions of the Royal Society* B 370(1674): 20140256.

Rock, P. 2014. 'The Public Faces of Public Criminology'. *Criminology & Criminal Justice* 14(4): 412–433.

Ross, A., C. Roux, T. Legrand and O. Ribaux. 2015. Introduction. *Australian Journal of Forensic Sciences* 47(1): 6–7.

Roux, C., and J. Robertson. 2009. 'The Development and Enhancement of Forensic Expertise: Higher Education and In-Service Training'. In J. Fraser and R. Williams, eds., *Handbook of Forensic Science*. Cullompton, UK: Willan.

Roux, C., B. Talbot-Wright, J. Robertson, F. Crispino and O. Ribaux. 2015. 'The End of the (Forensic Science) World as We Know It? The Example of Trace Evidence'. *Philosophical Transactions of the Royal Society* B 370(1674): 20140260.

Rowe, M. 2012. 'Just Like a TV Show: Public Criminology and the Media Coverage of "Hunt for Britain's Most Wanted Man"'. *Crime, Media, Culture* 9(1): 23–38.

Ruggiero, V. 2012. 'How public is public criminology?' *Crime, Media, Culture* 8(2): 151–160.

Saks, M.J., and J.J. Koehler. 2005. 'The Coming Paradigm Shift in Forensic Identification Science'. *Science* 309(5736): 892–895.

Sanders, C.B., and L. Eisler. 2014. 'Engaging and Debating the Role of Public Criminology: An Introduction'. *Radical Criminology* 4: 9–16.

Shelton, D.E. 2008. 'The "CSI Effect": Does It Really Exist?' *National Institute of Justice Journal* 259. www.nij.gov/journals/259/pages/csi-effect.aspx.

Shelton, D.E., Y.S. Kim and G. Barak. 2006. 'Study of Juror Expectations and Demands concerning Scientific Evidence: Does the "CSI Effect" Exist?' *Vanderbilt Journal of Entertainment & Technology Law* 9: 331–369.

Sherman, L. 2009. 'Evidence and Liberty: The Promise of Experimental Criminology'. *Criminology and Criminal Justice* 9(1): 5–28.

Skolnick, J.H. 1995. 'What Not to Do about Crime'. The American Society of Criminology 1994 Presidential Address. *Criminology* 33(1): 1–15.

Thompson, W.B. 2011. 'What Role Should Investigative Facts Play in the Evaluation of Scientific Evidence?' *Australian Journal of Forensic Sciences* 43(2–3): 123–134.

Tittle, C.R. 2004. 'The Arrogance of Public Sociology'. *Social Forces* 82(4): 1639–1643.

Turner, E. 2013. 'Beyond "Facts" and "Values": Rethinking Some Recent Debates about the Public Role of Criminology'. *British Journal of Criminology* 53(1): 149–166.

Uggen, C., and M. Inderbitzin. 2010. 'Public Criminologies'. *Criminology and Public Policy* 9(4): 725–749.

Vuille, J. 2013. 'Admissibility and Appraisal of Scientific Evidence in Continental European Criminal Justice Systems: Past, Present and Future'. *Australian Journal of Forensic Sciences* 45(4): 389–397.

Wacquant, L. 2011. 'From "Public Criminology" to the Reflexive Sociology of Criminological Production and Consumption, A Review of *Public Criminology?* by Ian Loader and Richard Sparks'. *British Journal of Criminology* 51(2): 438–448.

Young, J. 2004. 'Voodoo Criminology and the Numbers Game'. In J. Ferrell, K. Hayward, W. Morrison and M. Presdee, eds., *Cultural Criminology Unleashed*, 13–27. London: Glass House Press.

Zahn, M. 1999. 'Thoughts on the Future of Criminology'. The American Society of Criminology 1998 Presidential Address. *Criminology* 37(1): 1–16.

Zedner, L. 2007. 'Pre-Crime and Post-Criminology?' *Theoretical Criminology* 11(2): 261–281.

Part II

Forensic practices and crime regulation

6

Forensic-led regulation strategies

Are they fit for security problem-solving purposes?

Frank Crispino and Claude Roux

Despite previous warnings regarding some forensic malpractices and questions about forensic science's scientific underpinnings (Huber 1991; Giannelli 2002; Saks and Koehler 2005; Pyrek 2007), the report of the US National Academy of Sciences *Strengthening Forensic Science in the United States: A Path Forward* (National Research Council 2009) shook the forensic science community. It presented this discipline as undefined, fragmented and without relevant dedicated research, served by uncontrolled laboratories with weak scientific understandings, where employees were unaware of many cognitive biases attributable to the organization of their services as well as dependency on police forces (Edwards 2009). Although less polemical and more constructive, a similar Canadian review found results in agreement with the American report (Pollanen et al. 2013). Indeed, worldwide reactions to the NAS Report implicitly recognized the relevancy of the criticisms at an international level (Margot 2011a; Margot 2011b; Mnookin et al. 2011; Ross 2011; Robertson et al. 2013). Only a few managers and forensic scientists contextualized the NAS Report findings, both integrating previous reports of the same vein by the NAS and reframing them in a more systemic analysis of failures of the criminal justice system (police, prosecution, forensic providers, trier of fact), underlining that forensic scientists had not waited for such a report to address these critiques (Kaye 2010; Melson 2010). However, even these few scientists who extended the debate to the security system as a whole expressed their agreement with the mainstream of commentators, who focused on addressing 'issues of accuracy, reliability, and validity in the forensic science disciplines' (recommendation 3 of the NAS Report). Even if quality management processes had already been implemented in many facilities as a general policy adopted to ensure traceability and reliability within a laboratory (Crispino et al. 2001), the NAS Report summoned forensic science to provide transparency and robustness in how conclusions were reached to courts of law, which induced mandatory compliance with procedures and rules of justice systems. This move found in the implementation of quality system models a solution to such a requirement, leading to the splitting of forensic data and of sophisticated techniques into specialized fields, framed in the quality triangle of standardization, accreditation and certification (Lentini 2009; Hazard et al. 2013). However, this response, at the very least, does not seem to address the NAS Report's criticisms of fragmentation. In fact, there is a more fundamental question: Is such a forensic-led regulation strategy viable for more general security problem-solving purposes? To address this question, it is pertinent to understand the origins and goals of current quality management strategies in forensic science (part 1), to identify some of the limitations (part 2) and finally to propose complementary solutions to the reliability and efficiency of forensic science to a more general security involvement (part 3 and conclusion).

The origins and goals of current quality management strategies in forensic science

In general, certification and accreditation rightly appear as the way not only to counter the deficiencies of forensic science but also to regulate a large number of very diverse laboratories in order to establish confidence in the criminal justice system. For example, in the US more than 200 forensic labs at national, state, county and city jurisdictions are regulated this way[1] (Jonakait 1991; Giannelli 2008; Zimmerman 2011; Siegel 2013; Lord Thomas 2015). The process of certification and accreditation offers a comprehensive response to legitimate, but not necessarily scientifically supported, accusations against forensic science as the main body at fault for miscarriages of justice (Collins and Collins 2009; Neufeld and Scheck 2010). Fundamentally, the process surely comes out as a prerequisite for sharing evidence between laboratories, for feeding databases and for international cooperation in the fight against crime (Malkoc and Neuteboom 2007; Padar et al. 2015).

Nevertheless, the process of certification should also primarily be understood as the achievement of an older quality management conception, which began in the 1970s through proficiency tests (Peterson et al. 1978; Lentini 2009; Robertson et al. 2010). Through inter-laboratories tests, the process aimed at detecting pitfalls in the conduct of forensic examinations for the sake of the laboratories that volunteered to participate. Even if these tests are still carried out today, their intrinsic limits are recognized. For example, what does a failure of a single test mean? Does a successful test guarantee the absence of any error in a daily routine? As a result, they are complemented by individual certification and institutional accreditation procedures. Currently, these components are overarched by general requirements imported from the industrial and commercial arena, with ISO 17025 for the competence of testing and calibration laboratories at laboratory level, but also a still debatable ISO 17020 for the operation of various types of bodies performing inspection dedicated to crime scene units. These systems are understood as performers of their 'parent organizations, or authorities, with the objective of providing information about the conformity of inspected items with regulations, standards, specifications, inspection schemes or contracts' (www.iso.org/obp/ui/#iso:std:iso-iec:17020:ed-2:v1:en).

Notwithstanding the requisite adaptation of these general requirements to the crime laboratory at hand (such as ASTM E1732 for standardizing terminology in the US, CAN–P–1578 guidelines for the accreditation of forensic testing laboratories in Canada, AS 5388 Australian Standards on forensic analysis, etc.) and interrogations about the organizational links existing between crime scene units and forensic laboratories, such general requirements were clearly adopted to secure well-defined notions of scientific traceability and reliability of the examinations performed to the recipients of the service (police corps, attorneys, trier of fact), beyond the more formal and juridical chain of custody. It is worth remembering that traceability is an objective concept that can be summarized as 'nothing is hidden and everything is written'. Through this concept, each step of the process can be followed and understood. On the other hand, reliability is a subjective concept: no case is undertaken from a biased point of view or with a priori assumptions, so that the customers (judges, police) can trust the results provided (Crispino et al. 2001). Interestingly, ISO 17025 (but also ISO 17020) focuses on traceability, while most criticisms raised in the NAS Report relate to reliability.

Regardless, accreditation remains especially legitimate because it relies on quality procedures usually validated by relevant scientific working groups of the various forensic fields such as the European Network of Forensic Science Institutes (ENFSI) or a special committee of an authoritative body (e.g., the Organization of Scientific Area Committees [OSAC] of the American National Institute of Standards and Technology [NIST] that recently replaced the American Scientific Working Groups, although the latter appeared to be closer to the practitioners). The accreditation itself is delivered by a variety of bodies dedicated to forensic science that have flourished around the world, such as the Laboratory Accreditation Board of the American Society of Crime Laboratory Directors (ASCLD/LAB), the Forensic Specialties Accreditation Board (FSAB), the National Association of Testing Authorities (NATA) in Australia and the European Cooperation for Accreditation (EA). At the individual level, certification is generally awarded by professional organizations, such as the American College of Forensic Examiners Institute (ACFEI), to their members, notwithstanding uncontrolled questionable credentials (Ciedel 2012). But once granted, this attribute is mainly dependent on the personal deontology of the individual fellows, with few, if any effective policies available to regulate them. This lack of effective policies is due to a variety of factors—the private and volunteer status of the organization, financial constraints or fear about publicly admitting powerlessness to monitor (Melson 2012). Finally, the very concept of accreditation could become operatively senseless not only for security, but also justice purposes, because of the high complexity and low consensus surrounding the analysis of uncontrolled traces for reconstructing a single event, for which quality management procedures emphasize fragmented protocols.

However, quality management is not the appropriate focus, as Willis (2014) maintains:

> it is necessary to refocus on people. Forensic science is not a bundle of tasks or routine processes although it includes these. It needs productive thinking, problem solving, cognitive ability and decision-making about which, when and why. None of this is at variance with accreditation. In fact, if used in a continuous improvement way, accreditation acknowledges these skills. However, the more fragmented the process becomes, the less accreditation may help address the need for an overall approach to the questions raised to help solve crime and evaluate findings in the judicial process. (Willis 2014, 505)

The need to establish confidence with stakeholders (often justice representatives only) is well understood. However, from this consensus a culture has emerged that is dictated by the quality movement coming from the manufacturing economic model (Speaker 2009a, Willis 2010). In this culture, new business relationships between customers (defence attorneys, prosecutors, but also law enforcement agencies) and forensic science service providers are defined. It remains unclear if such a move is a consequence of, or an incentive for, a contested neoliberal conception of security at large, and policing in particular (Roberts 1996; Koppl 2005; Lawless 2010; Lawless and Williams 2010; Lawless 2011; Maguire et al. 2012; McAndrew 2012; Jackson 2013; Gallop and Brown 2014; Gallop and Squibb-Williams 2015). Following this credo, quality management should both optimize the quality of the forensic service provision and lessen its costs (Houck et al. 2009; King and Maguire 2009; Speaker 2009b; Speaker and Fleming 2010; Newman et al. 2011; Bonetti et al. 2012; Stimson 2013; Ludwig et al. 2014; Speaker 2015), even if pioneers of scientific quality expressed concerns about its misappropriation both by analysts, who would only understand quality management to control and upgrade their technical strategies (devices and analysis), and administrators, who would focus on the managing of the life of the laboratory through general instructions (Dupont 1998; Suzuki 1998).

At this stage, we ought to ask the question: Since quality management is specific to any sector that wants to be competitive while being effective and efficient through quality standards met by monitoring and evaluating the different stages of a process, did not this management perspective in terms of performance lose sight of the very mission of forensic science?

Limitations

Indeed, as forensic science is embedded in a complex investigation process (Brown and Willis 2010; Julian and Kelty 2015), isn't there a risk to letting the stakeholders believe in a quality assurance, uniquely grounded on accreditation procedures, that is misleading (Stauffer and Schiffer 2007; Willis 2010; Willis 2011; Ross 2013), since it confirms only that the entire process in the laboratory has been mastered and is trustworthy? Worse, such localized considerations could prevent forensic practitioners from identifying where the problems really lie with regard to the criminal justice system (Hazard et al., 2013). To summarize, the last 2015 annual report of the chief scientist adviser of the UK government sounds the alarm about the excesses of the policy England and Wales have chosen, that of privatization of forensic science services that should have been secured and regulated by quality management accreditation and certification. Although 'it has saved costs, reduced case turnaround times, maintained quality and, to some extent, inspired innovation ... the way services are procured has become increasingly fragmented, threatening future innovation and potentially undermining public confidence in the criminal justice process' (Gallop and Squibb-Williams 2015, 12).

But, in reality, the challenge extends well beyond the single experimental forensic provision, as it indicates the difficulty in stretching this model to the whole investigative phase, even when the latter is restricted to its scientific aspect. Indeed, most of the existing standards focus on the analysis stage, not even taking into consideration pre- and post-laboratory stages, namely, the crime scene performance and the interpretation of the results, for intelligence purposes or for court. Failure to consider forensic science in its totality (Roux et al. 2012) has an obvious impact on the effectiveness of quality assurance as it is currently designed. 'The forensic science community struggles today with the comprehensive quality approach because it failed to develop its own approach, instead mistakenly copying the work from the manufacturing sector' (Hazard et al. 2013, 1772).

It is also recognized that the nature of forensic science is still being debated. Adopting a more holistic view of forensic science questions the way we define rules of conduct and quality procedures for a body of knowledge whose epistemological nature is still debated (Kirk 1963; Ginzburg 1984; Evett 1996; Cleland 2001; Cleland 2002; Kennedy 2003; Koppl et al. 2008; Houck 2010; Evett 2015). Is forensic science a science in its own right, a police practice or a set of disconnected, enabled disciplines called 'forensics' when devoted to the courtroom (Roux et al. 2012)? While the conception of this domain is still at stake, is it wise to adopt a purely commercial regulation strategy? Indeed, Hazard et al. noticed that 'Although it was relatively straightforward to define and implement a quality system with laboratory procedures, it is a whole other problem with scene examination or opinion development' (2013, 1772).

Regardless, it seems obvious that the object of interest—the trace or mark—defines the forensic science domain. To be differentiated from an item that is a controlled sample from a known population, the trace is generally a unique specimen, degraded, mixed, of bad quality, of an inferred source of interest and produced during another inferred[2] action of interest (Margot 2011b; Margot 2014). Despite this realistic statement, the trace remains the most reliable source of information to reconstruct an event under investigation, within a holistic approach (Kind 1994; Kind 1999; Delémont et al. 2014). Of course, scientific process should not worsen the little available information provided by the trace. As such, chain of custody and analytical traceability are relevant constraints. Standardization offers a further relevant means to enable critical surveys of forensic analysis and allow for national and international data sharing. But it also raises the question of where uncertainty lies in forensic science. Does it make sense to secure the forensic analysis phase further, when jurists, sociologists and criminologists try to better assess what modern evidence is (Tillers 1983; Tillers 1989; Patenaude 2001; Lagnado 2011; Tillers 2011), when they defend a silo-dismantling approach (Kelty et al. 2013; Lord Thomas 2015) and when even judges question both their ability to manage or understand scientific evidence and the unscientific chess game led by prosecution and defence lawyers behind the adversarial procedure (Judge Edwards 2012; Laurin 2013)? Ironically, the questions about standardization draw law and security closer to long existing scientific questions about relevancy and interpretation (Appell et al. 1904; Finkelstein and Fairley 1970; Aitken and Stoney 1991; Robertson and Vignaux 1995; Evett 1996; Evett 1998; Taroni et al. 1998; Aitken and Taroni 2004; Tillers 2007; Champod and Evett 2009; Aitken et al. 2011; Tillers 2011a; Tillers 2011b; Biedermann 2013; Roberts and Aitken 2014; Taroni et al. 2014; Evett 2015).

At the least, the focus on traditional quality management appears to remove opportunities for an alternative conceptualization approach that would better focus on formation, education, selection and supervision of practitioners (Horswell 2004; Kelty and Julian 2010; Kelty and Julian 2011a; Kelty and Julian 2012; Crispino et al. 2014), or define dedicated forensic science research (Kelty and Julian 2011b; Margot 2011b; Mnookin et al. 2011), which would address the various types of inferences developed at the early phase of the investigation (Peirce 1898; 1995, Ginzburg 1984; Ginzburg 1989; Baber et al. 2006; Pape 2008; Schuliar and Crispino 2013; Hazard 2014; Bitzer et al. 2015). Finally, do certification and quality management strive to help or to coerce practitioners (Crispino et al. 2001; Kolowski 2015)?

Without denying that standard operating procedures also aim at reducing cognitive biases (Dror et al. 2013; Dror 2016), there is no question that they are not an exclusivity of forensic science, but a sociological if not political self-evident fact (Tversky and Kahneman 1974; Plous 1993). Hence, where is the rationale for imposing legitimate reliability and transparency of forensic practice—focused and restricted at court level (McCartney 2015)—while permitting a variable geometry for decision makers, whose understanding of forensic probative value should certainly be enhanced as a prerequisite (Providers 2009; Vuille 2013; Crispino et al. 2014)? Worse, focusing on bias, instead of raising awareness among forensic scientists about cognitive bias, could delay their core research, which is to understand the occurrence of available traces in criminogenic vs usual daily situations (Champod 2014). As Ribaux wrote in Chapter 2 of this book, 'The narrowness of traditional views on forensic science does not allow the structured, useful and comprehensive exploitation of all data whose treatment should fall under its purview', even ignoring that the experience of forensic practitioners is not critically taken into account within the current practice, as it certainly could be at least for intelligence purposes.

In such circumstances, we ought to ask the question: Are current forensic-led regulation strategies fit for security problem-solving purposes? Looking at the flexibility, skill, adaptability and innovation of organized crime in comparison to not only an apparent quality management silo culture, but also the poor efficiency of trace exploitation (Ribaux and Talbot Wright 2014), the present chapter would answer this question in the negative, as far as this question equates whether quality management policies are appropriate for policing (be it intelligence-led, problem-solving or even community-oriented (Ratcliffe 2011). But, as our critical analysis was framed within a holistic perspective, it should also be remembered that the ambivalent role of forensic science is also inherited from the difficulties in configuring security and justice through coherent strategies and organizations (Brodeur and Shearing 2005). Hence, no real other criminological alternatives can be proposed at this point.

Complementary Solutions

Understanding traditional quality management policies (part 1) and their limitations (part 2), and considering social, economic and also political constraints lend support to a rethinking of current trace management models (Collins 2013; Fisher 2013; Gialamas 2013; Lucas 2013). Since some proponents of straight quality management policies suggest looking to the quality management practice in the medical field (Christian 2011), a more general clinical approach within forensic science inspired by this field of practice invites a more thorough survey (Margot 2011b; Pottier and Planchon 2011). Indeed, medical science is aimed not only at curing a single case but also preventing illness through a symptom watch network or identifying an epidemic through repetition of cases, just as forensic science is not restricted to presenting evidence in courts but could also nurture prevention and intelligence schemes at tactical, operational and strategic levels (Ribaux 2014). Hence, mimicking medical quality procedures could possibly address the present deficiencies of forensic quality management-led regulations. For instance, whereas three levels of intervention and responsibility are easily identified in the medical organization—the paramedics or frontbench, the specialists at the other end and the general practitioner who rationalizes the efficiency of this structure either for the sake of the patient or of public health, all of them educated in a medical paradigm that lets them understand each other—the situation is blurred for forensic science. Crime scene examiners are generally considered to be trace providers for detectives, even if they do not see themselves that way (Ludwig et al. 2012); it is difficult to identify general practitioners able to enter into discussions with overspecialized and independent experts. The comparison with medical practice could support the hypothesis that high quality also depends on the way a forensic science culture is assimilated (into specific education/training and workplaces) and understood from a systemic point of view, which could invite questioning the philosophy of clients, customers and providers (Kobus et al. 2011) to arrive at a more collaborative approach relying on an epistemology based on the trace, the fundamental element of forensic science (Margot 2014). It seems that forensic-led regulations largely contributed to the closure of the UK Forensic Science Service, unanimously considered an international reference for interpretative operative research that could not be supported by the private sector (Commons 2011; Evett et al. 2012; Logan 2012; Gallop and Brown 2014). The same paradigm continues to contribute to, if not justify, closing down seminal forensic science fields such as trace evidence departments (Roux et al. 2015; Stoney and Stoney 2015). We should therefore seriously assess the consequences of such regulations before continuing in that direction. Actually, with the advent of the digital era, few investigations are conducted today without numerical traces. As a result, the volume and variety of data has dramatically increased in the early phase of an investigation. Since it is hard to conceive the integration of these data flows through external, systematically accredited laboratories, why not appraise the push they induce for a more collective security approach, and why should traditional forensic traces be excluded from such consideration?

Conclusion

Questioning security regulation strategies opens a Pandora's box. In particular it reminds us that 'forensic intelligence and crime investigation are about crime reconstruction. Such a logic can hardly be mechanized since it calls for imagination, drawing analogies and associating ideas' (see Ribaux and Caneppele, 'Forensic intelligence', chapter 12, in this volume). How much of these skills have to be standardized, and how can they be standardized? While it seems a collaborative approach relying on an epistemology based on the trace would go a long way to addressing this challenge, only time will tell. In the meantime, we invite the reader to contrast the current, inconsistent regulation of security through technical constraints with Goldstein's 38-year-old warning: 'All bureaucracies [are] becoming so preoccupied with running their organizations and getting so involved in their methods of operating that they lose sight of their primary purposes for which they were created' (Goldstein 1979, 236–237).

Notes

1 For an idea of the present US provision, see www.ksg.harvard.edu/netgov/html/research_dna_cj_labs.htm.

2 It should be remembered that 'to infer' means 'to develop a hypothesis in conditions of uncertainty'.

References

Aitken, C., P. Roberts and G. Jackson. 2011. *Fundamentals of Probability and Statistical Evidence in Criminal Proceedings. Guidance for Judges, Lawyers, Forensic Scientists and Expert Witnesses*. London: Royal Statstical Society.

Aitken, C., and D. Stoney. 1991. *The Use of Statistics in Forensic Science*. Chichester, West Sussex, England: CRC Press.

Aitken, C., and F. Taroni. 2004. *Statistics and the Evaluation of Evidence for Forensic Scientists*. Chichester, West Sussex, England: John Wiley & Sons Ltd.

Appell, P., J.-G. Darboux and H. Poincaré. 1904. *Rapport du 20 août 1904 de la commission Appell, Darboux, Poincaré lors de la 2ème révision du procès de Dreyfus*. Paris: Cour de Cassation.

Association of Forensic Science Providers. 2009. 'Standards for the Formulation of Evaluative Forensic Science Expert Opinion'. *Science & Justice* 49(3): 161–164.

Baber, C., P. Smith, J. Cross, J. Hunter and R. McMaster. 2006. 'Crime Scene Investigation as Distributed Cognition'. *Pragmatics & Cognition* 14(2): 357–382.

Biedermann, A. 2013. 'Your Uncertainty, Your Probability, Your Decision'. *Frontiers in Genetics* 4. https://dx.doi.org/10.3389%2Ffgene.2013.00148.

Bitzer, S., N. Albertini, E. Lock, O. Ribaux and O. Delémont. 2015. 'Utility of the Clue—From Measuring the Investigative Contribution of Forensic Science to Supporting the Decision to Use Traces'. *Science & Justice* 55(6): 509–513.

Bonetti, J., M. Crowley, K. Johnson, M. Khalil, K. Sween and T. Brettell. 2012. '2012 Student Paper: Forensic Science Administration and Ideals for Laboratory Management'. *Forensic Science Policy & Management: An International Journal* 3(1): 20–23.

Brodeur, J., and C. Shearing. 2005. 'Configuring Security and Justice'. *European Journal of Criminology* 2(4): 379–406.

Brown, S., and S. Willis. 2010. 'Complexity in Forensic Science'. *Forensic Science Policy & Management: An International Journal* 1(4): 192–198.

Champod, C. 2014. 'Research Focused Mainly on Bias Will Paralyse Forensic Science'. *Science & Justice* 54(2): 107–109.

Champod, C., and I. Evett. 2009. 'Evidence Interpretation: A Logical Approach'. In A. Jamieson and A. Moenssens, eds., *Wiley Encyclopedia of Forensic Science*, 968–976. Oxford: Wiley-Blackwell.

Christian, D. 2011. 'How the Clinical Laboratory Improvement Amendments (CLIA) Can Improve Forensic Laboratory Quality'. *Forensic Science Policy & Management: An International Journal* 2(1): 18–27.

Ciedel, A., Director. 2012. *Frontline: The Real CSI*.

Cleland, C. 2001. 'Historical Science, Experimental Science, and the Scientific Method'. *Geology* 29(11): 987–990.

Cleland, C. 2002. 'Methodological and Epistemic Differences between Historical Science and Experimental Science'. *Philosophy of Science* 69: 474–496.

Collins, J., and J.J. Collins. 2009. 'The Wrongful Conviction of Forensic Science'. *Forensic Science Policy & Management: An International Journal* 1(1): 17–31.

Collins Jr, J. 2013. '10 Criteria Defining a Model Forensic Science Laboratory'. *Forensic Science Policy & Management: An International Journal* 4(1–2): 38–56.

Crispino, F., Q. Rossy, O. Ribaux and C. Roux. 2014. 'Education and Training in Forensic Intelligence: A New Challenge'. *Australian Journal of Forensic Sciences* 47(1): 49–60.

Crispino, F., P. Touron, A. Abd ElKader, and C. Curran. 2001. 'Quality Management in a New Forensic Laboratory: A Constraint or a Tool?' *Interfaces* 26(2): 3.

Delémont, O., P. Esseiva, F. Been and L. Benaglia. 2014. 'La police scientifique au-delà de ses frontières actuelles: la perspective de nouvelles connaissances'. *Revue internationale de criminalistique et de police technique et scientifique* 67(3): 283–304.

Dror, I. 2016. 'Cognitive Neuroscience in Forensic Science: Understanding and Utilizing the Human Element'. *Philosophical Transaction of the Royal Society B* 370. DOI: 10.1098/rstb.2014.0255.

Dror, I., S. Kassin and J. Kukucka. 2013. 'New Application of Psychology to Law: Improving Forensic Evidence and Expert Witness Contributions'. *Journal of Applied Research in Memory and Cognition* 2: 78–81.

Dupont, A. 1998. *The Human Dimension: The Sense of Responsibilities and Notion of Expert*. 12th INTERPOL Forensic Science Symposium, Lyon, France: The Forensic Sciences Foundation Press.

Edwards, H., Honorable, Committee Co-Chair. 2009. *Strengthening Forensic Science in the United States: A Path Forward*, 12. Washington, DC: The National Academies Press.

Edwards, H. 2012. 'Judge Harry T. Edwards: How Reliable Is Forensic Evidence in Court?' *Frontline: The Real CSI*. G. Gavett, Director.

Evett, I. 1996. 'Expert Evidence and Forensic Misconceptions of the Nature of Exact Science'. *Science & Justice* 36(2): 118–122.

Evett, I. 1998. 'Towards a Uniform Framework for Reporting Opinions in Forensic Science Casework'. *Science & Justice* 38(3): 198–202.

Evett, I. 2015. 'The Logical Foundations of Forensic Science: Towards Reliable Knowledge'. *Philosophical Transaction of the Royal Society B* 370. DOI: 10.1098/rstb.2014.0263.

Evett, I., S. Pope and G. Tully. 2012. 'Forensic Science: The Police Piper Calls the Tune'. *The Law Society Gazette*. London. www.lawgazette.co.uk/law/forensic-science-the-police-piper-calls-the-tune/68187.article.

Finkelstein, M. and W. Fairley. 1970. 'A Bayesian Approach to Identification Evidence'. *Harvard Law Review* 83(3): 489–517.

Fisher, B. 2013. 'A "Gold Standard" Forensic Laboratory Model'. *Forensic Science Policy & Management: An International Journal* 4(1–2): 3–6.

Gallop, A., and J. Brown. 2014. 'The Market Future for Forensic Science Services in England and Wales'. *Policing: A Journal of Policy and Practice*: 254–264.

Gallop, A., and A. Squibb-Williams. 2015. Forensic Science in Context. In Sir M. Walport, Government Chief Scientific Adviser, *Forensic Science and Beyond: Authenticity, Provenance and Assurance. Evidence and Case Studies*, 12–16. London, UK: Government Office for Science.

Gialamas, D. 2013. 'A Review and Commentary on the Model Forensic Science Laboratory'. *Forensic Science Policy & Management: An International Journal* 4(1–2): 29–37.

Giannelli, P. 2002. 'Fabricated Reports'. *Criminal Justice* 16(4): 49–50.

Giannelli, P. 2008. 'Wrongful Convictions and Forensic Science: The Need to Regulate Crime Labs'. *North Carolina Law Review* 86: 163–235.

Ginzburg, C. 1984. 'Morelli, Freud, and Sherlock Holmes: Clues and Scientific Method'. In U. Eco and T. Sebeok, eds., *The Sign of Three: Dupin, Holmes, Peirce*, 81–118. Bloomington & Indianapolis: Indiana University Press.

Ginzburg, C. 1989. 'Traces. Racines d'un paradigme indiciaire'. In *Mythes, emblèmes, traces*, 139–180. Paris: Flammarion.

Goldstein, H. 1979. 'Improving Policing: A Problem-Oriented Approach'. *Crime & Delinquency* 25: 236–258.

Hazard, D. 2014. 'La pertinence en science forensique: Une (en)quête épistémologique et empirique'. Doctorat, Université de Lausanne.

Hazard, D., E. Stauffer and P. Margot. 2013. 'Forensic Science and the Paradigm of Quality'. In G. Bruinsma and D. Weisburd, eds., *Springer Encyclopedia of Criminology and Criminal Justice*, 1773–1782. New York: Springer.

Horswell, J. 2004. 'Crime Scene Investigation and Third Party Quality Systems Accreditation'. In J. Horswell, ed., *The Practice Of Crime Scene Investigation*, 67–82. Chichester, West Sussex, England: CRC Press.

Houck, M. 2010. 'An Investigation into the Foundational Principles of Forensic Science'. PhD diss., Curtin University of Technology.

Houck, M., R. Riley, P. Speaker and T. Witt. 2009. 'FORESIGHT: A Business Approach to Improving Forensic Science Services'. *Forensic Science Policy & Management: An International Journal* 1(2): 85–95.

Huber, P. 1991. *Galileo's Revenge: Junk Science in the Courtroom*. New York: Basic Books.

House of Commons. 2011. The Forensic Science Service. All Science and Technology Committee. London: The Stationery Office Limited: 95.

Jackson, G. 2013. 'The Impact of Commercialization on the Evaluation of DNA Evidence'. *Frontiers in Genetics* 4. https://doi.org/10.3389/fgene.2013.00227.

Jonakait, R. 1991. 'Forensic Science: The Need for Regulation'. *Harvard Journal of Law and Technology* 4: 109–191.

Julian, R., and S. Kelty. 2015. 'Forensic Science as "Risky Business": Identifying Key Risk Factors in the Forensic Process from Crime Scene to Court'. *Journal of Criminological Research, Policy and Practice* 1(4): 195–206.

Kaye, D. 2010. 'The Good, the Bad, the Ugly: The NAS Report on Strengthening Forensic Science in America'. *Science & Justice* 50(1): 8–11.

Kelty, S., and R. Julian. 2010. 'Identifying the Skills and Attributes of Good Crime Scene Personnel'. *Australasian Policing* 2(2): 40–41.

Kelty, S., and R. Julian. 2011a. 'Success in Forensic Science Research and Other Collaborative Projects: Meeting Your Partners' Expectations'. *Forensic Science Policy & Management: An International Journal* 2(3): 141–147.

Kelty, S., and R. Julian. 2011b. 'What Makes a Good Crime Scene Examiner?' *Royal Canadian Mounted Police Gazette* 73(1): 24–25.

Kelty, S., and R. Julian. 2012. 'The Effectiveness of Forensic Science in the Criminal Justice System. The 7 Key Attributes of Top-Performing Crime Scene Examiners'. *Hobart, Tasmania, Australia, Tasmanian Institute of Law Enforcement Studies*: 2.

Kelty, S., R. Julian and A. Ross. 2013. 'Dismantling the Justice Silos: Avoiding the Pitfalls and Reaping the Benefits of Information-Sharing between Forensic Science, Medicine and Law'. *Forensic Science International* (1–3): 8–15.

Kennedy, D. 2003. 'Forensic Science: Oxymoron?' *Science* 302: 1625.

Kind, S. 1994. 'Crime Investigation and the Criminal Trial: A Three Chapter Paradigm of Evidence'. *Journal of the Forensic Science Society* 34(3): 155–164.

Kind, S. 1999. *The Sceptical Witness*. London: Hodology Ltd.

King, W., and E. Maguire. 2009. 'Assessing the Performance of Systems Designed to Process Criminal Forensic Evidence'. *Forensic Science Policy & Management: An International Journal* 1(3): 159–170.

Kirk, P. 1963. 'The Ontogeny of Criminalistics'. *The Journal of Criminal Law, Criminology and Police Science* (54): 235–238.

Kobus, H., M. Houck, P. Speaker, R. Riley and T. Witt. 2011. 'Managing Performance in the Forensic Sciences: Expectations in Light of Limited Budgets'. *Forensic Science Policy & Management: An International Journal* 2(1): 36–43.

Kolowski, J. 2015. 'The Challenge of Accreditation for Forensic Laboratories within the Good/Fast/Cheap Performance Management Paradigm'. *Forensic Research & Criminology International Journal* 1(1). http://medcraveonline.com/FRCIJ/FRCIJ-01-00001.pdf.

Koppl, R. 2005. 'How to Improve Forensic Science'. *European Journal of Law and Economics* 20: 255–286.

Koppl, R., R. Kurzban and L. Kobilinsky. 2008. 'Epistemics for Forensics'. *Episteme* 5(2): 141–159.

Lagnado, D. 2011. 'Thinking about Evidence'. In P. Dawid, W. Twining and M. Vasilaki, eds., *Evidence, Inference and Enquiry*, 183–224. Oxford: Oxford University Press.

Laurin, J. 2013. 'Remapping the Path Forward: Toward a Systemic View of Forensic Science Reform and Oversight'. *Texas Law Review* (91): 1051–1118.

Lawless, C. 2010. 'A Curious Reconstruction? The Shaping of "Marketized" Forensic Science'. Discussion Paper. London School of Economics and Political Science.

Lawless, C. 2011. 'Policing Markets: The Contested Shaping of Neo-Liberal Forensic Science'. *British Journal of Criminology* 51: 671–689.

Lawless, C., and R. Williams. 2010. 'Helping with Inquiries or Helping with Profits? The Trials and Tribulations of a Technology of Forensic Reasoning'. *Social Studies of Science* 40(5): 731–755.

Lentini, J. 2009. 'Forensic Science Standards: Where They Come From and How They Are Used'. *Forensic Science Policy & Management: An International Journal* 1(1): 10–16.

Logan, A. 2012. 'The Destruction of the Forensic Science Service'. *The Law Society Gazette*. www.lawgazette.co.uk/law/the-destruction-of-the-forensic-science-service/67018.article.

Lord Thomas, C. 2015. 'The Legal Framework for More Robust Forensic Science Evidence'. *Philosophical Transaction of the Royal Society B* 370. DOI: 10.1098/rstb.2014.0258.

Lucas, D. 2013. 'The Forensic Sciences: Ideally, How Might They be Delivered?' *Forensic Science Policy & Management: An International Journal* 4(1–2): 7–22.

Ludwig, A., T. Edgar and C. Maguire. 2014. 'A Model for Managing Crime Scene Examiners'. *Forensic Science Policy & Management: An International Journal* 5(3–4): 76–90.

Ludwig, A., J. Fraser and R. Williams. 2012. 'Crime Scene Examiners and Volume Crime Investigations: An Empirical Study of Perception and Practice'. *Forensic Science Policy & Management: An International Journal* 3(2): 53–61.

Maguire, C., M. Houck, R. Williams and P. Speaker. 2012. 'Efficiency and the Cost-Effective Delivery of Forensic Science Services: Insourcing, Outsourcing, and Privatization'. *Forensic Science Policy & Management: An International Journal* 3(2): 62–69.

Malkoc, E., and W. Neuteboom. 2007. 'The Current Status of Forensic Science Laboratory Accreditation in Europe'. *Forensic science International* 167(2–3): 121–126.

Margot, P. 2011a. 'Commentary on *The Need for a Research Culture in the Forensic Sciences*'. *UCLA Law Review* 58: 795–801.

Margot, P. 2011b. 'Forensic Science on Trial—What Is the Law of the Land?' *Australian Journal of Forensic Sciences* 43(2–3): 89–103.

Margot, P. 2014. 'Traçologie: la trace, vecteur fondamental de la police scientifique'. *Revue internationale de criminologie et de police technique et scientifique* 67(1): 72–97.

McAndrew, W. 2012. 'Is Privatization Inevitable for Forensic Science Laboratories?' *Forensic Science Policy & Management: An International Journal* 3(1): 42–52.

McCartney, C. 2015. 'Forensic Data Exchange: Ensuring Integrity'. *Australian Journal of Forensic Sciences* 47(1): 36–48.

Melson, K. 2010. 'Embracing the Path Forward: The Journey to Justice Continues'. *Criminal and Civil Confinement* 36: 197–232.

Melson, K. 2012. 'Codes of Ethics in Forensic Science Societies: The Organizational Parameters of Morality and Conduct'. In J. Upshaw Downs and A.R. Swienton, eds., *Ethics in Forensic Science*, 81–135. Oxford: Academic Press.

Mnookin, J., S. Cole, I. Dror, B. Fisher, M. Houck, K. Inman, D. Kaye, J. Koehler, G. Langenburg, D. Risinger, N. Rudin, Siegel J and D. Stoney. 2011. 'The Need for a Research Culture in the Forensic Sciences'. *UCLA Law Review* 58: 725–779.

National Research Council. 2009. *Strengthening Forensic Science in the United States: A Path Forward*. Washington, DC: The National Academies Press.

Neufeld, P., and B. Scheck. 2010. 'Making Forensic Science More Scientific'. *Nature* 464: 351.

Newman, J., D. Dawley and P. Speaker. 2011. 'Strategic Management of Forensic Laboratory Resources: From Project FORESIGHT Metrics to the Development of Action Plans'. *Forensic Science Policy & Management: An International Journal* 2(4): 164–174.

Padar, Z., M. Nogel and G. Kovacs. 2015. 'Accreditation of Forensic Laboratories as a Part of the "European Forensic Science 2020" Concept in Countries of the Visegrad Group'. *Forensic Science International: Genetics Supplement Series* 5: e412–e413.

Pape, H. 2008. 'Searching for Traces: How to Connect the Sciences and the Humanities by a Peircean Theory of Indexicality'. *Transactions of the Charles S. Peirce Society: A Quarterly Journal in American Philosophy* 44(1): 1–25.

Patenaude, P. 2001. 'De l'expertise "forensique" et de la décision judiciaire: Domaines fertiles pour un effort de compréhension et de cohérence'. *Revue de droit de l'Université de Sherbrooke* 32: 3–58.

Peirce, C. 1898, 1995. *Le raisonnement et la logique des choses*. Paris.

Peterson, J., E. Fabricant, K. Field and J. Thornton. 1978. *Crime Laboratory Proficiency Testing Research Program*. Washington, DC: US Government Printing House.

Plous, S. 1993. *The Psychology of Judgment and Decision Making*. New York: McGraw-Hill.

Pollanen, M., M.J. Bowes, S.L. VanLaerhoven, J. Wallace, eds. 2013. *Forensic Science in Canada. A Report of Multidisciplinary Discussion*. Toronto: University of Toronto, Centre for Forensic Science and Medicine.

Pottier, P., and B. Planchon. 2011. 'Les activités mentales au cours du raisonnement médical diagnostique'. *La Revue de médecine interne* (32): 383–390.

Pyrek, K. 2007. *Forensic Science under Siege: The Challenges of Forensic Laboratories and the Medico-Legal Investigation System*. San Diego, CA: Library of Congress.

Ratcliffe, J. 2011. *Intelligence-Led Policing*. Cullompton: Willan.

Ribaux, O. 2014. *Police scientifique. Le renseignement par la trace*. Lausanne: Presses polytechniques et universitaires romandes.

Ribaux, O., and B. Talbot Wright. 2014. 'Expanding Forensic Science through Forensic Intelligence'. *Science & Justice* 54(6): 494–501.

Roberts, P. 1996. 'What Price a Free Market in Forensic Science Services? The Organization and Regulation of Science in the Criminal Process'. *British Journal of Criminology* 36(1): 37–60.

Roberts, P., and C. Aitken. 2014. *The Logic of Forensic Proof: Inferential Reasoning in Criminal Evidence and Forensic Science*. London, Royal Statistical Society.

Robertson, B., and B. Vignaux. 1995. *Interpreting Evidence. Evaluating Forensic Science in the Courtroom*. New York: John Wiley & Sons Inc.

Robertson, J., K. Kent and L. Wilson-Wilde. 2013. 'The Development of a Core Forensic Standards Framework for Australia'. *Forensic Science Policy & Management: An International Journal* 4(3–4): 59–67.

Robertson, J., H. Metz, N. Scudder and V. Hodgson. 2010. 'A Quality System Review: Australian Federal Police Forensic and Data Centres'. *Forensic Science Policy & Management: An International Journal* 1(4): 209–213.

Ross, A. 2011. 'Forensic Science in Australia—Can We Learn from International Reports?' *Australian Journal of Forensic Sciences* 43(2–3): 135–145.

Ross, A. 2013. 'Balancing Forensic Effectiveness (Accreditation and Standards) with Forensic Efficiency'. *Efficient Forensic Science: Are We Using Our Experts Effectively? A Symposium for Lawyers, Forensic Scientists, Medical Professionals and Others*. Sydney Masonic Centre, Australia: Australian Academy of Forensic Sciences.

Roux, C., F. Crispino and O. Ribaux. 2012. 'From Forensics to Forensic Science'. *Current Issues in Criminal Justice* 24(1): 7–24.

Roux, C., B. Talbot-Wright, J. Robertson, F. Crispino and O. Ribaux. 2015. 'The End of the (Forensic Science) World as We Know It? The Example of Trace Evidence'. *Philosophical Transaction of the Royal Society B* 370. DOI: 10.1098/rstb.2014.0260.

Saks, M., and J. Koehler. 2005. 'The Coming Paradigm Shift in Forensic Identification Science'. *Science* 309: 892–895.

Schuliar, Y., and F. Crispino. 2013. 'Semiotics, Heuristics and Inferences Used by Forensic Scientists'. In J. Siegel and P. Saukko, eds., *Encyclopedia of Forensic Sciences*, 2nd ed., 3: 310–313. Waltham: Academic Press.

Siegel , J. 2013. 'Criteria and Concepts for a Model Forensic Science Laboratory'. *Forensic Science Policy & Management: An International Journal* 4(1–2): 23–28.

Speaker, P. 2009a. 'The Decomposition of Return on Investment for Forensic Laboratories'. *Forensic Science Policy & Management: An International Journal* 1(2): 96–102.

Speaker, P. 2009b. 'Key Performance Indicators and Managerial Analysis for Forensic Laboratories'. *Forensic Science Policy & Management: An International Journal* 1(1): 32–42.

Speaker, P. 2015. 'Financial Management of Forensic Science Laboratories: Lessons from Project FORESIGHT 2011–2012'. *Forensic Science Policy & Management: An International Journal* 6(1–2): 7–29.

Speaker, P., and A. Fleming. 2010. 'Benchmarking and Budgeting Techniques for Improved Forensic Laboratory Management'. *Forensic Science Policy & Management: An International Journal* 1(4): 199–208.

Stauffer, E., and B. Schiffer. 2007. 'La certification de forensicien: concepts de base et regard critique sur l'expérience américaine'. *Revue internationale de criminalistique et de police technique* 60(4): 461–478.

Stimson, W. 2013. 'Measuring Operations with Forensic Systems Analysis'. *Forensic Science Policy & Management: An International Journal* 4(3–4): 79–86.

Stoney, D.A., and P.L. Stoney. 2015. 'Critical Review of Forensic Trace Evidence Analysis and the Need for a New Approach'. *Forensic Science International* 251: 159–170.

Suzuki, T. 1998. *The Concept of Quality System: Global Approach, Certification or Accreditation: Its Practical Utilization and Problems*. 12th INTERPOL Forensic Science Symposium Lyon: The Forensic Sciences Foundation Press.

Taroni, F., A. Biedermann, S. Bozza, P. Garbolino and C. Aitken. 2014. *Bayesian Networks for Probabilistic Inference and Decision Analysis in Forensic Science*. Chichester, West Sussex, England: Wiley.

Taroni, F., C. Champod and P. Margot. 1998. 'Forerunners of Bayesianism in Early Forensic Science'. *Jurimetrics Journal* 38: 183–200.

Tillers, P. 1983. 'Modern Theories of Relevancy'. *Wigmore on Evidence* 1A, Sec. 37. SSRN: https://ssrn.com/abstract=739786.

Tillers, P. 1989. 'Webs of Things in the Mind: A New Science of Evidence'. *Michigan Law Review* 87: 1225–1258.

Tillers, P. 2007. 'Introduction: Visualizing Evidence and Inference in Legal Settings'. *Law, Probability and Risk* 6: 1–4.
Tillers, P. 2011. 'Are There Universal Principles or Forms of Evidential Inference? Of Inference Networks and Onto-Epistemology'. In P. Dawid, W. Twining and M. Vasilaki, eds., *Evidence, Inference and Enquiry*. British Academy Publications Online.
Tillers, P. 2011a. 'The Structure and the Logic of Proof in Trials'. *Law, Probability and Risk* 10: 1–6.
Tillers, P. 2011b. 'Trial by Mathematics—Reconsidered'. *Law, Probability and Risk* 10(3): 167–173.
Tversky, A., and D. Kahneman. 1974. 'Judgment under Uncertainty: Heuristics and Biases'. *Science* 185: 1124–1131.
Vuille, J. 2013. 'Admissibility and Appraisal of Scientific Evidence in Continental European Criminal Justice Systems: Past, Present and Future'. *Australian Journal of Forensic Sciences* 45(4): 389–397.
Willis, S. 2010. 'Power, Process, People—A Pesentation on Quality and Competence in Forensic Science Delivered at EAFS2009'. *Science & Justice* 50(1): 23–25.
Willis, S. 2011. 'The Highs and Lows of Accreditation'. *Forensic Science Policy & Management: An International Journal* 2(2): 75–80.
Willis, S. 2014. 'Accreditation—Straight Belt or Life Jacket?' *Science & Justice* 54(6): 505–507.
Zimmerman, R.J. 2011. '10 Best of Good Laboratory Practices for Forensic Facilities: A Key to Satisfying Daubert's Gatekeeper and Rule 702'. *Forensic Science Policy & Management: An International Journal* 2(4): 187–197.

7

Forensic practices and policies

Jan De Kinder

Introduction

During their meeting on 9 June 2016, the European Council of the Ministers of Justice and Home Affairs approved an action plan to establish a European Forensic Science Area 2020 (EFSA 2020). The first decision for the establishment of such an area had already been taken in December 2011, when two needs were identified: to effectively and appropriately exchange scientific evidence between member states of the European Union, and to include expert opinions from one member state in the judicial processes of another. Both decisions were based on the increasing importance of forensic evidence in criminal matters. Additionally, the law enforcement and judicial authorities have to be confident that the forensic data they rely on is of high quality, irrespective of the jurisdiction under which the evidence is produced or processed.

An initial but significant step toward achieving these goals was taken in 2008 with the Prüm Decisions 2008/615/JHA and 2008/616/JHA of 23 June, enabling the cross-border exchange of DNA profiles, fingerprinting data and vehicle registration data. This decision is currently being implemented in the EU member states. In order to guarantee the quality of the data, an additional Council Framework Decision 2009/905/JHA was taken on 30 November 2009 establishing an obligatory accreditation of forensic service providers carrying out laboratory activities concerning DNA and fingerprints.

For more than a decade, the European Network of Forensic Science Institutes (ENFSI) had as a major aim the accreditation of its members according to the ISO17025 or ISO17020 standard. Currently, all institutes that have been members for more than three years are accredited. As a result of this move toward accreditation as a prerequisite for mutual trust, national legislatures have taken over mandating accreditation for all the forensic science deliverers, even in fields other than DNA and fingerprints.

The implementation of the above-mentioned action plan depends on the forensic structures in place in the respective member states. These differences are due to a series of factors, such as different legal systems, already existing organizations, historical decisions and traditions. Furthermore, the operating framework of forensic science service delivery is different in each country—there is no 'one solution fits all'.

This chapter explores a number of differences between West European and North European countries. For this purpose, a short questionnaire was developed and sent to the representatives of the ENFSI members in Belgium, Finland, France, Germany, The Netherlands and Sweden (see www.enfsi.eu for further information). The answers are presented and discussed in this chapter.

Governmental structures

There are different structures in place within the public realm of authority that cooperate in order to provide full forensic service in a given country, covering crime scene analysis as well as the main forensic fields (for the forensic laboratories). The examination of living persons or corpses will be dealt with in the section on legal medicine.

Germany

According to the German constitution, the primary responsibility for policing lies with the 16 German states (Lander). Each state has a state Criminal Police Office, Landeskriminalamt, which provides forensic examinations, among other things. Crime scene units are also part of the police organization, in general connected to larger police departments.

The Federal Criminal Police Office, the Bundeskriminalamt (BKA), serves as the central point for police information and communication. As such, the BKA is also the international contact point, i.e., the national central office for Interpol, Europol and the Schengen Information System. In the area of forensic science, the BKA coordinates and provides information services to the police forces of the German states. The federal police (Bundespolizei) and customs also provide forensic services.

Sweden

The Swedish National Forensic Centre (NFC), formerly the National Laboratory of Forensic Science (SKL), is an independent unit within the Swedish Police with the overall responsibility for forensic examinations. NFC comprises the national forensic laboratory in Linköping and regional forensic laboratories in Stockholm, Gothenburg and Malmö. In 2015, the 436 employees at the NFC, serving the whole country of Sweden, performed more than 120,000 forensic investigations and analyses in all forensic areas except forensic medicine. Crime scene units are part of the Swedish police. The NFC has a national responsibility to monitor, evaluate, harmonize and assure the quality of all forensic methods throughout the whole forensic process—at the crime scene, in the laboratory and in the digital forensic field.

Belgium

Belgium has a complex system in which the Federal Police carry out serious crime scene analysis and local police units sometimes perform volume crime scene analysis.

The National Institute for Forensic Science and Criminology (NICC/INCC) is an independent federal scientific institute performing forensic analysis in about ten different areas (DNA, drugs, toxicology, firearms, toolmarks, arson, gunshot residues, fibres, paint, glass and security inks). It is also the custodian of the national DNA databases. It belongs to the Department of Justice but is directly accountable to the minister of justice. Other forensic areas (fingerprints, audio and video analysis and marks) are the responsibility of the central unit of the Federal Police. The NICC/INCC also conducts scientific research in order to develop new techniques or to increase the knowledge base. Interestingly, it also oversees a criminology department.

France

There are two police forces in France and they have different forensic laboratory structures. Each organization oversees its own scene of crime units. The Gendarmerie has a central laboratory, the Institut de Recherche Criminelle de la Gendarmerie Nationale (IRCGN), which is located in Pontoise (near Paris). Within the National Police, the Institut National de Police Scientifique (INPS) has five laboratories (LPS for Laboratoires de police scientifique), which are situated in Lille, Paris, Lyon, Marseille and Toulouse.

Finland

The National Bureau of Investigation Forensic Laboratory (NBIFL) in Vantaa is part of the Finnish national police. It serves the entire country. The crime scene units are part of the Finnish local police. The NBIFL has a coordinating role in assuring the quality of the whole forensic chain by carrying out audits, providing training and preparing standard operating procedures.

The Netherlands

The Netherlands Forensic Institute (NFI), situated in Den Haag, is part of the Ministry of Security and Justice. It serves the whole country for a full range of forensic services. The crime scene units are part of the Netherlands police force.

Additional information on these forensic institutes can be found on the website of the European Network of Forensic Science Institutes (www.enfsi.eu), which also provides links to the websites of the individual organizations.

In the examples above, crime scene units are part of the police organization in all the countries studied. Forensic laboratories can belong either to the police structure or to the justice department. They can be engrafted on different places in the police structure to evidence a certain degree of independence. In Belgium, there is a historical division of forensic science disciplines between the Federal Police and the federal forensic laboratory.

Although currently much effort is being made to increase and improve the *science* in forensic *science* delivery, the status of that focus differs across organizations, ranging from police laboratories to scientific institutes entitled to conduct scientific research and develop new techniques.

Organization of legal medicine

Although forensic medicine is an intrinsic part of forensic science, the delivery of these services is mostly provided by another organization. This may have to do with the extensive education required to become a legal examiner as well as the need to be connected to a different infrastructure. Specialized scanning instruments and support from other medical experts can be an added value.

Within the countries taking part in this study, only in the Nethlands, and to some extent, in France do forensic laboratories provide legal medicine services. In the Netherlands, these are provided by the NFI on a state level. One of the two police forces in France, the Gendarmerie, has a legal medical unit as part of its forensic institute, the IRCGN, which is composed of three units: anthropology, thanatology and odontology. The NFI noted that the combination of forensic science and legal medicine in a single organization stimulates good communication between experts in each field. Although there is a big difference in culture between forensic science and legal medicine, close collaboration between these services will clearly lead to a better performing juridical system. The current fragmented state in other jurisdictions is due to historical

Table 7.1 Organization of legal medical services for living persons and corpses, by country

Country	*Provision of legal medical services*
Belgium	Independent legal examiners, mostly connected to a specialized faculty at a university
Finland	National Institute for Health and Welfare
France (partially)	Specialized hospital services
Germany	Specialized faculties at universities
Sweden	National Board of Forensic Medicine

developments as well as to the advantages legal medicine received from being hosted in medical or academic environments: the availability of a number of colleagues specializing in different medical areas. In other countries, legal medicine is provided by independent organizations, as demonstrated in Table 7.1.

It should be noted that in some countries, a regional structure (private doctors, emergency units at hospitals) exists that cooperates with the above-mentioned institutes for the examination of living persons as well as for the external examination of the deceased. They can identify the need for a more profound examination (autopsy) where the cause of death is violent or unknown.

Stakeholders

Requests that these organizations provide analyses come from the authorities conducting the criminal investigation. These authorities are determined by national law and are specified in Table 7.2.

A number of particularities can be observed from this data. This diagram clearly shows who is responsible for crime investigation. In the Nordic countries, it is the police, while for Belgium, France and the Netherlands, this responsibility is shared with the prosecutor's office and/or independent judges (Netherlands: rechter-commissaris, Belgium: onderzoeksrechter or juge d'instruction, France: juge d'instruction). In Belgium, the investigation is headed by the prosecutor or an independent judge. An examination of the effects of these differences on the use of forensic

Table 7.2 Authorities entitled to request a forensic analysis from the public forensic laboratory, by country

	Requesting authority		
Country	*Juridical*	*Police investigators*	*Defence actors*
Belgium	Yes (prosecutor, investigative judge and judge)	Not directly, except for the forensic disciplines provided by the police	No
Finland	Yes	Yes	No
France	Yes (prosecutor, investigative judge and judge)	Yes, but only in the first days of the investigation	No
Germany	Yes	Yes	No
Sweden	Yes	Yes	Yes
The Netherlands	Yes (prosecutor, investigative judge and judge)	Yes	No

science in criminal investigations is beyond the scope of this chapter, but it would be a very interesting research topic.

If there is a charge for the forensic analysis, the bill is sent, along with the expert opinion, to the requesting organization that has the structure necessary to pay for these services. Different and sometimes very complicated structures are in place in different countries. The goals of this billing vary: control over the number of requests, the creation of a bar to be reached before requesting analysis, charging the costs of the forensic analysis to the convicted offender or commercial market consultation.

It is quite remarkable that only in Sweden can defence attorneys ask the forensic laboratory to perform an analysis of the evidence material. Further research is needed to see how this matter is handled in other countries.

Activities of private forensic providers

Apart from public forensic laboratories, a number of countries also have private service providers. These can be active in a limited number of forensic fields or provide a large spectrum of forensic services, as is the case in the United Kingdom. This section provides an overview of the current situation in the countries that were queried.

Within the European Union, the framework decision requires an accreditation of forensic service providers who perform laboratory analysis in the fields of DNA and fingerprints. This requirement also applies to private forensic providers.

Table 7.3 Activities of private providers of forensic services and the relevant quality requirements in each country

Country	*Private forensic providers*
Belgium	A variety of private companies, independent experts and universities provide services in particular forensic fields (DNA, toxicology, firearm analysis, bullet trajectory analysis, legal medicine, etc.). New legislation is being prepared outlining the requirement of ISO17025 for accreditation. Also, lists of experts in different fields of expertise will soon be established.
Finland	Only the national NBIFL can use other laboratories on a subcontracting basis. There are strong accreditation requirements for the subcontractors.
France	There is a wide range of experts in different fields of forensics, but only a few carry out multidisciplinary analysis. There is no objective quality control on their practice except in DNA profiling where each expert has to perform external quality controls organized by the national agency for the safety of drugs and health products (ANSM) twice a year.
Germany	A few private providers are active in different fields (e.g., toxicology, DNA analysis, handwriting and document analysis).
Sweden	Minor companies and consultants offer forensic services. They act under a varying level of quality requirements.
The Netherlands	There are a couple of private providers. The juridical authority that requests an analysis should take an expert who has been certified by the central certification authority (NRGD). If not, he or she should provide an explanation for deviating from this list.

This table shows that the tradition of using private experts is stronger in France and Belgium. The other countries also have a number of private providers, restricted to specific roles. The existence of private providers allows those requesting a forensic analysis to choose between different providers. If only one provider is active, a failure in its operation will have a more severe effect on the timely delivery of expert opinions than when there are multiple providers. It would be possible to redirect the request for an expert opinion to another laboratory not impacted by the problem. Competition between multiple providers is an incentive toward a better product and/or a better service.

However, if too many providers are present in a single forensic field, the resulting fragmentation of the work will lead to reduced experiences gained in the laboratory, with a consequent failure to improve or a decline in the quality of work. Furthermore, the high cost of automation cannot be financed by the laboratory, which will result in an overall high cost for this type of analysis.

Subcontracting could be an interesting possibility for public service providers to have routine analysis performed in private, fully automated laboratories at a low cost. An example of this is the DNA-profiling of the convicted offenders in Belgium, which is subcontracted by the Justice Department. It also provides a way of dealing with temporary increases in casework.

The quality requirements imposed on the private providers are currently becoming more and more explicit. New legislation is available or on the way to ensure the quality of the forensic services being provided by the private sector.

Rarely requested forensic casework and second opinions

There is a great diversity in the requests for forensic analysis, and each type of question has a particular frequency. Some examinations are very common and can even be considered 'volume' examinations. These require the availability of a forensic examination on request; important investments in order to keep the apparatus state-of-the-art and maintained according to specifications; having the consumables available and personnel who are competent to do that type of examination. For the uncommon type of examination, this cost is too high to be carried by a medium size forensic laboratory. What are the solutions that these forensic laboratories propose in order to meet the needs of their customers?

Germany

The German police forensic laboratories cover a huge range of forensic methods. Some special services are only provided by one or two laboratories, but all forensic laboratories know the scope of the other labs. If the circumstances and the importance of the case call for the development of new methods, this is done. In these cases, particular attention is given to a proper validation before using the new method in providing an expert opinion.

Sweden

The NFC holds methods and competence for several seldom used methods. NFC also requests analyses from approved institutes, companies and experts, e.g., for audio analysis, and bears the costs for the requested services. The NFC cooperates with universities in research and development (R&D) projects and activities, but seldom turns to universities in casework, mainly due to the lack of validated methods.

Belgium

Forensic advisers assist the magistrate in locating the laboratory with the capacity to provide an answer to the question at issue. Laboratories that have a quality system in place are privileged over others. These laboratories can be part of a private provider, a university or a forensic laboratory in another country. The final decision lies with the requesting authority, but in general the proposals are followed.

France

In the INPS, certain analyses are performed in only one of the five labs. If the INPS does not perform a particular kind of analysis, it is up to the investigators or the magistrate to find a lab able to do it (university, research centre, other public lab, private experts, etc.). This person or organization usually has to be on a list of judicial experts. If not, the magistrate must justify his or her choice.

Finland

The NBIFL uses all the relevant labs in Finland and also those abroad, if necessary. The NBIFL has a good budget for buying services on a subcontracting basis.

The Netherlands

If the NFI is not able to handle the request, the police or the juridical authority will contact universities or private providers.

From these answers, it is clear that solutions are first sought within the structure itself. Second, national solutions are privileged over international solutions. A similar question occurs when a second opinion is requested. This may occur when there is some doubt, either on the part of the prosecutor or of the defence attorney, concerning the results obtained. These results are given in Table 7.4.

Table 7.4 Reactions of the public forensic laboratory when a second opinion is requested of an analysis that has already been performed by this organization

Country	*Second opinion*
Belgium	The juridical authority can request second opinions from a private provider of the relevant forensic services either after consultation with the NICC/INCC or directly without notification.
Finland	Requests for second opinions are very rare, since the NBIFL has a stable and highly respected position in the Finnish criminal justice system. The NBIFL may use forensic laboratories from neighbouring countries.
France	In France, the defence asks the investigating judge, since he or she is the only one who can decide to request further analysis or a second opinion. The second opinion must be delivered by another expert, public or private (for example, INPS can be charged with a second opinion on the cases carried out by the IRCGN).
Germany	In cases where a second opinion is requested, most often the BKA is asked. But second opinions may also be provided by a different LKA.

(continued)

Table 7.4 Reactions of the public forensic laboratory when a second opinion is requested of an analysis that has already been performed by this organization *(continued)*

Country	*Second opinion*
Sweden	Requests for second opinions are presented to the NFC, which recommends approved institutes, companies and experts for this purpose. Requests are still in some cases handled directly by the police or the prosecutor.
The Netherlands	For DNA, there is a second laboratory that is recognized by the government. In other fields, the second opinion can be obtained from a private provider or a lab from a neighbouring country (e.g., the NICC/INCC in Belgium).

The increase in demands for forensic services and the current economic downturn have led to closer collaboration between the public and private providers of forensic science. This can take the form of a complete transfer of a particular service (e.g., the DNA profiling of all convicted offenders) or subcontracting with private industry in case the public forensic laboratory does not have the capacity to meet the requests from criminal investigators. The public forensic laboratory remains in charge of the forensic analyses but arranges for some of them to be performed by a private partner.

Most of the above-mentioned forensic laboratories collaborate closely with universities for carrying out research projects in order to increase the forensic knowledge base and methods of analysis.

Currently, the public forensic service of the UK government, the Forensic Science Service, has been forced to cease its activities, leaving an almost completely private market.

Conclusion

In conclusion, there are two linked questions that can help to clarify the source of important differences between countries.

First, two situations appear to be in opposition: on the one hand, countries where a government agency has all the competencies regarding forensic analysis and, on the other hand, countries where multiple actors can play different roles, be they public or private.

Spreading forensic services across multiple institutions may be risky. First, there is what could be called an 'incoherency hazard' at various levels. It may lead to a loss of the global view of the case flow and to a poor evaluation of what investments are needed and which public strategies to develop. This is clearly linked to the difficulty in having a clear overview of all the services provided. In this context, it may be difficult to trace every case or piece of evidence, but also to fine-tune the forensic interventions in a case. If DNA and fingerprints are stored in different organizations, it may be difficult to systematize the analysis of the print before trying to extract DNA from it.

On another level, the multiplication of actors in the very same field can cause serious problems regarding knowledge and experience accumulation. It can be difficult, in smaller structures, to develop a highly specialized expertise. This can have a greater impact on complex cases than on routine analysis. In contrast, second opinions are easier to obtain in a diversified forensic landscape. It can lead to citizens having higher confidence in forensic interventions.

Regarding the costs, the multiplication of structures can lead to loss of efficiency (seldom-used hardware, higher prices for reagents, etc.) on large-scale analysis. It also causes the multiplication of accreditation costs. On the other hand, concurrency can lead to better prices, even if this is far from certain for all forensic disciplines and interventions.

Furthermore, smaller structures can lack a proper quality control system, since they don't reach the critical mass needed to be able to install the required equipment and procedures.

Accreditation systems are crucial in a diversified context because they can lead to the generalization of best practices—promoting the systems that are more efficient and also harmonizing the forensic landscape, making it easier to communicate and cooperate between different organizations.

A second question follows logically: what if some of the forensic organizations are private?

First, it should be stated that competition can lead to a decrease in costs and the resulting prices. Furthermore, private offers will concentrate on the most lucrative analysis and neglect the others. The latter will remain government expenses, making it impossible to compensate costs and benefits. This can lead to a classic situation: privatization of benefits and nationalization of costs.

As a matter of principle, it is dubious that a sovereign state can legitimately delegate one part of its fundamental privileges to private organizations, be they companies or universities. Justice is not meant to be privatized.

It can also be problematic to give evidence in criminal cases to private actors because of confidentiality concerns.

This leads to a final observation: not all public organizations are equal. Thus, police laboratories may appear less independent than public but structurally separated ones. For instance, the Belgian NICC is, by law, independent and has no hierarchical relationship with police or magistrates. It should be remembered that, besides scientific criteria, political and legal criteria can contribute to legitimizing forensic laboratories.

Thus, the structure of forensic expertise has to be clearly linked to scientific, legal, economic and political choices. There is no such thing as a natural system. So it has always been.

Acknowledgements

The author would like to thank the representatives of the above-mentioned forensic laboratories for answering the questionnaire. He also thanks Christophe Mincke, head of the NICC criminology department, for his support.

8

The practice of crime scene examination in an intelligence-based perspective

Olivier Delémont, Sonja Bitzer, Manon Jendly and Olivier Ribaux

Introduction

Crime scene examination can be summarized in simple terms as the processing of a location where a potentially criminal activity occurred. The first aim of this examination is to record and document the scene to be investigated. The second is to search for physical remnants of this activity that could contribute to identifying the individuals involved, reconstructing the sequence of events and, more generally, providing answers to a systematic questioning about the criminal activity (who, what, where, when, why and how?) (Delémont et al. 2014).

This chapter does not intend to educate on the practice of crime scene examination, to present state-of-the-art techniques for searching a crime scene or collecting and securing specimens. Instead, it describes how this practice is currently embedded within police institutions and the difficulties that ensue from its integration in different forensic science models. This chapter suggests that crime scene examination be formalized—from the decision to attend a scene to the selection of traces to process—to cement its place in both policing models and, in a wider perspective, in the understanding of crime.

Perpetuating the view inherited from the pioneers of the discipline, crime scene examination is commonly considered the starting point of forensic investigations (Wyatt 2014; Ludwig et al. 2012; Julian et al. 2012). Traces recovered during the examination of the scene provide information and items to feed different scientific operations. The results of this forensic science work then serve the whole investigative process and, eventually, the production of evidence for court purposes (Barclay 2009; Cole 2013). For instance, a bloodstain collected from the crime scene with a suitable swabbing technique will lead to a DNA profile through PCR amplification and genotyping. Compared to the profiles of individuals stored in a national DNA database, under restrictive legal conditions, it may reveal information about the *source* of the stain, i.e., the person whose blood it comes from. This finding may be used during a trial as proof of the presence of the individual at the crime scene.

The traditional conception of crime scene examination as a starting point is justified in a procedural conception, given that it precedes further forensic actions or examinations. But considering the more global perspective of the practice of forensic investigation within the criminal event under scrutiny, this conception is disputable. Although the criminal act may be a single and isolated event, due, for instance, to a peculiar combination of factors, it is more often than not a symptom of a more global activity: one of a series committed by a prolific offender, one sign of a general criminal trend that takes advantage of passing opportunities, etc. Many criminological theories emphasize that a criminal act is rooted in a context, or set of situations, that can be expressed in social, environmental or behavioural terms. The event for which the scene examination is undertaken is often not the starting point of the criminal history of the offender or of this type of crime. It is therefore highly beneficial to consider the processing of crime scene examinations within the general criminal context in which the activity occurred, beyond the confines of the specific case (Ribaux et al. 2010b). Past criminal events and past investigations provide knowledge that assists the examination of a crime scene; the outcomes of the current examination generate intelligence to direct future investigations.

This chapter adopts the perspective of an intelligence-based crime scene examination. But before further developing this perspective, we seek to shed light on the current difficulties that crime scene examiners face.

Crime scene examination and police activities

The disparity in definition and integration of forensic science within police institutions

Due to its close interconnections with traditional police investigations, crime scene examination remains essentially a responsibility of police institutions, undertaken by crime scene examiners or forensic units. But except for this institutional anchorage, great disparity exists in the way crime scenes are processed over space—countries, regions or jurisdictions—and also over time (Ribaux et al. 2010a). This disparity results from several dimensions that are important to acknowledge.

The legal system, and especially the distinction between adversarial and inquisitorial jurisdictions, is the first parameter that shapes the roles and functioning of police actions. Inevitably, it influences both crime scene attendance (i.e., the decision to deploy crime scene examiners) and the strategy of crime scene examination. The debates in court over the options that were chosen and strategies used at the scene seem to hang like the sword of Damocles over crime scene examiners practising in the adversarial system (Wilson-Kovacs 2014). Procedural issues, especially related to the chain of custody, seem to draw most of the attention, far more than in the practice described in inquisitorial systems.

In addition, organizational and managerial issues, while occurring far away from the concern of the scene investigation, can also have a strong influence on the way scene examinations are carried out and on their outcomes. We observe a wide spectrum of managerial models for the implementation of forensic science in police institutions, especially regarding crime scene examination. At one end of this spectrum, some models rely on the separation of the forensic work in relation to the crime scene between (a) crime scene examiners, with limited scientific training, and (b) specialized forensic scientists. This model is in line with the more general practice of forensic science depicted by Margot, who compares it to medicine: 'Forensic science is like a hospital serviced by clerics and nurses for most of the activities, and brain surgeons and cardiologists for highly specialised areas of medicine, but with no medical doctor in the middle' (Margot 2011, 800). At the other end of the spectrum, we find managerial models promoting the assignment of more generalist crime scene investigators that take charge of the processing of a crime scene and many of the further scientific operations performed on the items collected at the scene (Bitzer et al. 2016; Ribaux et al. 2010a). These models also strongly shape the way the work of crime scene examiners is perceived, by themselves and by criminal investigators. As many studies conducted in the UK highlight, several models of police integration of crime scene examiners are encountered, ranging from a purely technical role of evidence collectors to a recognized expert role of reflexive specialist advisers. These different integration models, and the professional recognition they encompass, are, of course, closely related to the managerial views of the role of forensic contributions in police and security issues. And they also have an impact on the adherence to the institution and its values, and to the sense of commitment. Indirectly, such factors affect the effectiveness and efficiency of the contribution of forensic science and of crime scene examination (Wilson-Kovacs 2014; Ludwig et al. 2012; Wyatt 2014).

Several studies show that crime scene examiners are often considered to have a special position within police institutions, with a job not always perceived as being aligned with institutional missions. This is further accentuated by recruitment policies moving toward increasing civilianization of crime scene examiners, essentially driven by economic incentive, and leading to tensions between civilians—often university graduates—and sworn officers (Wilson-Kovacs 2014; Ribaux et al. 2010a). In some institutions, crime scene examination units are also still labelled as the units where officers not competent or motivated enough to integrate into crime investigation units were sent to.

Before proceeding, it is necessary to bring formal clarification and reach semantic consensus. The disparity in models of integration of forensic science in police institutions, and of crime scene investigation in particular, is obvious. Because we aim to discuss the place of crime scene examination in an intelligence-based perspective, we seek to go beyond this diversity and the terminological subtleties that surround it. As a consequence, we have to adopt a consensus on some key definitions. In this chapter, the terms 'crime scene examiner' and 'crime scene investigator' refer to the trained professional whose work consists in processing crime scenes in order to document and collect physical traces that could potentially yield information about a known or alleged criminal activity. These terms are used regardless of the level of training or education, the recruitment scheme (civilians or sworn officers) or the model of integration in police institutions. We pretend that crime scene examination falls entirely under the forensic science umbrella. While a minor portion of the forensic community persists in considering it as an external operation of sample collection, crime scene investigation is more often described as a core activity of forensic science (Cole 2013).

The word 'trace', mentioned in the definition of crime scene examiner, refers here to remnants of past events that are present at the crime scene. The historical conception of forensic science describes the 'trace' as a *physical* remnant, characterized by a materiality that can be measured, described, compared, etc. (Margot 2014). With the advent of information and communications technology, the notion of 'trace' has expanded and encompasses also *digital* remnants. Some of these physical and digital remnants at the crime scene have been produced or exchanged during the criminal activity, and crime scene examiners are confronted with the challenge of detecting and distinguishing the traces that are related to the criminal activity from the traces produced during other actions taking place—before or after—at that place. The traces 'become signs when detected, recognised, collected and measured; an interpretation process aims at transforming them into clues in order to reconstruct what occurred' (Ribaux et al. 2016, 545–546). While locutions such as 'physical evidence', 'forensic items' and 'forensic artefacts' are sometimes used in the scientific literature with some conceptual subtleties, we prefer the generic term 'trace'.

Frictions in the practice of crime scene examination

Crime scene examination is shaped by a dichotomy that ensues from the fact that its practice is strongly anchored both in police activity and within the forensic science discipline, and from the gap between the conceptual and actual practice.

Forensic doctrine

Like blinkers that prevent a horse from moving away from its path, forensic science as a system tends to drive all efforts toward what is perceived as its main (if not exclusive) objective: the production of evidence for court. The majority of the forensic professionals who structure the doctrine of forensic science are working in academic institutions and centralized forensic laboratories. These institutions hire university graduates and renowned scientists who contribute to the vast majority of the publications in forensic science. Since the main concerns of the forensic academic unit and forensic laboratories are oriented toward the legal system, and the court trial as its final end, the court's requirements inevitably affect the activities and the perception of the role of the discipline (Mnookin et al. 2011). This paradigm, centred on the production of evidence for court and directly inherited from the judicial branch that sets up the trial as fundamental nucleus, strongly structures the forensic doctrine. This doctrine, consequently, shapes a conceptual practice of the discipline that is articulated around core issues such as the validation of the analytical chains, the pressure to achieve accreditation, the structuring of uniform interpreting schemes, the breaking up of forensic activities into highly specialized silos and the preoccupation for avoiding miscarriage of justice (Ribaux et al. 2010b; Resnikoff et al. 2015). Through education and training, this perception of forensic science imposes its methods and finality on the practice of crime scene investigation. Books and manuals focus mainly on the application of techniques and procedures, and legally acceptable trace collection, evidence preservation and contamination avoidance are the pillars of the training in crime scene examination. Or, as highlighted by Wyatt (2014) in his study considering crime scene investigators' everyday work and training, 'For the CSI, adherence to contamination avoidance protocol is seen as second nature' (Wyatt 2014, 445) and 'the message of the exercises was that trace collection and contamination avoidance is a three-fold process of correctly collecting, packaging and signing and sealing the packaging' (449).

Discrepancy between doctrine and actual practice

The reality of the practice of crime scene examination unveils a gap between practice and doctrine. While crime scene examiners acknowledge the importance of the procedures in contributing to the legal acceptance of their work before a court (documentation, chain of custody, etc.), as well as their role to detect, collect and secure pieces of evidence, they also move away from the concepts relayed by the doctrine for their everyday work. They recognize that the investigation of major crimes is mainly driven by the production of evidence for court issues (Wilson-Kovacs 2014), but at the same time they emphasize a wider contribution to several aspects of the investigation: the reconstruction of the sequence of events, the generation of intelligence and ideas in collaboration with investigators and crime analysts, the linkage of cases through physical traces, etc. (Resnikoff et al. 2015). Crime scene examiners emphasize this wider contribution mainly in relation to the investigation of volume crimes, but not only. Crime scene examiners state that they experience fundamental differences between the concepts they are taught through training, guidelines and manuals and the 'knowledgeable, expert, evidential use of trace' they gain with their experience (Wilson-Kovacs 2014, 774). This statement may also arise partly due to the fact that the doctrine advocates either very general principles (e.g., chain of custody, scene preservation) or, at the opposite extreme, very specific procedures (e.g., operating procedures to detect fingermarks with powder, to collect a shoemark from a wooden floor or to collect a DNA contact trace with a swab). But the two extreme levels of generality, while providing the legal frame and the collection of technical protocols, do not address the concrete and recurrent problem that crime scene examiners have to solve on a daily basis: how to process a crime scene, how to detect relevant traces, how to select the traces to collect, how to communicate with other stakeholders and what type of decision-making process must be undertaken. By nature, the doctrine is rather oriented toward the past by fixing good practices and preventing past errors from reoccurring. But it provides very little help in tackling new situations and new opportunities that societal changes involve.

The example of digital traces is in this regard very illustrative. The use of digital technology devices (smartphones, computers, tablets, etc.) has long been adopted by modern society, and almost everyone uses them on a daily basis. Naturally, these instruments and the data they contain become traces of our activities, including traces in relation to criminal offences, and not only in relation to cyber- or technological crimes. Yet, these traces, encountered by crime scene examiners on most of the scenes they attend, are more often than not considered by the forensic doctrine as a separate type of trace, requiring special procedures that are not explained in training and manuals for crime scene examiners but disseminated within a dedicated community under the banner of digital forensics. Faced with new challenges, the doctrine reacts with a breaking down into specialized subdisciplines and a multiplication of technical procedures, increasing the hiatus with the actual practice of crime scene examination.

Torn between conceptual and actual views of their practice, between the court-oriented inclination of forensic science and the security/crime reduction issues of police institutions they serve, crime scene examiners are (to paraphrase an image from Pierre Margot) 'like drivers in the mist'.[1] Although scientific skills and technical procedures are necessary to assess whether the work is correctly undertaken and will not hamper the criminal justice system, these are not sufficient to guarantee effective investigation of the several types of crime scenes. Other parameters, strongly related to the human factor, have been shown to play a crucial role in the quality of crime scene investigation outcomes (Wilson-Kovacs 2014). In corroboration, Australian researchers have identified seven critical skills that characterize crime scene examiners who outperform their peers (cognitive abilities, knowledge base, experience, work orientation, communication skills, professional demeanour and approach to life). It is interesting to notice that only one is related, in very general terms, to training and education ('knowledge base') while four are linked to the personality and the social aspect of the individual (Kelty et al. 2011).

The need for a situated identity for crime scene examination

The discrepancy that we have been highlighting between the forensic doctrine, or at least one of its main branches, and actual praxis is symptomatic of an unease that exists in situating the requirements and aims of crime scene investigation. This leads to a confrontation of entrenched views (see, for instance, Cole (2013)). In this chapter, we go beyond this debate and the question whether crime scene examiners are better incorporated within law enforcement or within external scientific agencies, a question whose relevance is attenuated by findings about the critical skills for crime scene examiners. Crime scene examination needs to define its professional identity and develop a methodological framework to support an integrated and scientific contribution to police investigation, criminal justice and security issues. The practice of crime scene examination needs to be anchored in a proactive and adaptive structure that may not only be compatible with the different models but also acknowledges the several pieces of knowledge that are put into practice through the investigation of a crime scene. This formalization would certainly contribute to a clarification of the positioning of crime scene examination, as well as provide assistance to crime scene examiners in their decision-making process. Observations suggest, by the way, that crime scene examiners implicitly tend to embrace the use of such a scheme of knowledge with accumulation of experience (Ribaux 2014; Resnikoff et al. 2015; Wyatt 2014).

The three phases in the decision-making process

In the following sections, we discuss in more detail the manifold dimensions of knowledge that crime scene examiners may deploy within the course of their activities. To fully assess the utility of this framework, we first have to acknowledge the different steps that crime scene examination encompasses. The practice of crime scene examination can be broken down into a sequence of three fundamental decision phases (Bitzer et al. 2016).

Crime scene attendance

When judicial authorities or police forces are informed about the occurrence of a potential criminal activity or another event that could require investigation, a first decision takes place: the decision to attend the scene of the action in order to document, search, collect and secure traces. This first decision phase arises from the fact that law enforcement institutions have limited resources that do not allow the investigation of every event reported. Priority has to be given to attending certain scenes, while others may not even be investigated. Such prioritization is more often than not grounded in the legally perceived seriousness of the situation (e.g., major crimes vs volume crimes); nonetheless, it results in great variations between jurisdictions (Williams 2004), and we will see later that it may also be impacted by other considerations. Obviously, the outcome of this decision phase will have a major influence on the information at disposal for subsequent investigations: if a scene is not attended, no physical trace will be available to assist further security or judicial steps, or only through the analysis of objects collected at the scene by uniformed police officers.

Crime scene investigation (in the narrow sense of the term)

This phase in the decision-making process encompasses in fact a series of choices that crime scene examiners are faced with from the moment they arrive at a scene until their departure with collected traces and items. This includes in particular (but not exclusively) the delimitation of the location to examine, the strategy for the investigation of the scene, the material and resources invested, the assessment of the traces to search for in priority and the selection of traces to collect and secure. This phase of crime scene investigation will involve the use of techniques and the application of procedures that often constitute the core of the training and education programme of crime scene examiners.

Triage

Items and traces collected at the crime scene are not all analysed, or not all immediately. Crime scene examiners have to decide which trace to process for further analysis in order to gain more information, either by in-house treatment within a police forensic unit or by submitting to an external laboratory. This step, known as 'triage' or 'triaging decision', takes place away from the crime scene, generally in the office. In principle, every single trace was collected at the crime scene for a given purpose and its potential for delivering useful intelligence. As such, it may be expected that every collected trace be submitted for further analysis. This situation almost prevails in the investigation of volume crimes where a strict selection already occurs on the scene, resulting in a limited amount of collected traces. For serious crimes, the collection of samples on the scene tends to be more massive, leading to further decisions about which traces to analyse, or which have priority.

In principle, these three phases are clearly separated in time: the triaging decision occurs after the completion of the scene investigation, which follows the decision to attend the scene. But it is obvious that they are intertwined: crime scene attendance has a decisive influence on the later phases, since when scenes are not attended by a crime scene examiner, the result is either an absence of physical traces for the offence under investigation or a collection of objects by an individual (generally a sworn officer) with little to no forensic background.[2] Similarly, the choices made during the scene investigation are oriented by the early decision of further analysis. Being aware that limited resources will be dedicated to a case afterward, or in accordance with institutional protocols, crime scene examiners restrain the collection to a selection of the detected physical traces (only one or two DNA swabs in the case of burglary, for instance). Notwithstanding, we consider these three phases of decision separately in the next section to clearly understand how they may be affected by the manifold dimensions of knowledge.

Intelligence assisting crime scene examination: the manifold knowledge dimensions

As previously discussed, crime scene examination should not be regarded as mainly a procedural driven activity. Techniques, methods, protocols and procedures exist and make a significant contribution to the detection of pertinent traces and the securing of evidence. But they are not sufficient to ground the practice of crime scene examiners. Crime scene examiners also rely heavily on an informal and largely tacit corpus of knowledge, often referred to as 'experience'. Crime scene examiners use several types of information to guide their daily practice: 'intelligence helps provide strategies for the search of traces and can assist in selecting which types of traces should be favoured and where they should be looked for' (Ribaux et al. 2010b, 14).

In order to better tackle the manner in which multifaceted knowledge may support crime scene examiners' decisions, the distribution of the different types of information in a formal framework is useful. Such an architecture has been suggested as the formalization of crime scene examination methodologies embedded in intelligence-led style of management (Ribaux et al. 2010b; Ribaux et al. 2010a; Bitzer et al. 2016). This anchoring encompasses two aspects: (1) crime scene examination is fed with intelligence, as already highlighted in the previous paragraph; (2) crime scene examination, generating clues and information from objective remnants of a past action, is a major contributor of crime intelligence (see Ribaux and Caneppele, 'Forensic intelligence', chapter 12, in this volume). While this second aspect—the production of intelligence—is of utmost importance in intelligence-led and problem-oriented policing (Ribaux 2014), we concentrate in this chapter on the contribution that distinct facets of knowledge can make toward crime scene examination.

A framework of knowledge dimensions

The management of intelligence for crime scene examination can be shaped into a framework of knowledge. Current refinement status of such a framework tends to structure it around four dimensions: the strategic context, the criminal background, the situational analysis and the physical environment. A fifth dimension, the utility of the clue, is also proposed for the triaging decision.

Strategic Dimension

The strategic dimension comprises the general frame to which the investigation process belongs. It encompasses all the factors extrinsic to the event under scrutiny, but that influence its enquiry. Depending on the broader context, the strategic dimension groups together several spheres, in particular:

- the legal framework, which dictates formal rules guiding the investigation, and determines the perceived seriousness of the event;
- political guidance, which defines security issues and priorities;
- policing emphases inclining the strategies and activities of law enforcement bodies; and
- managerial aspects, including decisions and constraints, related to the level of available resources, the workload and the possibility to schedule scene attendance.

The legal, political, policing and managerial spheres in which crime scene examination takes place decisively shape the general contours of the practice. Organizations, embedded in legal and political systems, following policing models, and taking into account available resources (persons, skills, material and technology), set periodically revisable objectives and priorities that are implemented into management rules. The management rules compose the mesh that inclines the three decision phases previously described in a certain direction. Undeniably, the decision to attend the scene, as well as the resources that are allocated to the processing of the crime scene (if attended), are framed by this strategic dimension. This influence is epitomized in the traditional distinction between major crimes (homicides, sexual offences, robberies, etc.) and volume crimes (burglaries, street robberies, thefts, criminal damages, etc.). Based primarily on the perceived criminal seriousness of the event, the importance of the damage or the value of loot, this distinction imposes on crime scene examiners by setting priorities for attendance and strategies of crime scene examination. Attendance is mandatory at homicide scenes, and resources in terms of time, material and personnel are massive. At the opposite end, car thefts, even if perpetrated in a way favourable to the production of traces, are not systematically subject to forensic scrutiny. The same scheme applies with attempted offences, which are seldom attended because they are considered less serious in a criminal law perspective, even if they could have been perpetrated by prolific offenders and/or could be rich in traces.

On the one hand, the strategic dimension has a major impact on the work of crime scene examiners, but on the other, the latter have very little latitude to alleviate or reorient this influence. Such orientation may be achieved in a medium or longer term with a reinforced forensic awareness among policymakers.

Criminal background

As emphasized in the preamble to this chapter, most of the situations that are subject to crime scene investigation are not unique or particular events. Prolific offenders commit repetitive crimes, making a substantial contribution to overall criminal activity, and recurring opportunities result in criminal episodes that encompass several individual cases. Criminal events are, more often than not, linked to others. Considering the whole range of linked events unveils valuable information for crime detection and repression, as well as for prevention and dissuasion purposes. The pivotal role of physical and digital traces for the detection and structuring of repetitive crime series has already been recognized (Rossy et al. 2013), acknowledging the contribution of forensic intelligence for crime analysis. Here, we want to make explicit the reverse effect, i.e., how the knowledge of the criminal environment may assist crime scene examination.

In addition to strategic issues, knowledge of the criminal background may also influence the general practice of crime scene investigation. Awareness and understanding of the topical structure of criminality, current criminal trends and pending series of repetitive crimes provide pieces of information that may impact on the decisions to attend a scene and the strategy to investigate it. If a new case can be associated with a known series of crimes or a critical phenomenon, crime scene examiners tend to consider it more important, increasing the propensity to investigate the scene (Resnikoff et al. 2015). But in our opinion, the main benefit of an informed perception of the criminal environment is felt in the processing of the scene itself and the choices regarding the traces to search for and collect. Hence, if a new case is recognized as potentially part of a known series of events, the information already available from the previous events can be used to orient the search for traces. The knowledge of the criminal environment is an actionable intelligence that shapes the crime scene examination by aiming at (a) confirming that the specific case belongs to a presumed repetitive activity, and (b) providing an added value of information. The utility of the traces detected during the scene examination is then not only determined by their potential to deliver information about the identity of the offender or their actions on the specific event, but also and more importantly for their potential to shed light on new aspects of the criminal activity of the prolific offender or a criminal phenomenon.

An illustration of the influence of criminal intelligence on the processing of crime scenes is briefly presented here; full details can be found in Ribaux et al. (2010a). A series of burglaries perpetrated with a similar modus operandi was subject to forensic investigations by distinct crime scene examiners. Each case was mainly investigated as an isolated event. And for each case, a DNA swab of the broken and extracted door lock cylinder was collected. DNA profiling of the traces always resulted in the same DNA profile but its source remained unknown since no correspondence appeared with the indexes of arrestees and convicted offenders in the national DNA database. In a first approach, considering each single case, the obtaining of this DNA profile was considered a successful result for at least three reasons: (1) the location of the trace (broken door cylinders) was highly relevant to the offence, (2) the obtained profile was a complete profile of a single contributor, and (3) the DNA profile allowed confirmation of the links with previous cases. But in terms of knowledge about the repetitive criminal activity, the accumulation of corresponding DNA profiles was of very limited utility: it enabled attribution of newly committed cases to the offender, but provided no added value about the identity of the perpetrator(s). Finally, on one of the subsequent cases, in addition to swabbing the broken door cylinder, a crime scene examiner decided to extend his investigation to other types of traces. He searched for fingermarks on a jewellery box that was presumably handled by the offender, although several other persons had also legitimately touched this box, considerably affecting the relevance of enhanced traces. Fingermarks were detected and their comparison with the national fingerprint database led to a correspondence with the prints of a known offender. Further police investigations led to the arrest of this known offender and two accomplices. One of the accomplices turned out to be the source of the DNA profile collected on the many door lock cylinders. This example shows how knowledge of the topical criminal environment can act as an actionable intelligence to direct the examination of a crime scene and to favour the use of uncertain or incomplete traces with the aim of providing an added value of information.

The dimension of knowledge pertaining to the criminal environment is, of course, linked to the intelligence awareness of police institutions and to their ability to produce, structure and disseminate timely intelligence through the institution. But this knowledge does not solely depend on what is institutionally produced (for instance, through crime analysis units); it also rests on informal exchanges and discussions between crime scene examiners and detectives, as well as on the personal experience gained by each examiner through the investigation of previous cases (Resnikoff et al. 2015).

Situational analysis

The criminal event under investigation constitutes a specific *situation* where an offender interacted in a given time frame with an immediate environment and a suitable target (possibly a victim) (Clarke and Eck 2005; Cohen and Felson 1979). The understanding of this situation and of the several potentialities of interaction that it implies is also a critical dimension that guides the process of crime scene investigation. This dimension of knowledge can be schematically depicted as the criminological chapter of the reasoning at the crime scene, since it is close to the models of crime understanding that have formed the basis of situational approaches of crime prevention. It consists in finding out the actual opportunities created by the triangle 'offender-target-environment', and in unveiling the physical interactions that ensued from these opportunities. In other words, the evaluation of the situation is an attempt by the crime scene examiner to understand the immediate environment where the crime took place, to figure out the constraints and obstacles that the offender had to overcome in committing his crime, and to reconstruct by reasoning the sequence of past events. This situational analysis reveals hypothetical interfaces (or contact points) between the offender and the environment or between the offender and the victim. By 'walking in the offender's shoes' or 'thinking like offenders', crime scene examiners attempt to locate remnants left on the scene by the offender or objects he was using. This is also how crime scene examiners assess the level of pertinence of the traces they search for or detect.

To perform this situational analysis, crime scene examiners rely, of course, on their personal skills: an acute sense of observation and reasoning abilities to perceive the details of the immediate environment, and imagine possible actions that could have caused them. Criminological education, providing a better perception of the mechanisms and the ecology of crime (see Leclerc, 'Boosting crime scene investigations capabilities through crime script analysis', chapter 9, in this volume), can also substantially improve the ability to decipher the peculiarities of the situation and guide the search for traces. It is interesting, in this perspective, to remember that Locard, one of the pioneers of forensic science, was known to explore obscure districts of cities he visited to learn more about criminals and their habits (Roux et al. 2012). Since that time, forensic science, essentially dragged by a technological wave, has moved some distance from the study of crime and criminals. Criminology is now seldom included in training provided to crime scene examiners or even in the general education of police officers.

In addition, crime scene examiners can also benefit from 'external' sources of information that can provide actionable intelligence. Crime scene examiners have always considered the information obtained from victims or witnesses to target potential pertinent traces (Wyatt 2014). And recent expansion in information and communication technologies (e.g., CCTV, smartphone and various tracking devices) has created new sets of opportunities by widening the availability of images witnessing criminal actions or events (Milliet et al. 2014). For instance, after a robbery, it has become common practice to first and foremost scrutinize CCTV sequences in order to analyse the actions of the perpetrators and target relevant interfaces where traces will be sought during the examination of the scene.

Physical environment

While traces are the main object of crime scene examiners' scrutiny, the knowledge dimension pertaining to them obviously plays a crucial role in the practice of crime scene examination.

Reasoning about the physical environment aims at assessing the chances to detect, enhance and/or collect traces at a crime scene. It consists in an evaluation made by the crime scene examiner that takes into account the likelihood of the presence of a trace at a specific physical place and the possibility of retrieving information from this trace. This dimension relies on the actual knowledge of two different aspects: (a) the science of traces, i.e., the different types of traces and their survival at the crime scene considering their genesis, transfer and persistence mechanisms, contamination issues, etc. and (b) the technical possibilities of detecting and collecting them. Crime scene examiners use this knowledge in combination with the physical context of the scene where the offence took place to form their decisions regarding crime scene attendance and the strategy for scene investigation. For instance, they may decide to omit crime scene examination if the location where the offence occurred has been highly modified or even cleaned after the crime. Or, if they attend the scene, they will consider what they know about different traces in order to choose which traces to target and select adequate technical means.

Since this is the principal concern of forensic training and manuals, it is probably the level of knowledge in which crime scene examiners are mainly educated. Moreover, driven by quality management purposes, forensic policies tend to promote the development of good practice manuals and standard operating procedures that delineate this corpus of knowledge. Statistics on trace collection and analysis outcomes are compiled and they support the inductive forming of general rules (Mapes et al. 2016; Baechler 2016). In line with the general trend of evidence-based practice of scientific disciplines, this set of rules is expected to form the basis for the decision-making process regarding trace detection and collection at the crime scene. But more often than not, the criteria that guide such inductive studies are centred on a cost-effectiveness approach (e.g., considering the chance of obtaining a DNA profile from a trace—maximization of the analytical outcome) rather than on the informative contribution to the reconstruction of the case or to the understanding of the criminal environment.

Utility of the clue

Studying in detail the triage decision step that follows crime scene examination, Bitzer et al. suggest that an additional dimension of knowledge is involved in this decision, and by anticipation, may also affect the previous steps of crime scene attendance and investigation (2016). The utility of the clue encompasses the expected added value that may be obtained through the analysis of a trace. It is therefore intimately related to the context of a specific case and depends on the intrinsic information potential of the trace (considering the criminal background, the immediate analysis and the physical environment). But at the same time, it is restrained by the information already available at the time of the decision (Bitzer et al. 2015). While this dimension has been shown to play a role in the specific context that was studied, it is still debatable whether it can be generalized to other legal, organizational or managerial environments.

Hierarchy and impact on the decision-making processes of crime scene examination

This analysis and formalization of the different dimensions of intelligence that shape the practice of crime scene examination brings out a hierarchal structure (Figure 8.1). This hierarchy relates to a degree of proximity with the actual work at the crime scene. The physical environment includes the knowledge that is directly related to the forensic work at the scene: it conditions the technical skills and operations related to the treatment of each trace. The situational and criminal dimensions have a wider perspective and insight into the forensic work at the scene, by considering factors that may affect the organization and the strategy of this work in relation to the circumstances of the case and its potential links with other criminal activities. This hierarchy of proximity should, however, not be seen as a hierarchy of importance. Depending on the context and circumstances of an event, one of these dimensions of knowledge may prevail over the others and influence in a decisive manner the examination of the crime scene. But this is not a constant situation, and priorities change over situations, and even over time during the course of an investigation.

This is, for instance, the case with (possible) homicide cases where the strategic dimension inexorably constrains the police enquiry in general, including the forensic work. In such situations, if the offender is at large, resources and priorities are definitely aimed at identifying, locating and arresting him. Some forensic actions may contribute to the timely production of intelligence for this very first chapter of the investigation, especially by exploiting digital traces and rapid indicative or identification methods. But the more traditional (and time-consuming) practice of crime scene examination, encompassing a systematic and meticulous search of traces at the scene, is then postponed; operational constraints have priority.

The formalization of crime scene investigation practice within a framework of knowledge—for instance through the architecture depicted in the previous sections—intends to focus attention on the wide scope of knowledge and skills that crime scene examiners have to assimilate, far beyond the traditional view of technical evidence collectors. It also highlights the contribution that related disciplines, such as criminology or crime analysis, bring to forensic science for a practice of crime scene examination anchored in intelligence-led policing.

Possible pitfalls of the intelligence-based practice of crime scene examination

The demonstrable benefits from an intelligence-based crime scene examination have often been associated with the investigation of repetitive crimes. Certainly, the integration of information from previous cases hypothetically linked with a new offence provides convincing examples of

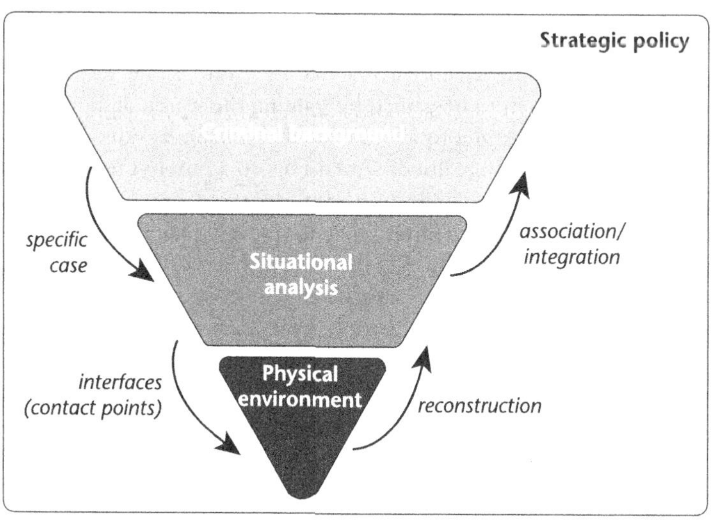

Figure 8.1 Formal structure of intelligence layers shaping the practice of crime scene examination (adapted from Ribaux 2014, 322)

intelligence (namely, criminal background) assisting the search for traces (Ribaux et al. 2010a). But the serial character of the offence must not be seen as a requisite for a practice grounded in intelligence, nor even as an opposition to a case-by-case approach. Although a majority of offences have a repetitive dimension (Farrell and Pease 2014), it should not be denied that certain crimes are singular events, either by nature or contingency. For instance, the vast majority of homicides are unique crimes and do not correspond to a repetitive criminal activity (Cusson 1999). While very popular in the public fantasy, serial killers cause only a tiny proportion of homicides; most perpetrators (in common law) commit only one homicide. The investigation of such crimes emphasizes the importance of focusing on 'The Case', in an approach that could seem tailored to the situation and almost unique. It is true, then, that the criminal background dimension makes a fairly limited, if not non-existent, contribution in such investigations. However, the other knowledge dimensions (the strategic context, the situational understanding of the case, the physical environment of the scene and the utility of the clue) still significantly shape the overall examination of the crime scene. Moreover, observation from actual practice suggests that recollection and confrontation with past cases is a key process that enriches a case-by-case approach. Crime scene examiners base their reasoning on the perception of the actual situation and on the analogy they can draw from previous cases (Houck et al. 2012). They often remember situations they have encountered and learn from successes and mistakes that have been made to attune a suitable strategy to apply to new cases. Thus, even a practice of crime scene examination oriented toward singular offences is, in fact, anchored in an intelligence-based perspective (similar to an informal case-based reasoning), and produces valuable knowledge for future investigations.

The articulation of crime scene examination in relation to available crime intelligence raises the spectre of a possible deleterious influence on the rigour of the investigation. The issue of cognitive bias influencing decisions in forensic science is much debated (see, for instance, Kassin et al. (2013), Champod (2014)), and it is clearly beyond our scope to expand on this delicate topic. However, it must be recognized that intelligence-based crime scene examination is in essence oriented by the available information, which may, as such, influence the overall strategy of scene investigation in a particular direction. The risks of contextual bias, confirmation bias or selective perception—for instance, by focusing on the search for traces that can corroborate a preconception based on a priori knowledge—is definitely latent. But we claim that this risk should not count against a practice of crime scene examination rooted in intelligence. There is too much to be gained by framing the search and detection of traces in a fully informed perspective. And a totally unbiased approach to crime scene investigation, in addition to being practically unrealistic, would rely on a purely mechanical application of procedures, while the detection and collection of relevant traces requires a cognitive approach founded on mainly abductive reasoning. Incentives for mitigating possible deleterious influences of cognitive bias should, however, be provided, in particular by setting up a culture of demonstrable critical thinking and a permanent concern for challenging preconceptions (Ribaux et al. 2010a). We also strongly believe that reinforcing the teaching of scientific method as the skeleton for crime scene investigation will contribute to a balanced practice of intelligence-based crime scene examination limiting adverse effects (see da Agra, 'Criminology and forensic science as a *Unitas Multiplex*: an epistemological approach', chapter 2, in this volume). The pivotal role of crime scene examination for security and criminal investigation purposes, using and producing intelligence, must be fully acknowledged. Consequently, training and education of crime scene examination should move away from the sole focus on quality issues such as good practices and standard operating procedures, and reinforce its anchoring in forensic science, criminology and crime analysis.

Conclusion: Where Next?

Crime scene examiners are facing a professional environment that is definitely more complex than in the past. Ongoing dependence of police activities on science and technology tends to promote a wider use of forensic contributions (Ludwig et al. 2012; Wilson-Kovacs 2014). No longer restricted only to the production of scientific evidence supporting the prosecution of criminal investigation, forensic science is expected to serve security issues through the provision of intelligence. This is certainly desirable, but it also substantially extends the scope of actions for crime scene examiners. Crime scene examination becomes a cornerstone of security and judicial processes. The role of the trace in the massive policing efforts following the 13 November 2015 Paris attacks epitomizes this trend. While arriving for a routine search of premises in a Brussels neighbourhood, police officers were fired at by three men. One of them was killed and the two others fled. The scene examination in the flat led to the detection of fingermarks from Salah Abdeslam, a presumed central protagonist of the Paris attacks (*Le Monde* 2016). This finding was a crucial breakthrough, and Abdeslam was arrested three days later.

In parallel, today's society is experiencing rapid changes echoing the evolution of computer and communication technologies, characterized by the very quick diffusion of their products within daily routine activities (use of computers, smartphones, connected objects, the Internet of things, etc.). This trend creates not only new opportunities for illicit actions but also traces that provide new opportunities to gain information about these illicit actions, as well as about more conventional offences. Crime scene examiners are thus faced with a new dimension of the investigation field, calling for an expansion of their awareness, knowledge and skills. Digital traces are encountered on almost every crime scene, and their multiplicity and volatility increases the complexity of the work of crime scene examiners. While often handled as a separate discipline (referred to as *digital forensics*), mainly in response to the technological specialization that it encompassed in the very beginning of the digital age, the search, detection, collection and use of digital data should enter, if this has not already happened, into the scope of activities of crime scene examiners. The risk of engorgement resulting from the proliferation of traces on the crime will, as a necessary consequence, require an increase of knowledgeable selectivity. In our opinion, this calls for conceptual frameworks that could help to analyse the complexity of the task and provide assistance in the setting up of operational strategies to process scenes of crime. The structuring of the manifold dimensions of intelligence may bring a substantial contribution in this perspective.

Notes

1 Pierre Margot used the image to illustrate the situation of forensic scientists; it also encompasses crime scene examiners. 'Forensic science is essentially a research-oriented endeavour that is limited by the quality of traces criminals leave and by the lack of circumstantial knowledge. Forensic scientists are like drivers in the mist' (Margot 2011, 799).

2 In some institutions, police officers themselves collect objects they think could be suitable in further forensic examinations.

References

Baechler, S. 2016. 'Study of Criteria Influencing the Success Rate of DNA Swabs in Operational Conditions: A Contribution to an Evidence-Based Approach to Crime Scene Investigation and Triage'. *Forensic Science International: Genetics* 20(January): 130–139.

Barclay, D. 2009. 'Using Forensic Science in Major Crime Inquiries'. In J. Fraser and R. Williams, eds., *Handbook of Forensic Science*, 337–358. Cullompton: Willan Publishing Ltd.

Bitzer, S., N. Albertini, E. Lock, O. Ribaux and O. Delémont. 2015. 'Utility of the Clue—From Assessing the Investigative Contribution of Forensic Science to Supporting the Decision to Use Traces'. *Science and Justice* 55(6): 509–513.

Bitzer, S., O. Ribaux, N. Albertini and O. Delémont. 2016. 'To Analyse a Trace or Not? Evaluating the Decision-Making Process in the Criminal Investigation'. *Forensic Science International*, 1–10. https://doi.org/10.1016/j.forsciint.2016.02.022.

Champod, C. 2014. 'Research Focused Mainly on Bias Will Paralyse Forensic Science'. *Science and Justice* 54(2): 107–109.

Clarke, R.V., and J.E. Eck. 2005. 'Crime Analysis for Problem Solvers in 60 Small Steps'. Washington, DC: Center for Problem-Oriented Policing.

Cohen, L.E., and M. Felson. 1979. 'Social Change and Crime Rate Trends: A Routine Activity Approach'. *American Sociological Review* 44(4): 588–608.

Cole, S.A. 2013. 'Forensic Science Reform: Out of the Laboratory and into the Crime Scene'. *Texas Law Review* 91: 123–136.

Cusson F. 1999. 'Les meurtriers qui tuent de nouveau'. In J. Proulx, M. Cusson and M. Ouimet, eds., *Les violences criminelles*, 131–156. Laval: Les Presses de l'Université Laval.

Delémont, O., E. Lock and O. Ribaux. 2014. 'Forensic Science and Criminal Investigation'. In G. Bruinsma and D. Weisburd, eds., *Encyclopedia of Criminology and Criminal Justice*, 1754–1763. New York: Springer Science+Business.

Farrell, G., and K. Pease. 2014. 'Prediction and Crime Clusters'. In G. Bruinsma and D. Weisburd, eds., *Encyclopedia of Criminology and Criminal Justice*, 3862–3870. New York: Springer Science+Business.

Houck, M., F. Crispino and T. McAdam. 2012. *The Science of Crime Scenes*. San Diego: Academic Press publications.

Julian, R.D., S.F. Kelty and J. Robertson. 2012. '"Get It Right the First Time": Critical Issues at the Crime Scene'. *Current Issues in Crimnal Justice* 24(1): 25–37.

Kassin, S., I. Dror and J. Kukucka. 2013. 'The Forensic Confirmation Bias: Problems, Perspectives, and Pproposed Solutions'. *Journal of Applied Research in Memory and Cognition* 2(1): 42–52.

Kelty, S.F., R.D. Julian and J. Robertson. 2011. 'Professionalism in Crime Scene Examination: The Seven Key Attributes of Top Crime Scene Examiners'. *Forensic Science Policy & Management: An International Journal* 2(4): 175–186.

Le Monde. 2016. 'Six questions sur l'arrestation de Salah Abdeslam'. *Le Monde*, 19 March 2016. www.lemonde.fr/attaques-a-paris/article/2016/03/19/arrestation-de-salah-abdeslam-les-questions-qui-se-posent_4886384_4809495.html.

Ludwig, A., J. Fraser and R. Williams. 2012. 'Crime Scene Examiners and Volume Crime Investigations: An Empirical Study of Perception and Practice'. *Forensic Science Policy & Management: An International Journal* 3(2): 53–61.

Mapes, A.A., A.D. Kloosterman, V. Van Marion and C.J. De Poot. 2016. 'Knowledge on DNA Success Rates to Optimize the DNA Analysis Process: From Crime Scene to Laboratory'. *Journal of Forensic Sciences* 61(4): 1055–1061.

Margot, P. 2011. 'Commentary on the Need for a Research Culture in the Forensic Sciences'. *UCLA Law Review* 58(3): 795–801.

Margot, P. 2014. 'Traçologie: la trace, vecteur fondamental de la police scientifique'. *Revue internationale de criminologie et de police technique et scientifique* 67(1): 72–97.

Milliet, Q., O. Delémont and P. Margot. 2014. 'A Forensic Science Perspective on the Role of Images in Crime Investigation and Reconstruction'. *Science & Justice* 54(6): 470–480.

Mnookin, J.L., S.A. Cole, I.E. Dror, B.A.J. Fisher, M.M. Houck, K. Inman, D.H. Kaye, J.J. Koehler, G. Langenburg, M.D. Risinger, N. Rudin, J. Siegel and D.A. Stoney. 2011. 'The Need for a Research Culture in the Forensic Sciences'. *UCLA Law Review* 58(3): 725–780.

Resnikoff, T., O. Ribaux, A. Baylon, M. Jendly and Q. Rossy. 2015. 'The Polymorphism of Crime Scene Investigation: An Exploratory Analysis of the Influence of Crime and Forensic Intelligence on Decisions Made by Crime Scene Examiners'. *Forensic Science International* 257(December): 425–434.

Ribaux, O. 2014. *Police scientifique. Le renseignement par la trace*. Presses Polytechniques et Universitaires Romandes.

Ribaux, O., A. Baylon, E. Lock, O. Delémont, C. Roux, C. Zingg and P. Margot. 2010a. 'Intelligence-Led Crime Scene Processing. Part II: Intelligence and Crime Scene Examination. *Forensic Science International* 199(1–3): 63–71.

Ribaux, O., A. Baylon, C. Roux, O. Delémont, E. Lock, C. Zingg and P. Margot. 2010b. 'Intelligence-Led Crime Scene Processing. Part I: Forensic Intelligence. *Forensic Science International* 195(1–3): 10–16.

Ribaux, O., F. Crispino, O. Delémont and C. Roux. 2016. 'The Progressive Opening of Forensic Science toward Criminological Concerns'. *Security Journal* 29(4): 543–560.

Rossy, Q., S. Ioset, D. Dessimoz and O. Ribaux. 2013. 'Integrating Forensic Information in a Crime Intelligence Database'. *Forensic Science International* 230(1–3):137–146.

Roux, C., F. Crispino and O. Ribaux. 2012. 'From Forensics to Forensic Science'. *Current Issues in Criminal Justice* 24(1): 7–24.

Williams, R. 2004. 'The Management of Crime Scene Examination in Relation to the Investigation of Burglary and Vehicle Crime'. Home Office RDS Online Report 24/04. London: Durham University.

Wilson-Kovacs, D. 2014. '"Backroom Boys": Occupational Dynamics in Crime Scene Examination'. *Sociology* 48(4): 763–779.

Wyatt, D. 2014. 'Practising Crime Scene Investigation: Trace and Contamination in Routine Work'. *Policing and Society* 24(4): 443–458.

9

Boosting crime scene investigations capabilities through crime script analysis

Benoit Leclerc

Introduction

The analysis of crime event patterns in space and time, understanding opportunities to offend, and preventing crime events from occurring in the first place best characterizes environmental criminology/crime science (Wortley and Mazerolle 2008)—a field of criminology for which the theoretical foundations started to emerge around 30 years ago (e.g., Clarke 1980; Cohen and Felson 1979; see Leclerc and Wortley 2013 for a historical overview of rational choice). Environmental criminology primarily originated from grouping three key theoretical approaches to crime events: (1) routine activity approach (Cohen and Felson 1979; Felson 2008), (2) crime pattern theory (Brantingham and Brantingham 1978, 1984), and (3) the rational choice perspective (Cornish and Clarke 1986, 2008). Taken together, these approaches form opportunity theories of crime (Felson and Clarke 1998). For a detailed review of these approaches, I refer the reader to one of the editions of the *Environmental Criminology and Crime Analyst* textbook (Wortley and Mazerolle 2008; Wortley and Townsley 2016).

The field of environmental criminology is mainly driven by reducing crime rather than developing or testing general theories of crime, which fundamentally falls outside traditional criminology. Any theoretical advancement in this field is achieved with practical implications in mind—theoretical contributions must enhance the potential of and facilitate crime prevention practices. Situational crime prevention is the approach through which crime prevention initiatives are developed and applied (e.g., Clarke 1980, 1997). Based on the assumptions that crime is the outcome of an interaction between the offender and the situation and that opportunities play a powerful role in generating crime (Clarke 2008), successful situational crime prevention measures consist of reducing crime opportunities and controlling crime precipitators. Twenty-five techniques have been classified according to five prevention strategies: (1) increasing risk of offending, (2) increasing efforts for offending, (3) reducing rewards associated with offending, (4) removing excuses justifying offending, and (5) reducing provocations that can precipitate offending (Cornish and Clarke 2003). The practice of situational crime prevention is closely linked to script analysis, since its main requirement is to understand how crime is committed.

In this chapter, I first show that scripting the process of crime scene investigation itself could not only provide investigators with a clear template on how to systematically investigate a crime scene but also boost their capability of successfully identifying and apprehending offenders. Second, I argue that crime scene investigators and police forces in general could use offender scripts to systematically track down the crime-commission process of offenders to support and guide their investigation.

The concept of script

Script analysis originated from the notion of schemas in cognitive psychology. A schema is a cognitive structure that contains assumptions and expectations about the social world based on past behaviour and experience. Schemas essentially assist people navigating the social world every day. For instance, each person has accumulated knowledge about him/herself, other people, how to interact with others and what sequence of actions to follow in order to achieve desired goals. Accordingly, different forms of schemas exist (e.g., self-schemas, person schemas, relational schemas, event schemas) (Augoustinos et al. 2006; Baldwin 1992; Fiske and Taylor 1991). The event schema refers specifically to scripts. An event schema is a knowledge structure that organizes the sequence of actions to adopt in a particular context to achieve an outcome. Schank and Abelson (1977) illustrated the concept of scripts by using the now classic example of eating in a restaurant; that is, the sequence of actions that must be taken by the customer of a restaurant. The customer must enter the restaurant; wait to be seated; get the menu; order; eat; get the cheque; pay and exit (for other applications of script analysis in psychology, see Leclerc 2013a).

Offender scripts (aka crime scripts)

In relation to criminology specifically, Clarke and Cornish (1985) provided four decision-making models, one of which was target selection. Recognizing the limitations of this model, Cornish (1994) borrowed the script concept from cognitive psychology in order to provide a framework to systematically identify and investigate each stage of the crime-commission process of a specific crime, the decisions and actions that must be taken at each stage and the resources required for successful completion of the crime. In the study of crime events, environmental criminologists and crime analysts must complete a thorough analysis of the crime through the investigation of a number of basic questions that capture the circumstances of offenses, such as Who was involved? What happened? Where did it happen? When did it happen? and How was it perpetrated? (Clarke and Eck 2005). Script analysis targets the last question in particular—how the crime was committed—and situates this process back into its context, thus taking into account the circumstances under which the script was executed. Put simply, applied to crime, the script concept makes the crime-commission process much easier to identify and understand, and as a result, boosts the potential for crime prevention.

The typical sequence of the stages of a script is presented in Table 9.1. As an illustration, a hypothetical example of a street robbery script of an adult stranger is shown (see Leclerc 2013a). As seen in Table 9.1, applied to crime, the script represents the complete step-by-step sequence of actions adopted prior to, during and following the commission of a particular crime. Apart from identifying the crime-commission process, the powerful benefit of breaking down the script is to provide an intervention-point for each stage of the script to disrupt its execution and thus prevent offending. Rather than trying to prevent crime taken as a whole or as a single event, each stage can be targeted for prevention purposes. For instance, situational prevention measures could be designed to target the preparation stage. Other measures could be developed to address the entry stage, and so on. In the end, the more stages in the script, the more intervention-points to guide prevention efforts.

Table 9.1 Script stages used in crime script analysis

Script stages	*Script actions*
Preparation	Get a weapon, select co-offenders
Entry	Enter neighbourhood, go to public park
Precondition	Look for potential victims
Instrumental precondition	Identify and select a potential victim
Instrumental initiation	Approach and verbally intimidate a potential victim
Instrumental actualization	Assault
Doing	Take money and other valuables
Postcondition	Threaten the victim to not report victimization
Exit	Walk away

Source: Adapted from Leclerc 2013a

Table 9.2 The application of script analysis to the main actors during crime events

Dimension	*Offender*	*Victim*	*Guardian*
Objective pursued by actor during event	Commit crime	Avoid victimization	Intervene
Focus of script analysis	Crime-commission process	Self-precautionary process	Intervention process
Prevention purpose	Disrupt script	Facilitate script	Facilitate script

Source: Leclerc 2013a

Crime prevention agent scripts

One recent innovation in crime scripts was to demonstrate that scripts can also be performed through the eyes of potential victims and guardians against crime (Leclerc 2013a, 2017). The objective of performing offender scripts (typically referred to as crime scripts) is to identify each stage of the crime-commission process in order to obtain a fuller range of intervention-points to disrupt scripts before crime completion (see Table 9.2). In regard to potential victims, however, the objective of the actor is to avoid victimization, not to commit crime. Accordingly, script analysis from the perspective of the potential victim aims to identify the behavioural sequence leading to non-victimization, that is, the self-precautionary process that potential victims should adopt to avoid victimization (see Smith 2017 for examples of victim scripts). Finally, with respect to potential guardians against crime willing to interfere, the objective is to intervene in order to successfully prevent crime. Therefore, the goal of script analysis is to identify the intervention process likely to lead to a successful intervention. With victim and potential guardian scripts, the ultimate objective for crime prevention is to facilitate the execution of the script, not disrupt it. In these two cases, situational crime prevention techniques would be designed to facilitate each stage of the script.

The intervention script model developed by Leclerc and Reynald (2015) offers an example for what could be achieved in the context of crime scene investigations. The intervention script contains 12 stages that guardians must follow in order to intervene (either indirectly or directly) and prevent crime in public settings (see Figure 9.1). Leclerc and Reynald also mapped hypothetical prevention techniques onto the script to show how the intervention process could be facilitated (see Table 9.3). This work provides a clear illustration of how script can be used from the perspective of potential guardians who may prevent crime.

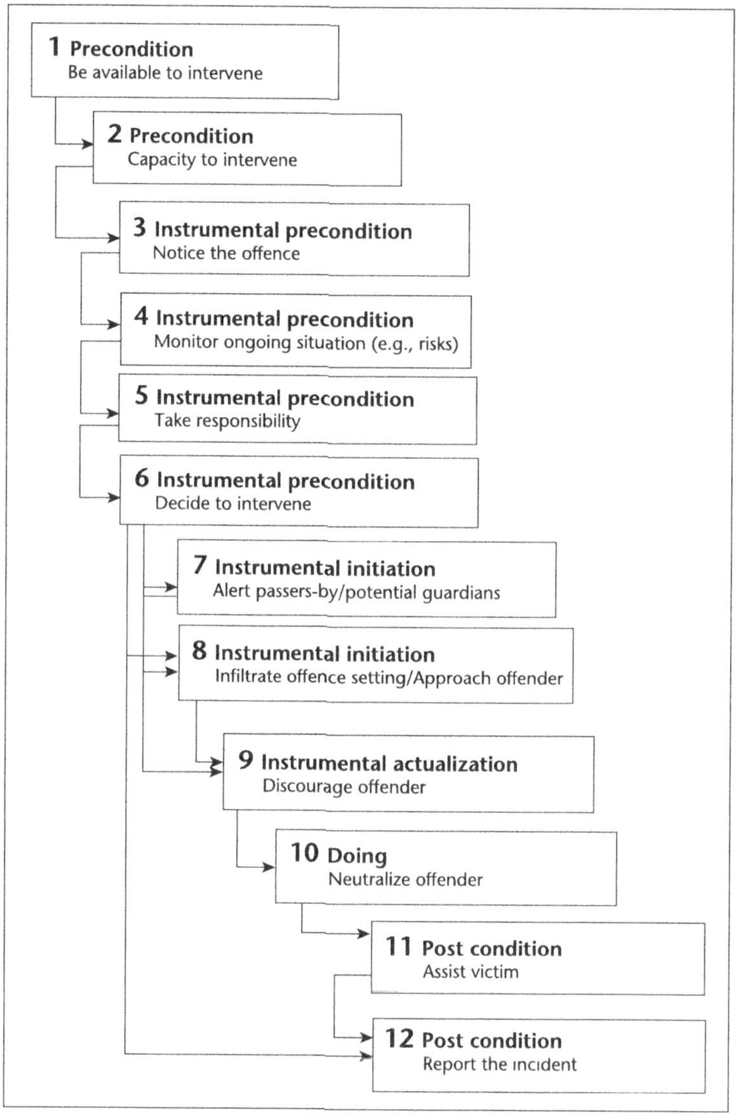

Figure 9.1 Intervention script of capable guardians against crime in public settings

Scripts for crime scene investigators

Crime scene investigation scripts

As pointed out by Leclerc (2013b), crime script analysis can be applied to any human behavioural sequence, which includes virtually anyone who is involved in a crime event, including those who can reduce, prevent or investigate crime. The 'process' followed by police officers, detectives, medical examiners, crime scene investigators and so forth during crime scene investigations can be scripted and generate a wide range of intervention-points to facilitate investigations and, as a result, enhance opportunities to successfully apprehend offenders. In fact, any behavioural

Table 9.3 Situational prevention strategies and techniques to facilitate guardianship at selected steps of the intervention script

Step of script	*Situational crime prevention strategy*	*Situational crime prevention techniques*
1. Availability to intervene	Reduce the effort Reduce the risk	*Encourage accessibility and usage of public setting* *Design spaces that are aesthetically pleasing *Facilitate accessibility and encourage steady flow of users *Increase surveillance and encourage safety
2. Capacity to intervene	Reduce the effort Reduce the risk	*Increase physical capacity* *Provide free self-defence training sessions
3. Notice the offence 4. Monitor the offence	Reduce the effort	*Facilitate natural surveillance* *Create clear lines of sight *Manipulate physical design to ensure windows face public space *Use CCTV
5. Take responsibility	Provide excuses Increase rewards	*Encourage collective awareness* *Use signage/announcements to promote vigilance and raise awareness of safety precautions *Use signage/announcements to promote civic responsibility to assist victims *Introduce and promote community awards* *Provide awards for civic engagement in the prevention of crime
6. Decide to intervene	Provide excuses	*Promote active guardianship* *Use publicity campaigns to encourage intervention *Shaming of inaction *Ensure that police contact information is readily available
7. Alert passers-by	Reduce the effort	*Increase communication potential* *Encourage presence of onsite place managers *Mobilize community watch groups *Install emergency alarm systems
8. Approach offender 9. Discourage offender	Increase the reward Provide excuses	*Promote citizen intervention laws* *Provide and raise awareness of citizens' legal arrest powers *Introduce incentives for intervention* *Public commendation and/or monetary rewards/ compensation *Increase social capacity* *Publicize police guidelines to manage dangerous situations (e.g., hostage situations)
10. Neutralize offender	Reduce the effort Reduce the risk	*Increase physical capacity* *Provide free self-defence training sessions
11. Assist victim	Provide excuses	*Create social pressure* *Penalties for failing to assist victims in need *Use publicity campaigns to encourage victim assistance
12. Report the incident	Reduce the effort Provide excuses	*Provide accessible channels of communication* * Increase availability of emergency phone booths *Introduce incentives for reporting* *Public commendation and/or monetary rewards/ compensation *Use mechanical surveillance* *Use monitored CCTV cameras

Source: Leclerc and Reynald 2015

sequences for which an outcome can be clearly identified can be analysed through script analysis.

Drawing on Leclerc and Reynald (2015), I argue that the process of crime scene investigations can also be scripted and provide intervention-points to facilitate its execution. The National Institute of Justice in the US (2000, 2013) provides a guide that can be used in crime scene investigations. This guide contains five general stages: (1) arrival at the scene/initial response and prioritization of efforts, (2) preliminary documentation and evaluation at the scene, (3) processing the scene, (4) completing and recording the crime scene investigation, and (5) crime scene equipment. Each of these stages also comprises a series of mini-stages. In total, there are 26 different stages outlined in the guide (see Table 9.4). The document also provides information on the tasks to be completed during crime scene investigations at each stage. Similarly, Fisher and Fisher (2012) also cover a range of stages (e.g., when officers first arrive at the scene and when crime scene investigators evaluate the scene). However, Fisher and Fisher's work focuses on particular types of techniques/examinations, such as footprints, firearms, explosives and drugs and toxicology, rather than detailing all the stages during crime scene investigations.

The National Institute of Justice (2000, 2013) guide offers a rough step-by-step description of the actions adopted in crime scene investigations. Coupled with empirical evidence, this guide

Table 9.4 Step-by-step guide for crime scene investigations

Five general stages	*Mini-stages*
1. Arriving at the scene: initial response/ prioritization	1. Initial response/receipt of information 2. Safety procedures 3. Emergency care 4. Secure and control persons at the scene 5. Boundaries: identify, establish, protect and secure 6. Turn over control of the scene and brief investigators in charge 7. Document actions and observations 8. Establish a command post and make notifications 9. Manage witnesses
2. Preliminary documentation and evaluation of the scene	1. Conduct scene assessment 2. Conduct scene 'walk-through' and initial documentation 3. Note-taking and logs
3. Processing the scene	1. Determine team composition 2. Ensure contamination control 3. Documentation 4. Prioritize collection of evidence 5. Crime scene search methods 6. Collect, preserve, inventory, package, transport and submit evidence 7. Detailed crime scene evidence collection
4. Completing/recording the crime scene investigation	1. Establish crime scene debriefing team 2. Perform final survey of the crime scene 3. Documentation of the crime scene 4. Acknowledge specialized crime scene circumstances
5. Crime scene equipment	1. Initial responding officer(s) 2. Crime scene investigator/evidence technician 3. Evidence collection kits

Source: Adapted from National Institute of Justice 2013

could be used as a template to develop a detailed, evidence-based script for crime scene investigators specifically. However, there are a number of issues to consider beforehand. First, the stage depicting the arrival at the scene/initial response and prioritization of efforts is performed by officers who are the first professionals to arrive at the scene, not crime scene investigators. Essentially, this means that the involvement of officers on the scene is a process in itself performed by actors other than crime scene investigators, which ideally requires its own script. Second, the last stage of the guide (i.e., crime scene equipment) cannot be conceptualized as a stage in the process (this point also applies to a number of mini-stages), but mainly a list of different tools that can be used by crime scene investigators during the investigation. In a script, crime scene equipment (or props) is typically included at each relevant script stage to enhance the comprehensiveness of the actions undertaken by the actor (i.e., offender or guardian) and how the actions can be performed in the script.

Related to the first issue presented above is the involvement of a number of different professionals at different stages during crime scene investigations, which complicates the process of crime scene investigation (Bradbury and Feist 2005)—an issue that taps into the effective management of crime scene investigations as well (Julian et al. 2012). The decision to deploy crime scene investigators on a crime scene in the first place appears simple, but varies according to a number of factors, such as the type of crime, availability of crime scene investigators, work prioritization, time and experience (Bradbury and Feist 2005; Julian et al. 2012; Ribaux et al. 2010). Consequently, it is possible that the roles of different professionals also overlap, especially when crime scene investigators are needed but not available to attend a crime scene (Bradbury and Feist 2005). There are further issues raised in the literature, such as the lack of collaboration and communication between crime scene investigators and other professionals involved, such as detectives (Bradbury and Feist 2005).

Going back to the first issue, scripting is easier to perform from the perspective of a single actor. This means that the process of crime scene investigation should be deconstructed from the perspective of each professional involved, that is, officers who first arrive at the scene, medical examiners, detectives, crime scene investigators and so on. In the end, the sequence of actions performed by each professional involved in crime scene investigations should be scripted, which would streamline the different processes in place for each actor and also help clarify and address the issues reported above. Scripts could provide each professional with a systematic template to follow during crime scene investigations. Where crime scene investigations differ substantially according to the type of crime, different scripts could also be developed accordingly. For illustration purposes, there may exist two general scripts for crime scene investigators—one for interpersonal crimes and one for property crimes.

The main point is that if a script can be generated for crime scene investigators, then each stage of the script can be used as an intervention-point to address current issues reported in the literature and thus facilitate crime scene investigations. For instance, going back to the guide provided by the US Department of Justice (2013) (see Table 9.4), the stage of preliminary documentation and evaluation at the scene consists of three mini-stages: (1) conducting scene assessment, (2) conducting scene 'walk-through' and initial documentation, and (3) note-taking and logs. Conducting scene assessment involves a number of actions, such as conversing with the first responders regarding observations and activities and evaluating safety issues that may affect all personnel entering the scene. In a similar fashion to Leclerc and Reynald (2015), situational prevention techniques could be applied to facilitate those actions, which could then increase the likelihood of crime scene investigators providing assistance for identifying offenders. Reducing efforts, decreasing the risks and increasing rewards associated with the investigation, and providing excuses to boost the likelihood of successfully conducting the investigation, all have the potential to be applied to crime scene investigations to facilitate the tasks of conversing with first responders and evaluating safety issues that may affect all personnel entering the scene, for instance.

Offender scripts for crime scene investigations

Besides scripting crime scene investigations, script analysis can be performed on the offender's crime-commission process, which has been the focus of most script research in criminology so far. Crime scene investigators, in theory, focus on what is referred to as 'offender modus operandi'—the strategies adopted by offenders to commit their crime successfully. Offender modus operandi is naturally incorporated into a script analysis—it is at the core of a crime script. Crime scripts thus provide a template to systematically investigate offender modus operandi. Most importantly, this template identifies all the stages of the crime-commission process of a specific crime, as well as providing insights into the underlying offender decision-making process.

The study of offender modus operandi implies 'thinking thief' (Ekblom 2007). The literature suggests that crime scene investigators, once on the crime scene, will be 'thinking thief' for amassing physical evidence to help identify offenders (Ribaux et al. 2010). 'Thinking thief' is arguably a fundamental requirement for understanding how crime is committed, which is consistent with the approach of environmental criminology and, most specifically, script analysis. Crime scene investigators have to put themselves in the shoes of offenders to understand what happened during the crime and the circumstances under which the crime was committed. However, the literature indicates that attending a crime scene is not mandatory for crime scene investigators—the potential for attendance varies according to a number of situational factors (Bradbury and Feist 2005; Resnikoff et al. 2015). This reality is obviously problematic if there is no opportunity for an investigator to examine a crime scene from the perspective of the offender. From the approach of environmental criminology, it becomes quite impossible to script the crime-commission process of offenders in the absence of human resources capable of 'thinking thief'. The availability of an investigator appears to be a fundamental precondition for scripting in this context.

Assuming that a crime scene is attended by crime scene investigators, the efforts of the investigation would be typically directed only at the crime scene itself, that is, the location where the crime was committed. However, script analysis has the potential to pinpoint further 'contact points' between the offender and victim for analysis, especially for serious crimes such as homicide and sexual offences. For instance, Leclerc, Wortley and Smallbone (2011) identified the general script followed by child sexual offenders. In this script, there are several contact points between the offender and the victim. For stranger offending, stages during which the offender and the victim interact in a different location may include when the offender first encounters the victim and when the offender proceeds to the location where sexual contact occurs. In fact, Beauregard et al. (2007) found that serial sexual offenders may use a number of different locations to commit their crime, which include the location where the victim is left alone after crime. Similarly, Leclerc, Wortley and Smallbone (2010) observed that a number of child sexual offenders use different locations to obtain sexual contact with the same victim over a period of time. In short, it appears logical for crime scene investigations to move beyond examining only the location where the crime was committed and investigate other locations where the offender and victim converged in time and space during the entire crime-commission process. To some extent, this suggestion taps into the concept of secondary crime scene described in the literature, but secondary crime scenes generally relate only to immediate spaces next to the location where the crime was committed (e.g., kitchen next to a bedroom) (Bertino and Bertino 2012). In summary, by breaking down the crime-commission process into a number of stages, a crime script offers the opportunity (and raises awareness of the potential) of uncovering and investigating crime-commission stages that complement the stage during which the crime is committed, and these could be examined as well. In turn, this practice has the potential to boost the likelihood of identifying offenders.

Conclusion

The utility of script analysis for investigating, reducing and preventing crime is exceptionally relevant. The strengths of script analysis are numerous (Leclerc 2016). Crime script analysis is systematic, compatible, resilient, insightful, practical and theoretically grounded. For instance, it has the power to break down a complex sequence of actions into a series of stages, which provides a structure and therefore simplifies complex behavioural processes through a systematic approach. Most importantly for crime scene investigations, crime script analysis is also practice-oriented, since it has the capacity to generate a wide range of intervention-points for situational prevention, thus providing opportunities for examining behavioural processes in order to ultimately address crime problems. Crime scene investigation is another important area that can be improved through crime script analysis. The application of script analysis to crime scene investigations appears promising.

References

Augoustinos, M., I. Walker and N. Donaghue. 2006. *Social Cognition: An Integrated Introduction*, 2nd ed. London: Sage Publications.

Baldwin, M.W. 1992. 'Relational Schemas and the Processing of Social Information'. *Psychological Bulletin* 112(3): 461–484.

Beauregard, E., J. Proulx, D.K. Rossmo, B. Leclerc and J.-F. Allaire. 2007. 'Script Analysis of the Hunting Process of Serial Sex Offenders'. *Criminal Justice and Behavior* 34(8): 1069–1084.

Bertino, A.J., and P. Bertino. 2012. *Forensic Science: Fundamentals and Investigations*, 2nd ed. Boston, MA: Cengage Learning.

Bradbury, S.A., and A. Feist. 2005. *The Use of Forensic Science in Volume Crime Investigations: A Review of the Research Literature*. Research Development and Statistics Directorate. London: Home Office.

Brantingham, P.J., and P.L. Brantingham. 1978. 'A Theoretical Model of Crime Site Selection'. In M. Krohn and R. Akers, eds., *Crime, Law, and Sanctions*, 105–118. Beverly Hills, CA: Sage.

Brantingham, P.J., and P.L. Brantingham. 1984. *Patterns in Crime*. New York: MacMillan.

Clarke, R.V. 1980. '"Situational" Crime Prevention: Theory and Practice'. *British Journal of Criminology* 20(2): 136–147.

Clarke, R.V. 1997. 'Situational Crime Prevention: Successful Case Studies'. Guilderland, NY: Harrow and Heston.

Clarke, R.V. 2008. 'Situational Crime Prevention'. In Wortley and Mazerolle, *Environmental Criminology and Crime Analyses*, 178–194.

Clarke, R.V., and D.B. Cornish. 1985. 'Modeling Offenders' Decisions: A Framework for Research and Policy'. In M. Tonry and N. Morris, eds., *Crime and Justice: An Annual Review of Research*, 6: 147–185. Chicago: University of Chicago Press.

Clarke, R., and J. Eck. 2005. 'Crime Analysis for Problem Solvers in 60 Small Steps'. Washington, DC: US Department of Justice Office of Community Oriented Policing Services. www.popcenter.org.

Cohen, L.E., and M. Felson. 1979. 'Social Change and Crime Rate Trends: A Routine Activity Approach'. *American Sociological Review* 44(4): 588–608.

Cornish, D.B. 1994. 'The Procedural Analysis of Offending and Its Relevance for Situational Prevention'. In R.V. Clarke, ed., *Crime Prevention Studies*, 3: 151–196. Monsey, NY: Criminal Justice Press.

Cornish, D.B., and R.V. Clarke. 1986. 'Introduction'. In D.B. Cornish and R.V. Clarke, eds., *The Reasoning Criminal: Rational Choice Perspectives on Offending*. New York: Springer-Verlag.

Cornish, D.B., and R.V. Clarke. 2003. 'Opportunities, Precipitators and Criminal Decisions: A Reply to Wortley's Critique of Situational Crime Prevention'. In M. Smith and D.B. Cornish, eds., *Crime*

Prevention Studies: Theory for Practice in Situational Crime Prevention, 16: 41–96. Monsey, NY: Criminal Justice Press.

Cornish, D.B., and R.V. Clarke. 2008. 'The Rational Choice Perspective'. In Wortley and Mazerolle, *Environmental Criminology and Crime Analysis*, 22–47.

Ekblom, P. 2007. 'Thinking Thief: Crime Frameworks for Design against Crime'. Paper presented at the Design Against Crime Research Centre, UK, London.

Felson, M. 2008. 'Routine Activity Approach'. In Wortley and Mazerolle, *Environmental Criminology and Crime Analyses*, 70–77.

Felson, M., and R.V. Clarke. 1998. *Opportunity Makes the Thief: Practical Theory for Crime Prevention*. Police Research Series paper 98. London: Home Office.

Fisher, B.A.J., and D.R. Fisher. 2012. *Techniques of Crime Scene Investigation*, 8th ed. Boca Raton, FL: CRC Press.

Fiske, S.T., and S.E. Taylor. 1991. *Social Cognition*, 2nd ed. New York: McGraw-Hill.

Julian, R., S. Kelty and J. Robertson. 2012. '"Get It Right the First Time": Critical Issues at the Crime Scene'. *Current Issues in Criminal Justice* 24(1): 25–37.

Leclerc, B. 2013a. 'New Developments in Script Analysis for Situational Crime Prevention: Moving beyond Offender Scripts'. In B. Leclerc and R. Wortley, eds., *Cognition and Crime: Offender Decision-Making and Script Analyses*, 221–236. Crime Science Series. London, UK: Routledge.

Leclerc, B. 2013b. 'Script Analysis for Crime Controllers: Extending the Reach of Situational Prevention'. In S. Caneppele and F. Calderoni, eds., *Organized Crime, Corruption, and Crime Prevention: Essays in Honour of Ernesto U. Savona*, 13–20. New York: Springer.

Leclerc, B. 2016. 'Crime Scripts'. In R. Wortley and M. Townsley, eds., *Environmental Criminology and Crime Analysis*, 2nd ed., 119–141. London, UK: Routledge.

Leclerc, B. 2017. 'Script Analysis and the SCRIPT Acronym'. In B. Leclerc and E.U. Savona, eds., *Crime Prevention in the 21st Century: Insightful Approaches for Crime Prevention Initiatives*, 49–58. New York, NY: Springer.

Leclerc, B., and D. Reynald. 2015. 'When Scripts and Guardianship Unite: A Theoretical Script Model to Facilitate Intervention by Capable Guardians'. *Security Journal*, DOI:10.1057/sj.2015.8.

Leclerc, B., and R. Wortley. 2013. 'The Reasoning Criminal: Twenty-Five Years On'. In B. Leclerc and R. Wortley, eds., *Cognition and Crime: Offender Decision-Making and Script Analyses*, 1–11. Crime Science Series. London, UK: Routledge.

Leclerc, B., R. Wortley and S. Smallbone. 2010. 'Investigating Mobility Patterns for Repetitive Sexual Contact in Adult Child Sex Offending'. *Journal of Criminal Justice* 38(4): 648–656.

Leclerc, B., R. Wortley and S. Smallbone. 2011. 'Getting into the Script of Adult Child Sex Offenders and Mapping out Situational Prevention Measures'. *Journal of Research in Crime and Delinquency* 48(2): 209–237.

National Institute of Justice (US) (Technical Working Group on Crime Scene Investigation). 2000. 'Crime Scene Investigation: A Guide for Law Enforcement'. Research report. US Dept. of Justice, Office of Justice Programs, National Institute of Justice. Florida: Purdue University.

National Institute of Justice (US) (Technical Working Group on Crime Scene Investigation). 2013. 'Crime Scene Investigation: A Guide for Law Enforcement'. Research report. US Dept. of Justice, Office of Justice Programs, National Institute of Justice. Florida: Purdue University.

Ribaux, O., A. Baylon, E. Lock, O. Delémont, C. Roux, C. Zingg and P. Margot. 2010. 'Intelligence-led Crime Scene Processing. Part II: Intelligence and Crime Scene Examination'. *Forensic Science International* 199 (1–3): 63–71.

Resnikoff, T., O. Ribaux, A. Baylon, M. Jendly and Q. Rossy. 2015. 'The Polymorphism of Crime Scene Investigation: An Exploratory Analysis of the Influence of Crime Scene and Forensic Intelligence on Decisions Made by Crime Scene Examiners'. *Forensic Science International* 257 (December): 425–434.

Schank, R., and R.P. Abelson. 1977. *Scripts, Plans, Goals and Understanding: An Inquiry into Human Knowledge*. Hillsdale, NJ: Erlbaum.

Smith, M.J. 2017. 'Expanding the Script Analytic Approach Using Victim Narratives: Learning about Robberies of Taxi Drivers from the Drivers Themselves'. In B. Leclerc and E.U. Savona, eds., *Crime Prevention in the 21st Century: Insightful Approaches for Crime Prevention Initiatives*, 77–98. New York: Springer.

Wortley, R., and L. Mazerolle, eds., 2008. *Environmental Criminology and Crime Analyses*. Cullompton, UK: Willan.

Wortley, R., and M. Townsley, eds., 2016. *Environmental Criminology and Crime Analyses*. 2nd ed. London: Routledge.

10
The CSI effect

Simon A. Cole and Glenn Porter

The application of forensic science and technology within the criminal justice system has witnessed a cyclical relationship between the media and fictional popular culture. Nineteenth-century creators of the literary genre of detective fiction were notably influenced by real-life figures from the criminal justice system. Edgar Allan Poe's detective, Dupin, was modeled on the French minister of police, Vidocq. Scotland Yard detective Charley Field was evidently the model for Dickens's Inspector Bucket (Summerscale 2008). Most famously, the Scottish medico-legalist Joseph Bell is known to have been the inspiration for Arthur Conan Doyle's enduringly popular private detective, Sherlock Holmes (Crowther and White 1988). Like the fictional character he invented, Conan Doyle himself also investigated real cases such as the alleged wrongful conviction of George Edalji in 1903. The cyclical relationship between forensic science and popular culture signifies 'art imitating life imitating art imitating life' (Risinger 2006, 2).

Sherlock Holmes also developed into more than just a popular culture reflection of the 'real' phenomena of detection and forensic science. Some perceive Holmes to have directly influenced the development of forensic science itself. Somewhat more narrowly, Mark Twain is often treated as having contributed to the development of fingerprint identification through his depiction of the technique, first in *Life on the Mississippi* and, more extensively, by his lawyer-detective-scientist character David 'Pudd'nhead' Wilson (Federal Bureau of Investigation 1991; Chinn 2000; Mnookin 2001; Cole 2007).

From a more contemporary perspective, television dramatizations like *CSI*, *Criminal Minds*, *NCIS* and others portray a more modern methodical approach to investigation using a combination of forensic science, psychology and high technology that currently incorporates fictional technologies, such as artificial intelligence, predictive computing and so on, that may not be fictional in the near future. Detective intuition or hypothetico-deductive reasoning are replaced by high-tech evidence enhancement, high visibility through public surveillance systems, and identity searches processed by computer databases. While the characterization of the scientist or scientist/cop as protagonist hero has been modernized, the basis of the narratives has remained stubbornly consistent with conventional narrative themes. There have, however, been small changes such as a greater emphasis on teamwork, consistent with modern working environments, as opposed to individual genius, and a notable shift in gender balance (Nolan 2007).

The common theme across most popular culture artefacts depicting crime-solving often characterizes the offender's appearance, social background, ethnicity, gender and other stereotypical constructs in ways that dramatize either the violation of the victim, the effect of crime, or methods of solving and linking the crime to the offender. The typical narrative is a moralistic one, which portrays the criminal justice system as a perfect arbitrator of justice. Notably absent when crime is depicted within popular culture are any social causes of crime like poverty, mental health, social-economic and relationship pressures, etc. Rather, the portrayal is often a sanitized version of criminal activity in which the criminal act is punished, justice is served to victims and, based on a highly moralistic narrative, good always triumphs over evil.

While Stevens (2011) suggests that the media and popular culture shape social perspectives and opinions while influencing public policies, claims about a 'CSI effect' propose that actors involved in a criminal trial may confuse the dramatization of crime with reality. More disturbing would be the notion that the offender's guilt (or innocence) is based on the same narrative constructs devised by dramatic representations. In reality, the truth is most often more nuanced.

There are two types of influence that are considered within the purview of the 'CSI effect': (1) media reporting factual accounts of crime within news outlets (printed press, television, social media, internet news sources) and (2) fictional representations of crime through creative sources such as novels, television dramas and motion picture films. Both popular culture sources, factual or fictional, are carefully constructed within a narrative framework so the consumers of the material (including the news) may engage, understand and sympathize with the characters and ultimately be entertained. Entertainment is the primary objective of popular culture artefacts. The intention of both sources (news and fiction) is to replicate life and the consequences of crime and to resonate with the audience. The difficulty some members of the general public may find in separating the depiction of real life from reality gives rise to the concept of the 'CSI effect' and its possible disruptive influence on the criminal justice system.

The creation of the detective

The vocation of detective coalesced during the nineteenth century and quickly became a functioning part of professionalizing police organizations. This occurred around the same time the iconic fictional detective figures became idolized within popular culture. Shpayer-Makov (2011, 2) suggests within England 'the figure of the detective embodied characteristics that caught the imagination of the public from the top of the social pyramid all the way down ... By the First World War, the English detective, whether official or private, stood out as a central figure in the gallery of English archetypes. The fame of Scotland Yard transcended national boundaries and reached the far corners of the world, maintaining this special status to this day'. Further, 'it is difficult to differentiate between their authentic life and what was written about them at the time, as their public image became an integral part of their history' (Shpayer-Makov 2011, 1–2).

Poe and Dickens are generally viewed as 'the principal inventors of the "permanently popular" literature of detection for their respective countries' (Thomas 1999, 40). Poe's 'The Murders in the Rue Morgue', generally considered the advent of detective fiction, was published in 1841, and the first English detective story is dated to 1849 (Summerscale 2008). Dickens's *Bleak House* appeared in 1853, and Wilkie Collins's *Woman in White* in 1859. Detective fiction was 'sometimes anticipating the actual technologies being developed by forensic science, sometimes appropriating or popularizing them' (Thomas 1999, 288). The rise of detective fiction provoked anxiety. In the early twentieth century, there were widespread concerns that detective fiction had pernicious effects on the reading public: 'As early as 1894, newspapers reported that detective fiction has real effects ("Every Man His Own Holmes", *New York Times* 1894).

Headlines such as "Sherlock Holmes Annoys Paris Police: Vogue of the Stage Detective Leads to Criticism of City's Criminal Hunters" (*New York Times* 1908) illustrate particular anxieties about the translation of and difference between the real and the representational' (Littlefield 2011).

These anxieties, of course, anticipated the vaunted CSI effect that so many imagine to be a peculiar attribute of our own age. To the contrary, Littlefield (2011, 141–142) argues,

> While there was not a singular term (as with the 'CSI Effect') to describe and encapsulate anxieties about fictional representations of police work, news stories were rife with criticism about the detectives of stage, screen, and page. Indeed, there was a general trend in major American papers (the *New York Times* and the *Chicago Daily Tribune*) between 1894 and 1935 to enumerate and describe the influence of fictional representations of detective work on the opinions of average citizens. These anxious discourses can be broken into four categories: concern about audience gullibility, distrust of spectacular fiction, apprehension about the public's heightened expectations of scientific detective work, and fears about the education of criminals.

This shows 'that the question of distillation—is CSI representing real forensic science?—dates back at least an entire century to scientific detective fiction' (Littlefield 2011, 146).

Television

With the advent of mass visual media—television—new opportunities emerged for popular culture to reflect criminal investigation and legal process. Crime shows made up one-third of prime-time television programming by 1960. From that date through the 1990s, crime shows averaged around one-fourth of prime-time television programming, with the peak being 40 percent in 1975. 'Overall, the proportion of television time devoted to crime and violence makes crime the largest single subject matter on television, with crime themes found across all types of programming' (Surette 1998, 35–36). In the 1960s, the popular television serial *Perry Mason* depicted a heroic defence lawyer who routinely proved criminal defendants innocent at the dramatic denouements of criminal trials. 'The Perry Mason syndrome', the supposed effect that this skewed portrayal of the American criminal justice system might have had on the American public's perception of the American criminal justice system, generated some modest comment (Mann 2006). More directly related to the issue of science and technology was the 1970s programme *Quincy, M.E.*, in which a medical examiner solved crimes using scientific evidence. But these programmes did not provoke the sort of media frenzy that would be generated three and four decades later under the label 'CSI effect'.

CSI

The police procedural drama became perhaps the most dependable formula for television drama. The solving—and, in some cases, adjudication—of crime provided endless dramatic storylines. Seemingly limitless variations on the theme were possible by varying the characters, the setting or the overall ambiance of the programmes—gritty or funny; glamorous or 'realistic'; and so on.

However, with the limited exception of *Quincy*, one variation that had enjoyed little success involved placing science, rather than the less scientific aspects of policing—questioning witnesses, interrogating suspects, chasing people and other 'action'—at the centre of the programme. This changed in 2000, with the nearly simultaneous development of *Waking the Dead* in the United Kingdom and *CSI* in the United States. These programmes made science the driver of the investigation; the more traditional police investigative techniques were pushed to the background. The forensic technicians moved from supporting to leading roles. To serve the needs of television entertainment, the programmes fudged things substantially by allowing their scientist protagonists also to engage in traditional police activities such as interrogating witnesses and suspects, chasing down perpetrators and using firearms, which is usually denied their real-life counterparts. But the shows, especially *CSI*, were driven by and promulgated the slogan 'people lie', but science offers only truth (Nolan 2007).

Over the next several years, *CSI* enjoyed remarkable success. One sign of success was its generation of two spin-off programmes, *CSI: Miami* and *CSI: New York*. Another was its success in the international market, driven by its glamorous American locations and production values (Horan 2007; Knox 2007). Yet another was its success in the rerun market, driven by its capsulated structure, with minimal character story arcs, so that any episode could easily be viewed alone and out of order. There was a period in the first decade of the twenty-first century in which it seemed like viewers with broadband television access (such as cable or satellite) could watch *CSI* at any time of the day or night. Still another measure of success was the number of imitators it spawned, as competitor networks sought to compete with *CSI*'s success—*Without a Trace*, *Numb3rs*, *Criminal Minds*, *N.C.I.S.: Naval Criminal Investigative Service*, *The Closer*, *Crossing Jordan*, *Bones*, and *The Evidence*. Finally, there were the ratings. The original *CSI* was for a time the most popular series on US television, and it was in the top ten for eleven years. *CSI* was named the most watched show in the world five times. At the height of their popularity, all three *CSI* franchises were in the top twenty US programmes.

Twenty-first-century forensic science

Why did this happen? Again, reflecting 'real-life', surely actual developments in forensic science played a role. Forensic science made a number of important developments during the couple of decades preceding the advent of *CSI* that may have fostered the view among television producers that forensic science was increasingly important in police work. These developments included new technologies and gadgets for detecting and visualizing trace evidence. The development of forensic DNA profiling, a forensic technique of perhaps unprecedented power, captured the public imagination through events like the O.J. Simpson trial and the exposure of wrongful convictions by the Innocence Project (Aronson 2007; Lynch et al. 2008; Kaye 2010). But, while less glamorous than DNA profiling, the most important developments probably lay in computing. The ability to compile and search databases consisting of DNA profiles, fingerprints and toolmark images presented significant changes in forensic science. Computing also heralded countless other less noticeable changes, such as increased ability to visualize evidence and the introduction of information management systems.

In short, the vision of policing promulgated by *CSI* and its ilk, though undoubtedly exaggerated, romanticized, fantastic and even downright absurd, was not fabricated without some source of inspiration. It was an attempt, however risible, to reflect the creators' perception of actual developments occurring in authentic police work.

It is worth noting, of course, that this perception may well have been quite off. Criminologists have generally found that forensic services are grossly underused in police investigations. This was the case in some early investigations in the 1980s (Ericson 1981). But, perhaps more surprisingly, it remained the case after the advent of forensic DNA profiling and computerization. While there is great variation among countries, jurisdictions, agencies and individuals, generally, criminologists have found that police perceived forensic science as a tool for bolstering solved cases, rather than solving them (Innes 2003; Pratt et al. 2006; Strom and Hickman 2010).

The CSI Effect

There is some evidence that prosecutors, specifically the National District Attorneys Association, sometime around 2002 began advocating the idea of treating *CSI* as a rhetorical resource for prosecutors due to its positive portrayal of state witnesses. However, within a short period of time, this original message got turned on its head. By the time the first media mention of a CSI effect appeared in the press in *Time* in 2002, the message was that *CSI* was damaging to prosecutors. Rather than being benefited by the positive media portrayal of their expert witnesses, prosecutors were quoted saying that *CSI* hampered them by 'raising expectations' for forensic evidence. Thus was begat the CSI effect, a fundamentally counterintuitive claim that the popularity of a television programme depicting state witnesses as dedicated, honest, truthful, intelligent and even glamorous benefited not the prosecutors who proffered their testimony but the defendants against whom their testimony was proffered. Why? The claim was that *CSI* perpetuated the notion that forensic science was enormously powerful and widely available and that most, if not all, criminal investigations could benefit from forensic analyses. This popular belief, it was claimed, would lead jurors and perhaps victims to be surprised, or even disappointed, if forensic evidence was not presented in a criminal case. It might make them reluctant to convict on circumstantial evidence alone, supposedly desiring the purportedly stronger proof that could be derived from forensic evidence. Thus, *CSI* supposedly harmed, rather than helped, prosecutors' chances of conviction. From the media's point of view, this new hypothesis was presumably more interesting than the intuitive one: man bites dog, rather than dog bites man.

To be sure, there were other voices that spoke to the media and tried to posit different 'effects' of the popularity of *CSI*. Defence attorneys did attempt to argue that *CSI*'s positive portrayal of forensic scientists should be expected to bolster their credibility in front of lay juries. And the producers of *CSI*, presumably defensive about the implicit claim that their creation was helping to set criminals free, began positing the claim that the real 'effect' of *CSI* was 'educational'. But, measured in sheer numbers, the prosecutors' message was by far the most prevalent (Harvey and Derksen 2009; Cole and Dioso-Villa 2009; Cole 2015).

Indeed, the term 'CSI effect' turned out to be highly resonant, suitable for appropriation by a variety of different constituencies. Everyone, it seemed, perceived a CSI effect and was happy to tell the media about it. The media was happy to comply, it has been suggested, because CSI effect stories were easy and cheap to 'localize' with a visit to the local crime laboratory and an interview with someone there, or an interview with a prosecutor and perhaps another legal professional. This was an important strategy during a period of crisis in the traditional news media due to the disruptive influence of new technology.

CSI and its effects

The various CSI 'effects' reported in the media, however, were wildly inconsistent. An effort to bring some sort of order to all these competing CSI effects resulted in classifying seven different CSI effects (Cole and Dioso-Villa 2007).

The perhaps canonical effect, the 'strong prosecutor's effect', is the claim that television programming is altering juror behaviour. Specifically, it is frequently claimed that *CSI* has increased juror expectations for forensic evidence in criminal trials. Because of *CSI*, jurors supposedly expect to see forensic evidence more often and expect it to be more probative. This, in turn, could lead to acquittals in cases where forensic evidence is absent or insufficiently probative. In other words, it is suggested that jurors are acquitting in cases lacking forensic evidence in which they would have convicted but for the creation of *CSI* and similar television programmes.

Many prosecutors also made a weaker claim, the 'weak prosecutor's effect'. This claim posited that *CSI* has altered prosecutor, not juror, behaviour. Claimed changes in prosecutorial behaviour include questioning potential jurors about their television viewing habits in *voir dire*, presenting 'negative evidence' testimony, discussing *CSI* in summations and requesting legally unnecessary forensic tests (Jenkins and Schuller 2007).

Some defence attorneys advance an opposite effect, the 'defendant's effect' (Godsey and Alou 2011). The claim is that *CSI* and similar television programming, through their positive and heroic portrayals of state-employed forensic scientists, enhance the perceived credibility of the government's forensic witnesses, thus advantaging the prosecution.

The producers of *CSI*, in rebutting charges that their product is contaminating the criminal justice system, appropriated the term 'CSI effect' and reinterpreted it as an educational effect on the general public. The 'producer's effect' holds that *CSI* teaches science to the American viewing public.

The 'educator's effect', in contrast, claims that *CSI* is attracting young people into careers in forensic science. Some media sources posit the 'police chief's effect'. This claim holds that *CSI* has educated criminals on how to avoid detection. Examples of the supposed police chief's effect include wearing gloves and dousing crime scenes with bleach. The victim's effect concerns the supposed effect of *CSI* programs on crime victims' behaviour. The claim is that victims have increased expectations that law enforcement will collect forensic evidence at a crime scene.

Others reinterpreted the CSI effect as the 'tech effect' (Shelton et al. 2006). They suggest that any apparent changes in juror behaviour should be attributed to real technological developments rather than to television programming's depiction of fantasized forensic techniques.

Although the media coverage portrays the CSI effect as a well-documented phenomenon, actual evidence of the various effects is difficult to come by. Media accounts rely largely on anecdotes and conclusory statements by various criminal justice system actors. Little reference is made to empirical data, and when such references are made, they usually note the absence of such data. A review of the socio-legal literature reveals a rather different picture. Most legal scholars characterize claims of the most commonly discussed CSI effect—the strong prosecutor's effect that would lead to wrongful acquittals—as speculative, and many suggest that the defendant's effect is equally plausible, even if mentioned less often by the media (Podlas 2006; Tyler 2006).

What was the CSI effect?

The *CSI* series has ceased production, albeit reruns remain in circulation, and discussion of the CSI effect appears to be waning (Cole 2015). What, then, was the CSI effect? Many different interpretations have been offered. One is that it simply represented a form of 'sour grapes' by attorneys, either disenchanted with the trial system generally or seeking to explain the outcome of a specific trial (Tyler 2006). More sweepingly, it has been argued that the CSI effect represents a concerted attack on the jury system altogether (Cole and Dioso-Villa 2009; Landry 2009). Still another explanation is that the anxious discussion about the CSI effect reflects law's anxiety about the growing power of science to resolve factual disputes (Cole and Dioso-Villa 2007; Machado and Santos 2011). Yet another is that the CSI effect represents an assertion of hegemony, by the media and its expert informants, over both the 'reality' of forensic science and the reality of the CSI effect itself (Landry 2009; Cole 2015). Others suggest that the CSI effect represents a 'media panic' (Tyler 2006; Cole and Dioso-Villa 2007; Okita 2007; Harvey and Derksen 2009). Note that the CSI effect itself is yet another turn in the cyclical relationship between the criminal justice system and the media. The CSI effect is a discourse about the pernicious effects of popular media on the criminal justice system. And yet, this discourse is itself primarily disseminated by the popular media. It may be suggested, therefore, that the CSI effect is an effort by media to sell still more media—in the form of stories about the pernicious effects of media! Moreover, still more turns of the cycle may be expected. For example, the very claim that there is a CSI effect and that it is 'real' may itself affect the behaviour of legal actors—such as judges being asked to rule on a motion to give a jury instruction to 'cure' the CSI effect. Thus, another interpretation of CSI effect discourse is that it simply represents efforts by legal adversaries to 'game' their trials by perpetuating the notion that their side is structurally disadvantaged in the trial process (Cole and Dioso-Villa 2007; Mopas 2007). In this sense, the CSI effect is only one illustration of the cyclical relationship between the criminal justice system and media, broadly constructed, a relationship which consists of 'art imitating life imitating art imitating life' (Risinger 2006, 2), potentially ad infinitum.

Much of the scholarly literature on the CSI effect can be assigned to one of four general approaches. One approach analyses the programme *CSI* and its spinoffs and imitators from the perspective of various disciplines including literary studies, visual studies, cultural studies, communication, anthropology, cultural criminology and so on (Allen 2007; Nolan 2007; Bonnycastle 2009; Dobson 2009; Glynn and Kim 2009; Hohenstein 2009; Turkel 2009). For example, Gever (2005) documents the idealized image of science found on *CSI*. Valverde (2006) also notes that *CSI* perpetuates the valorization of forensic evidence and the notion that it requires no interpretation. Kruse (2010) adds that forensic evidence on *CSI* is depicted as definitive, not susceptible to probabilistic reasoning. Based on an analysis of *CSI*'s first season, Cavender and Deutsch argue, '*CSI* combines the traditions of the crime genre with a new forensic realism to fuse the police and science with a convergent moral authority' (Cavender and Deutsch 2007, 68). And, based on an analysis of *CSI* episodes, Ley et al. (2012) argue that its portrayal of forensic DNA profiling supports an idealized perception of that technique.

A second approach repeats, in more sophisticated but often no less hyperbolic terms, the social problems claims about the CSI effect already made by media. For example, Durnal (2010) argues, 'The CSI effect is very real', based largely on anecdotes and surveys of legal actors. Similarly, Lawson (2009), apparently finding the term 'effect' too tame, refers to the 'CSI infection'.

A third approach is to empirically test the 'reality' of the CSI effect as a social problem. The theoretical foundation for such approaches was laid by Tyler (2006) for psychology and Podlas (2006) for communications. One methodological approach is to survey social groups involved in the criminal justice system. For example, Watkins (2004) surveyed attorneys. Thomas (2005, 2006), a county attorney, surveyed his own prosecutors. Robbers (2008) surveyed trial attorneys and judges. Stevens (2008, 2011) surveyed prosecutors. Hughes and Magers (2007) surveyed judges. Smith et al. (2008, 2011) surveyed legal professionals. Huey (2010) interviewed police officers. Prainsack and Kitzberger (2009) interviewed Austrian convicts. This study was replicated in Portugal, and the comparative results published as a book (Machado and Painsack 2012). Weaver et al. (2012) interviewed forensic science students. The potential actions of courts in response to a perception of the CSI effect were reviewed by Cole and Dioso-Villa (2011) and, in greater depth, by Feeler (2014).

Many others reported surveys of jurors or potential jurors. Podlas (2006) surveyed 306 college students and asked them to reach a verdict of guilty or not guilty, where the expected or 'legally correct' verdict for the case was not guilty. Podlas compared students who regularly watched forensic television programmes with those who did not and found that there were no significant differences in their decision-making processes or the handing down of 'not guilty' verdicts. The survey results did not indicate any increased expectation of forensic evidence by *CSI* viewers compared to non-*CSI* viewers (Podlas 2006). Shelton et al. (2006) administered a survey to 1,027 individuals called to jury duty in a county in southeast Michigan, USA. In both this study and a follow-up study of another county, they found increased expectations of forensic evidence, but that these expectations were not caused by *CSI* viewing. Rather, the authors suggest that the increased expectations of forensic evidence may reflect broader popular awareness of technological advances. Instead of a CSI effect, they posited a general 'tech effect' experienced by everyone (Shelton et al. 2009). Okita (2007) surveyed more than 1,200 Canadians about their attitudes toward forensic science. Like Shelton et al., Okita found that *CSI* viewers and non-viewers did not differ significantly in their perceptions of the accuracy and necessity of forensic science for investigating crimes. Indeed, in some cases non-viewers perceived forensic science to be more accurate than viewers did. However, Okita noted that even the differences between viewers and non-viewers that she did find were so small that they were unlikely to be operationalized, say, by producing different verdicts. In a series of studies, Smith et al. (2008) found evidence of changes in legal professionals' behaviour (the weak prosecutor's effect), and found evidence suggestive of the defendant's effect. But they found little evidence supporting the strong prosecutor's effect. Holmgren and Fordham (2011) analysed surveys of Canadian college students and Australian jurors. While they found that *CSI* did seem to influence perceptions of forensic evidence, they found no support for the claim that this influence alters jury verdicts. Wise (2009–2010) interviewed Australian police, forensic scientists and legal actors about how they changed their behaviour in response to *CSI*. Brewer and Ley (2010) surveyed potential jurors in the Milwaukee, Wisconsin area and found that television viewing increased viewers' perception of the power of forensic DNA evidence. However, they found no support for the claim that these individuals would produce biased jury verdicts. Baskin and Sommers's (2010) juror survey found support for both the strong prosecutor's and defendant's effects. Chan (2013) surveyed potential jurors in Malaysia and found support for the defendant's effect and the producer's effect.

Still others conducted jury simulations on college students (Reardon and O'Neil 2008; Smith et al. 2008). Podlas's second study included 538 mock jurors who deliberated in small groups about two crime scenarios where forensic evidence was neither necessary nor referenced. Podlas tested for the strong prosecutor's effect as measured by not guilty verdicts or wrongful acquittals for each scenario. She found no indication that *CSI*-viewing jurors acquitted in cases that warranted convictions, nor did she find that *CSI* viewers relied on forensic evidence to a greater degree than their non-*CSI* viewing counterparts (Podlas 2006–2007). Schweitzer and Saks (2007) tested 48 college students for both the strong prosecutor's effect and the defendant's effect. They found indirect evidence of an increased expectation of high-tech forensic science perhaps consistent with *CSI*'s depictions of forensic techniques, and a tendency to find less high-tech or glamorous techniques less convincing. Maeder and Corbett (2015) had similar findings. Likewise, in a study of 140 college students, Jenkins et al. (2008) found *CSI* viewers more sensitive to possible flaws in a forensic assay that was discussed in a mock trial transcript.

Some have sought to measure acquittal rates in trials (Loeffler 2006; Owens 2010). Loeffler (2006) found no evidence of an increase in acquittals after examining the acquittal rate of four large states. Cole and Dioso-Villa (2007) examined data on the jury acquittal rate in federal courts and found no discernible increase in acquittal rates following the advent of *CSI*. Looking at Canadian data, Dupont (2007) also found no discernible increase in acquittals that was attributable to *CSI*. Cole and Dioso-Villa (2009) compiled acquittal rates for all jury verdicts from the felony trial courts of eight states and the federal district courts. Linear regressions of acquittal rates before and after 2000, after the first airing of *CSI*, showed no statistically significant difference.

A fourth approach is to engage in critical scholarship that questions the claims promulgated by media and seeks to explore and explain how and why a discourse about a supposed CSI effect has arisen in the first place. Mopas argues, 'various actors are mobilizing the representations of forensics found on the show for different purposes' (Mopas, 2007, 111). Cole and Dioso-Villa

(2007) suggested that the CSI effect represented legal anxiety about the persuasive power of scientific evidence. In a subsequent analysis, they argued that the CSI effect represented a criminal law version of 'litigation anxiety' in civil law—the claim that the American courts were beset by an epidemic of over litigation (Cole and Dioso-Villa 2009). Similarly, Landry (2009) argues that CSI effect discourse represents a scapegoating of jurors and the jury system. Harvey and Derksen (2009, 21) argue 'that the media have turned the persistent effects of television on popular culture into a catchy phrase that encapsulates the latest installment of the public's long-term fascination with crime and mystery genres'. Cole (2015) argues that the CSI effect represents an assertion of hegemony by the media and its expert informants over both the 'reality' of forensic science and the reality of the CSI effect itself. In yet a further turn of the cyclical relationship, Machado and Santos's (2011) case study of Portuguese missing children cases explored the effect of CSI effect discourse on the press itself.

Conclusion

The proliferation and popularization of fictional crime television programmes like *CSI* has significantly impacted television audiences over the last decade. In particular, *CSI* syndication has been highly successful, and it offered a novel approach to the genre of detective fiction by making the protagonist the scientist rather than the police detective. This format, while retaining a highly moralistic narrative of good versus evil, depicted crime-solving as driven by a highly idealized notion of science as absolute truth. Claims about the disruptive nature of the CSI effect on the criminal justice system, however, are not well supported by research.

There may, however, be other impacts of media technology and the application of popular culture methods of visual communication—not generally discussed under the auspices of the term 'CSI effect'—that could disrupt or influence methods of presenting evidence within the criminal justice system. The telling of stories or presenting narratives through visual means has significantly increased in contemporary society (Porter 2007; Porter and Kennedy 2012; Porter 2013). Media and popular culture formats expose audiences to sophisticated visual narrative forms that can be compelling forms of communication. Regular exposure to visual forms of communication, in particular visual narrative structures, may have raised the confidence levels of legal actors engaging with visual material. However, any confidence in visual literacy skills is based on a visual narrative form that is constructed by the media or popular culture media material that has an agenda of entertainment with a low threshold for truth-telling. The difference in concepts of truth between the criminal justice system and the media are obvious. This mismatch becomes problematic when witnesses provide the criminal justice system with evidence that is generated from visual sources (i.e., closed-circuit television [CCTV]) (Porter 2009). Witnesses, including experts, may be overconfident in their ability to interpret visual evidence sourced from various media technology. Understanding visual evidence limitations and advantages requires a more rigorous and informed knowledge of visual culture rather than a reliance on lay experience with media and popular culture material (Porter 2007). The difficultly lies in understanding their limitations regarding visual literacy skills and knowledge.

This issue stems from the constant exposure to visual narrative forms produced by the media and popular culture industry. This is not the same as the CSI effect per se, but nevertheless is influenced by and allied with popular culture and modern forms of visual communication. Several Australian cases have highlighted the mismatch between experts' level of confidence when examining visual material and the empirical foundation of their analyses. Edmond and Wortley (2016) provide a comprehensive survey of cases involving anatomists in England and Australia identifying suspects from CCTV sources. Often a low standard of proof is exposed in cases in which anatomists provide identification evidence using low-quality visual sourced material (Edmond et al. 2009; Edmond et al. 2010). Porter (2012) also discusses experts interpreting visual evidence from crime scene photographs in an Australian coronial case. The Romuald Zak inquest in Western Australian Coroners Court (2007) witnessed several experts from disciplines such as anatomy, pathology and entomology providing evidence of questionable reliability based on their examination of crime scene photographs and not the physical evidence.

Perhaps the greater concern regarding how evidence is portrayed within the criminal justice system is not the supposed dangers commonly associated with the CSI effect but rather the presentation of visual evidence within a popular culture paradigm. Often visual media are synthesized within a constructed visual narrative to present both forms of visual material as a single, connected narrative, as when CCTV footage of an incident is combined with the arrest photograph of the accused. This practice places significant stress on the burden of proof and other evidential principles.

References

Allen, M., ed. 2007. *Reading CSI: Crime TV under the Microscope*. London: I.B. Tauris.

Aronson, J.D. 2007. *Genetic Witness: Science, Law, and Controversy in the Making of DNA Profiling*. New Brunswick, NJ: Rutgers University Press.

Baskin, D.R., and I.B. Sommers. 2010. 'Crime-Show-Viewing Habits and Public Attitudes toward Forensic Evidence: The "CSI Effect" Revisited'. *Justice System Journal* 31(1): 97–113.

Bonnycastle, K.D. 2009. 'Not the Usual Suspects: The Obfuscation of Political Economy and Race in *CSI*'. In M. Byers and V.M. Johnson, eds., *The CSI Effect: Television, Crime, and Governance*, 149–176. Lanham, MD: Lexington.

Brewer, P., and B. Ley. 2010. 'Media Use and Public Perceptions of DNA Evidence'. *Science Communication* 32(1): 93–117.

Cavender, G., and S.K. Deutsch. 2007. 'CSI and Moral Authority: The Police and Science'. *Crime Media Culture* 3(1): 67–81.

Chan, K.-W. 2013. 'An Investigation into the CSI effect on the Malaysian Population'. *Australian Journal of Forensic Sciences* 45(4): 417–430.

Chinn, S.E. 2000. *Technology and the Logic of American Racism*. London: Continuum.

Cole, S.A. 2007. 'Twins, Twain, Galton and Gilman: Fingerprinting, Individualization, Brotherhood and Race in Pudd'nhead Wilson'. *Configurations* 15(3): 227–265.

Cole, S.A. 2015. 'A Surfeit of Science. The "CSI Effect" and the Media Appropriation of the Public Understanding of Science'. *Public Understanding of Science* 24(2): 130–146.

Cole, S.A., and R. Dioso-Villa. 2007. 'CSI and Its Effects: Media, Juries, and the Burden of Proof'. *New England Law Review* 41(3): 435–469.

Cole, S.A., and R. Dioso-Villa. 2009. 'Investigating the "CSI Effect" Effect: Media and Litigation Crisis in Criminal Law'. *Stanford Law Review* 61(6): 1335–1373.

Cole, S.A., and R. Dioso-Villa. 2011. 'Should Judges Worry about the "CSI Effect"'? *Court Review* 47(1–2): 20–31.

Crowther, M.A., and B. White. 1988. *On Soul and Conscience: The Medical Expert and Crime*. Aberdeen: Aberdeen University Press.

Dobson, N. 2009. 'Generic Difference and Innovation in *CSI*: Crime Scene Investigation'. In M. Byers and V.M. Johnson, eds., *The CSI Effect: Television, Crime, and Governance*, 75–89. Lanham, MD: Lexington.

Dupont, B. 2007. 'The CSI Effect: Myths and Reality'. Paper presented at the 29th Annual Conference of the Canadian Identification Association, Montreal.

Durnal, E.W. 2010. 'Crime Scene Investigation (As Seen on TV)'. *Forensic Science International* 199(1–3): 1–5.

Edmond G., K. Biber, R. Kemp and G. Porter. 2009. 'Laws Looking Glass: Expert Identification Evidence Derived from Photographic and Video Images'. *Current Issues in Criminal Justice* 20(3): 337–377.

Edmond, G., R. Kemp, G. Porter, D. Hamer, M. Burton, K. Biber and M. San Roque. 2010. 'Atkins v The Emperor: The "Cautious" use of Unreliable "Expert" Opinion'. *International Journal of Evidence & Proof* 14 (2): 146–165.

Edmond, G., and N. Wortley. 2016. 'Interpreting Image Evidence: Facial Mapping, Police Familiars and Super-Recognisers in England and Australia'. *Journal of International and Comparative Law* 3(2): 473–522.

Ericson, R.V. 1981. *Making Crime: A Study of Detective Work*. Toronto: Butterworths.

Federal Bureau of Investigation. 1991. 'The Identification Division of the FBI: A Brief Outline of the History, Services, and Operating Techniques of the World's Largest Repository of Fingerprints'. Washington, DC: Federal Bureau of Investigation.

Feeler, W. 2014. 'Can Fiction Impede Conviction? Addressing Claims of a "CSI Effect" in the Criminal Courtroom'. *Mississippi Law Journal* 83(1): 1–57.

Gever, M. 2005. 'The Spectacle of Crime, Digitized: *CSI: Crime Scene Investigation* and Social Anatomy'. *European Journal of Cultural Studies* 8(4): 445–463.

Glynn, B., and J. Kim. 2009. 'Corpses, Spectacle, Illusion: The Body as *Abject* and *Object* in *CSI*'. In M. Byers and V.M. Johnson, eds., *The CSI Effect: Television, Crime, and Governance*, 93–110. Lanham, MD: Lexington.

Godsey, M.A., and M. Alou. 2011. 'She Blinded Me with Science: Wrongful Convictions and the "Reverse CSI-Effect"'. *Texas Wesleyan Law Review* 17(4): 481–497.

Harvey, L., and L. Derksen. 2009. 'Science Fiction or Social Fact? An Exploratory Content Analysis of Popular Press Reports on the CSI Effect'. In M. Byers and V.M. Johnson, eds., *The CSI Effect: Television, Crime, and Governance*, 3–28. Lanham, MD: Lexington.

Hohenstein, K. 2009. '*CSI* and *Law & Order:* Dueling Representations of Science and Law in the Criminal Justice System'. In M. Byers and V.M. Johnson, eds., *The CSI Effect: Television, Crime, and Governance*, 61–74. Lanham, MD: Lexington.

Holmgren, J., and J. Fordham. 2011. 'The CSI Effect and the Canadian and the Australian Jury'. *Journal of Forensic Sciences* 56(S1): S63–S71.

Horan, D. 2007. 'RTÉ and the *CSI* Franchise'. In M. Allen, ed., *Reading CSI: Crime TV under the Microscope*, 198–200. London: I.B. Tauris.

Huey, L. 2010. 'I've Seen this on *CSI*': Criminal Investigators' Perceptions about the Management of Public Expectations in the Field'. *Crime, Media, Culture* 6(1): 49–68.

Hughes, T., and M. Magers. 2007. 'The Perceived Impact of Crime Scene Investigation Shows on the Administration of Justice'. *Journal of Criminal Justice and Popular Culture* 14(3): 259–276.

Innes, M. 2003. *Investigating Murder: Detective Work and the Police Response to Criminal Homicide*. Oxford: Oxford University Press.

Jenkins, G., C. Do, K. Movshovich and R. Schuller. 2008. 'The CSI Effect: Mock Jurors' Sensitivity to the Reliability of Forensic Evidence'. Address at the Annual Meeting of the American Psychology–Law Society, Jacksonville, Florida.

Jenkins, G., and R. Schuller. 2007. 'The Impact of Negative Forensic Evidence on Mock Jurors' Perceptions of a Trial of Drug-Facilitated Sexual Assault'. *Law and Human Behavior* 31(4): 369–379.

Kaye, D.H. 2010. *The Double Helix and the Law of Evidence*. Cambridge: Harvard University Press.

Knox, S. 2007. 'Five's Finest: The Import of *CSI* to British Television'. In M. Allen, ed., *Reading CSI: Crime TV under the Microscope*, 183–197. London: I.B. Tauris.

Kruse, C. 2010. 'Producing Absolute Truth: *CSI* Science as Wishful Thinking'. *American Anthropologist* 112(1): 79–91.

Landry, D. 2009. 'Faux Science and the Social Construction of a Risk Society: A Burkean Engagement with the CSI Debates'. *Journal of the Institute of Justice and International Studies* 9: 145–156.

Lawson, T.F. 2009. 'Before the Verdict and beyond the Verdict: The *CSI* Infection within Modern Criminal Jury Trials'. *Loyola University of Chicago Law Journal* 41: 119–173.

Ley, B., N. Jankowski and P. Brewer, P. 2012. 'Investigating *CSI*: Portrayals of DNA Testing on a Forensic Crime Show and Their Potential Effects'. *Public Understanding of Science* 21(1): 51–67.

Littlefield, M.M. 2011. 'Historicizing CSI and Its Effect(s): The Real and the Representational in American Scientific Detective Fiction and Print News Media, 1902–1935'. *Crime, Media, Culture* 7(2): 133–148.

Loeffler, C. 2006. '"CSI" and the Criminal Justice System: Jury Trials'. *New Republic*. June 7.

Lynch, M., S.A. Cole, R. McNally and K. Jordan. 2008. *Truth Machine: The Contentious History of DNA Fingerprinting*. Chicago: University of Chicago Press.

Machado, H., and B. Prainsack. 2012. *Tracing Technologies: Prisoners' Views in the Era of CSI*. Farnham: Ashgate.

Machado, H., and F. Santos. 2011. 'Popular Press and Forensic Genetics in Portugal: Expectations and Disappointments Regarding Two Cases of Missing Children'. *Public Understanding of Science* 20(3): 303–318.

Maeder, E.M., and R. Corbett. 2015. 'Beyond Frequency: Perceived Realism and the CSI Effect'. *Canadian Journal of Criminology and Criminal Justice* 57(1): 83–114.

Mann, M. 2005/2006. 'The "CSI Effect": Better Jurors through Television and Science?' *Buffalo Public Interest Law Journal* 24: 211–237.

Mnookin, J.L. 2001. 'Fingerprint Evidence in an Age of DNA Profiling'. *Brooklyn Law Review* 67(1): 13–70.

Mopas, M. 2007. 'Examining the "CSI Effect" through an ANT Lens'. *Crime, Media, Culture* 3(1): 110–117.

Nolan, T.W. 2007. 'Depiction of the "CSI Effect" in Popular Culture: Portrait in Domination and Effective Affectation'. *New England Law Review* 41: 575–589.

Okita, K. 2007. 'The CSI Effect: Examining CSI's Effects upon Public Perceptions of Forensic Science'. MA thesis, University of Alberta.

Owens, E.G. 2010. 'Media and the Criminal Justice System'. http://dx.doi.org/10.2139/ssrn.1632396.

Podlas, K. 2006. '"The CSI Effect": Exposing the Media Myth'. *Fordham Intellectual Property, Media and Entertainment Law Journal* 16: 429–465.

Podlas, K. (2006–2007). 'The "CSI Effect" and Other Forensic Fictions'. *Loyola of Los Angeles Entertainment Law Review* 27: 87–125.

Porter G. 2007. 'Visual Culture in Forensic Science'. *Australian Journal of Forensic Sciences* 39(2): 81–91.

Porter G. 2009. 'CCTV Images as Evidence'. *Australian Journal of Forensic Sciences* 41(1): 11–25.

Porter G. 2012. 'Zak Coronial Inquest and the Interpretation of Photographic Evidence'. *Current Issues in Criminal Justice* 24(1): 39–49.

Porter G. 2013. 'Images as Evidence'. *Precedent* 119 (Nov/Dec): 38–42.

Porter G., and M. Kennedy. 2012. 'Photographic Truth and Evidence'. *Australian Journal of Forensic Sciences* 44(2): 183–192.

Prainsack, B., and M. Kitzberger. 2009. 'DNA behind Bars: Other Ways of Knowing Forensic DNA Technologies'. *Social Studies of Science* 39(1): 51–79.

Pratt, T.C., M.J. Gaffney, N.P. Lovrich and C.L. Johnson. 2006. 'This Isn't "CSI": Estimating the National Backlog of Forensic DNA Cases and the Barriers Associated with Case Processing'. *Criminal Justice Policy Review* 17(1): 32–47.

Reardon, M., and K. O'Neil. 2008. 'The "CSI Effect": Individual Differences'. Paper presented at the American Psychology-Law Society, Jacksonville, Florida.

Risinger, D.M. 2006. 'Boxes in Boxes: Julian Barnes, Conan Doyle, Sherlock Holmes and the Edalji Case'. *International Commentary on Evidence* 4(2): 1–90.

Robbers, M.L.P. 2008. 'Blinded by Science: The Social Construction of Reality in Forensic Television Shows and Its Effect on Criminal Jury Trials'. *Criminal Justice Policy Review* 19(1): 84–102.

Schweitzer, N.J., and M.J. Saks. 2007. 'The CSI Effect: Popular Fiction about Forensic Science Affects the Public's Expectations about Real Forensic Science'. *Jurimetrics* 47(3): 357–364.

Shelton, D.E., Y.S. Kim and G. Barak. 2006. 'A Study of Juror Expectations and Demands Concerning Scientific Evidence: Does the "CSI Effect" Exist?' *Vanderbilt Journal of Entertainment and Technology Law* 9: 331–368.

Shelton, D.E., Y.S. Kim and G. Barak. 2009. 'An Indirect-Effects Model of Mediated Adjudication: The CSI Myth, the Tech Effect, and Metropolitan Jurors' Expectations for Scientific Evidence'. *Vanderbilt Journal of Entertainment and Technology Law* 12: 1–43.

Shpayer-Makov, H. 2011. *The Ascent of the Detective: Police Sleuths in Victorian and Edwardian England.* Oxford: Oxford University Press.

Smith, S.M., M.W. Patry and V. Stinson. 2008. 'Exploring the CSI Effect: Is It Real? If so, What Is It?' Paper presented at the North American Correctional and Criminal Justice Psychology Conference, Ottawa.

Smith, S.M., V. Stinson and M.W. Patry. 2011. 'Fact or Fiction? The Myth and Reality of the CSI Effect'. *Court Review* 47(1–2): 4–7.

Stevens, D.J. 2008. 'Forensic Science, Wrongful Convictions, and American Prosecutor Discretion'. *Howard Journal* 47(1): 31–51.

Stevens, D.J. 2011. *Media and Criminal Justice: The CSI Effect.* Burlington, MA: Jones & Bartlett Publishers.

Strom, K.J., and M.J. Hickman. 2010. 'Unanalyzed Evidence in Law Enforcement Agencies: A National Examination of Forensic Processing in Police Departments'. *Criminology and Public Policy* 9(2): 381–402.

Summerscale, K. 2008. *The Suspicions of Mr. Whicher, or The Murder at Road Hill House*. London: Bloomsbury.

Surette, R. 1998. *Media, Crime, and Criminal Justice: Images and Realities*. Belmont, CA: Wadsworth.

Thomas, A. 2005. 'CSI: Maricopa County: The CSI Effect and Its Real-Life Impact on Justice'. www.maricopacountyattorney.org/Press/PDF/CSIReport.pdf.

Thomas, A. 2006. 'The CSI Effect: Fact or Fiction'. *Yale Law Journal* 115(70). http://yalelawjournal.org/forum/the-csi-effect-fact-or-fiction

Thomas, R.R. 1999. *Detective Fiction and the Rise of Forensic Science*. Cambridge: Cambridge University Press.

Turkel, W.J. 2009. 'The Crime Scene, the Evidential Fetish, and the Usable Past'. In M. Byers and V.M. Johnson, eds., *The CSI Effect: Television, Crime, and Governance*, 133–146. Lanham, MD: Lexington.

Tyler, T. 2006. 'Viewing *CSI* and the Threshold of Guilt: Managing Truth and Justice in Reality and Fiction'. *Yale Law Journal* 115(5): 1050–1085.

Valverde, M. 2006. *Law and Order: Images, Meanings, Myths*. Abingdon, UK: Routledge.

Watkins, M.J. 2004. 'Forensics in the Media: Have Attorneys Reacted to the Growing Popularity of Forensic Crime Dramas?' MA thesis, Florida State University.

Weaver, R., Y. Salamonson J. Koch and G. Porter. 2012. 'The CSI Effect at University: Forensic Science Students' Television Viewing and Perceptions of Ethical Issues'. *Australian Journal of Forensic Sciences* 44(4): 381–391.

Wise, J. 2009–2010. 'Providing the CSI Treatment: Criminal Justice Practitioners and the CSI Effect'. *Current Issues in Criminal Justice* 21(3): 383–399.

11

Forensic science and wrongful convictions

Joëlle Vuille and Christophe Champod

Introduction

In the 1990s, forensic science evidence, and forensic DNA analysis in particular, began being used to exonerate people who had been convicted of crimes they had not committed. This opened up the field of research into wrongful convictions in ways that had been previously unknown, and shed new light on the causes of erroneous verdicts. Eyewitness identification came under the spotlight as a major contributor to the conviction of the innocent, as did false confessions, prosecutorial misconduct, sloppy defence work and lying jailhouse informants (Scheck et al. 2001; Garrett 2011). Ironically, the use of forensic science evidence to exonerate the innocent also helped identify forensic science evidence itself as an important factor in the conviction of the innocent. If the causal link between scientific evidence of dubious quality and erroneous verdicts can certainly be questioned, as wrongful convictions are usually the result of a combination of shortcomings on the part of the criminal justice system and its actors, it is now established that misleading forensic science evidence is sometimes provided to the fact-finder, and this, in turn, increases the risk that an erroneous verdict will be meted out.

Indeed, hailed during many decades as a powerful weapon in the search for the (judicial) truth, forensic practitioners and forensic practices have recently come under the microscope of scholars, innocence advocates and public institutions, and the picture that has been drawn is far from ideal. In this chapter, we take a critical look at forensic science as a contributor to wrongful convictions, but also as a vehicle to obtain exonerations. We argue that forensic science evidence can be distorted in both enterprises, and that it is the forensic practitioner's professional responsibility to render her conclusions in ways that preclude their manipulation by parties, fact-finders and advocates. We then highlight the differences between Anglo-Saxon jurisdictions and courts in Continental Europe in their approach to forensic science and wrongful convictions and, finally, we make recommendations that the forensic community would be well advised to implement soon if they want to avoid further criticism and develop different practices in the future.

The role of forensic science and forensic practitioners in causing and detecting wrongful convictions

In the context of wrongful convictions, forensic science evidence must be examined in three different perspectives: when it implicates an innocent suspect, when it fails to exclude an innocent suspect and when it is used to obtain the exoneration of a convict whose guilt is doubted.

Forensic science evidence implicating an innocent

Forensic science evidence has been shown to contribute to the prosecution and conviction of the innocent in various ways: samples can get switched,[1] clerical errors can be made, contamination of crime-scene samples can occur,[2] contamination may happen in the laboratory,[3] the interpretation of results can be biased[4] or otherwise exaggerated (see the microscopic hair comparison controversy, below). Forensic practitioners can also willingly report false results to incriminate suspects whom they know to be innocent.[5] If such errors constitute mainly anecdotal evidence and are treated as anomalous, one issue has come to light in recent years that is pervasive, systemic and much more problematic: the apparent widespread use by forensic practitioners of insufficiently validated techniques combined with poorly defined reporting practices.

Indeed, in recent years, several reports have denounced the use of techniques put on the forensic market despite a lack of standards and insufficient empirical validation, and practices relying too much on the subjectivity of the individual analyst (National Research Council 2009; PCAST 2016; PCAST Addendum 2017). One prime example is bite mark evidence, sometimes considered the 'poster child of the failed, unscientific approaches historically accepted in all 50 US States' (Bowers 2017, 145). Bite mark analysis aims at comparing the teeth of a suspect with the bruises left on the skin of a victim. It rests on the assumptions that individuals' teeth are sufficiently different from one another to be distinguishable, that skin can capture that distinctiveness, that the analyst can correctly associate the teeth with the imprint left on the skin and that the analyst can give a scientifically valid estimate of the probative force of the association (Bowers 2017, 152).

The problem is that none of these assumptions has been established scientifically: even if the combination of the 32 teeth of the adult dentition can possibly be unique, it is not the case of the eight front upper-jaw teeth seen in a typical bite mark (and 'uniqueness' is a tautological argument anyway). Besides, teeth have five sides, whereas a bite only records one side of each tooth. Studies have found matches between dental casts from different people (PCAST 2016, 84). The human skin is not a good medium for recording bites, since significant distortion occurs; and the distortions produced by a bite are so variable and so substantial that they render the analysis almost impossible (PCAST 2016, 84). Several studies suggest that bite mark analysts don't consistently agree on whether a bruise found on a victim is a human bite mark or not (see the studies referenced in Bowers 2017, 156), and they do not consistently agree on whether a dentition produced a certain bite (see the studies referenced in PCAST 2016, 85, and National Research Council 2009, 173). Besides, there is no standard establishing the quality and number of characteristics necessary to reach the threshold where one can say that the 'match' between the mark and the dentition has some evidentiary value (NRC 2009, 176). If the American Board of Forensic Odontology has issued guidelines on a range of conclusions (ABFO *Diplomates Reference Manual* 2016), its members are not required to follow them, there is no guidance on how to apply the suggested criteria, and more importantly, the guidelines have no scientific basis but are merely the product of the authors' opinion. Moreover, the suggested conclusions rest on the flawed logic of addressing the probability of the propositions (i.e., whether the suspect is the biter or not) instead of offering the more appropriate assessment of the probability of the findings given the propositions relevant in the case. And even if an analyst could reliably match a dentition to a bite mark, there exists no scientific study to support the evidentiary value of that association, as the percentage of the population whose dentition could have produced a bite indistinguishable from the one under consideration is unknown (Bowers 2017, 155). Finally, many real-life cases attest to the fact that errors were made in casework and led to the prosecution or conviction of an innocent person.[6]

Another area under criticism is the microscopic examination of hair, which has similar limitations as bite mark evidence (Hsu 2015a, 2015b; Cole and Duster 2016; Norton et al. 2016). Despite concerns expressed through the years regarding the ability of forensic microscopists to draw robust conclusions from hair comparison (NRC 2009, 155; Risinger and Saks 2003; Smith and Goodman 1995; Garrett and Neufeld 2009), it is only recently that the FBI, in collaboration with the Innocence Project and the National Association of Criminal Defense Lawyers, has initiated a review of hundreds of cases of microscopic hair comparisons. The data gathered until April 2015 and covering the years 1972 to 1999 suggests that the results of such comparisons were overstated to favour the prosecution in more than 95 percent of cases, including in 32 death-penalty cases. The problem was not attributable to one incompetent individual, since 26 out of 28 examiners in the unit routinely exaggerated the probative weight of their observations.

The fact that insufficiently validated forensic techniques are finally coming under scrutiny must be saluted, but it is a shame that it took so many years for those weaknesses to be fully articulated and finally recognized.[7] Another collateral effect of this scrutiny is that it shed an unfavourable light on all forensic areas without acknowledging the contribution of forensic disciplines that are robust. This also shows that, contrary to an argument frequently presented in the literature, the pressures of adversarialism and the gatekeeping duty attributed to judges in US jurisdictions are insufficient to regulate the forensic community and ensure that the evidence used in criminal prosecutions is accurate and unbiased.

Forensic science evidence failing to exclude an innocent

Among the cases in which forensic science evidence contributed to the conviction of the innocent, one type raises particular issues: cases in which forensic practitioners failed to exclude a suspect who was in fact innocent, although the techniques used in the case indicated that the person identified was not the author of the crime. (We will not discuss here techniques whose discrimination power is too weak to exclude an innocent suspect.) In Brandon Garrett's analysis of the first 250 exoneration cases of the Innocence Project, evidence that should have been presented as being neutral or exculpatory for the suspect was in fact presented to the jury as being inculpatory in dozens of cases (Garrett 2011, 90; see also Cole 2012, 725). The Schiedam Park murder case in the Netherlands can help illustrate the point (Posthumus 2005; van Koppen 2008; Brants 2013). In 2000, a 10-year-old girl was murdered in a park as she was playing with her 11-year-old friend. Experts conducted DNA analysis on various samples taken from the victim and, although the yielded profiles were incomplete, considered that the results could be attributed to the same male, who was not the suspect in the case. The prosecution, who were convinced of the suspect's guilt since he had initially confessed (but later retracted his confession), invited the experts to not report the results as such. To the prosecutors, the experts reiterated their belief that the DNA came from the attacker, because it had been found both on the victim and on the murder weapon, after the children had played in water for some time. At trial, the prosecution told the court that anybody who had been in contact with the victim during the day could have left the DNA traces, and that the absence of the suspect's DNA did not support his non-involvement in the crime. The final report filed by the experts did not mention the fact that the same unknown male DNA had been found both on the victim and on the murder weapon, which was misleading at the very least. Of course, it could be argued that in such cases, the forensic practitioners are not as much to be blamed as the prosecution or even the legal system as a whole, since the final interpretation of what the evidence means in a given case is the court's and/or jury's responsibility (Collins and Jarvis 2009). If this argument has some merit from a legal point of view, it is, in our opinion, morally weak.

Using forensic science evidence to exonerate a convict

Forensic science evidence is often used to obtain the exoneration of a person earlier convicted of a crime. In this context, it is often said that forensic science evidence proves, or at least supports, the claims of *innocence* made by the person in question. But is the exoneree always factually innocent? Several scholars and practitioners have voiced their skepticism over the years (for a review, see Medwed 2008). The problem in this context is that scientific evidence used to exonerate the innocent is not held to the same standards of validity and robustness as the scientific evidence previously used to convict the person, and its interpretation can be asymmetrical (Edmond 2002). One example is the Mark Dallagher case in the UK, in which a man convicted of murder on the basis of earprint evidence found on a window was later exonerated because a DNA profile obtained from the mark did not match Dallagher's profile, leading to the conclusion that it demonstrated the erroneous nature of the earprint identification and Dallagher's lack of involvement in the crime (Schiffer and Champod 2008). Without claiming to know whether Mr Dallagher was in fact guilty or innocent of the crime for which he was initially convicted, we can say that the interpretation of the DNA evidence to exonerate him was over-simplistic. The presence of a DNA trace of unknown origin cannot in and of itself lead to the conclusion that the convict was innocent; a comprehensive interpretation of the evidence requires taking into account the probability of observing a DNA profile from an unknown person both under the hypothesis that Dallagher was the source of the earmark and under the hypothesis that he was not and that an unknown person was. Since the probability of detecting an unknown DNA profile on the window if Dallagher was the source of the earmark (because the DNA was on the surface for other, innocent, reasons) is not 0 percent, and the probability of an unknown person leaving their DNA on the mark if Dallagher was not the source of the mark is not 100 percent, one cannot deduce from the presence of an unknown DNA profile on or under the earprint that Dallagher did not leave the earprint on the crime scene. The case against Dallagher is still presented in the UK as the prime example of a miscarriage of justice caused by dubious earprint identification and ultimately revealed thanks to DNA profiling. The Law Commission (2009, 11), while reviewing the admissibility of expert evidence, stated: 'The prosecution had no choice but to drop its case against him as DNA evidence taken from the latent print unequivocally established that it had been left by someone other than D'. The DNA findings would certainly support the defence proposition, but would not make its case certain based on these DNA results only. There was no dispute as to the source of the DNA (Dallagher was not the source), but the crux of the matter revolves around the mechanisms whereby this DNA had been transferred. Listening by putting one's ear to the window is not the only possible mechanism. Even if the legal standard of proof in criminal matters is asymmetrical, the evaluation of the evidence is misleading if it considers only one side of the argument (here the defence perspective).

The forensic practitioner: a willing accomplice to judicial errors?

Why and how does the forensic practitioner contribute to erroneous verdicts? We have already mentioned the use of insufficiently validated techniques, which, unsurprisingly, can lead to erroneous verdicts. But even when well-established techniques are used, there is a risk that the forensic science evidence will contribute to erroneous verdicts because forensic practitioners sometimes lack transparency and because they often give conclusions in a contextual void, which allows advocates and fact-finders to distort them.

Lack of transparency

A lack of transparency has plagued many forensic fields for decades. Experts routinely testify that a suspect has been *identified* as the source of a fingermark found on the crime scene, an assertion sometimes nuanced by an indication that the result is (merely) the opinion of the analyst; shoe print analysts testify that a crime scene print *is compatible with* a reference shoe found at a suspect's place, not reporting the value of the evidence under an alternative (defence) hypothesis; DNA analysts report that a semen stain found on a rape victim matches the DNA profile of a suspect and that a random match has a probability of 1 in 30 gazillions, but gives no indication as to possibility that an *error was made* during the collection, analysis or interpretation of the evidence. Such conclusions conceal the limits of the inferences drawn by the analysts and can be misleading for the fact-finder, in different ways.

First, conclusions of identification convey the false idea that the expert has effectively designated the suspect as the source of the print, when in fact this decision can only be made by the fact-finder in view of the suspect population, and the other evidence against/in favour of the accused. Indeed, deciding to express a conclusion of identification goes beyond the forensic observations. It requires consideration of the size of the relevant population, jointly with a weighed assessment of losses associated with each possible decision. Such a holistic assessment cannot reasonably be asked of a forensic expert (see Biedermann, Bozza and Taroni 2016). Besides, a conclusion of identification conceals the various judgments made by the analyst when evaluating the evidence (i.e., whether the crime scene mark and the reference print share corresponding minutiae, how distortion accounts for or cannot account for differences, how rare the minutiae are, what the probability of an error is and thus, what the strength of the association is).

Second, conclusions that do not explicitly weight the value of the evidence under two competing hypotheses are useless at best and very misleading at worst. The case of Barry George can help illustrate this point. George was convicted for the murder of journalist Jill Dando after one gunshot residue (GSR) was found on his jacket one year after the facts (R. v. Barry George, Court of Appeal, [2007] EWCA Crim 2722). George had come to the attention of the police because he lived nearby, had a history of violence, a fascination for the victim and mental health issues. At trial, the court held that finding one GSR particle on George's jacket was compatible with him having shot Jill Dando a year earlier. On appeal, experts testified that, if the presence of a GSR was indeed consistent with George having shot a firearm, it was equally consistent with innocent presence, and in consequence, that the presence of that particle did not support one of the hypotheses considered over the other. George was acquitted.

Third, conclusions that do not incorporate the possibility that an error was made during the collection, transport, analysis or interpretation of the evidence are not transparent because mistakes are always possible. It is not currently customary for forensic practitioners to provide error rates for the techniques employed, and many in the forensic community would argue that forensic practitioners should not be required to do so. Requiring that error rates be disclosed is not new;

the request first emerged in the context of the early debates surrounding DNA evidence (Lempert 1995). It is true that laboratory error rates are difficult to estimate (National Research Council 1996), but if that is true for the forensic community, it is even more true for the defence and, eventually, for the fact-finder. Developing error rates for forensic techniques should, in the long run, be an endeavour organized systematically in the various forensic communities and not a question litigated again and again in individual cases (and not very transparently either, we guess).

Finally, it is customary in some forensic circles to prepare very short written reports and to wait for the parties to ask for details and explanations before elaborating on the exact meaning of the results. Such an approach (motivated by time constrains but also sometimes by comfort) prevents full transparency and deprives the parties of the guidance that the expert can bring in understanding the limitations of the forensic results.

Lack of context

Forensic practitioners have also contributed to the conviction of the innocent by providing conclusions in a factual void, i.e., out of the context of the case in which those conclusions would later be interpreted by attorneys and fact-finders. In the Anglo-American world, this has long been considered desirable, and recent research on contextual bias suggests that forensic practitioners can sometimes be influenced by irrelevant information about the case and that this can lead them to erroneous conclusions (Edmond et al. 2015; Stammers and Bunn 2015). In Continental Europe, where prosecution bias on the part of forensic practitioners has not (yet) been denounced as a major cause of erroneous forensic conclusions, it is not uncommon for forensic practitioners to consider that their conclusions can be useful to the case only if they are contextualized, and that providing uncontextualized conclusions can actually create a risk that they will be distorted (Champod 2014). The European Network of Forensic Science Institutes (ENFSI)[8] recently published a guideline encouraging its members to render activity-level conclusions in cases in which it is appropriate (ENFSI 2015; see also Champod et al. 2016 and Biedermann, Champod et al. 2016). This recommendation is based on the observation that it is sometimes necessary to evaluate forensic science evidence under activity level propositions in criminal cases, and that the task should not be left to lawyers and fact-finders who will most often resolve such issues on the basis of common sense, a poor substitute for scientific knowledge. Evaluating the evidence at the level of activities requires forensic practitioners to be aware of a number of elements from the case, which can create a risk of bias. We contend that measures should be put in place to protect experts from irrelevant information that could bias them, but we do not think that the risk of bias should preclude experts from ever evaluating evidence at the activity level. If such were the case, the cure would be far worse than the disease, and would create new risks for the sound evaluation of the evidence. Under the recommendations of the ENFSI, the forensic practitioner who is called to give activity-level conclusions should do so on the basis of statistical data when such data exists. In the absence of hard statistical data, the expert should use data derived from experiments conducted under controlled conditions, and, as a last resort, should give his opinion on the basis of his training and experience (making explicit that such is the case). Whatever the data used, the expert must express her opinion in a written report, shared with the parties in a timely manner. In that respect, local practices that allow an expert to provide a written report as to source and conjecture as to activities once she is heard in court do not allow for a transparent, balanced and robust evaluation of the evidence.

The importance of contextualization can be illustrated by the case of Juan Rivera, accused of raping and murdering 11-year-old Holly Staker in 1992 in Illinois.[9] Rivera was convicted after he confessed to the crime, although no physical evidence linked him to the crime. In 2004, semen found on vaginal swabs taken from the victim was found not to match him. The prosecution considered that this new evidence did not support Rivera's innocence, and suggested that the semen came from Holly having had consensual sex with another man prior to the murder. The prosecution provided no evidence for the fact that an 11-year-old girl had an active sex-life and its case was further undermined by the testimony of experts who argued that, after intercourse, semen tends to flow downwards in the vagina into the woman's underwear as she goes about her daily activities. Since Holly had been wearing the same underwear since the morning of the crime and no sperm had been found on it when it was examined, the experts' assessment had to support Rivera's innocence.

There is an old adage that absence of evidence is not evidence of absence (see for instance Gill 2014, xii). In a criminal case, however, this reasoning can be misleading. The absence of findings often supports the hypothesis that the defendant did not commit the crime, against the alternative hypothesis. And yet, it is not uncommon for such absence of evidence not to be considered seriously and to be casually explained away. It is the forensic practitioner's responsibility to point out such misguided reasoning to the parties and fact-finders, by offering a comprehensive assessment of the evidence, i.e., not one limited to source.

The European perspective

The debate around forensic science evidence and its contribution to wrongful convictions has been most prevalent in the United States and the Anglo-Saxon world more generally. But what about Europe? Have the same problems been identified in Europe or have European jurisdictions been able to protect themselves against the excesses of forensic practitioners identified in the United States, Canada or Australia? When considering forensic science and wrongful conviction in Europe, it is important to distinguish between the United Kingdom and Continental Europe.

In the United Kingdom, the debate around forensic science evidence and its role in the conviction of the innocent has been vivid for many years. The Runciman report, which investigated the wrongful convictions of the Birmingham Six, among others, recommended the creation of the Criminal Cases Review Commission, which was set up in 1995 and is now tasked with the referral of cases to the appeal court in cases of doubtful convictions.[10] Forensic science practices are also regularly debated in the public forum, notably through the judgments of the Court of Appeal (see, for instance, R. v. T [2010] All ER (D) 240 (Oct)., R. v. Paul E. Gray [2003] EWCA Crim 1001, R. v. Adams [1996] 2 Cr App R 467, [1996] Crim LR 898, CA and R. v. Adams [1998] 1 Cr App R 377; R. v. Doheny and Adams [1997] 1 Crim App R 369).

In Continental Europe, no institution exists for the systematic review of possible cases of wrongful convictions. All (national) criminal procedures allow for the revision of an erroneous verdict, but no initiative has been created to this date to allow for the critical review of alleged wrongful convictions by independent parties (although the Dutch Commissie Evaluatie Afgesloten Strafzaken [CEAS] could be an exception in Continental Europe; see DeRoos and Nijboer 2011). Innocence movements have also failed, until now, to gain momentum, and their actions remain marginal. (Again, one exception to this rule could be the Netherlands, where some scholars have long been vocal about possible miscarriages of justice, and where instances of wrongful convictions are well documented and have been discussed in the public forum.) As a consequence, data on wrongful convictions is difficult to gather and the role of forensic science evidence in wrongful convictions in Continental Europe has not been as visible as in Anglo-Saxon jurisdictions. Cases exist where misleading scientific evidence formed the basis of a verdict later declared erroneous by a superior court, but they remain isolated.[11] Does this mean that all is well in the European forensic science landscape? We doubt it. Everyday casework suggests that forensic practitioners face many of the same challenges in Europe as they do elsewhere, even if the institutional structure of laboratories and procedural roles played by the parties could to some extent act as protective factors against the production and use of erroneous forensic science evidence (the fact that in most European jurisdictions, the investigation of the case is in the hands of a neutral magistrate certainly protects the defence against partisanship and bias on the part of scientific experts, for instance).

The way forward

If forensic practitioners want to reclaim power over their role in the criminal justice system, we contend that they should first become more transparent in their conclusions, by making the limits of their conclusions explicit to the fact-finder, and more courageously, by taking it upon themselves to contextualize their results. Even in well-established disciplines such as fingerprint comparisons, conclusions that conceal the limits of the inferences drawn by the expert should be abandoned. In their stead, we advocate for the use of conclusions that explicitly account for the probability of an adventitious match and for the possibility that an error was committed during the analysis and/or interpretation of the evidence. The fact that such numbers are currently difficult to produce should not prevent analysts from adopting such a framework.

It is also important to establish whose responsibility it is, in the criminal justice system, to sound the alarm if it becomes apparent that scientific evidence is being used in a way that is not warranted by the content of the expert's conclusions. Forensic scientists cannot deliver their report and then remain silent if they see that their conclusions are being used in a way that is scientifically unwarranted. One fundamental building block toward reclaiming power is to agree on a reporting scheme that is based on sound logical principles. The ENFSI guideline constitutes without a doubt a first step in that direction. It is unfortunate, however, to see how difficult it is for this guideline to be considered a standard in the community (Biedermann et al. 2017).

As mentioned earlier, since the National Research Council released its report in 2009, the forensic sciences have come under a lot of scrutiny from external bodies, and this has been resented by (at least a part of) the forensic community. The responses elicited by the PCAST report are telling in this context, both in their tone and content (see Federal Bureau of Investigation 2016 and National District Attorneys Association 2016; a statement made by Attorney General Loretta Lynch is reported by Fields 2016). We respectfully submit that external bodies would not have had to put forensic practices and practitioners under the microscope if the latter had done a better job at regulating themselves to begin with. The attitudes that we have witnessed in reaction to the recent criticisms have often been complacent and self-righteous, and have lacked the honest self-assessment necessary to reform practices that, in all fairness, were sometimes questionable. The forensic community must acknowledge the errors of the past and take responsibility for the future. Instead of dismissing critics with dubious arguments, forensic practitioners should recognize that some of the techniques used in the past were not solid enough to support convictions, and either conduct the necessary research to validate them or abandon them altogether. Forensic science practice needs in-depth reform, based on fundamental research and open debate, in collaboration with the justice system, and not the small anecdotal changes conceded grudgingly under the pressure of external forces and primarily aimed at preserving the stakeholders' professional reputation and comfort.

Acknowledgement

Joëlle Vuille thanks the Swiss National Science Foundation for their financial support (grant PZ00P1_154955 / 1).

Notes

1 Consider, for example, a Swiss case in which the buccal swabs from two individuals were switched when they were processed at the booking station. Both profiles were loaded on the national DNA database. A stain later collected from a crime scene thus produced a correspondence to the wrong individual. It is only thanks to the suspect's constant denial and a further police investigation that the error was uncovered (Tribunal cantonal de Neuchâtel, jugement du 31 juillet 2014, CPEN.2014.16/der). On errors commonly found in a DNA laboratory, see Kloosterman, Sjerps and Quak (2014) (who should be commended for their efforts in transparency, as they are the only analysts to our knowledge to have published internal data on errors so widely).

2 As in the Meyrargue murders case in France; see, for instance, www.francetvinfo.fr/societe/justice/adn-piece-maitresse-ou-traitresse.html (retrieved 8 February 2017). See also the Phantom of Heilbronn case in Germany, a spectacular case of contamination that did not lead to any wrongful conviction but raised serious questions as to certain forensic practices (Himmelreich 2009). Another case that is worth indicating is the wrongful conviction of Farah Abdulkadir Jama in Australia following a contamination of the intimate swabs taken from a woman who was thought to have been sexually assaulted. It transpired that Mr Jama's DNA was transferred to the swabs through contamination. Another young woman, who had had consensual intercourse with him, had been examined in the same room shortly before the assaulted woman (Vincent 2010).

3 The Adam Scott case in the UK is the prime example of such an event (see Gill 2014, as well as the report of the Forensic Science Regulator, available at www.gov.uk/government/publications/forensic-science-regulators-report-on-the-dna-contamination-case-at-lgc-forensics). A plastic tray that contained Scott's saliva was reused, by mistake, to process evidence from a rape. An association between the DNA profiles was detected and led to Scott being charged with the crime. The laboratory staff spotted an analogous contamination in another case one day after Scott's analysis, but did not check back on the previous days immediately. Only after five months did the Prosecution drop the charges, thanks to the efforts of a police investigator who was doubtful of Scott's involvement and had gathered additional exonerating evidence. Contaminations in the laboratory that could lead to an adventitious correspondence are rare, and laboratories implement quality assurance to prevent them, but they can occur. DNA scientists have invested a lot of resources in estimating the adverse probability of a random match, but, at times, these very small estimates blind scientists and other actors of the judicial system to the small probability of a laboratory error, which should also be accounted for.

4 The seminal case in matters of cognitive biases certainly being the wrongful prosecution of Brandon Mayfield after the 2004 Madrid station attacks. See Office of the Inspector General (2006).

5 Think of Fred Zain or Annie Dookhan, for example. On so-called forensic fraud, see Turvey (2013).

6 See the cases of wrongful convictions and indictments identified by the Innocence Project: www.innocenceproject.org/cases-where-dna-revealed-that-bite-mark-analysis-led-to-wrongful-arrests-and-convictions/ (accessed 8 February 2017). The phenomenon is not limited to the US, since in Switzerland, in 2007, a serial killer was exonerated of one of the murders for which he had been convicted on the basis of bite mark evidence: www.tagblatt.ch/altdaten/tagblatt-alt/tagblattheute/hb/schauplatz/tb-sa/art797,63904 (accessed 8 February 2017).

7 In a landmark case recently decided by the California Supreme Court, the conviction of William Richards was overturned after a bite mark expert recanted testimony given a decade earlier, in which he had declared that a bite mark found on the hand of a murder victim was *consistent with* Richards' dentition. For a review of legal precedents, the growing doubts and the scientific challenges associated with bite mark evidence, see Saks et al. 2016. The Bill Richards case is all the more important that the exoneration was made possible by a new law that allows convictions to be overturned when experts recant their earlier testimony because of an advance in science or technology (something that had been impossible until then, the argument being that an expert can never be wrong since his conclusions merely reflect his personal opinion). See Smith (2016).

8 ENFSI brings together more than 60 laboratories and aims at sharing common quality standards and exchanging knowledge and expertise. ENFSI has the privileged status of an EU monopolist and has strong collaboration ties with Europol, CEPOL, Eurojust and Interpol.

9 www.innocenceproject.org/cases/juan-rivera/ (last retrieved 8 February 2017).
10 See www.ccrc.gov.uk and its Scottish counterpart, the Scottish Criminal Cases Review Commission (SCCRC), http://sccrc.org.uk/.
11 See, for example, the Donald Stellwag and de Montgazon cases in Germany, the Amanda Knox case in Italy and the Lucia de B. and Putten cases in the Netherlands.

References

ABFO (American Board of Forensic Odontology). 2016. *Diplomates Reference Manual*. https://abfo.org/resources/abfo-manual.

Biedermann, A., S. Bozza and F. Taroni. 2016. 'The Decisionalization of Individualization'. *Forensic Science International* 266: 29–38.

Biedermann, A., C. Champod, G. Jackson, P. Gill, D. Taylor, J. Butler, N. Morling, T. Hicks, J. Vuille F. and F. Taroni. 2016. 'Evaluation of Forensic DNA Traces When Propositions of Interest Relate to Activities: Analysis and Discussion of Recurrent Concerns'. *Frontiers in Genetics*, 7. https://dx.doi.org/10.3389%2Ffgene.2016.00215.

Biedermann, A., C. Champod and S. Willis. 2017. 'Development of European Standards for Evaluative Reporting in Forensic Science'. *The International Journal of Evidence & Proof* 21(1–2): 14–29.

Bowers, C.M. 2017. 'Bite mark evidence'. In W.J. Koen and C.M. Bowers, eds., *Forensic Science Reform: Protecting the Innocent*, 145–166. London: Academic Press.

Brants, C. 2013. 'Wrongful Convictions and Inquisitorial Process: The Case of the Netherlands'. *University of Cincinnati Law Review* 80(4): 1069–1114.

Champod, C. 2014. 'Research Focused Mainly on Bias Will Paralyse Forensic Science'. *Science and Justice* 54(2): 107–109.

Champod C., A. Biedermann, J. Vuille, S. Willis and J. De Kinder. 2016. 'ENFSI [European Network of Forensic Science Institutes] *Guideline for Evaluative Reporting in Forensic Science: A Primer for Legal Practitioners*'. *Criminal Law and Justice Weekly* 180(10). www.criminallawandjustice.co.uk/issue/Vol180-No10.

Cole, S.A. 2012. 'Forensic Science and Wrongful Convictions: From Exposer to Contributor to Corrector'. *New England Law Review* 46(4): 711–736.

Cole, S.A., and T. Duster. 2016. 'Microscopic Hair Examination and the Sociology of Science'. *Contexts* 15(winter): 28–35.

Collins, J.M., and J. Jarvis. 2009. 'The Wrongful Conviction of Forensic Science'. *Forensic Science Policy and Management* 1(1): 17–31.

De Roos, T.A., and J.F. Nijboer. 2011. 'Wrongfully Convicted: How the Dutch Deal with the Revision of Their "Miscarriages of Justice"'. *Criminal Law Forum* 22(4): 567–591.

Edmond, G. 2002. 'Constructing Miscarriages of Justice: Misunderstanding Scientific Evidence in High Profile Criminal Appeals'. *Oxford Journal of Legal Studies* 22(1): 53–89.

Edmond, G., J.M. Tangen, R.A. Searston and I.E. Dror. 2015. 'Contextual Bias and Cross-Contamination in the Forensic Sciences: The Corrosive Implications for Investigations, Plea Bargains, Trials and Appeals'. *Law, Probability & Risk* 15(1): 1–25.

ENFSI. 2015. *Guideline for Evaluative Reporting in Forensic Science: A Primer for Legal Practitioners*. http://enfsi.eu/sites/default/files/documents/external_publications/m1_guideline.pdf.

Federal Bureau of Investigation. 2016. Comments on: President's Council of Advisors on Science and Technology, Report to the President, *Forensic Science in Federal Criminal Courts: Ensuring Scientific Validity of Pattern Comparison Methods*. 20 September 2016. www.fbi.gov/file-repository/fbi-pcast-response.pdf/view.

Fields, G. 2016. 'White House Advisory Council Report Is Critical of Forensics Used in Criminal Trials'. *Wall Street Journal*, 20 September 2016. www.wsj.com/articles/white-house-advisory-council-releases-report-critical-of-forensics-used-in-criminal-trials-1474394743.

Garrett, B. 2011. *Convicting the Innocent*. Cambridge: Harvard University Press.

Garrett, B.L., and P.J. Neufeld. 2009. 'Invalid Forensic Science Testimony and Wrongful Convictions'. *Virginia Law Review* 95(1): 1–97.

Gill, P. 2014. *Misleading DNA Evidence: Reasons for Miscarriages of Justice*. Amsterdam: Academic Press/Elsevier.

Himmelreich, C. 2009. 'Germany's Phantom Serial Killer: A DNA Blunder'. *Time*, 27 March 2009. http://content.time.com/time/world/article/0,8599,1888126,00.html.

Hsu, S. 2015a. 'FBI Admits Flaws in Hair Analysis over Decades'. *Washington Post*, 18 April 2015. www.washingtonpost.com/local/crime/fbi-overstated-forensic-hair-matches-in-nearly-all-criminal-trials-for-decades/2015/04/18/39c8d8c6-e515-11e4-b510-962fcfabc310_story.html?utm_term=.74811005505b.

Hsu, S. 2015b. 'After FBI Admits Overstating Forensic Hair Matches, Focus Turns to Cases'. *Washington Post*, 20 April 2015. www.sbs.com.au/news/article/2015/04/22/after-fbi-admits-overstating-forensic-hair-matches-focus-turns-cases.

Kloosterman, A., M. Sjerps and A. Quak. 2014. 'Error Rates in Forensic DNA Analysis: Definition, Numbers, Impact and Communication'. *Forensic Science International: Genetics* 12: 77–85. https://doi.org/10.1016/j.fsigen.2014.04.014.

The Law Commission. 2009. *The Admissibility of Expert Evidence in Criminal Proceedings in England and Wales—A New Approach to the Determination of Evidentiary Reliability*. A Consultation Paper. www.lawcom.gov.uk/expert_evidence.htm Consultation Paper No 190.

Lempert, R.O. 1995. 'The Honest Scientist's Guide to DNA Evidence'. In B.S. Weir, ed., *Human Identification: The Use of DNA Markers*, vol. 4, 119–124. Dordrecht: Kluwer Academic Publishers.

Medwed, D.S. 2008. 'Innocentrism'. *University of Illinois Law Review* 5: 1549–1572.

National District Attorneys Association (NDAA). 2016. 'Forensic Science in Criminal Courts: Ensuring Scientific Validity of Feature-Comparison Methods'. www.ciclt.net/ul/ndaajustice/PCAST/NDAA%20PCAST%20Response%20FINAL.pdf.

National Research Council, Committee on DNA Technology in Forensic Science. 1996. *The Evaluation of Forensic DNA Evidence*. Washington, DC: National Academies Press.

National Research Council. 2009. *Strengthening Forensic Science in the United States: A Path Forward*. Washington, DC: National Academies Press.

Norton, J., W.E. Anderson and G. Divine. 2016. 'Flawed Forensics: Statistical Failings of Microscopic Hair Analysis'. *Significance* 13(2): 26–29.

Office of the Inspector General. 2006. *A Review of the FBI's Handling of the Brandon Mayfield Case*. US Department of Justice. https://oig.justice.gov/special/s0601/final.pdf.

President's Council of Advisors on Science and Technology (PCAST), Executive Office of the President. 2016. *Forensic Science in Criminal Courts: Ensuring Scientific Validity of Feature-Comparison Methods*. https://obamawhitehouse.archives.gov/sites/default/files/microsites/ostp/PCAST/pcast_forensic_science_report_final.pdf.

PCAST. 2017. *An Addendum to the PCAST Report on Forensic Science in Criminal Courts*. 6 January 2017. https://obamawhitehouse.archives.gov/sites/default/files/microsites/ostp/PCAST/pcast_forensics_addendum_finalv2.pdf.

Posthumus, Frits. 2005. *Evaluatieonderzoek in de Schiedammer parkmoord*. www.geenstijl.nl/paginas/rapportmoord.pdf.

Risinger, D.M., and M.J. Saks. 2003. 'Rationality, Research and Leviathan: Law Enforcement Sponsored Research and the Criminal Process'. *Michigan State DCL Law Review* 4: 1023–1050.

Saks, M.J., T. Albright, T.L. Bohan, B.E. Bierer et al., 2016. 'Forensic Bitemark Identification: Weak Foundations, Exaggerated Claims'. *Journal of Law and the Biosciences* 3(3): 538–575.

Scheck, B., P. Neufeld and J. Dwyer. 2001. *Actual Innocence: When Justice Goes Wrong and How to Make It Right*. New York: Signet.

Schiffer, B., and C. Champod. 2008. 'Judicial Error and Forensic Science: Pondering the Contribution of DNA Evidence'. In R. Huff and M. Killias, eds., *Wrongful Conviction: International Perspectives on Miscarriages of Justice*, 33–55. Philadelphia: Temple University Press.

Smith, J. 2016. 'Junk Science on Trial in Bill Richards Bite-Mark Appeal'. *Intercept*, 6 May 2016. https://theintercept.com/2016/05/06/junk-science-on-trial-in-bill-richards-bite-mark-appeal.

Smith, C.A.S., and P.D. Goodman. 1995–1996. 'Forensic Hair Comparison Analysis: Nineteenth Century Science or Twentieth Century Snake Oil'. *Columbia Human Rights Law Review* 27: 227–291.

Stammers, S., and S. Bunn. 2015. *Unintentional Bias in Forensic Investigation*. London: Houses of Parliament, Parliamentary Office of Science and Technology.

Turvey, B.E. 2013. *Forensic Fraud: Evaluating Law Enforcement and Forensic Science Cultures in the Context of Examiner Misconduct*. Waltham, MA: Academic Press.

Van Koppen, P.J. 2008. 'Blundering Justice'. In R.N. Kocsis, ed., *Serial Murder and the Psychology of Violent Crimes*, 207–228. Totowa, NJ: Humana Press.

Vincent, F.H.R. 2010. *Inquiry into the Circumstances That Led to the Conviction of Mr Farah Abdulkadir Jama*. Melbourne: Victorian Government Printer.

12
Forensic intelligence

Olivier Ribaux and Stefano Caneppele

In this chapter, the term 'intelligence' is progressively integrated into the dominant conceptualizations that traditional forensic science laboratories implement in serving justice systems. Forensic intelligence thus expands the narrower scope of forensic science. The latter's frame of reference eventually changes when its contribution to security studies and proactive styles of policing is envisaged. A generic forensic intelligence process is presented, which provides forensic science with a global framework demonstrating the possible collaboration between many new professions and forensic scientists who are interested in crime intelligence.

Introduction

Forensic intelligence brings together two terms whose definitions are the object of many interpretations. Depending on the position adopted, forensic intelligence can even be considered an oxymoron, or, at least, as highlighting tensions inherent in the articulation of security and justice systems. Indeed, 'forensic', etymologically, designates the context of a court of law. Crime intelligence (the conjunction of criminal intelligence analysis and crime analysis, following Ratcliffe [2008]) covers a much broader scope. Beyond its role in investigative procedures, it is often related to security studies. This field has travelled some distance from the legalist approach to crime problems.

Nevertheless, there are many incentives for adopting the proposed articulation. The narrowness of traditional views on forensic science does not allow the structured, useful and comprehensive exploitation of all data whose treatment should fall under its purview. This is particularly evident in its allegiance to justice systems, which themselves struggle to adapt to increased human traceability and the harm caused by innovative crime systems. Consequently, a reform movement within forensic science is gaining greater recognition. It proceeds by progressively expanding the role of forensic science, from its narrower interpretation to its integration into proactive styles of policing and security studies. A logical framework that allows the gradual integration of ideas under the heading 'intelligence' supports this expansion.

A generic forensic intelligence process developed in the scientific literature will be described here (Morelato et al. 2014). It aims at:

(1) Facilitating the debate around the protection of civil liberties;
(2) Questioning efficiency as the primary, or sole, criterion in forensic work;

(3) Serving training and education purposes;
(4) Leading to realistic computerizations; and
(5) Showing how forensic science can collaborate with a broad set of new professions related to security.

Defining forensic science: from a structural to a procedural view

Currently, the dominant practice in forensic science splits the treatments of data collected at scenes into specialized fields, called forensic disciplines. This division follows different dimensions: the types of forensic data (e.g., pattern evidence such as fingermarks, shoemarks or toolmarks; trace evidence and DNA), the use of sophisticated techniques (e.g., separation methods in analytical chemistry or image acquisition and processing techniques) and limited fields of investigations where the analysis of the material collected has a particular legal relevancy (e.g., illicit drugs, fire and firearms investigations). This fragmented view has been called forensics (Roux et al. 2012; see Crispino and Roux, 'Forensic-led regulation strategies: are they fit for security problem-solving purposes?', chapter 6, this volume) and is based on the following postulates:

- It clearly distinguishes police work from sciences serving justice purposes.
- It is implemented through an independent organization responding to specific demands from authorities, such as commissioned expertise. Such a structure is implemented under the form of the so-called traditional forensics laboratory.
- The sciences concerned are directly related to fundamental disciplines, such as chemistry, physics or computer science.
- Terms used in the literature such as 'client' or 'forensic science provider' emphasize the existence of a public/private management system delineating services and products offered to various actors/figures, mostly belonging to justice systems (some laboratories also respond to private demands).

The basic tenet of these forensics structures is mandatory compliance with procedures and rules of justice systems. Since the publication in 2009 of the US National Academy of Sciences report criticizing flawed practices, the use of methods which lack scientific foundations, and unstandardized procedures across laboratories (NAS 2009), pressure on forensic laboratories has increased. Subsequently, the major trend in response to this criticism has been the implementation of quality systems. Fundamental sciences and practices developed in common industrial laboratories have served as a reference. Forensics has thus almost no epistemology of its own within this frame of reference (see Crispino and Roux, chapter 6, this volume).

On this fragmented view of forensics, internal cohesive forces inevitably weaken until the question arises: is there any justification or advantage to maintaining a single forensic laboratory? The failure to provide a convincing answer to this elementary question is illustrated by the closure of many such laboratories around the world, or of some of their economically less viable components. In particular, trace evidence departments are in jeopardy, despite the richness of the information conveyed (Stoney and Stoney 2015). The most obvious gap in this conception, beyond lack of identity of a discipline, is its failure to consider crime scene investigations (Ludwig et al. 2012; Roux et al. 2012; Resnikoff et al. 2015). This disregard creates a serious void in conceptualizing the whole treatment of forensic data.

A procedural view of forensic science

The view privileged in this chapter is procedural; it considers how information is processed transversally, rather than focusing on the way forensic activities are organized (Williams 2007). For this purpose, we define in Figure 12.1 a global process for forensic science. It is inspired by

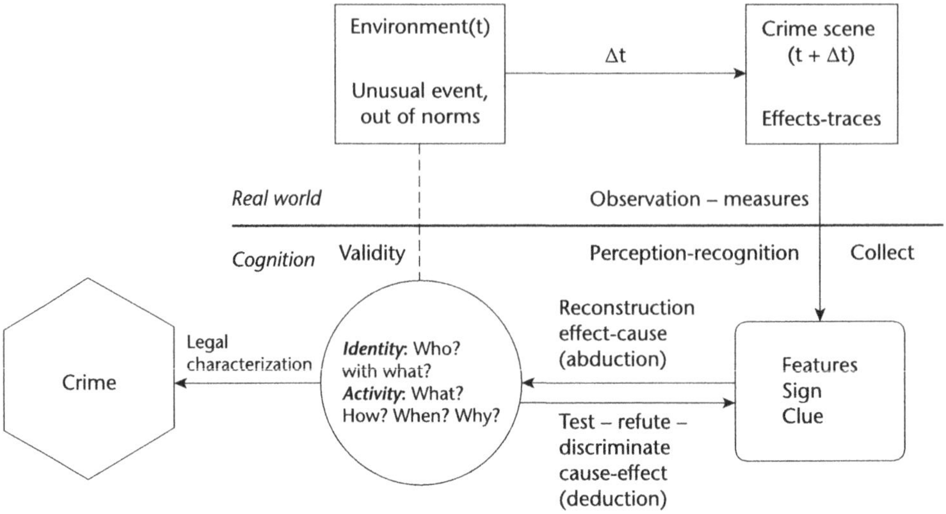

Figure 12.1 Global forensic process

The activity perturbs the environment and causes exchanges of material (application of Locard's postulate). This material is dispersed and delineates the crime scene. Investigations lead to the detection of traces, which are observed, collected, measured and recognized as relevant. Results of observations and features extracted become signs that indicate aspects of the activity through reconstruction (logical abduction). More than one hypothesis may explain observations. Rival hypotheses and their logical consequences are tested through experiments. In function of their resistance, they are discriminated and reformulated and beliefs in their validity adapted. Hypotheses are eventually developed in regard to their relevancy for legally characterizing the case.

Inman and Rudin (2001) and Roux et al. (2012). It outlines the logical treatment of information accessible from singular cases, toward their use in justice systems. This description is transversal and generic. This means it is independent from how the various figures/actors are organized, how their roles and functions are distributed, the type of material exchanged, as well as the techniques used to detect, observe and measure it.

The procedural view derives directly from the richer interpretation of Locard's postulate. Hence, it situates the trace as the common object of study (see Margot, 'Traceology, the bedrock of forensic science and its associated semantics', chapter 3, this volume). The trace is the effect, the vestige of an unusual activity perturbing the environment, whatever the nature and the size of the material exchanged. It is the elementary information on which the activity of interest is logically reconstructed. The trace follows a long path and may be used under many forms before eventually being presented at a court of law. We consider that it becomes evidence only when it supports a court's decision-making process (see Margot, chapter 3, this volume), whatever its use in earlier phases of the logical process. This logical transformation from the trace to evidence aims at making actionable the information conveyed.

Of course, forensic science cannot be considered in isolation. Justice systems still mostly define the context, whatever the vision adopted. In a procedural view, however, forensic science demonstrates its own epistemology and benefits from a greater latitude for its development.

Scope of the narrower view of forensic science

Bringing a transversal view into the fragmented practice of forensics is the principal merit of the so-called Bayesian community (see Margot, chapter 3, this volume). It developed a rational model for assessing the strength of the information conveyed by a trace, and for integrating it into the global decision-making process of a court of law. Forensic science thus retakes the initiative in relation to the exploitation of its object of study.

The model's contribution can be situated within our forensic science framework (Figure 12.2). The Bayesian model clarifies the respective positions of actors/figures when an expertise is commissioned. The so-called Likelihood Ratio (LR), derived from Bayes' theorem, is defined as the province of the scientist, while the client, it is assumed, deals with other terms of the formula. The clients here are mostly a court of law or an authority that commissions an expertise. This approach postulates that the core of the forensic expertise resides in the capacity to evaluate uncertain information through subjectively stated probabilities, and to combine them coherently. Hence, the rationalization efforts focus on intensively 'probabilizing' the process, but keeping in its own hands a very limited part of it (Biedermann 2015). The LR is deductive in nature: propositions are assumed to be given (see Figure 12.2).

Occasionally, a broader contribution of forensic science to the whole process is recognized. Forensic science goes beyond the LR by providing opinions on other terms of the formula. However, such contributions are allowed under very restrictive conditions: 'another situation where scientists may legitimately formulate probabilities is when they intervene at the investigative

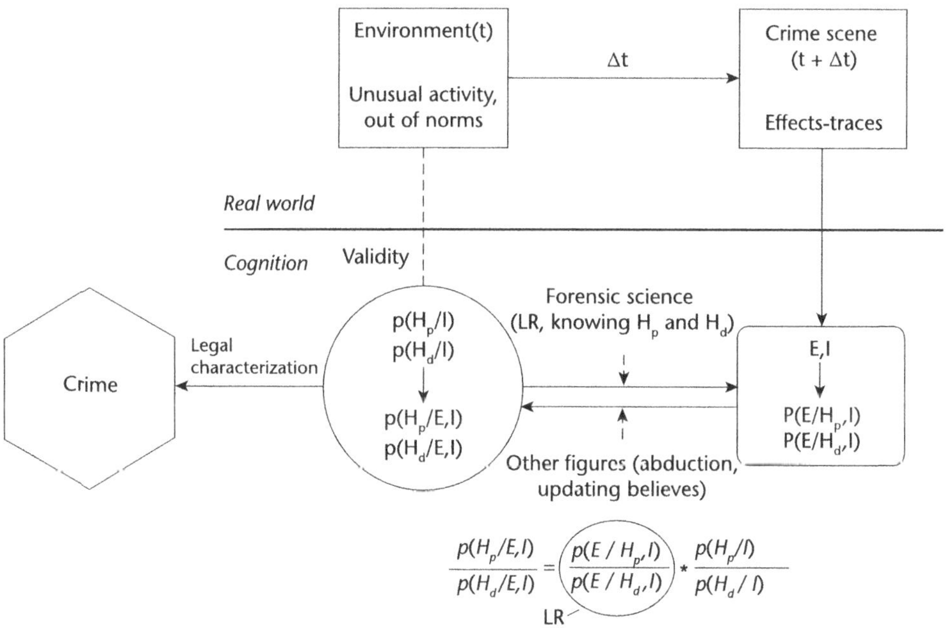

Figure 12.2 How probabilistic inferences situate narrower visions of forensic science

H_p and H_d are the hypotheses remaining after investigations. At this stage, they are preferably termed 'propositions', rather than 'hypotheses'. A formula derived from Bayes' theorem expresses how relative beliefs in these hypotheses, interpreted within specific circumstances (I), change with new observations (E). The likelihood ratio (LR) delineates the territory of forensic science. It demands an evaluation of the observations extracted from a trace, supposing that H_p and H_d are true. It is thus deductive in nature. The other terms are the province of other figures of the court process. One of the advantages of this conception is the universality of the model. It applies whatever the type of traces under consideration and across justice systems.

phase and express, for example, an opinion about a matter that can reasonably be confined to technical and scientific considerations only (e.g., the cause of a technical failure, cause of a fire, etc.)' (Biedermann 2015, 146). This opening remains very narrow. Support provided to a client for formulating propositions is also only reluctantly admitted. Inman and Rudin (2001) recognize that this is where the experience of the scientist is the most useful—and the least recognized!

Delineation of an area for forensic intelligence

There is a growing consensus that recognizes other poorly formalized forms of forensic work scattered across justice systems and the police (e.g., crime scene investigation). They concern the abductive part of the forensic process (reconstructing the activity, developing hypotheses) rather than evaluating already stated propositions. Some within the academic community, however, judge this logic to be insufficiently mature, and scientists operating in forensic laboratories by and large concur. Abduction is not sufficiently mathematized, while forensic science at a court of law must provide protagonists with transparency and robustness in how conclusions are reached. The difficulties in expressing the logic consequently exceed the threshold for a science dedicated to justice systems.

This is exactly the postulate forensic intelligence does not take as granted. Etymologically, investigation contains the Latin root *vestigium*, which means the vestige or the trace. Investigation expresses the central role of detecting, collecting, recognizing and interpreting trace in the whole crime investigation process, not only in the evaluation of given propositions (LR). In comparison with the forensics view, forensic intelligence addresses a significant gap. The police already take the initiative in this area and create good practices, but with weak scientific grounding. This creates a context with great potential for missing information or misinterpreting data. Forensic intelligence considers participation in the structuring and implementation of these processes one of the responsibilities of forensic science.

In summary, the dominant view of a forensic expert's role within forensic science explicitly covers only a very small part of the global treatment of traces. This view masks the variety of uses of information conveyed by traces, the need for integration with other data and the missed opportunities for conducting investigations, particularly in the earlier phase of crime investigation. These gaps are already evident at the crime scene.

Forensic intelligence and crime investigation are about crime reconstruction. Such a logic can hardly be mechanized since it calls for imagination, drawing analogies and associating ideas. Some aspects can nevertheless be rationalized and structured, even if not readily mathematizable. Forensic intelligence postulates that these efforts bring greater efficiency and robustness to justice procedures globally than the proliferation of costly measures of control externally proposed in the traditional model. The scientific consolidation of these wider territories dramatically reduces risk of error and augments transparency in the conduct of crime investigations.

Differentiated contexts for the application of the forensic science process

Kind (1994) provides a useful positioning of forensic activities within the whole criminal investigation process. He provides a first structure and allows the progressive integration of the concept of intelligence (see also Delémont et al. 2014). At least four different contexts (Kind calls them chapters) can be postulated: They have differentiated implications for the way to logically apply the forensic process, prior to a court's final decision (see Figure 12.3).

In the first two chapters of the investigation (see Figure 12.3), the main question is to link activities to persons, while the next two chapters deal with connecting persons to activities. At this point the logic is reversed, from being more abductive in the early phase to becoming

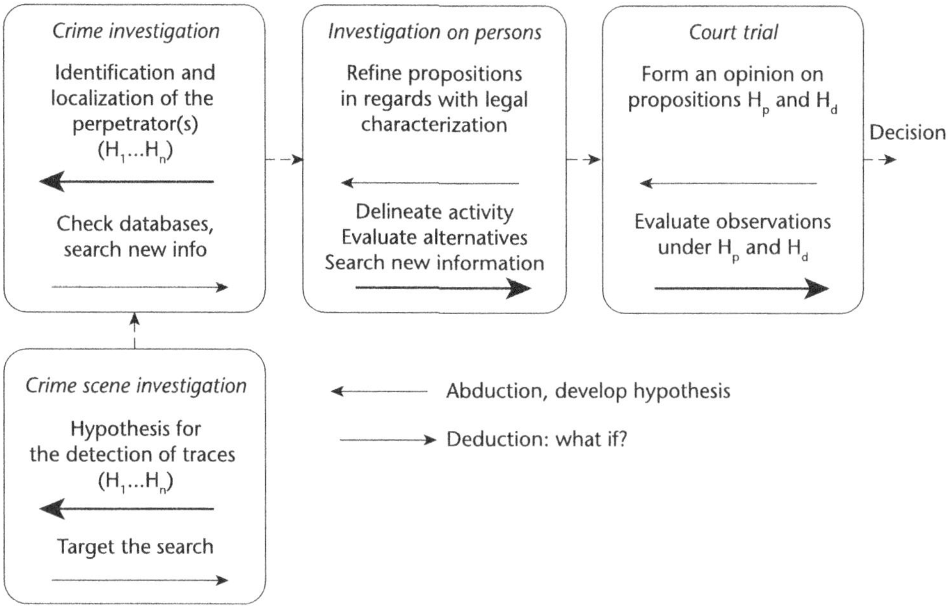

Figure 12.3 The criminal investigation process as four chapters inspired by Kind

Crime scene investigation requires the intensive development of hypotheses about what occurred with the intent of collecting relevant traces of the activity or noticing their astonishing absence. They are relevant in the sense of being related to the case, as well as adding value for the variety of tasks distributed over the chapters (Bitzer et al. 2015). Those traces will first find their utility in supporting the identification and localization of potential perpetrators. But they also serve to legally characterize the crime. The next step means that persons are under investigation. New scope for the activities can be delineated, for instance, through operations such as the search of the home of the person. Legal characterization is now crucial. It demands adaption of hypotheses until they reach the form of propositions (both the defence and the prosecutors proceed) relevant for informing the court's judgments. The court trial itself, then, is the place for debating propositions (and occasionally raising new ones) to reach a verdict. The sequence is not perfect. When a person is stopped in the street wearing a gun without authorization or carrying an unknown suspect substance, this may lead directly to the initiation of an investigation of that person to search for possible illegal activities. When informants point to persons, investigations of these (networked) persons also start immediately in order to delineate their activities.

more deductive leading to the court trial. This progression is compounded by the increased stability of hypotheses along the whole process. In the early phase, there are incentives for imagining a broad range of possibilities for explaining all the information available. At the other end, propositions have been refined and stabilized.

Forensic intelligence as interpreted traces supporting decision-making

Figure 12.3 describes the many treatments the trace follows until it reaches a court of law, where it becomes evidence. The framework suggested by Bitzer et al. (2015) helps further structure the process.

A detected trace is first found factually relevant, i.e., linked to the event under consideration. It is useful, i.e., helps in the resolution of the task. It is usable, i.e., understandable for its users. Such a gradual interpretation allows a first link to be drawn with the term intelligence.

Indeed, in its broader interpretation, intelligence is the accurate, timely and useful product of logically processing information (Ribaux et al. 2003). It influences decision-making. On this interpretation, evidence is a particular form of intelligence obtained from a trace, as it has been evaluated with the objective of supporting a court's decision-making process. Judging by the amount of attention the trace attracts, it is probably the most visible and studied form of intelligence. Yet, it has been demonstrated that only a tiny part of existing traces are detected, analysed and eventually used by a court of law (Bradbury and Feist 2005). Moreover, the resolution of only few cases can be attributed to traces (Brodeur 2010). Thus, the focus on the court trial calls into question the effectiveness and efficiency of forensic science (Roux et al. 2014). Why engage so many resources if forensic science's influence on the outcome of justice systems is negligible?

In response, forensic intelligence argues that many opportunities to use the informative potential of traces are missed and that a systematic identification of the variety of its actual contributions is needed (Delémont et al. 2014).

Such decisions already come up in crime scene investigation (see Delémont et al., 'The practice of crime scene examination in an intelligence-based perspective', chapter 8, this volume). For instance, a sequence of shoemarks is found at the scene of a burglary. This sequence may lead to the assumption that the perpetrator moved toward an object that has potentially been touched (contact point). A fingermark found on the object may, in turn, lead to the burglar. In this situation, the sequence of shoemarks was assumed relevant, useful and usable in making a decision relative to the task (collecting traces). This reasoning is independent of whether the shoemarks will subsequently also play a role at a court of law. These shoemarks have acquired the status of intelligence because they have provided support in guiding actions that help resolve the task. There is no evaluative model of the efficiency of forensic science that integrates such determinant contributions.

Some typologies illustrating the variety of the kinds of intelligence provided by traces have been proposed (e.g., Ribaux et al. 2006) (see Table 12.1). They provide elementary building blocks. Looking for decision-making points where traces are used in practice, as well as evaluating this contribution, is, however, at the top of forensic intelligence's research agenda.

One important characteristic of crime has still not been taken into account: forensic science work has been considered as a response to events, on a case-by-case basis, while certain forms of criminality are highly concentrated and repetitive. What role can traces play in this perspective?

Forensic intelligence, repetitive crimes and crime analysis

The repetitive nature of certain forms of crimes has long been recognized (Ratcliffe 2008): crime concentrates in place and time; it often reaches the same (type of) victims and some offenders are known to be 'prolific'.

The elementary inferences described above can thus be linked to form a chain in many practical situations. When a DNA profile allows the identification of a suspect, police can take actions against this person—for example, interviews or a search at his or her home. When shoes are collected in the course of these operations, sole patterns are systematically compared with those collected previously at different scenes. Similarities found extend the scope of the investigation to other cases. The person's mobile phone may, in turn, indicate connection with criminal networks. These kinds of inference structures are frequently used for uncovering part of the broader activity of a person under arrest.

The information conveyed by traces is also used for detecting crime repetitions prior to an arrest. When used systematically, traces are extremely powerful for this purpose. A typology for structuring the contribution can be defined (Table 12.2). Of importance in terms of intelligence is the evaluation of the impact of linking activities on investigations. The variety of forms this intelligence (usefulness) can take increases dramatically.

Table 12.1 Examples of forensic intelligence related to investigations

Types of inference	*Example of intelligence provided*	*Usefulness/possible actions taken*
Suggesting a possible frame (possible sources for the trace)	A fingermark found at the scene is compared to fingerprints of known persons stored in a database. The interpretation of this comparison may point to the source of the trace.	An investigation against the person begins.
	A partial DNA profile extracted from a biological trace collected at a scene is compared with a database, providing a frame of possible sources.	Focus the search to a limited set of persons (frame).
Identifying a substance	A powder found on a person is identified as an illicit substance.	Decide to keep the person in jail for further investigations.
	A red substance found on the floor is identified as human blood.	Envisage the hypothesis of a homicide, and take measures accordingly.
Suggesting the description of an object or a person	A red paint fragment is recovered at a car accident. The make and model of the car at its source is determined.	Police call the public for assistance and check databases of the car's owners according to this information.
	DNA has been extracted from biological traces. It provides the gender of the person, as well as indications about the human appearance of the source.	Police target their search according to the physical profile determined.
Reconstructing the modus operandi	Debris found at the scene is compared to images taken by witnesses, allowing the development of possible scenarios for the origin and cause of the fire, and establishing its criminal nature.	Start an investigation for arson.
Assembling pieces of same origin	Pieces of a single body are found at different places.	Link investigations that may have started independently.
Situating trace in time (Weyermann and Ribaux 2012)	The time since the person died has been evaluated by the examination of the body and the use of forensic entomology.	Test scenario and adapt actions in function of chronologies.
Localization of trace	The signal of a mobile phone belonging to a missing person is localized.	Orient the search for the missing person.
	Specific plants, soil and fibres are found on an abandoned body.	Reorient the investigations. If a place is determined, search for possible source for the fibres.
Linking individuals	Fibres are exchanged between shirts of persons.	Orient the investigation by supposing a link between the two individuals.
Linking persons to objects	The DNA profile of a person is found on the screen of a computer.	Evaluate consequences that the person is a possible user of the computer.
Linking objects	A list of calls to/from a mobile phone collected from an arrested person is made.	Search for accomplices or detect/consolidate knowledge on the structure of a criminal network.

Table 12.2 Examples of forensic intelligence related to crime repetitions

Types of inference	*Example of intelligence provided*	*Usefulness/possible action taken*
The same source—person	DNA profile found at a scene is the same as a DNA profile found at another scene.	Investigations are linked together and information joined. This synthesis allows a better description of the profile of the perpetrator.
The same source—object	A bullet found at one scene is assumed to have been fired by the same gun as another bullet found at another scene.	Investigations are linked together, and information joined. The synthesis reorients investigations.
The same type of source—object/substance	An illicit substance found on an individual is linked with (comes from the same batch as) the illicit substance found on another person.	The substance comes from the same network, and investigations can be linked.
	From images and paint specimens found at the scene, robbers have used the same make and model of car in break and enter of jewellery store.	Envisage the possibility that perpetrators belong to the same group. Recent stolen cars of this make and model are searched for in order to extend investigations and anticipate next cases.
	An increase in the use of guns of a certain make and model is observed from bullets and a cartridge found at scenes (Hannam 2010).	Possibility of a new organized crime network and its consequences has to be envisaged.

Forensic intelligence and intelligence-led policing

The contribution of forensic intelligence seems, at this point, related only to crime investigations. Its contribution is, however, far broader. Linking activities and persons is part of the understanding of crime systems and mechanisms. This knowledge, in turn, allows the design of proactive actions aimed at disrupting those activities. From investigating the past, forensic intelligence turns to anticipating the future.

For instance, traces can support the detection of the activity of a serial offender through the comparison of DNA profiles collected at different scenes. Then the synthesis of all the information collected on each case in the series may cause a pattern to emerge. This pattern shows regularities in the behaviour of the offender that can be used to anticipate his or her further activities. Intelligence partly provided by traces thus indicates how preventive/repressive measures can be envisaged and planned to mitigate an activity causing harm.

This switch from reactive to proactive policing changes the reference for forensic science and also connects to the global field of security and policing, in particular to problem solving (see Cusson, 'A method that combines criminology and forensic science', chapter 4, this volume) or, broadly, to the so-called intelligence-led style of policing. Since the late 1980s, intelligence-led policing models have developed, principally in the UK (Ratcliffe 2008). As early as 1996, Tilley and Ford (1996) regretted that forensic science was not sufficiently connected to the new developments in policing high-volume crimes. This was confirmed by subsequent audits (Blakey 2002), as well as when globally evaluating the variety of contribution of forensic science (Bradbury and Feist 2005).

This recognized potential needed to be further investigated and expounded. A definition of a forensic intelligence process has been proposed for this purpose (Morelato et al. 2014; Baechler

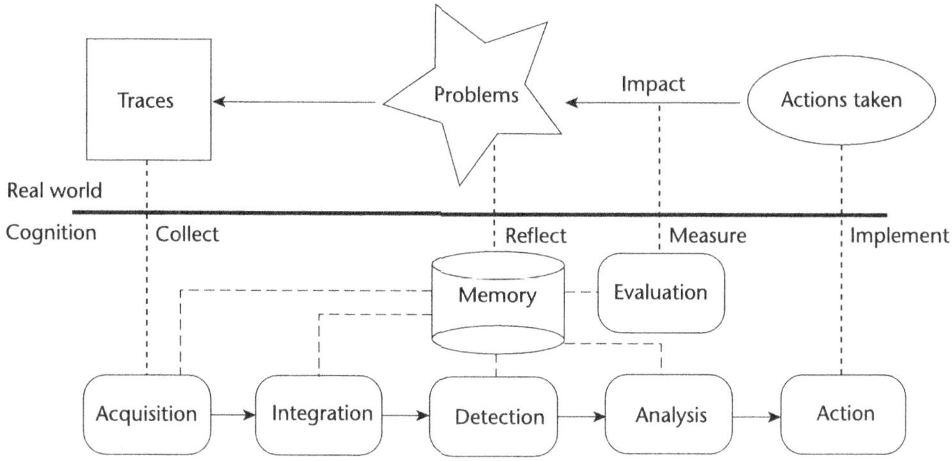

Figure 12.4 Forensic intelligence process, inspired by Ribaux (2014)

Repeated harmful or unlawful activities cause problems. They generate traces that have to be detected and collected. Features are extracted from traces (acquisition). This data is entered into a memory and linked to the knowledge already available on certain problems (integration). Repetitions are detected, for instance, through the search of tendencies, clusters or elementary links, and grouped into new problems (detection). Problems detected are analysed in order to determine their cause (analysis). This analysis allows the design and the choice of a response to the problem (action). Actions are eventually deployed, and their impact on the problem has to be systematically evaluated.

et al. 2015) (see Figure 12.4). The SARA (scanning, analysing, response, assessment) methodology developed for supporting problem-oriented and community policing (see Cusson, chapter 4, this volume) has inspired the description of this process. The forensic intelligence process, however, focuses on the use of traces. It is generic since it does not depend on the type of traces under consideration. It is iterative in the sense that it ensures the continuous follow-up of problems. And it relates to intelligence since the main objective is to lead to recommendations on how to deploy measures for responding to problems.

It can be instantiated for monitoring high-volume crimes (Ribaux et al. 2006), the systematic linkage of false ID documents (Baechler et al. 2013), illicit markets on the Internet or any other types of repetitive problems (Morelato et al. 2014). Of course, each adaptation demands the integration of specificities associated with the problem under scrutiny or the nature of the traces treated.

It is not easy to discern which elements of the architecture of the process—and at which level of detail—are generic transversally. Such discernment is related to a subtle modelling activity. Many aspects of its elementary functions have, however, been identified with some genericity (Morelato et al. 2014). For example,

- methodology for linking cases can be based on measure of similarities, i.e., the definition of 'distances' calculated between vectors of features extracted from traces (Esseiva et al. 2003; Baechler et al. 2013);
- analysis can be oriented by the detection of tendencies in the data, such as the increase or drop in the appearance of a specific characteristic of a certain type of trace collected in a time series. For instance, an increase in the appearance of a certain type of sole pattern in

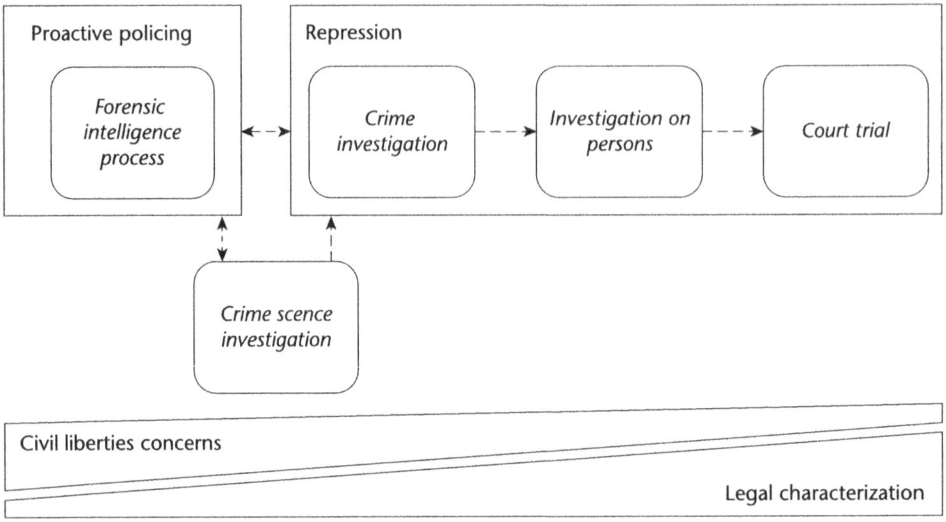

Figure 12.5 The use of forensic science in proactive policing

The use of forensic intelligence in proactive policing may orient crime investigation and crime scene investigation (see Délemont et al., chapter 8, this volume). Conversely, lessons learned from investigations feed knowledge on crime systems and mechanisms. The legal context in which those activities are carried out changes dramatically, as proactive policing needs the collection of data and may be closely related to surveillance. Concerns about civil liberties are thus a priority, while the analytical activity takes distance from a too legalist approach of criminal behaviour. When the investigation of the case progresses, legal characterization is a priority, and the judge orders intrusive measures for this purpose.

the traces collected during a certain period in a specific region may indicate the activity of a single perpetrator (Albertetti et al. 2016); and

- clusters in the data are detected, for instance, the grouping of characteristics of the chemical profile of illicit seized substances (Esseiva et al. 2003).

The whole articulation of forensic intelligence can now be formulated in Figure 12.5.

Building capacities for articulations with other types of data

Forensic intelligence proposes that traces left by the activity of interest receive much more attention as elementary building blocks producing intelligence for guiding investigations and orienting policing. In recent times, investigators have relied principally on interviews of witnesses, victims or suspects. This activity has not been abandoned, but few investigations are conducted now without numerical traces extracted from electronic devices. The volume and variety of information accessible in the early phase of an investigation has thus dramatically increased, necessitating new frameworks for their integration with more traditional types of data. The formalized model for accessing scientific expertise through an external laboratory in a formal and punctual manner cannot work in these conditions. Investigations thus become naturally much more collective and interdisciplinary. On a serious case, interdisciplinary teams are now ready to intervene rapidly in certain countries (Barclay 2009), while laboratories tend to define new roles for coordinating scientific information and ensuring more fluidity in the process (Schuliar and Crispino 2013). The future will demand much more work for formalizing such a collective process in order to favour hypothesis development and management, which are at the core of crime investigation.

Traces have rarely been considered as central in crime linkage systems and crime analysis. Such processes are founded to a greater extent on modus operandi or other behavioural aspects related to the activity of the perpetrator. They therefore leave very implicit the reconstruction phase at the core of the forensic process: the activity took place in the past, and modus operandi can be assumed only on the basis of the interpretation of relics of the event. This hole in the reasoning process may lead to missing essential points. Modus operandi is systematically the result of a reconstruction, even when the action has been filmed (images are definitely traces of the activity). How many homicides, for example, are lacking in the data because the investigative process failed to analyse sufficiently deeply suicides or accidents? The systematic use of traces in comparing crimes is far from effective. Structures for this purpose must still be defined by starting from the generic process presented.

Conclusion

This chapter contributes to articulating the pervasive message in this handbook: The study of crime cannot totally abstract from understanding the disturbances caused by unusual specific activities occurring on a physical/digital substrate. This is not only a technical problem; this is much more an information-processing problem calling for solid logical foundations—the proper use of information conveyed by traces.

By filling an alarming gap in crime investigation and broader policing, forensic intelligence contributes to restoring a broader position for forensic science. It demands the more offensive and explicit integration of information conveyed by traces. A solid framework is urgently needed, since the increase in human traceability demands changes in the way investigations are conducted and proactive policing envisaged.

Traditional physical traces often come late in the investigative process, more often under the form of a commissioned expertise carried out by an independent laboratory and dedicated to a court of law. Conversely, numerical traces are used very early in crime investigations, even before crimes are perpetrated, through communication monitoring. Numerical traces are *voluminous*, of great *variety* and demand *velocity* in their treatments. Their *validity* is often questionable. They have a great informational *value*. These 5 Vs are well-known signs that investigation and intelligence has entered into big data space. Methodologies for exploring those spaces are only in their infancy.

The view of forensic intelligence presented in this chapter shows how the richness of the concept of trace can be used for this purpose.

References

Albertetti, F., L. Grossrieder, O. Ribaux and K. Stoffel. 2016. 'Change Points Detection in Crime-Related Time Series: An On-line Fuzzy Approach Based on a Shape Space Representation'. *Applied Soft Computing* 40(C): 441–454. http://dx.doi.org/10.1016/j.asoc.2015.12.004.

Baechler, S., M. Morelato, O. Ribaux, A. Beavis, M. Tahtouh, P. Kirkbride, P. Esseiva, P. Margot and C. Roux. 2015 'Forensic Intelligence Framework. Part II: Study of the Main Generic Building Blocks and Challenges through the Examples of Illicit Drugs and False Identity Documents Monitoring'. *Forensic Science International* 250 (May): 44–52.

Baechler, S., V. Terrasse, T. Fritz, J.-P. Pujol, O. Ribaux and P. Margot. 2013. 'The Systematic Profiling of False Identity Documents: Method Validation and Performance Evaluation Using Seizures Known to Originate from Common and Different Sources'. *Forensic Science International* 232(1–3): 180–190.

Barclay, D. 2009. 'Using Forensic Science in Major Crime Inquiries'. In J. Fraser and R. Williams, eds., *Handbook of Forensic Science*, 337–358. Cullompton: Willan.

Biedermann, A. 2015. 'The Role of the Subjectivist Position in the Probabilization of Forensic Science'. *Journal of Forensic Science and Medicine* 1(2):140–148.

Bitzer, S., N. Albertini, E. Lock, O. Ribaux and O. Delémont. 2015. 'Utility of the Clue—From Measuring the Investigative Contribution of Forensic Science to Supporting the Decision to Use Traces'. *Science & Justice* 55(6): 509–513.

Blakey, D. 2002. 'Under the Microscope Refocused. A Revisit to the Thematic Inspection. Report on Scientific and Technical Support'. Ditchling: Her Majesty's Inspectorate of Constabulary.

Bradbury, S.-A., and A. Feist. 2005. 'The Use of Forensic Science in Volume Crime Investigations: A Review of the Research Literature', Online Report, Home Office, London, 43/05. www.gov.uk/government/uploads/system/uploads/attachment_data/file/115849/hoor4305.pdf (accessed 23 September 2017).

Brodeur, J.-P. 2010. *The Policing Web*. New York: Oxford University Press.

Delémont, O., O. Ribaux and E. Lock. 2014. 'Forensic Science and Criminal Inquiry'. In G.J.N. Bruinsma and D.L. Weisburd, eds., *Encyclopedia of Criminology and Criminal Justice*, 1754–1762. Berlin: Springer.

Esseiva, P., L. Dujourdy, F. Anglada, F. Taroni and P. Margot. 2003. 'A Methodology for Illicit Heroin Seizures Comparison in a Drug Intelligence Perspective Using Large Databases'. *Forensic Science International* 132(2): 139–152.

Hannam, A.G. 2010. 'Trends in Converted Firearms in England & Wales as Identified by the National Firearms Forensic Intelligence Database (NFFID) between September 2003 and September 2008'. *Journal of Forensic Sciences* 55(3): 757–766.

Inman, K., and N. Rudin. 2001. *Principles and Practice of Criminalistics: The Profession of Forensic Science*. Boca Raton, FL: CRC Press LLC.

Kind, S.S. 1994. 'Crime Investigation and the Criminal Trial: A Three Chapter Paradigm of Evidence'. *Journal of the Forensic Science Society* 34(3): 155–164.

Ludwig, A., J. Fraser and R. Williams. 2012. 'Crime Scene Examiners and Volume Crime Investigations: An Empirical Study of Perception and Practice'. *Forensic Science Policy & Management: An International Journal of Police Science and Management* 3(2): 53–61.

Morelato, M., S. Baechler, O. Ribaux, A. Beavis, M. Tahtouh, P. Kirkbride, C. Roux and P. Margot. 2014. 'Forensic Intelligence Framework. Part I: Induction of a Transversal Model by Comparing Illicit Drugs and False Identity Documents Monitoring'. *Forensic Science International* 236 (March): 181–190.

National Research Council. 2009. *Strengthening Forensic Science in the United States: A Path Forward*. Washington, DC: The National Academies Press.

Ratcliffe, J. 2008 *Intelligence-Led Policing*. Cullompton, UK: Willan.

Resnikoff, T., O. Ribaux, A. Baylon, M. Jendly and Q. Rossy. 2015. 'The Polymorphism of Crime Scene Investigation: An Exploratory Analysis of the Influence of Crime and Forensic Intelligence on Decisions Made by Crime Scene Examiners'. *Forensic Science International* 257 (December): 425–434.

Ribaux, O. 2014. *Police scientifique. Le renseignement par la trace*. Lausanne: Presses Polytechniques et Universitaires Romandes.

Ribaux, O., A. Girod, S. Walsh, P. Margot, S. Mizrahi and V. Clivaz. 2003. 'Forensic Intelligence and Crime Analysis'. *Probability, Law and Risk* 2(2): 47–60.

Ribaux, O., S.J. Walsh and P. Margot. 2006. 'The Contribution of Forensic Science to Crime Analysis and Investigation: Forensic Intelligence'. *Forensic Science International* 156(2–3): 171–181.

Roux, C., F. Crispino and O. Ribaux. 2012. 'From Forensics to Forensic Science'. *Current Issues in Criminal Justice* 24(1): 7–24.

Roux, C., R. Julian, S. Kelty and O. Ribaux. 2014. 'Forensic Science Effectiveness'. In G.J.N. Bruinsma and D. Weisburd, eds., *Encyclopedia of Criminology & Criminal Justice*, 1795–1804. Berlin: Springer.

Schuliar, Y., and F. Crispino. 2013. 'Semiotics, Heuristics, and Inferences Used by Forensic Scientists'. In M. Houck and J.A. Siegel, eds., *Encyclopedia of Forensic Science*, 2nd ed., 310–313. Waltham: Academic Press.

Stoney, D.A., and P.L. Stoney. 2015. 'Critical Review of Forensic Trace Evidence Analysis and the Need for a New Approach'. *Forensic Science International* 251 (June): 159–170.

Tilley, N., and A. Ford. 1996. 'Forensic Science and Crime Investigation'. In B. Webb, ed., *Crime Detection and Prevention*, 73. London: Police Research Group, Home Office.

Weyermann, C., and O. Ribaux. 2012. 'Situating Forensic Traces in Time'. *Science and Justice* 52(2): 68–75.

Williams, R. 2007. 'Policing and Forensic Science'. In T. Newburn, ed., *Handbook of Policing*, 760–793. Cullompton: Willan.

13

Prevention and forensic science

How forensic evidence supports prevention

Nick Tilley and James French

Crime, crime prevention and forensic science

A crime occurs when a sufficiently motivated offender meets a sufficiently suitable target with nothing or no one able to stand between them, effectively either to hold back the offender or to protect the target (Cohen and Felson 1979; Felson 1986).

Almost all of us can be tempted to commit a crime and most of us have succumbed at some point (Gabor 1994; Tilley 2013). We drive above the speed limit, fail to pay fares on public transport, pilfer from our employers, understate our incomes in our tax returns, over-claim expenses or welfare benefits, exaggerate losses to insurance companies, assault others when angry or inebriated, steal from shops or libraries, drop litter or commit some other offence. Likewise, most of us have been targets of crime or have possessed typical targets of crime. We have been physically or sexually assaulted, been pickpocketed, fallen for a scam of some sort, suffered a burglary or car theft or been deliberately short-changed in shops. Saying that almost all of us have offended in at least some way and at some time does not mean that we are all equally likely to offend. Some people over some periods commit crime at a high rate. Along similar lines, although most of us will have been victims at some point, a few of us are victimized repeatedly (Farrell and Pease 1993; Everson and Pease 2001; Pease 1998).

Patterns of crime across space and time are a function of the supply, distribution and movement of those sufficiently motivated to commit crime, of targets that are attractive enough to tempt potential offenders and of those who can effectively stand between them (Cohen and Felson 1979). Crime concentrations are found in conditions where likely offenders and suitable targets converge in the absence of effective intermediaries (Wortley and Mazerolle 2008). The routines of everyday life, often shaped by the layout of cities, produce the patterns of encounter that lie behind observable crime patterns (Brantingham and Brantingham 1984).

Crime prevention involves efforts either to reduce the supply of those sufficiently motivated (and able) to offend or of targets that are sufficiently suitable for the offender, or to increase the supply of intermediaries able to stand between suitable targets and likely offenders (Felson and Eckert 2016; Tilley 2009).

Crime prevention is oriented to the future. It tries to avert events that would otherwise happen. It is akin to public health, which is concerned with preventing diseases or accidents (Brantingham and Faust 1976; van Dijk and de Waard 1991). Primary prevention in relation to crime and public health focuses on whole populations. Secondary prevention focuses on populations that are known to be at heightened risk. Tertiary prevention focuses on those whose past experience or activity show them to be at risk of further problems.

Forensic science has historically been orientated to the past: to help determine whether an incident involved criminal behaviour and to help identify or eliminate suspects in relation to a specific crime. The application of forensic science may identify (or eliminate) populations from which a suspect is likely to come. It may also contribute to the implication of specific individuals. More broadly, it assists in the process of reconstructing criminal events in space and time. In courts of law, forensic evidence can be used either as part of the case against someone or to show that a suspect should be acquitted. A major aim of forensic science is to improve the chances that the guilty will be convicted and more importantly still that the innocent will be exonerated. A key role of the forensic scientist has been to assist the court in reaching its decision.

There is a growing knowledge-base for forensic scientists to draw on to identify, collect, analyse, interpret and present evidence relating to crime events and those who may be suspected of committing specific offences. There are active and important research programmes oriented to improving forensic techniques and our capacity to interpret evidence in the service of traditional aims. Unfortunately, it has been repeatedly found that forensic science is not well used even in its traditional role, at least as regards volume crimes, and this has been the case over a sustained period (Tilley and Townsley 2009; Ludwig and Fraser 2014). In addition to technical improvements in forensic technique, there appear to be widespread continuing needs for improvements in the systems that provide for its effective use in its traditional role of contributing effectively to criminal investigations. Specific recurrently identified weaknesses include: limited forensic knowledge and training among investigators, poor communications, poor use of resources and poor timeliness (ibid.). The degree to which forensic science can be used in the investigation of volume crime will also depend on the financial resources that are available. Furthermore, questions and concerns have been raised regarding the scientific basis of a number of forensic science disciplines. These debates culminated in the publication of the report on *Strengthening Forensic Science in the United States* by the National Academy of Sciences in 2009 (NAS 2009).

Ostensibly, forensic science, as a backward-looking enterprise oriented to serving the interests of justice for specific individuals, has rather little to contribute to crime prevention, which is forward looking and oriented to averting harms to unknown populations. Conventionally, forensic science is deemed to play its part through its specialist role in assisting detection and investigation within the criminal justice process. The remainder of this chapter will try to show ways in which forensic science may already be supporting crime prevention, even when that is not its main focus. More ambitiously, it will then lay out an agenda for forensic scientists to make a much larger contribution to crime prevention in the future. Having said that, it is important to note that the justice-focused role of forensic science is crucial. The crime prevention role envisaged later in this chapter is not an alternative. Rather, it builds on some skills and habits of thought that forensic scientists already have. Moreover, the types of contribution to crime prevention envisaged turn on the development and use of robust forensic techniques and frameworks for interpreting evidence in a logical, balanced and rigorous manner.

Preventive supports of forensic science

When the sentences passed on active offenders involve incarceration, those offenders are prevented from committing crimes in the community. They are incapacitated while in prison. Vollaard (2011) shows that the incarceration of prolific offenders in the Netherlands produced preventive effects (see also Zimring and Hawkins 1995 for an overview of what research can tell us about incapacitation and its effects). Where forensic scientists have played a part in the detection and conviction of incarcerated prolific offenders, they have thereby contributed to crime prevention. Moreover, if offenders who are apprehended are provided with effective treatments that inhibit later offending, then forensic scientists involved in their detection and conviction will have played a role in leading them to that treatment. And there is some evidence that some treatment programmes can be effective in preventive terms for some offenders (Tilley 2009).

The prospect of enhanced risks of detection created by forensic science may contribute to general deterrence. In particular, the capacities of forensic science displayed in popular television programmes may plausibly lead to a 'CSI effect', according to which an exaggerated impression of the technical potential of forensic science leads offenders to overestimate the risks from offending, leading them to commit fewer crimes. The extent to which jurors expect and demand scientific evidence in criminal cases and the degree to which this may be influenced by popular culture have been considered in the literature (see Shelton et al. 2006 and Tyler 2006). However, we know of no empirical studies that have systematically tested hypotheses regarding offenders. It is also possible that offenders may have developed a greater awareness of forensic strategies and therefore engage in counter-forensic efforts in an attempt to evade detection. Again, we know of no systematic evidence on this.

The development and expansion of DNA databases and the growing ability to produce DNA profiles successfully from very small quantities of material should have enhanced these effects by increasing rates of detection, by speeding up detection and by heightening perceived risks to likely offenders. Moreover, they may add specific deterrence in that once an arrestee has had their DNA profile entered into a DNA database they will know that their chances of being detected while committing some future crime is increased. Notwithstanding this, our increased ability to generate profiles from smaller and smaller quantities of material gives rise to a range of interpretation issues that relate to mixtures, contamination and transfer. Further research in these areas will assist in the process of analysing and interpreting profiles that are generated in casework.

The preventive potential of forensic science

We now move to ways in which forensic science might play a broader role in crime prevention than it has as traditionally understood. This section is in two parts. The first discusses a strategic framework for greater application of forensic science to crime prevention. The second outlines specific ways in which forensic science may be used within that framework.

A strategic framework for using forensic science for preventive purposes

The most effective general approach to crime reduction in policing is 'problem-oriented policing' (POP) (Weisburd and Eck 2004; Weisburd et al. 2010). The so-called SARA process lies at the heart of POP as it is most often implemented (Eck and Spelman 1987; Sidebottom and Tilley 2011). SARA refers to Scanning, Analysis, Response and Assessment. Scanning involves identifying specific recurrent problems that fall to the police, including crimes. Analysis involves developing and testing conjectures about the conditions creating or enabling the specified problems, especially those that might be open to preventive attention. Response involves the formulation and delivery of a preventive strategy that follows from the analysis, in other words, finding what conditions might realistically be open to intervention by the police, partner or other third party who might be persuaded to act. Assessment involves efforts to determine whether the preventive measures are in practice delivering their intended effects.

Rather than a fixed linear process, SARA is best thought of as an iterative one with feedback from later stages to earlier ones. Herman Goldstein, who invented POP (1979, 1990), advocated POP as a general approach to wash through all ranks and all specialisms in police agencies. Third parties feeding into policing would likewise align to POP and the SARA process. Indeed, in England and Wales, where partnerships between agencies in the service of crime reduction have been put on a statutory footing, POP is now often described as 'Problem-Oriented Partnership' to capture the joint responsibility for delivering crime prevention across agencies (Bullock et al. 2012). What might be the role of forensic science in this?

First, POP largely describes the scientific method. Given their scientific orientation, forensic scientists should be able to help police and their partners engage in that open, critical, empirical theory-testing and theory-refinement process required of POP. Second and more specifically, forensic scientists are well placed to help identify and analyse specific crime problems, and also work through potential solutions to them.

The scanning side of POP is not confined to identifying problems that have already taken hold. It also involves searching for warning signs of problems that are just around the corner and might be pre-empted by early intervention. Forensic science has a potential role to play here too.

New crimes and new methods of committing old crimes evolve continuously. Offenders adapt to changed circumstances, exploiting newly discovered crime opportunities and circumventing preventive strategies that have been put in place to try to thwart them. There are various sources of information on emergent crime problems, including police officers, victimization surveys, Crime Stoppers organizations, etc. Forensic scientists, notably crime scene examiners for crimes in physical space, are well placed to work out how crimes are being committed and to identify emergent trends. Those involved in digital forensics are well placed to work out how crimes are being committed in cyber space. The advantage in both cases is that early warnings may enable adaptations to be made speedily to avoid the crime harvest that would otherwise follow.

Forensic science also has a role to play in analysing problems and helping to identify responses. In engineering, progress is made through the identification and correction of fault. Forensic scientists functioning in like manner would be in a position to examine crimes as failures to prevent crime. Identifying repeat failures to prevent crime because of the presence (or absence) of the same attribute could be invaluable in pointing out where we should try to take remedial action.

An example may help to make clear how this could work (Clarke and Mayhew 1988). Suicide has not in all jurisdictions at all times been a crime, but it was an offence in England and Wales before 1962. Suicide rates in England and Wales dropped steadily with the replacement of toxic gas by non-toxic gas for heating and cooking in domestic premises, as shown in Figure 13.1. As can be seen, the overall drop in suicide matched closely the fall in suicide using domestic gas. This is not to say that the gas supply caused suicide. However, the gas supply permitted and in this sense facilitated it. For many individuals, even though numerous alternative suicide methods are available, the convenience of a poisonous gas supply was sufficient to allow suicidal intentions readily to be acted on, so much so that the removal of that method produced a substantial fall in the overall suicide rate. The change in gas supply was certainly not made with the prevention of suicide in mind. The reduction in suicide instead was a happy, unintended by-product. What the example does show, however, is that detailed analysis of modus operandi might help identify families of incident (comparable to suicides using the domestic gas supply) that could be prevented by changing the opportunity (say removing the supply of that convenient method for taking one's life). In fact, just this type of learning has happened in relation to suicide, where requiring that paracetamol tablets be sold in blister packs rather than bottles has made it more difficult for those tempted to commit suicide to wash a handful down quickly and thereby kill themselves.

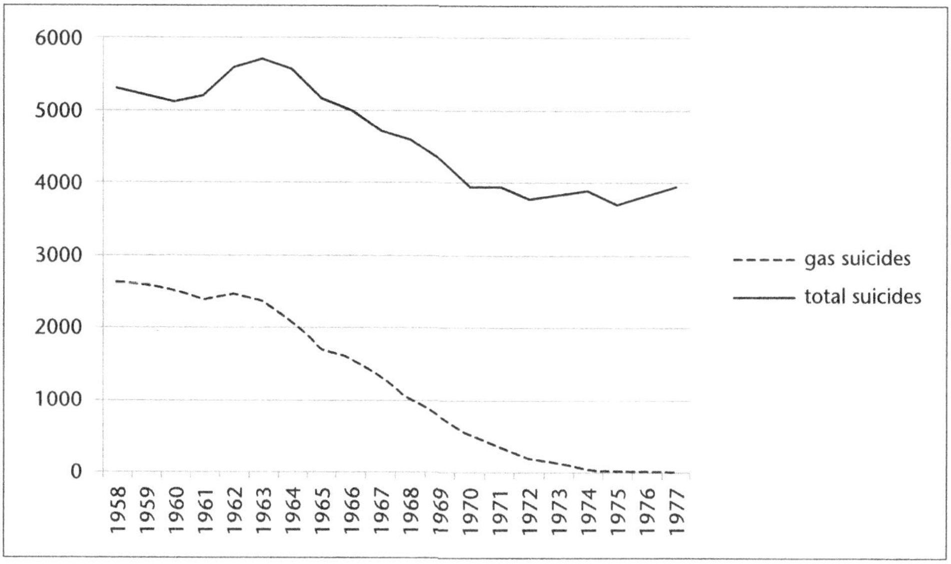

Figure 13.1 All suicides and suicides by gas, England and Wales, 1958–1977

Crime scene examiners and forensic scientists are well placed to analyse in detail the crime opportunities (preventive failures) being exploited by offenders in physical spaces. Forensic accountants might do the same for fraud. Forensic investigators of all forms of cyber crime are equally in a strong position to perform the same role in relation to crimes that occur in cyber rather than physical space.

One of the key tools developed for POP is the problem-analysis triangle (PAT). The PAT uses the insight noted at the start of this chapter: for a crime to occur, a likely offender has to encounter a suitable target in the absence of a capable guardian. Subtract the likely offender or suitable target or add capable guardianship and the offence will not take place. Locations vary in the guardianship they provide for potential victims. The sides of PAT thus relate to targets (or victims), offenders and locations. In the next section, we turn specifically to examples of ways in which forensic science can help identify suitable targets that need to be made less suitable, offenders who need treatment or diversion and locations that call for greater guardianship.

Specific preventive uses of forensic science

REDUCING THE SUPPLY OF SUITABLE TARGETS AND OF PROLIFIC OFFENDERS

There is a large body of research on repeat victimization (Farrell and Pease 1993, 2017). This suggests ways in which the preventive potential of forensic science may be enhanced. For diverse offence types across a wide range of jurisdictions, it has been found consistently that those who suffer a crime are at increased risk of another and that this increased risk fades quickly. Furthermore, it is found that the same offenders tend to be those that commit the repeat crimes (Everson and Pease 2001; Bernasco 2008). Lastly, those committing the repeat crimes tend to be prolific (Everson and Pease 2001). This pattern provides opportunities to target enhanced efforts at detection, notably those aiming to collect trace material that would (a) establish the probability that the same offender was, indeed, responsible for offences in the series, (b) associate relevant contact trace materials (notably fingerprints and DNA profiles) to those already on the database, and (c) increase the chance that the offender would subsequently be apprehended (such as application of grease to surfaces liable to be touched by offenders to provide high-quality fingermarks and of property marking fluids such as Smartwater that the offender is liable to pick up when committing an offence).

The phenomenon of repeat victimization creates an opportunity for those involved in forensic science activities to contribute to crime prevention in a second way. It provides the scope for the crime scene investigator to give timely advice to the victim on steps they can take to reduce their risk of a repeat incident. Given the time spent at the scene of the crime in comparison to the first officer who attends, crime scene examiners are well placed to warn the victim of the raised risk they face, especially in the short term. Moreover, crime scene examiners' work in reconstructing the ways in which particular offences were committed and their broader expertise in understanding how crimes are committed puts them in an especially strong position to provide bespoke advice to a victim on what they might do in order to reduce the risk of further incidents.

Reducing the supply of likely offenders

SHORTENING CRIMINAL CAREERS

Criminal careers research shows that offending peaks early and most criminal careers are short (Farrington 1986). Research also shows that prolific young offenders are versatile (Farrington 1998). Catching offenders late in their criminal careers clearly risks missing the preventive potential that might be realized by their early identification and the effective inhibition of subsequent offending.

Putting the DNA profile of those apprehended the first time they are arrested onto a DNA database (Leary and Pease 2003), even if they are not subsequently processed by the criminal justice system, may produce preventive benefits in two ways.[1] First, it may act as a deterrent in that the (perceived) risks of being caught for a future crime are increased. Second, those who are caught (by whatever means) for a second offence can then be steered toward responses designed to pre-empt the take-off of a criminal career. Those responses might, for example, include 'targeted deterrence' techniques that emphasize the enhanced level of enforcement applied to those caught a second time (see Kennedy 2009; Kennedy et al. 2017); restorative conferences that confront those in embryonic criminal careers with the harmful personal consequences of their offences (see Braithwaite 1989; Hayes 2007; Lauwaert 2015); the mobilization of third-party informal control over those involved (Mazerolle and Ransley 2005); more or less levered changes in routine activities that could expose the offender to fewer opportunities, temptations or peer pressures for continued offending (Schaefer et al. 2016); some form of cognitive behavioural treatment to improve the reasoning skills of those beginning to choose to offend and so on (see Tilley 2009 for a brief overview). The problem of selecting the best response to those whose behaviour reveals them possibly to be on the cusp of an active criminal career is not the problem for forensic scientists. Their work might, however, help identify repeat offenders sooner than would otherwise be the case. Those in other agencies can then steer them toward preventive treatments.

CATCHING PROLIFIC OFFENDERS

The identification of series of serious crimes and the detection of their perpetrators is clearly important for public protection. Forensic evidence can help identify series. If sufficiently similar individual identifiers are found across scenes of several offences, even if the person involved is not yet known, this suggests the same offender. Moreover, if across a series there are, say, three with stains yielding the same DNA profile and one where there is also a fingermark and another three with the same fingermark, including the one linking fingermark to DNA profile, we have evidence of a series of six offences (Leary 2001). The integration of forensic intelligence and crime data in an intelligence database is outlined by Rossy et al. (2013). Through this integration and the sharing of the database, the Swiss authorities are able to link repeat offences via matches and traces and are able to understand the geographical extent of serial offenders. Meanwhile, De Ceuster et al. (2012) discuss the utility of a pan-European ballistic database to assist in the detection of offences linked by, for example, a common firearm. Ribaux et al. (2003) also discuss the feasibility of using forensic data to identify series of linked crimes across space and time. Clearly, linkages can be extended in more or less fuzzy ways using other cross-type identifiers. Geographic profiling can then help narrow the probable range of suspects, given what research tells us about the ways in which the geographical distribution of crimes reflects routine activities (Rossmo 1979). Armed with this information, investigators can target their enquiries to try to find the perpetrators whose apprehension is important for preventive reasons.

DISRUPTING CRIMINAL NETWORKS

Offending normally involves third parties: there are, of course, victims; many offences are committed not by isolated individuals but by associates; complex offences occur in stages, which may include the collection of tools to commit the crime, selection of target, commission of the crime, departure from the crime scene and capitalization on the potential benefits from the crime. The term 'crime script' has come to be used to describe the steps involved in committing a given type of crime, and these stages leave their traces and normally involve third parties (Cornish 1994; Lacoste and Tremblay 2003; Hancock and Laycock 2010; Brayley et al. 2011). An armed robbery, terrorist attack and theft of vehicle for export are three examples. Even when not meeting the definition of 'organized crime', many offences involve the activities of loose networks. Identifying such networks and their members is important for understanding local drivers of crime. With such understanding, promising methods of disruption can be developed, for example by focusing enforcement activity on key members.

Forensic science has a potential role here in that it can help find out who is related to whom by virtue of transferred contact trace materials and the co-presence of trace materials from different individuals who associate with one another in the course of conducting criminal enterprises. Mobile phone and other developments in digital forensics may also be especially important here. With regard to trace evidence, the detection of materials relating to the production of explosive devices or the distribution of illegal drugs or firearms through using our understanding of the behaviour and dynamics of trace materials may also be of value.

Finding unsafe locations to make them safer

At any level of resolution, crime is found to be concentrated (Tilley 2009). Some countries have much higher crime rates than others. Within countries, some regions have much higher crime rates than others. Within regions, some districts have much higher crime rates than others. Within districts, some neighbourhoods have much higher crime rates than others. Within neighbourhoods, some streets have much higher crime rates than others. These forms of concentration can be uncovered using police data, but techniques from forensic science could be used to identify some otherwise unnoticed high levels of concentration for preventive attention. Signs of criminal activity may be left that can be retrieved and analysed. An example may help here. Parks can be sites for criminal and antisocial behaviour. In a recent research project in Australia, the local refuse collectors, over a period of a year, collected and coded refuse collected from public open spaces in an area of concern (Tseloni and Tilley 2016). The refuse types included condoms, beer cans, drug paraphernalia, weapons, etc. Counts of these were used as indicators of concentrations of public space criminal and antisocial behaviour. The materials collected are clearly open to forensic examination to determine whether the people involved were repeat users of the open space or whether they were a changing population, with implications for the preventive strategies that could then be formulated.

Implementing preventive forensic science

If forensic science is to play a part in the problem-solving strategy and, more especially, to contribute in the specific ways outlined in this chapter, the following would be required. There would need to be a central depository of information on crime scene examinations and on forensic examinations as they relate to individual cases. There would also need to be resources for conducting timely and imaginative aggregate analyses of emerging patterns using these data, with a view to discerning preventive opportunities. In practice, such developments would be very challenging. Cases lodged using only standard codes are liable to miss the atypical and novel. Data mining tools that are capable of dealing with text will be needed. Moreover, forensic scientists would need to develop the skills in and habits of providing accounts of cases that are open to systematic interrogation. In those jurisdictions where the work of forensic science is spread among many private suppliers, this will not be easy.

In the UK, an example of the kind of national record-keeping that is open to this form of analysis is the National Ballistics Intelligence Service (NABIS), which has developed a database that identifies and tracks recovered ballistic items, records details of recovered items and allows recovered items to be linked to people, other items, objects and crime groups. This database appears currently to be used mainly for investigation, but it also permits strategic analysis of the 'extent of illegal possession, supply and use of firearms and directing proactive work upstream' (www.nabis.police.uk/Database, accessed 14 June 2016). This latter is clearly preventive in orientation.

Conclusion

This chapter has tried to imagine an extended role for forensic science in preventing crime. Although traditionally forensic science has focused on identifying those who have committed crime (or demonstrating the innocence of suspects), we have tried to show that a widened preventive contribution is possible. Some preventive functions of forensic science are built into its traditional role, notably the contribution to the conviction of offenders who are then processed in preventive ways through the criminal justice system, either through incapacitation or treatment. Other preventive benefits may be produced by media-induced exaggerations of the capacities of forensic science that may lead some would-be offenders not to commit crime because of the enhanced perceived risk of apprehension brought about by clever forensic scientists and advanced forensic techniques. The development of the DNA database constitutes a widely known major development in forensic science (alongside improvements in techniques for collecting and analyzing stains, which increase its discriminative powers) that may have increased perceived risks of apprehension at the margins with preventive benefits. So far, so good.

What we have tried to do, however, is to illustrate a range of other ways in which forensic science might be drawn into contributing to crime prevention. Some of these are suggested by findings of criminological research. Others draw on exemplars of prevention where there seem to be promising contributions that those involved in forensic science might in principle make.

Much of what has been suggested in this chapter is speculative. Determining whether any of the potential preventive benefits can in practice be realized in the ways mooted here in a cost-effective way would require a substantial investment of time and money, perhaps best achieved in demonstration projects.

Finally, to reiterate a point made earlier, none of what has been said should in any way be taken to suggest that the justice-oriented casework of forensic science should cease to be its core function. Nor is it to say that the research endeavours targeting improvements in the range and accuracy of forensic analyses and interpretations are not important. Rather, the question raised (at the invitation of the editors of this volume) has been whether there are improved preventive side-benefits that could be achieved by more effectively mobilizing what is done to make an increased contribution to the crime prevention agenda.

Note

1 Against this, there are risks to civil liberties from keeping records of those against whom there is insufficient evidence to proceed in a given case.

References

Bernasco, W. 2008. 'Them again? Same Offender Involvement in Repeat and Near Repeat Burglaries'. *European Journal of Criminology* 5(4): 411–431.

Braithwaite, J. 1989. *Crime, Shame and Reintegration*. Cambridge: Cambridge University Press.

Brantingham, P.J., and P.L. Brantingham. 1984. *Patterns in Crime*. New York: Macmillan.

Brantingham, P., and F. Faust. 1976. 'A Conceptual Model of Crime Prevention'. *Crime and Delinquency* 22(3): 284–296.

Brayley, H., E. Cockbain and G. Laycock. 2011. 'The Value of Crime Scripting: Deconstructing Internal Child Sex Trafficking'. *Policing: A Journal of Policy and Practice* 5(2): 132–143.

Bullock, K., R. Erol and N. Tilley. 2012. *Problem-Oriented Policing and Partnerships*. London: Routledge.

Clarke, R.V., and P. Mayhew. 1988. 'The British Gas Suicide Story and Its Criminological Implications'. In M. Tonry and N. Morris, eds., *Crime and Justice*, vol. 10, 79–116. Chicago: University of Chicago Press.

Cohen L., and M. Felson. 1979. 'Social Change and Crime Rate Trends: A Routine Activity Approach'. *American Sociological Review* 44(4): 588–608.

Cornish, D.B. 1994. 'The Procedural Analysis of Offending and Its Relevance for Situational Prevention'. In R.V. Clarke, ed., *Crime Prevention Studies*, vol. 3, 151–196. Monsey, NY. Criminal Justice Press.

De Ceuster, J., R. Hermsen, M. Mastaglio and R. Nennstiel. 2012. 'A Discussion on the Usefulness of a Shared European Ballistic Image Database'. *Science and Justice* 52(4): 237–242.

Eck, J.E., and W. Spelman. 1987. *Problem-Solving: Problem-Oriented Policing in Newport News*. Washington, DC: Police Executive Research Forum.

Everson, S., and K. Pease. 2001. 'Crime against the Same Person and Place: Detection Opportunity and Offender Targeting'. In G. Farrell and K. Pease, eds., *Repeat Victimization*. Crime Prevention Studies, vol. 12, 199–220. Monsey, NY: Criminal Justice Press.

Farrell, G., and K. Pease. 1993. *Once Bitten, Twice Bitten: Repeat Victimisation and the Implications for Crime Prevention*. Crime Prevention Unit Paper 46. London: Home Office.

Farrell, G., and K. Pease. 2017. 'Preventing Repeat Crime Concentration'. In N. Tilley and A. Sidebottom, eds., *Handbook of Crime Prevention and Community Safety*, 2nd ed., 143–156. London: Routledge.

Farrington, D. 1986. 'Age and Crime'. *Crime and Justice* 7: 189–250.

Farrington, D. 1998. 'Predictors, Causes, and Correlates of Male Youth Violence'. *Crime and Justice* 23: 421–475.

Felson, M. 1986. 'Linking Criminal Choices, Routine Activities, Informal Control, and Criminal Outcomes'. In D. Cornish and R. Clarke, eds., *The Reasoning Criminal: Rational Choice Perspectives on Offending*, 119–128. New York: Springer.

Felson, M., and M. Eckert. 2016. *Crime and Everyday Life*. 5th ed. London: Sage.

Gabor, T. 1994. *Everybody Does It! Crime by the Public*. Toronto: University of Toronto Press.
Goldstein, H. 1979. 'Improving Policing: A Problem-Oriented Approach'. *Crime and Delinquency* 25: 236–258.
Goldstein, H. 1990. *Problem-Oriented Policing*. New York: Wiley.
Hancock, G., and G. Laycock. 2010. 'Organised Crime and Crime Scripts: Prospects for Disruption'. In K. Bullock, N. Tilley and R.V. Clarke, eds., *Situational Prevention of Organised Crimes*, 172–192. Cullompton, UK: Willan.
Hayes, H. 2007. 'Reoffending and Restorative Justice'. In G. Johnstone and D. Van Ness, eds., *Handbook of Restorative Justice*, 426–444. Cullompton, UK: Willan.
Kennedy, D. 2009. *Deterrence and Crime Prevention: Reconsidering the Prospect of Sanction*. London: Routledge.
Kennedy, D., M. Kleiman and A. Braga. 2017. 'Beyond Deterrence: Strategies of Focus and Fairness'. In N. Tilley and A. Sidebottom, eds., *Handbook of Crime Prevention and Community Safety*, 157–182. 2nd ed. London: Routledge.
Lacoste, J., and P. Tremblay. 2003. 'Crime Innovation: A Script Analysis of Patterns in Check Forgery'. In M.J. Smith and D.B. Cornish, eds., *Theory for Practice in Situational Crime Prevention*, 171–198. Crime Prevention Studies, vol. 16. Monsey, NY: Criminal Justice Press.
Lauwaert, K. 2015. 'Restorative Justice and Restorative Justice Practices'. In K. Lauwaert and I. Aertson, eds., *Desistance and Restorative Justice*, 38–53. Leuven: European Forum for Restorative Justice.
Leary, R. 2001. *Evaluation of the Impact of the FLINTS Software System in West Midlands and Elsewhere*. London: Home Office.
Leary, R., and K. Pease. 2003. 'DNA and the Active Criminal Population'. *Crime Prevention & Community Safety—An International Journal* 5(1): 7–12.
Ludwig, A., and J. Fraser. 2014. 'Effective Use of Forensic Science in Volume Crime Investigation: Identifying Recurring Themes in the Literature'. *Science and Justice* 54(1): 81–88.
Mazerolle, L., and J. Ransley. 2005. *Third Party Policing*. Cambridge: Cambridge University Press.
National Research Council. 2009. (NAS 2009) *Strengthening Forensic Science in the United States: A Path Forward*. Washington, DC: The National Academies Press.
Pease, K. 1998. *Repeat Victimisation: Taking Stock*. Crime Detection and Prevention Series Paper 90. London: Home Office.
Ribaux, O., A. Girod, S.J. Walsh, P. Margot, S. Mizrahi and V. Clivaz. 2003. 'Forensic Intelligence and Crime Analysis'. *Law, Probability and Risk* 2(1): 47–60.
Rossmo, K. 1979. *Geographic Profiling*. Baton Rouge, FL: CRC Press.
Rossy, Q., S. Ioset, D. Dessimoz and O. Ribaux. 2013. 'Integrating Forensic Information in a Crime Intelligence Database'. *Forensic Science International* 230(1–3): 137–146.
Schaefer, L., F. Cullen and J. Eck. 2016. *Environmental Corrections*. Los Angeles: Sage.
Shelton, D., Y. Kim and G. Barak. 2006. 'A Study of Juror Expectations and Demands concerning Scientific Evidence: Does the "CSI Effect" Exist?' *Vanderbilt Journal of Entertainment & Technology Law* 9(2): 331–368.
Sidebottom, A., and N. Tilley. 2011. 'Improving Problem-Oriented Policing: The Need for a New Model?' *Crime Prevention and Community Safety* 13(2): 79–101.
Tilley, N. 2009. *Crime Prevention*. London: Routledge.
Tilley, N. 2013. *Analyzing and Responding to Repeat Offending*. Problem-Solving Tools Series Problem-Oriented Guides for Police, no. 11. Washington, DC: Community Oriented Policing Service, US Department of Justice.
Tilley, N., and M. Townsley. 2009. 'Forensic Science in UK Policing: Strategies, Tactics and Effectiveness'. In J. Fraser and R. Williams, eds., *Handbook of Forensic Science*, 359–379. Cullompton, UK: Willan.
Tseloni. A., and N. Tilley. 2016. 'Choosing and Using Statistical Sources in Criminology: What Can the Crime Survey for England and Wales Tell Us?' *Legal Information Management* 16: 78–90. doi:10.1017/S1472669616000219.
Tyler, T. 2006. 'Viewing CSI and the Threshold of Guilt: Managing Truth and Justice in Reality and Fiction'. *Yale Law Journal* 115(5): 1050–1085.
van Dijk, J.J.M., and J. de Waard. 1991. 'A Two-Dimensional Typology of Crime Prevention Projects: With a Bibliography'. *Criminal Justice Abstracts* 23: 483–503.
Vollaard, B. 2011. *Preventing Crime through Selective Incapacitation*. Tilec Discussion Paper, no. 2011–001. Tilburg, The Netherlands: Tilburg Law and Economics Center, Tilburg University, 2010.
Weisburd, D., and J. Eck. 2004. 'What Can the Police Do to Reduce Crime, Disorder and Fear?' *Annals of the American Political and Social Sciences* 593(1): 42–65.

Weisburd, D., C.W. Telep, J.C. Hinkle and J.E. Eck. 2010. *The Effects of Problem-Oriented Policing on Crime and Disorder*. Crime Prevention Research Review, no. 4. Washington, DC: US Department of Justice, Office of Community Oriented Policing Services.
Wortley, R., and L. Mazerolle. 2008. *Environmental Criminology and Crime Analysis*. London: Routledge.
Zimring, F., and G. Hawkins. 1995. *Incapacitation*. New York: Oxford University Press.

14

Evaluating the consumption of illicit drugs via wastewater analysis

How forensic indicators are used in open and confined settings

Pierre Esseiva, Lisa Benaglia, Frederic Been and Frank Zobel

Principles of wastewater-based epidemiology (WBE)

Wastewater analysis relies on the principle that every substance, either licit or illicit, consumed by human beings leaves a trace materialized under the form of a metabolized product (the unchanged substance and/or a mixture of metabolites) that will be excreted via urine and faeces. These are conveyed through the sewer network to a wastewater treatment plant (WWTP) where they can be detected and quantified (Daughton 2001). Zuccato first implemented this approach in 2005 to monitor the consumption of illicit drugs in the city of Milan (Zuccato et al. 2005). Inspired by the results of this first study, many scientists around the world focused their efforts to refine the scientific grounds of this discipline and proposed applications in various directions. In the scientific literature, this approach has been referred to as sewage- or wastewater-based epidemiology (SBE or WBE).

Numerous researchers have successfully implemented this approach to detect traces of illicit drug use among selected communities across the world. WBE has been identified by the European Monitoring Centre for Drugs and Drug Addiction (Castiglioni et al. 2016) as a complementary technique to estimate illicit drug use at the community level. The United Nations Office for Drugs and Crime (UNODC) has also recognized the potential of this approach. Since 2011, an international competence network, supported by funding from the European research program Horizon 2020, has been organizing an annual international sampling campaign to monitor illicit drug use in different cities across Europe and overseas (Castiglioni et al. 2016; Thomas et al. 2012).

In the past decade, it has been demonstrated that WBE is an excellent tool for obtaining near real-time data about consumption of illicit drugs in a target area. Because it can be deployed rapidly and without too much effort compared to self-report surveys, regular sampling campaigns can be set up that can act as a monitoring tool to detect trends and spot new patterns in drug use.

Wastewater sampling

Sampling is one of the most challenging and important aspects of WBE (Ort et al. 2010a). It must be set up carefully in line with the scientific question one seeks to answer. Sampling designs range from taking simple grab (punctual) samples to composite sampling approaches, which consist in aggregating multiple samples collected in a time-, volume- or flow-proportional manner. These issues have been extensively studied by Ort and his colleagues (Ort et al. 2010b) and efforts have been made to propose a best-practice method, improving the comparability of results from different locations. In particular, flow-proportional (ideally continuous) composite sampling has been recommended as the most appropriate strategy for collecting representative wastewater samples (Ort et al. 2010b). Because this method is not a simple matter to implement, a discrete approach is generally adopted. Yet, this should ideally be characterized by high sampling frequencies (i.e., sampling every 5 to 10 minutes or more), in order to account for the potentially important variations in analyte[1] concentration and flows that can occur during the sampling period. Sampling is typically performed over 24 hours in order to obtain a global overview of analyte loads (in milligrams or grams) reaching the wastewater treatment plant (WWTP) over the course of a day. Composite samples are generally collected using automatic samplers (i.e., a pump connected to a fridge installed at the inlet of the WWTP), which gather subsamples according to the selected sampling mode (i.e., time-, volume- or flow-proportional). While being more tedious, composite sampling improves the representativeness of the collected samples, an important aspect when one seeks to monitor the content of wastewater over longer periods.

Chemical analysis

The analysis of very tiny amounts (in the nanograms per litre range, or lower) of target compounds in the composite sample requires highly selective and sensitive analytical methods. The technique of choice is generally liquid chromatography (LC) for the separation, coupled with a tandem mass spectrometer (MS/MS) or a high-resolution mass spectrometer (HRMS) for detection (Bijlsma et al. 2014). Prior to instrumental analysis, a crucial step consists in preparing samples in order to minimize the effects of the matrix as well as to pre-concentrate the target analytes. This is often performed using solid-phase extraction (SPE), a technique based on the adsorption of the target compounds onto a solid phase, allowing a concentration factor of 100 or more. Yet, thanks to recent advances in instrumental techniques, alternative and less time-consuming methods have been implemented, e.g., 'dilute and shoot' (O'Brien et al. 2014) and large volume injection (Berset et al. 2010).

From substance quantitation to back-calculation of substance use

Wastewater monitoring campaigns will initially aim at determining if illicit drugs are present, hence potentially consumed, to detect changing trends or highlight the emergence of a new substance. However, the most interesting aspect consists in going further and inferring how much of an illicit drug is consumed and, by extension, how many doses are consumed, or even how many people are concerned (i.e., prevalence) (Burgard et al. 2014).

Calculating the quantity of illicit drugs consumed by the population connected to a specific catchment based on the amount of the target biomarker is feasible (Zuccato et al. 2008), even though this inference can become more complex depending on the target substance (often requiring knowledge about degradation and/or the metabolization processes of the substance). To obtain this information, the daily mass load of target residues has first to be estimated. This is done by multiplying the target biomarker concentration, measured in the collected composite samples (in nanograms per litre), by the wastewater flow at the influent of the WWTP (in litres per day). To move on to the next stage, i.e., estimating the daily consumption of a parent illicit drug, it is necessary to account for the excretion rate of the target biomarker (parent compound or metabolite). For example, after consumption of cocaine, approximately 32.5 percent on average of the initial dose will be excreted in the form of benzoylecgonine (major urinary metabolite of cocaine) (Khan and Nicell 2011). Therefore, if we measure 100 mg as daily mass loads of benzoylecgonine in wastewater, this corresponds to a daily consumption of pure cocaine of approximately 323 mg $\left(\frac{100}{0.325} \times \frac{303\ (\textit{molecular weight of cocaïne})}{289\ (\textit{molecular weight of benzoylecgonine})}\right)$.

Comparing results coming from different cities or countries is also often proposed in the literature, but it is not a simple matter and requires calculating so-called 'per capita loads'. To achieve this, it is essential to know the size of the contributing population served by the WWTP in order to obtain population normalized figures (i.e., mg/day•1000 inhabitants), which account for differences in the size of the population between sampling locations. This composes the per capita loads and consists of the unit of choice for comparative studies.

Various strategies have been proposed to account for or estimate the size of the contributing population. The first and most static approach consists in collecting census data for the WWTP under investigation. Yet, this data comes with significant uncertainties—e.g., administrative regions may not coincide with geographic catchments of WWTP, estimates of the population may be outdated (O'Brien et al. 2014)—and, furthermore, it does not account for population fluctuations due to commuters or seasonal effects (e.g., holidays or special events).

The use of hydrochemical parameters like biological oxygen demand, nitrogen, phosphorus or ammonium has also been investigated. Been et al. (2014) demonstrated that ammonium levels provide indications about the contributing population and reflect variations in the size of the contributing population due to commutes (i.e., weekdays versus weekends) or seasonal effects (e.g., holidays). Alternative approaches based on the measurement of pharmaceuticals, personal care products and endogenous compounds have also been suggested (O'Brien et al. 2014; Chen et al. 2014). While requiring additional analysis, these methods all provided good estimates of the size of the population and were successfully implemented in wastewater monitoring campaigns. However, none of the methods developed to date allows accurate estimates of the population size to be easily obtained, and there is still no consensus in the scientific community about which method to adopt. Yet, for systematic comparative studies, a harmonized and accurate approach to assessing the size of the contributing population is needed. When the focus is on monitoring illicit drug use over longer periods in a specific location, accounting for fluctuations in the population is less critical. In fact, variations in drug loads have been shown to be orders of magnitude larger compared to changes in the size of the population (Been et al. 2014; Lai et al. 2015).

Uncertainties measurement

Uncertainties related to WBE cannot be disregarded or ignored. In each of the aforementioned steps (i.e., wastewater sampling, sample preparation, analysis, mass loads and consumption estimates), uncertainties exist and propagate across the results. Even if uncertainties regarding the analysis of illicit drug residues are well understood, they remain key variables that go along with uncontrolled uncertainties. The major uncertainties are linked to the measurement of the size of the contributing population and the excretion rates of the unchanged parent compound and/or its metabolites (intra- and inter-individual variation as well as differences due to the administration route). The impact of these uncertainties increases as one back-calculates the amounts of substance initially consumed. Interesting approaches based on Bayesian modelling and Markov Chain Monte Carlo simulations (Been et al. 2016b) have been proposed to account for the interaction of these diverse sources of error and estimate the total uncertainty (Jones et al. 2014). Furthermore, this type of model allows the integration of other knowledge about illicit drug use (e.g., general population surveys, seizures). Thus, more realistic estimations, in the form of probability distributions, about the amounts of substance consumed or the prevalence of illicit drug use in a given population can be obtained.

Applications and Limitations

Monitoring trends and patterns

One of the most interesting applications of WBE is its potential to study long-term trends and patterns in illicit drug use in a specific area (van Nuijs et al. 2011). The possibility of following the consumption of a population nearly in real time, compared to traditional tools which take much longer to set up, offers new perspectives to understanding and investigating the phenomenon. In the following example (see Figure 14.1), one can observe the different patterns of consumption of MDMA and methamphetamine (MA) that can be highlighted through wastewater analysis. MDMA consumption clearly presents an increase during the weekend, while MA stays stable over the whole week. This difference is not really a surprise: MDMA is typically a party drug whose use is mainly recreational (e.g., nightclubs), while MA consumption concerns mainly regular (heavy/addicted) users (Zobel et al. 2015). Therefore, it is not surprising that the so-called 'weekend effect' is absent, since dependent users will use similar amounts every day. Even if these results confirm what is already known among addiction researchers, they are supported here by objective observations.

Taking the example of cannabis and the hot topic about its legalization/decriminalization, the combination of WBE and population surveys data could offer essential information for evaluating the impact of such a significant change in illicit drug policy. It is a safe bet that never-ending debates will take place between supporters and opponents of cannabis legalization and one of the main arguments will be focused on the change in usage patterns: increase, stabilization or decrease in the prevalence of cannabis use (Cressey 2015). Wastewater-based epidemiology could be one of the key instruments in unveiling the evolution of cannabis use in society. Indeed, if the situation before the change in the legislation is monitored, the initial 'background level' of consumption may be assessed (see Figure 14.2 showing the situation of cannabis consumption in the city of Lausanne in 2014). By doing a continuous study, objective data would be acquired to evaluate both the short- and long-term impact of legalization/decriminalization policy. It is likely that after such a change in regulation of marijuana, an increase of prevalence will take place as observed in Colorado (Reed 2016). However, it is not certain that this situation will last forever.

This real-time observation is therefore of great value in monitoring the evolution of cannabis use and could be seen as a sort of 'whistle-blower', highlighting significant changes in consumption patterns that require the deployment of a specific strategy (e.g., self-report questionnaire) to better understand the reasons for these changes, for example, if the increase is among minors or other vulnerable groups.

Cannabis legalization initiatives will also present arguments about its capability to 'eradicate the black market'. In Colorado, for example, this question has been raised (Miron 2014) and no clear answers are currently available. One could imagine that having an adequate supply on offer would result in no room in the market for illicit production and sales. With WBE, it is possible to estimate the amounts of illicit drugs used in a specific catchment and, by accounting for the size of the contributing population, also to estimate the per capita usage. Combining this data with retail statistics, it would be possible to evaluate whether quantities sold are compatible with the (expected)

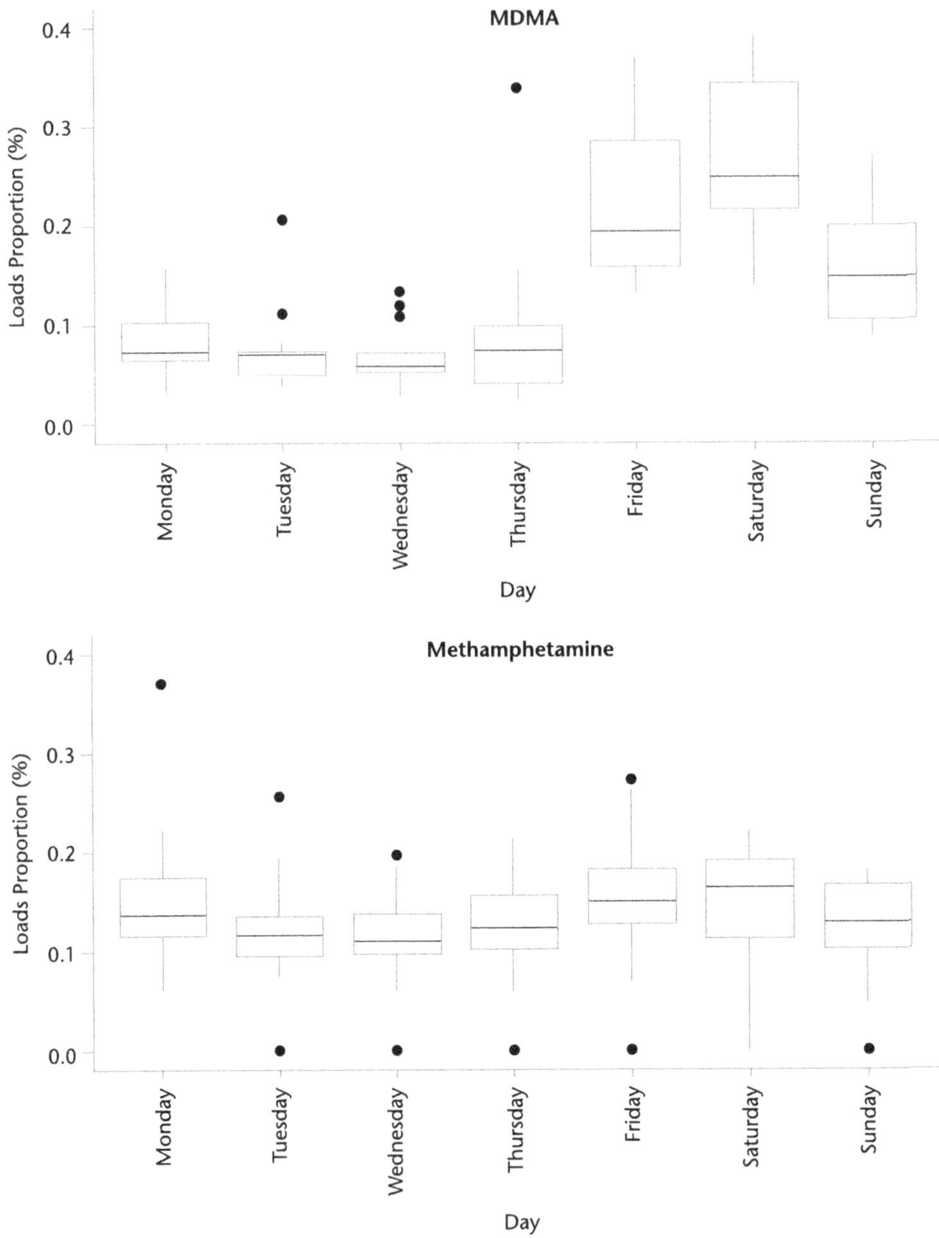

Figure 14.1 Weekly pattern consumption of MDMA and methamphetamine in 13 Swiss cities measured over a single-week period in 2014

consumption estimates derived from WBE. Of course, there are variables that are difficult to account for, like the proportion of the cannabis bought that is really consumed, the size of an individual dose and even the consumption habits of users. However, the comparison of these two sources of data could be used in a strategic perspective in order to obtain a better overview of the situation, in particular if monitoring is carried out routinely and over longer periods. If cannabis

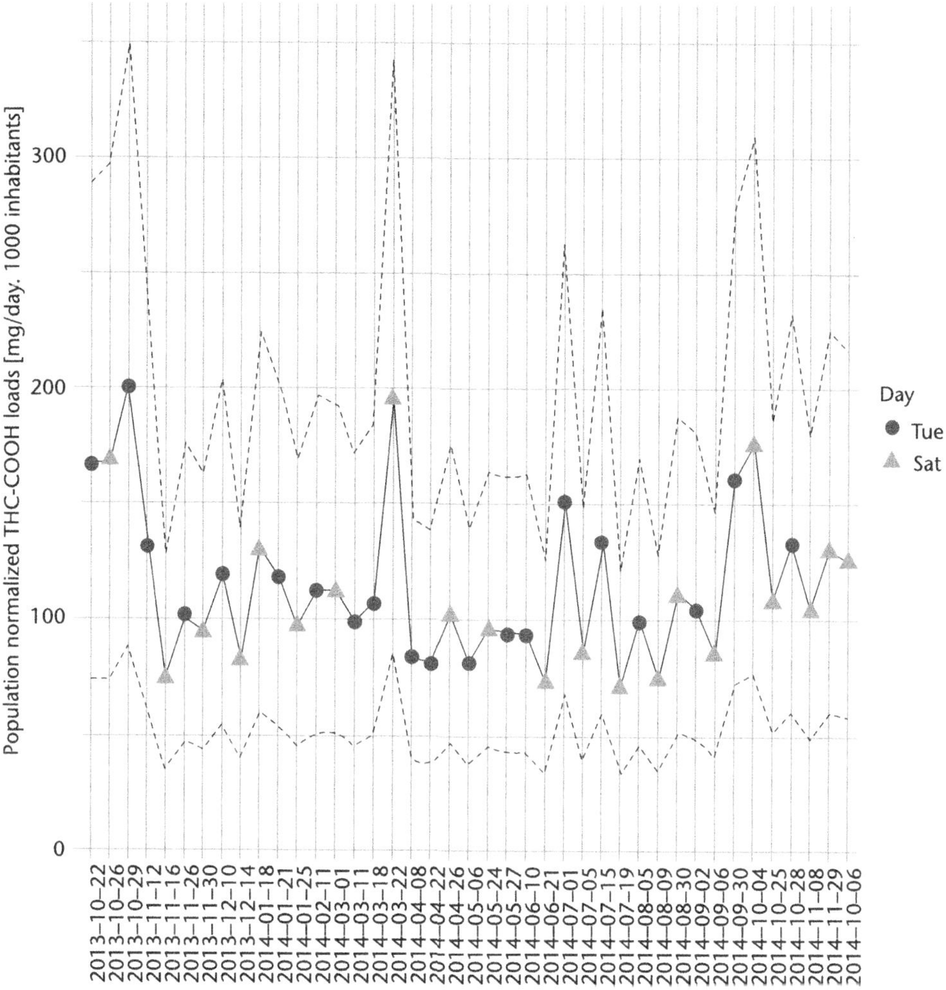

Figure 14.2 Annual evolution of THC-COOH loads (the target metabolites of THC) measured between October 2013 and December 2014 in Lausanne

came to be legalized, the comparison between wastewater-based estimates and sales statistics would provide evidence on which to assess the existence, or not, of an alternative (black) market. Of course, such conclusions should be taken with extreme caution, mainly due to the uncertainties associated with the back-calculation process of illicit drug use from WBE. However, depending on the magnitude of the observed differences, some hypotheses could still be formulated. For example, if back-calculated estimates are clearly lower than sales figures, one could imagine that the cannabis sold in the area is not consumed on site. Again, alternative explanations could be found, among them the use by or the export of the drugs to people from other regions. Since it is possible to buy quite large amounts of cannabis per person and per transaction—28.5 grams per day in the states of Colorado and Washington, while in Colorado, non-residents are allowed to purchase up to a quarter of that amount (Pardo 2014)—the occurrence of this kind of behaviour is not a surprise. However, a comparison with WBE data could give some hints about the extent of this phenomenon. Because cannabis sales in the states of Colorado and Washington are strictly controlled, it should be possible to differentiate purchases made by residents and non-residents. This would make it possible to have an idea about the cannabis loads (as THC-COOH or THC) expected from the consumption by the resident population. Again, if differences were to be highlighted, in particular if measured loads were lower than expected, this could suggest that some residents are reselling some or all of their purchase outside the state. Of course, this kind of hypothesis needs to be compared with and validated in the light of other sources of data (e.g., police statistics about people apprehended for cannabis trafficking). Nonetheless, these examples show how WBE data can be used to support research hypotheses.

The approach presented here is valuable for all types of illicit drugs. Both public health authorities and law enforcement agencies are interested in obtaining this 'big picture'. Knowing through WBE, that heroin consumption is stable, for example, could be seen as good news, in the sense that it suggests a stable number of users consuming this product. For public health authorities, it is important to have information about their capacity to cover and assist injecting drug users. Wastewater-based epidemiology can provide them with complementary data to assess whether current measures make it possible to reach the majority of heroin users, especially with regard to treatment and harm reduction programs, such as needle and syringe exchanges, opioid substitution treatment, HIV testing and counselling and antiretroviral therapy. As shown later in this chapter, additional valuable information can be derived from WBE when combined with other data sources.

Wastewater-based epidemiology could also be used in a more strategic perspective. For example, our research team received a request from a law enforcement department regarding the prevalence of the consumption of synthetic illicit drugs in a specific city, by focusing on wastewater analysis at the main wastewater treatment plant of the city. This question was addressed in a highly politicized atmosphere, as the Regulatory Authority accused local law enforcement of being indulgent toward the trafficking of these specific substances. The situation was, however, quite different in a law enforcement perspective. Efforts were concentrated on the two major and best-organized traffics, namely, in cocaine and heroin, and there were next to no resources to cover an additional criminal organization. Wastewater analysis was then an excellent opportunity to appraise the actual consumption of these substances in the area. The results obtained for two consecutive years are presented in Figure 14.3.

Clearly, cocaine is the main substance of use. Again, this was not a surprise, since both public health authorities and law enforcement already had that information. The most interesting aspect concerns the consumption of synthetic products, in particular amphetamine and methamphetamine, whose respective loads are only a few grams per day. It is important to specify that the residence time of the wastewater in the sewers in this case is inferior to the time at which degradation could occur (Khan and Nicell 2011; van Nuijs et al. 2011). Thus, there is strong evidence that during the investigation periods, the consumption of these two amphetamine-type stimulants (ATS) was very low and that they did not represent major issues. This was rather good news for the police, since it confirmed their vision and knowledge about the illicit drugs scene in the city. It was also good news from a public health perspective because it suggested that the consumption of these two products was limited.

It is also important to mention that there are additional benefits to a continuous rolling analysis. While the situation of methamphetamine and amphetamine appeared not to be a major concern for the two years under study, having a systematic and (almost) real-time snapshot of the situation offers an efficient and relevant tool to detect trend changes that would require adaptations in both law enforcement strategies and public health responses.

The results also indicate that MDMA (methylenedioxymethamphetamine) is the ATS most prevalent in the city, in line with previous studies (Been et al. 2016a). It is mainly consumed during the weekend, in a recreational setting. Measured amounts are not alarming and are

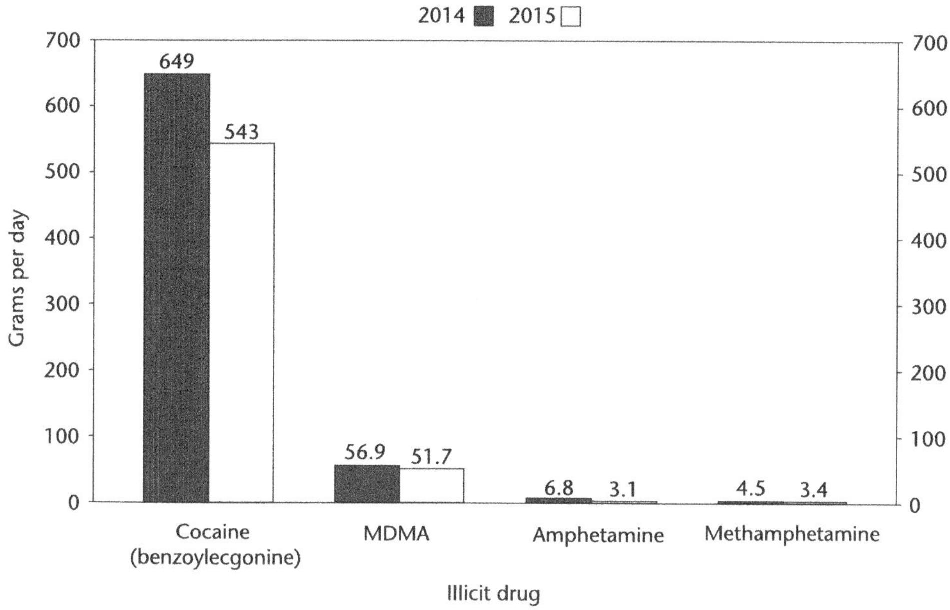

Figure 14.3 Daily average consumption of pure illicit drug in 2014 and 2015 in a specific city

comparable to the data presented in other studies (Ort et al. 2014), suggesting that there is not the critical mass necessary to have significant open street trafficking, and its consumption is the focus of a specific population (i.e., partygoers).

Spatial differences

Since 2010, a European initiative (SCORE—Sewage Analysis CORe group) bringing together experts working on the analysis of illicit drugs in wastewater, has been promoting an international study aiming at comparing the pattern of illicit drug use between major European cities (Ort et al. 2014) as well as proposing harmonized and best-practice procedures to improve the comparability of WBE campaigns (Castiglioni et al. 2016). The results obtained have been in agreement with traditional surveillance and epidemiological data available. Globally, the results obtained have not revealed any particularity about illicit drugs in Europe not already known from other indicators. However, the major advantage of this approach lies in the level of detail that can be achieved when investigating spatial differences.

The analysis of methamphetamine in Switzerland is an interesting example that illustrates the utility of this approach. Figure 14.4 clearly highlights the differences between Swiss regions. In general, the Latin cantons (Italian and French speaking) are characterized by no or less methamphetamine consumption compared to the German speaking areas of Switzerland.

One discrepancy concerns the canton of Neuchâtel. While located in the French-speaking region, it shows the highest per capita methamphetamine loads. Investigating these surprising results, we found confirmation of the phenomenon from the canton's law enforcement agencies. Indeed, the police were aware of the existence of a specific group of methamphetamine users in the area. In this situation, WBE confirms what was already known by people on the frontline of the problem of illicit drug use. Yet, a closer analysis of Figure 14.4 reveals additional pertinent information. For example, as already discussed, methamphetamine use is not a concern for

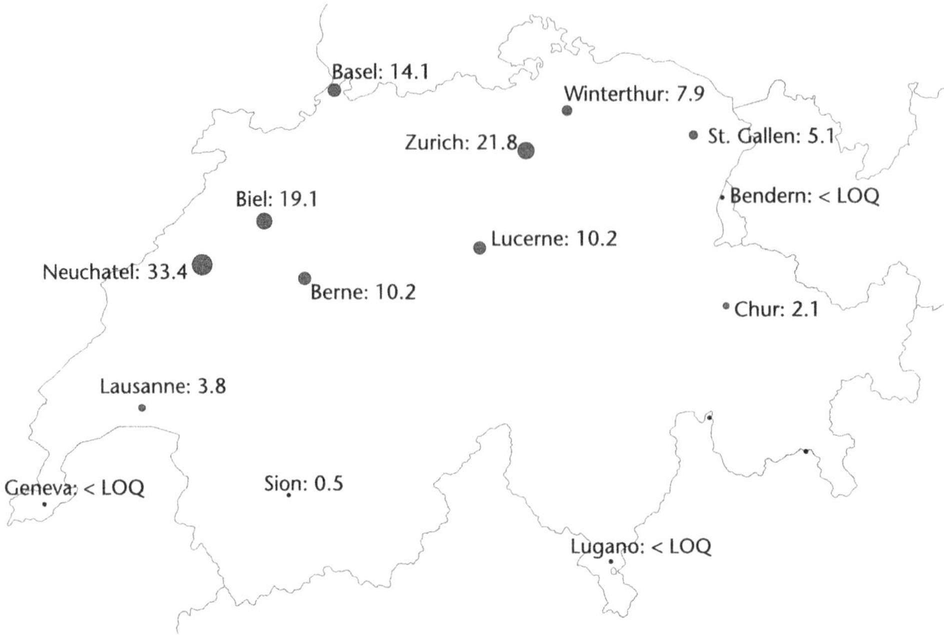

Figure 14.4 Population normalized loads [mg•day•1000 inhabitants] for methamphetamine measured in Switzerland and Liechtenstein

Geneva or Lausanne. In a sense, this is good news for public health and law enforcement, since they can continue to focus their efforts on other illicit drugs. However, in order to take advantage of the full potential of WBE, the spatial information has to be combined with the temporal dimension. Being able to draw an image of illicit drug use, as presented in Figure 14.3, in a systematic way (for example, every month) offers a more strategic overview of the phenomenon. In fact, at the present time, there is no tool that makes it possible to monitor, in quasi real-time, the evolution of methamphetamine consumption. Following the existing four pillars drug policy in force in Switzerland (prevention, therapy, harm reduction and repression) (FOPH 2016), this approach would be an efficient way to detect the appearance of a new problem allowing specific measures to be rapidly proposed and adopted (Burgard et al. 2014).

New patterns of consumption

Wastewater-based epidemiology has the potential to detect whether a specific product has been consumed—keeping in mind some limitations—and therefore is of particular interest when dealing with drugs known as 'new psychoactive substances' (NPS) observed in the illicit drug market. During 2015, more than 100 new products were reported (EMCDDA and Europol 2016), among them cathinones (more than 30 new substances), synthetic cannabinoids (30), phenethylamines (5), opioids (5), tryptamines (4), benzodiazepines (4) and arylalkylamines (4). The problem these substances present comes from the fact that their molecular structures are not controlled by international conventions (the 1961 United Nations Single Convention on Narcotic Drugs and the 1971 United Nations Convention on Psychotropic Substances). This ambiguity in the legislation benefits manufacturers and resellers who can openly offer their products on the Internet.

While political leaders warn about the dangers these drugs pose in their respective jurisdictions, and ask for information, it is difficult to provide a response with standard populations surveys or other harm reduction statistics. In fact, the population attracted by these new products (so-called 'psychonauts' looking to test new substances and explore their effects) is not easily reached and is not necessarily under treatment.

New psychoactive substances represent a particular challenge for WBE. Because of the large number of chemical forms (i.e., homologues) in which they can appear on the market, users are not all consuming the same product and, moreover, they often do not know exactly what they are taking. This is clearly different from traditional illicit drugs like cocaine or methamphetamine, whose users are always consuming the same principal ingredient. Furthermore, the metabolism and the quantity needed to reach a dose can be drastically different. For fentanyl derivatives like carfentanyl, for example, a dose is in the order of magnitude of 0.01 mg compared to 20 mg for cocaine (Goullé and Guerbet 2016). This clearly has an impact on WBE because the consumption of such a small quantity will result in very low concentrations in wastewater, too low to be detected with current analytical instruments. Passive sampling approaches, which make it possible to concentrate target analytes over longer periods of time, could be an alternative to conventional composite samples. Yet, no studies of this type have been carried out to date. Furthermore, non-targeted screening methods, based on high-resolution mass spectrometers, still lack the sensitivity to detect trace amounts of target compounds in complex matrices. A possible solution to partially overcome these problems could be using other sources of information to narrow down the number of target compounds and focus solely on those that, at a given time, appear to be of particular interest among drug users. As explained above, NPS are mainly sold on the Internet via dedicated websites. These can be monitored to extract information about the online market of NPS as well as to follow online discussions of customers and sellers. This approach aims at gathering information about the prevalence of use of specific NPS as well as the demand. This monitoring strategy could result in a list of the 'most wanted' or the 'most discussed' substances. Law enforcement and custom seizures are another source of data available to assess the occurrence of NPS and identify 'hot' products.

These complementary sources of data could be processed iteratively to continuously update knowledge about the use of illicit drugs. Furthermore, the 'entrance point' into the iterative mechanism is not crucial. For example, wastewater monitoring can detect the presence of a new compound or it can highlight a modification (e.g., increase) in consumption patterns of a specific product. The identified phenomenon can then be compared to information derived from Internet websites and forums to understand its 'popularity' (i.e., prevalence). If it appears that the phenomenon could become a threat to public health, authorities would have objective data at hand to establish priorities and thus propose relevant preventive and/or repressive measures quickly. The same approach is also applicable to new trends detected through web monitoring or when an important seizure of a specific NPS is made by law enforcement. These observations are key indicators of the appearance of a new phenomenon that needs to be investigated in order to be better understood. Wastewater analysis could then be deployed for confirming these observations as well as for providing an overview of the extent and evolution of this new phenomenon.

WBE's ability to detect the use of new substances and understand their consumption pattern demonstrates its potential to contribute to an early warning system and to offer an efficient approach to confirm and monitor a problematic situation.

The challenge of confined environments

Some initiatives have tried to go 'upstream' (Burgard et al. 2014) by targeting specific populations, like students (Burgard et al. 2013) and prisoners (Brewer et al. 2016; Postigo et al. 2011), or during specific events like music festivals (Lai et al. 2013). Targeting the evaluation of consumption in a closed or semi-closed environment[2] presents challenges mainly with regard to collecting composite samples and measuring flows. Indeed, sampling at the influent of a WWTP is easier, since access to the wastewater stream is generally not an issue and researchers can often benefit from the help of WWTP personnel. In a confined environment, deploying traditional sampling devices is more complicated due to limited accessibility (e.g., manholes) and/or low (intermittent) flows. Dedicated systems capable of dealing with low or intermittent flow and highly variable substance mass loads are required. Furthermore, it is sometimes not even possible to install an automatic sampler due to the difficulty of reaching the domestic sewer and accessibility to power. Due to their time integrative characteristic, the deployment of passive sampling devices like POCIS (polar organic chemical integrative sampler) in the wastewater stream could be an interesting alternative for monitoring the long-term consumption of illicit drugs or performing qualitative analysis of products that are present in low concentration (either because of their limited use, such as NPS, or because of the low dosage). One drawback associated with the use of passive sampling devices pertains to the calibration of the passive sampler, a necessity for inferring the concentration of the target metabolites, which can be quite difficult and time-consuming (Harman et al. 2011).

'Upstream' investigation also exposes ethical problems that are normally not raised when the analysis is performed 'downstream' at the WWTP (Hall et al. 2012; Prichard et al. 2014). Indeed, when WBE monitoring campaigns focus on the general population, confidentiality is guaranteed because it is not possible to identify an individual or a specific population. However, this is subject to discussion when a prison or a college is targeted. In these applications, there is a risk of stigmatizing the targeted population. It is thus necessary to ask for the appropriate authorization, inform the authorities in charge of the establishments and ensure that the results of the research are handled correctly. Regardless of the location, what is of utmost importance is that researchers and the responsible authorities agree on how the study should be carried out and, in particular, how the results should be used and divulged (e.g., anonymization).

Using WBE at the venue of a music festival will, unsurprisingly, demonstrate that illicit drugs are being consumed. Thus, one might question the utility of analyses. Music festivals are often called into question for being places where people come to consume illicit drugs. But WBE could be an ideal tool to overcome this stigmatization. As Lai et al. show (2013), consumption during a music festival was in the same order of magnitude as in the nearby urban area, except for MDMA use, which was higher at the festival venue. Similar results were observed at a similar event in Switzerland. Based on these results, festival organizers have objective evidence at hand to argue that music festivals do not particularly attract illicit drug users.

As is being done for cities, rough estimates of the quantity of illicit drugs consumed during the event can be made. This could be of interest to law enforcement as well as the security of the music festival in order to assess whether the current consumption of (and thus the demand for) illicit drugs is sufficient to attract dealers, who could potentially establish a market. This could be particularly interesting for MDMA, the only illicit drug that appeared to have a higher consumption rate at the music festival under study, which is consistent with its recreational use. In a Swiss study (Benaglia 2016), it was estimated that about 450 doses per day (with one dose being 120 mg of pure MDMA) were consumed on average. With the attendance of more than 60,000 persons per festival day, the authors suggest that the demand remains relatively small.

Focusing on a specific sewer pipe to investigate the consumption patterns of a confined population is also a possibility. Prisons are a good example of deploying WBE to assess the quantity of illicit drugs being used. It is an open secret that licit and illicit drugs are being used in prisons. Yet, this is kept quiet most of the time, perhaps because no one has an idea of the extent of the phenomenon. Moreover, the results of a WBE campaign in a prison could lead to a repressive response by penitentiary authorities—for example, eliminating family visits if

WBE shows an increase in drug loads after these take place, or increasing controls to prevent smuggling of illicit drugs. However, it is also possible to adopt more preventive and harm reduction approaches. Indeed, being informed about the type and amount of substances being consumed is the starting point to developing an efficient and adequate strategy for preventing their use but also offering adequate treatment for people concerned.

Evaluating the efficiency of prevention programs is a particularly interesting application of WBE. Once WBE has been performed in colleges, schools, prisons or music festivals, and a global picture of the consumption of illicit drugs is available, measures (e.g., prevention, repression) could be proposed to modify the current situation. WBE could be the ideal tool for monitoring the impact of such measures, mainly because it offers the possibility of acquiring results almost in real time and with less effort compared to self-report surveys. This allows a continuous monitoring of the situation and, thanks to the acquired data, fine-tuning interventions and adapting strategies. Still, WBE will not replace traditional criminological/epidemiological tools like self-report surveys. Traditional general population surveys will remain crucial to understanding the reasons and motivations behind the use of illicit drugs and/or the changes in patterns of consumption.

The need to combine complementary sources of data

As already mentioned, WBE needs to be combined with and contextualized in the light of other data. However, it has to be said that, until recently, this aspect was often minimized in most publications, since the focus was on more technical features. In this section, we present and discuss a study that exemplifies the added value of combining WBE with existing information. The example focuses on heroin use. Indeed, heroin users are likely the best-known illicit drug user population, mainly because most individuals are or have been in treatment (opioid substitution treatment) or attend needle and syringe exchanges and other harm reduction programs.

Combining WBE and traditional indicators is essential for evaluating reliability and pertinence of these new indicators. In the research by Been et al. (2015), WBE, as an indicator of drug use, was 'calibrated' using methadone. The idea behind this approach is that, the more we know about the consumption pattern of a specific product, the better we will be able to estimate the loads we expect to measure at the WWTP, thus allowing us to assess the reliability and pertinence of consumption estimates derived from WBE. Methadone is the product of choice, since it is being used in opioid substitution treatments, and relatively detailed figures about the quantities distributed per day and per patient are available. While its contribution is very limited, there are also figures about medical usage of methadone (e.g., for pain treatment). Finally, combining these figures allows us to estimate expected daily consumption. Wastewater-based estimates and prescription figures were totally in line, thus supporting the reliability of WBE. Various sources of data, to which WBE estimates can be compared, also exist for heroin-injecting users. Data coming from opioid substitution treatments and needle and syringe exchange programs can be used to infer the quantity consumed by this population. It should be mentioned that obtaining these estimates is not straightforward, since numerous sources of uncertainty exist (e.g., dosage and heroin purity, the percentage of syringes used to inject heroin). Trying to go a step further in the interpretation, one could infer that, because the different indicators provide comparable estimates about heroin consumption in the area under investigation, current figures about the heroin population (i.e., prevalence) are realistic. Furthermore, for public health stakeholders, this means that harm reduction measures in place cover the target population and that there is no (or at least only a limited) 'hidden' heroin user population.

Carrying on in this direction, one could try to perform the same interpretation for cocaine, where it could be estimated that the injecting population accounts for approximately 5 to 10 percent of the quantity of cocaine that is measured in wastewater. It means, in this case, that the majority of cocaine users are not known, perhaps due to the fact that this population is well integrated in the society.

In conclusion, there is a need to combine WBE with other indicators. This holds true also for estimates derived from traditional epidemiological and criminological indicators, since reliable conclusions can be drawn only when a body of indicators points in the same direction.

Notes

1 An analyte is a substance, compound or chemical species that is of interest in an analytical procedure.
2 In a WBE context, studies performed in a closed or semi-closed environment rely on sampling and analysis from the sewer system of a defined subpopulation (closed environment, such as prisons), or from the sewer system to which a defined subpopulation contributes significantly (semi-closed environment, such as a music festival). This is different from traditional studies where the sampling is done in a wastewater treatment plant collating the wastewater of an entire city and in such a way that it is not possible to identify a specific contributing population.

References

Been, F., L. Benaglia, S. Lucia, J.-P. Gervasoni, P. Esseiva and O. Delémont. 2015. 'Data Triangulation in the Context of Opioids Monitoring via Wastewater Analyses'. *Drug and Alcohol Dependence* 151(June): 203–210.

Been, F., L. Bijlsma, L. Benaglia, J.-D. Berset, A.M. Botero-Coy, S. Castiglioni, L. Kraus, F. Zobel, M.P. Schaub … and C. Ort. 2016a. 'Assessing Geographical Differences in Illicit Drug Consumption: A Comparison of Results from Epidemiological and Wastewater Data in Germany and Switzerland'. *Drug and Alcohol Dependence* 161(April): 189–199.

Been, F., L. Rossi, C. Ort, S. Rudaz, O. Delémont and P. Esseiva. 2014. 'Population Normalization with Ammonium in Wastewater-Based Epidemiology: Application to Illicit Drug Monitoring'. *Environmental Science & Technology* 48(14): 8162–8169.

Been, F., C. Schneider, F. Zobel, O. Delémont and P. Esseiva. 2016b. 'Integrating Environmental and Self-Report Data to Refine Cannabis Prevalence Estimates in a Major Urban Area of Switzerland'. *International Journal of Drug Policy* 36(October): 33–42.

Benaglia, L. 2016. 'Monitoring Illicit Drug Consumptions through Wastewater Analysis in a Music Festival'. Paper presented to the School of Criminal Justice, University of Lausanne.

Berset, J.-D., R. Brenneisen and C. Mathieu. 2010. 'Analysis of Licit and Illicit Drugs in Waste, Surface and Lake Water Samples Using Large Volume Direct Injection High Performance Liquid Chromatography–Electrospray Tandem Mass Spectrometry (HPLC–MS/MS)'. *Chemosphere* 81(7): 859–866.

Bijlsma, L., R. Serrano, C. Ferrer, I. Tormos and F. Hernández. 2014. 'Occurrence and Behavior of Illicit Drugs and Metabolites in Sewage Water from the Spanish Mediterranean Coast (Valencia Region)'. *Science of the Total Environment* 487(July): 703–709.

Brewer, A.J., C.J. Banta-Green, C. Ort, A.E. Robel and J. Field. 2016. 'Wastewater Testing Compared with Random Urinalyses for the Surveillance of Illicit Drug Use in Prisons'. *Drug and Alcohol Review* 35(2): 133–137.

Burgard, D.A., C. Banta-Green and J.A. Field. 2014. 'Working Upstream: How Far Can You Go with Sewage-Based Drug Epidemiology?' *Environmental Science and Technology* 48(3): 1362–1368.

Burgard, D.A., R. Fuller, B. Becker, R. Ferrell and M.J. Dinglasan-Panlilio. 2013. 'Potential Trends in Attention Deficit Hyperactivity Disorder (ADHD) Drug Use on a College Campus: Wastewater Analysis of Amphetamine and Ritalinic Acid'. *Science of the Total Environment* 450(April): 242–249.

Castiglioni, S., L. Vandam and P. Griffiths. 2016. *Assessing Illicit Drugs in Wastewater.* European Monitoring Centre for Drugs and Drug Addiction, Luxembourg: Publications Office of the European Union.

Chen, C., C. Kostakis, J.P. Gerber, B.J. Tscharke, R.J. Irvine and J.M. White. 2014. 'Towards Finding a Population Biomarker for Wastewater Epidemiology Studies'. *Science of the Total Environment* 487(1): 621–628.

Cressey, D. 2015. 'The Cannabis Experiment'. *Nature* 524(7565): 280–283.

Daughton, C. 2001. 'Emerging Pollutants, and Communicating the Science of Environmental Chemistry and Mass Spectrometry: Pharmaceuticals in the Environment'. *Journal of the American Society for Mass Spectrometry* 12(10): 1067–1076.

EMCDDA and Europol. 2016. *2016 EU Drug Markets Report: In-Depth Analysis*. European Monitoring Centre for Drugs and Drug Addiction and Europol, Luxembourg: Publications Office of the European Union.

FOPH. 2016. Swiss Drug Policy, Swiss Federal Office of Public Health. www.bag.admin.ch/bag/en/home/aktuell/news/news5.html (accessed April 2016).

Goullé, J.-P., and M. Guerbet. 2016. 'Cannabinoïdes de synthèse et nouvelles drogues. Quoi de neuf?' *Revue Francophone des Laboratoires* 479: 33–42.

Hall, W., J. Prichard, P. Kirkbride, R. Bruno, P.K. Thai, C. Gartner, F.Y. Lai, C. Ort and J.F. Mueller. 2012. 'An Analysis of Ethical Issues in Using Wastewater Analysis to Monitor Illicit Drug Use: Ethical Issues in Wastewater Monitoring for Drug Use'. *Addiction* 107(10): 1767–1773.

Harman, C., M. Reid and K.V. Thomas. 2011. 'In Situ Calibration of a Passive Sampling Device for Selected Illicit Drugs and Their Metabolites in Wastewater, and Subsequent Year-Long Assessment of Community Drug Usage'. *Environmental Science & Technology* 45(13): 5676–5682.

Jones, H.E., M. Hickman, B. Kasprzyk-Hordern, N.J. Welton, D.R. Baker and A.E. Ades. 2014. 'Illicit and Pharmaceutical Drug Consumption Estimated via Wastewater Analysis. Part B: Placing Back-Calculations in a Formal Statistical Framework'. *Science of the Total Environment* 487(July): 642–650.

Khan, U., and J.A. Nicell. 2011. 'Refined Sewer Epidemiology Mass Balances and Their Application to Heroin, Cocaine and Ecstasy'. *Environment International* 37(7): 1236–1252.

Lai, F.Y., S. Anuj, R. Bruno, S. Carter, C. Gartner, W. Hall, K.P. Kirkbride, J.F. Mueller, J.W. O'Brien, J. Prichard, P.K. Thai and C. Ort. 2015. 'Systematic and Day-to-Day Effects of Chemical-Derived Population Estimates on Wastewater-Based Drug Epidemiology'. *Environmental Science & Technology* 49(2): 999–1008.

Lai, F.Y., P.K. Thai, J. O'Brien, C. Gartner, R. Bruno, B. Kele, C. Ort, J. Prichard, P. Kirkbride, W. Hall, S. Carter and J.F. Mueller. 2013. 'Using Quantitative Wastewater Analysis to Measure Daily Usage of Conventional and Emerging Illicit Drugs at an Annual Music Festival: Illicit Drugs in Music Event Wastewaters'. *Drug and Alcohol Review* 32(6): 594–602.

Miron, J. 2014. 'Marijuana Policy in Colorado'. Washington, DC: CATO Institute.

O'Brien, J.W., P.K. Thai, G. Eaglesham, C. Ort, A. Scheidegger, S. Carter, F.Y. Lai and J.F. Mueller. 2014. 'A Model to Estimate the Population Contributing to the Wastewater Using Samples Collected on Census Day'. *Environmental Science & Technology* 48(1): 517–525.

Ort, C., M.G. Lawrence, J. Reungoat and J.F. Mueller. 2010a. 'Sampling for PPCPs in Wastewater Systems: Comparison of Different Sampling Modes and Optimization Strategies'. *Environmental Science & Technology* 44(16): 6289–6296.

Ort, C., M.G. Lawrence, J. Rieckermann and A. Joss. 2010b. 'Sampling for Pharmaceuticals and Personal Care Products (PPCPs) and Illicit Drugs in Wastewater Systems: Are Your Conclusions Valid? A Critical Review'. *Environmental Science & Technology* 44(16): 6024–6035.

Ort, C., A.L.N. van Nuijs, J.-D. Berset, L. Bijlsma, S. Castiglioni, A. Covaci, P. de Voogt, E. Emke ... and K.V. Thomas. 2014. 'Spatial Differences and Temporal Changes in Illicit Drug Use in Europe Quantified by Wastewater Analysis: Wastewater Data Covering 24.74 Million People'. *Addiction* 109(8): 1338–1352.

Pardo, B. 2014. 'Cannabis Policy Reforms in the Americas: A Comparative Analysis of Colorado, Washington, and Uruguay'. *International Journal of Drug Policy* 25(4): 727–735.

Postigo, C., M.L. de Alda and D. Barceló. 2011. 'Evaluation of Drugs of Abuse Use and Trends in a Prison through Wastewater Analysis'. *Environment International* 37(1): 49–55.

Prichard, J., W. Hall, P. de Voogt and E. Zuccato. 2014. 'Sewage Epidemiology and Illicit Drug Research: The Development of Ethical Research Guidelines'. *Science of the Total Environment* 472(February): 550–555.

Reed, J., 2016. *Marijuana Legalization in Colorado: Early Findings*. Denver: Colorado Department of Public Safety.

Thomas, K.V., L. Bijlsma, S. Castiglioni, A. Covaci, E. Emke, R. Grabic, F. Hernández, S. Karolak and P. de Voogt. 2012. 'Comparing Illicit Drug Use in 19 European Cities through Sewage Analysis'. *Science of the Total Environment* 432(August): 432–439.

van Nuijs, A.L.N., J.-F. Mougel, I. Tarcomnicu, L. Bervoets, R. Blust, P.G. Jorens, H. Neels and A. Covaci. 2011. 'Sewage Epidemiology—A Real-Time Approach to Estimate the Consumption of Illicit Drugs in Brussels, Belgium'. *Environment International* 37(3): 612–621.

Zobel, F., C. Schneider and M. Marthaler. 2015. *Nouvelles Tendances dans le domaine des Drogues (NTD): La méthamphétamine en Suisse*. Lausanne: Addiction Suisse.

Zuccato, E., C. Chiabrando, S. Castiglioni, R. Bagnati and R. Fanelli. 2008. 'Estimating Community Drug Abuse by Wastewater Analysis'. *Environmental Health Perspectives* 116(8): 1027–1032.

Zuccato, E., C. Chiabrando, S. Castiglioni, D. Calamari, R. Bagnati, S. Schiarea and R. Fanelli. 2005. 'Cocaine in Surface Waters: A New Evidence-Based Tool to Monitor Community Drug Abuse'. *Environmental Health* 4(1): 14.

Part III

Forensic science and crime analysis

15

Reconstruction and study of offending trajectories through forensic evidence

An illustration using a forensic DNA database

Patrick P.J.M.H. Jeuniaux, Sabine De Moor, Luc Robert, Bertrand Renard, Caroline Stappers and Vanessa Vanvooren

Introduction

Offending trajectories, or 'criminal careers', have been studied in criminology since its origins (Piquero et al. 2003), and the usefulness of this concept has been discussed (Blumstein et al. 1988). Different sources (e.g., official records, self-reports) have been used to collect data, giving rise to important results on criminal careers themselves and on the methodologies employed to study them.

These studies constitute a particular case of the difficulties that exist in measuring crime, a more general concern that has been a topic of debate in criminological studies for many decades and that is commonly referred to as 'the dark figure of crime' (e.g., Biderman and Reiss 1967; Skogan 1977). Depending on our views on deviancy and crime, not all types of behaviour that some would label delinquent become known by third persons or by institutions (be they part of the criminal justice system or researchers or otherwise). The 'dark figure of crime' casts a shadow over what is known about crime and, all labelling questions aside, raises questions about how complete or representative crime data are, an issue that also touches on the validity of criminological research findings. Criminologists attempt to bridge the gap between crimes that are unknown and those that are known by seeking to extend methods and explore new sources of data. Although they are probably always 'guestimates' (de Castelbajac 2014), new types of data can be reliably used to at least shed light on what previously was part of the dark number of crime.

The issue of the dark number of crime is also important for the study of criminal careers. Much like a jigsaw puzzle, criminal careers need to be (re)constructed, just as a puzzle needs to be solved through assembling the various pieces of evidence that lie on the board. Moreover, as with a real puzzle, some pieces are easier to deal with than others, which may first lead to a biased reconstruction of the model. Finally, but contrary to the puzzle metaphor, we may never know when we are done with the reconstruction process. In other words, reconstructing offending trajectories is a challenge in itself.

The goal of this chapter is to study how forensic science can be used to cast its particular light on reconstructing criminal careers and study them. We organize our points in three stages.

First, we provide an overview of the study of criminal careers by briefly defining relevant concepts, evoking a few key research results, and explaining how different data sources help in studying criminal careers under different angles. One of these angles is forensic evidence. We discuss the advantages and disadvantages of using this type of data relative to other data types.

Second, we examine how a particular type of forensic evidence—forensic DNA data—can be used (as an indicator) to reconstruct criminal careers. To illustrate our claims, we proceed to a case study of the Belgian national forensic DNA database. We briefly explain the nature of the data, the process that generated it, and how this situation sets limits to our reconstruction attempt. Our dataset contains 7,535 offending trajectories. We describe the methodology that was used to derive them from the dataset and offer some statistics that give an idea of the interest of the dataset for future criminological research.

Third, we reflect on the specificity of forensic science (with a particular focus on forensic DNA data) as a potential source for research on criminal careers.

Theory: the study of criminal careers

In criminological research, the interest in the pattern of offending that takes place over the lifetime of individuals results in the examination of 'offending trajectories' or 'criminal careers'. But what is this concept and how is it useful?

The concept of criminal career

A criminal career can be defined as 'the longitudinal sequence of offences committed by an offender who has a detectable rate of offending during some period' (Blumstein et al. 1988, 2). This needs to be differentiated from the related concept of career criminals, which can be defined as 'persons who commit many crimes beginning at an early age and who persist in offending over the life course' (Paternoster 2014, 277). The study of criminal careers examines the involvement of individuals in criminal activity from a developmental or life-course perspective (DeLisi and Piquero 2011). The unit of analysis is not the crime but the individual who has committed the crime (Blumstein et al. 1988). This approach is longitudinal in the sense that the individual offender and his or her trajectory are studied over a period of time. The consistency or change of an individual over time can therefore be studied. Moreover, the individual's characteristics can be compared to one another.

Several dimensions pertaining to offending trajectories can be measured, including the beginning or onset of a criminal career (the age when it started, the seriousness and circumstances of the first offence), the duration of the career or career length (including the time elapsing between the first and the most recent offence), the end of the career (including why offenders cease to commit new offences, i.e., desistance from crime) and many other dimensions of offending (e.g., frequency, the specialization or versatility in terms of crime types or crime seriousness, escalation, de-escalation; Blumstein and Cohen 1987; DeLisi and Piquero 2011).

On the basis of these parameters, patterns and dimensions, many research questions can be asked (Townsley et al. 2005), including, Why do some people stop offending whereas others continue? What is the influence of age on the type of crimes committed? What are the characteristics of chronic offenders?

The modern approach to criminal careers can be traced back to a 1986 compendium entitled *Criminal Careers and 'Career Criminals'* by Blumstein and colleagues (Blumstein et al. 1986; Mazerolle 2014). The notion of criminal career is not a theory of crime per se but allows one to measure relevant quantitative variables that can be used in order to structure explanations of criminal activity (Blumstein et al. 1988). This approach provides fundamental knowledge on offending and supports evidence-based criminal justice policy (Farrington 2001). For instance, it can help in the design of better crime detection policies (Tilley and Townsley 2009).

There is an abundance of research about criminal careers (DeLisi and Piquero 2011; Laub and Sampson 2001; Piquero et al. 2003) and it would lead us too far afield to try to exhaustively cover core issues and debates here. Some key results are that: (1) careers show constancy and variation in terms of offending rate, persistence, and duration; (2) offending continuity is more common than discontinuity; (3) most offending careers are short; (4) some careers are long and persistent (i.e., so as to legitimate the use of expressions such as 'career criminal' or 'chronic criminal offender') and take up a large share of known crimes; (5) career criminals tend to commit more frequent and more serious offences; (6) an early age of career onset is consistently related to persistent and/or serious offending; (7) a criminal career frequently ends after the 20s and rarely starts after that age, whereas offenders aged 30 are likely to be persistent offenders; (8) most offenders are versatile and only a few are specialists, although there may be an exception for offenders of property crimes and violent crimes; and (9) as the criminal career is progressing, an increase of seriousness and specialization may appear. On the other hand, most offenders do not necessarily pass through an escalation of seriousness over time. These findings refer to patterns in criminal behaviour.

Data sources

Two types of sources are usually employed to collect data on criminal activities: (1) official records and (2) surveys. The first type results from the routine activity of institutions (e.g., recording arrests or convictions). The second type results from using recording instruments on specific occasions (e.g., victimization surveys, self-report crime surveys). These sources have their specific advantages and disadvantages and none is perfect.

The main problem with official records is their structural selectivity (i.e., bias). Indeed, their content depends on the recording process that is established by the authorities and that is influenced by many (factual, legal, organizational, institutional) factors, ranging from the ability to detect crimes to the political decision to devote resources to address criminality. Because official records represent a small portion of all crimes that have been committed, one may wonder whether they constitute a representative sample (Farrington 2001). Moreover, more serious and violent crimes and crimes perpetrated by prolific offenders may be over-represented in arrest data, whereas specialized offenders may be under-represented, since the former have a higher probability to be arrested and the latter a lower one (Lammers and Bernasco 2013).

Self-report crime surveys and victimization surveys have been used to search for information about criminality in addition to what is known on the basis of official crime records. Such surveys contributed to the unveiling of the large number of crimes that come to be unreported. Self-report crime surveys show that many more crimes are committed (over 20 times as many) than those we can see from conviction records (Farrington et al. 2013; Farrington and Ttofi 2014). For instance, many individuals reported being involved in a drug crime or carrying a weapon leading to public disorder without being arrested (Babinski et al. 2001).

Despite such methodological and empirical progress, the validity of self-reported crimes has been questioned. Whereas Kivivuori (2011) concludes that they are reliable in measuring the prevalence of crime in young populations, and Farrington (2001) claims that they are valid for young males, this validity is more uncertain for older and female populations. Moreover, according to Babinski et al. (2001), some high-frequency less-serious crimes (e.g., vandalism) and low-frequency more-serious crimes (e.g., assault) would show less in self-reports than in official records. Finally, there is the concern that most delinquents are likely to provide inaccurate self-reports, either intentionally or unintentionally (Auty et al. 2015).

Next to the official data and surveys, we find a third type of data source: operational devices (files, databases). Much like the official records, they concern information that is regularly collected by the authorities, but they are less administrative in nature in that they directly serve decisions taken to perform critical actions (e.g., finding criminals). Among these, we find law-enforcement intelligence databases and forensic science databases.

The main advantage of operational data sources over official data and self-report crime surveys is that they allow access to information on the criminal activities of unidentified offenders, i.e., offenders who are not known by the authorities (because they have never been caught). This point was clearly made for DNA databases by Lammers and colleagues. For instance, Lammers et al. (2012) studied the factors that influence the probability of arrest by comparing the characteristics of trajectories of offenders who were arrested to those who were not. Similar studies comparing arrested to non-arrested offenders involving other factors were later conducted (e.g., Lammers 2014; Lammers and Bernasco 2013). Additional research carried out with this type of data investigated patterns of co-offending criminality (Jeuniaux, Duboccage et al. 2015) and transnational offending (Bernasco et al. 2015), with the added advantage of including not only known offenders but also offenders that are not known to the authorities.

DNA evidence is not the only type of forensic evidence to which this approach can be applied: we think of fingerprints, shoe marks, earmarks, images, etc. (e.g., Rossy et al. 2013). However, DNA evidence is a very convincing way to determine that the same person was present at multiple crime locations (and possibly involved in different crimes), thanks to the high reliability of the criminal evidence based on DNA and its current quality standards. Moreover, the ability to link crimes to the same offender is important, recognizing that a small proportion of chronic offenders are responsible for a large share of all crimes (De Moor et al. 2016). For this reason, DNA-based datasets present an added value over sources that are not organized around the individuals (e.g., judicial dossiers, which naturally revolve around cases).

A major drawback of these operational sources is that they suffer from restrictions similar to those of official records, i.e., selectivity or bias. It is important to understand the nature of this selectivity. We discuss this issue in the next section.

Case study: reconstructing trajectories through forensic DNA data

In this section, we present a case study to show how the Belgian National Forensic DNA database can be used to reconstruct and study criminal careers. For short, we shall call it the 'National DNA database' (hereafter NDD). Because the NDD was established in 2002, we can cover a time frame of more than ten years of activities, hence one that is susceptible to capturing significant portions of offending trajectories. Our objective is to illustrate two things: (1) the methodological considerations that need to be taken into account when reconstructing the trajectories on the basis of the NDD and (2) the potential results that can be gathered from exploring the reconstructed trajectories.

A method for reconstructing trajectories based on DNA profiles

In order to reconstruct the criminal activities of offenders, we need to understand a few basic principles of how forensic DNA works, how it is used and recorded, and in what context it operates (for details, see Jeuniaux, Duboccage et al. 2015; Jeuniaux, Renard et al. 2015; Renard et al. 2013).

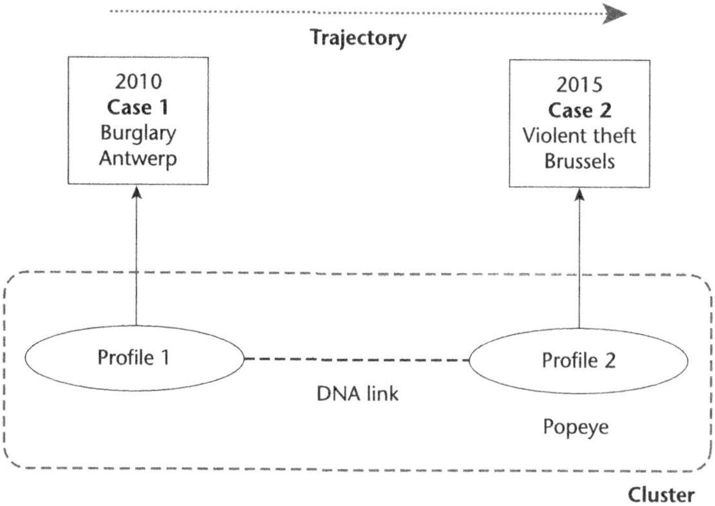

Figure 15.1 Example of a DNA-based trajectory

Three types of entities need to be distinguished in order to reconstruct trajectories: the case, the profile and the person. We illustrate this with a mock example (see Figure 15.1). An unknown male offender has left his DNA profile (Profile 1) in a case of burglary in Antwerp in 2010 (Case 1). Profile 1 is stored in the NDD but shows no match with previously stored profiles. Later the same offender (named 'Popeye') is convicted for a violent theft committed in Brussels in 2015 (Case 2). Because of this conviction, his DNA profile is sampled and sent to the NDD as Profile 2. A comparison of Profile 2 to the NDD shows that it is the same as Profile 1 (hence a 'DNA link' is drawn between the two profiles). A subsequent analysis shows that it is likely that the same person is the source of both profiles. When this happens, the NDD department establishes what is called in jargon a 'cluster'. A cluster is formed when a link between two profiles from different cases can be established. Therefore, through the existence of this cluster, Profile 1 and Profile 2 are associated with Popeye. What we call a trajectory is the ordered sequence of cases that belongs to the same particular individual (or cluster). In this example, our trajectory is the sequence Case 1–Case 2 associated to the cluster 'Popeye'.

The National Institute of Forensic Science and Criminology (INCC[1]) hosts the NDD. The department that runs the NDD within the INCC stores and manages the DNA profiles through a collection of software called the Combined DNA Index Systems (CODIS), whereas the administrative acts (receiving, recording, deleting, comparing, emailing, etc.) pertaining to the processing of the DNA profiles are recorded by a separate administrative database (ADMIN). The dataset that is analysed in this study is an extraction of the ADMIN database made on 10 May 2016. It is composed of 7,535 clusters, with their associated profiles and cases.

In Jeuniaux, Duboccage et al. (2015) and Renard et al. (2013), we described the process that leads to the records in the NDD. As shown in detail in those publications, the legal context has progressively been elaborated, first in 1999 and then in 2011, to place the use of forensic DNA under the control of the judiciary that from then on put particular constraints on the actions being performed. A simplified view of this chain of events is provided by Figure 15.2.

First, a crime is committed. If it is detected, a magistrate opens a case. The case may later be dropped or dismissed. If not dropped or dismissed, a trial may follow that may lead to a conviction. Second, depending on a variety of factors (e.g., the nature of the crime, the legislation, regional

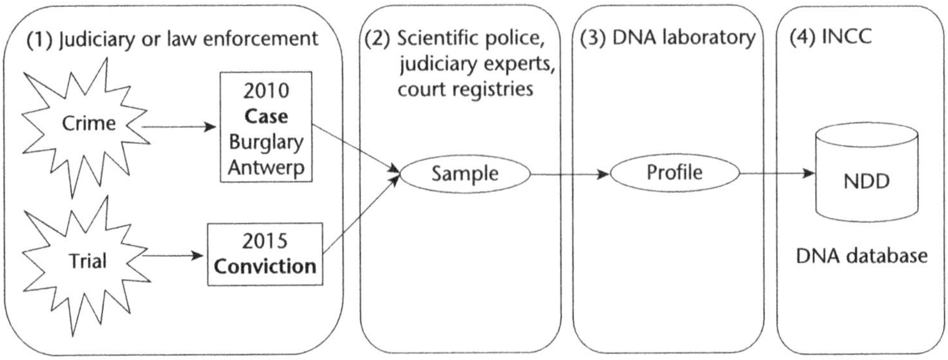

Figure 15.2 Simplified view of the process that leads to using the DNA database

policies), biological material may be sampled by the police from a crime scene, a victim, a suspect or a convicted offender. Third, the sample is sent to a DNA laboratory for analysis. When the results are available, they are sent to the magistrate and to the NDD. In the best situation, the results include a DNA profile that can be helpful to the criminal investigation or that can be processed by the NDD. Fourth, the NDD department at the INCC opens an administrative case to relate the criminal affair and a new DNA profile. The new DNA profile may be compared to the (old) profiles already stored in the NDD and to the profiles of certain international databases.[2] The NDD reports the result of the comparison to the magistrates. The two main possible results are positive or negative. A negative result means that there was no reliable match between the new profile and the old profiles. A positive result means that there was such a match and therefore that the same person is already registered, in association with another crime, in Belgium or another country. Finally, a profile can be stored in the NDD or deleted from the NDD.

We consider that there are four dimensions that impede our ability to reconstruct the (true) trajectories: (1) unit selectivity, (2) unit counting, (3) segment characterization, and (4) internal ordering. The problem of unit selectivity is the issue of the dark number cited above. It is important to realize that in the same way that not all crimes are detected, not all crimes lead to biological material being sampled, DNA profiles extracted from the sample and DNA profiles being stored in the NDD. Moreover, certain crimes will be under-represented in our dataset (e.g., white-collar crimes). Changes in legislation in 2011 led to an extension of the nature of crimes that lead to a DNA profile being generated on the basis of a conviction. The 2011 legislation also facilitates the transmission of DNA profiles to the NDD. As a result, after it came into force in 2014, more profiles and cases were available (e.g., there is a 41% increase of registered profiles in 2016 compared to 2013). Other historical events can be cited that impact the quantity and nature of the data.

The problem of unit counting concerns determining what constitutes a unit of analysis (or statistical unit). The constructs we are interested in are the crimes that composed the trajectory (see Figure 15.1). We shall therefore not count the DNA profiles (as we may have several profiles of the same individual for the same crime) but the crimes. Now, in order to run its operations, the NDD department needs to handle its forensic resource (the DNA data itself) but also perform administrative acts. Some important acts concern the reconciliation between the reality of the magistrate and the reality of the forensic DNA data handled by the NDD department. The department aims at categorizing each DNA profile within an administrative case (opened in the department) that is in a one-to-one correspondence with the judicial dossier (opened by a magistrate) that refers to a particular crime. As far as the data analysis is concerned, some work needs to be done to ensure that we do not count the same crime twice. Moreover, we are only interested in those crimes that were linked through their DNA, which requires at least two profiles (as in the example of Figure 15.1). Finally, we ignore the crimes that correspond to foreign profiles, since we usually receive no information on the nature of these crimes (because this aspect does not concern the NDD department).

The problem of segment characterization concerns the ability to describe the segments (i.e., the crimes) in each trajectory. Because it is not relevant to the activities of the NDD department to know the specifics of the criminal affairs, such information is usually scarce. It would be interesting to know the nature, location and time of the crime, but we have only approximate indicators for this information.

The nature of the crime can be approached by using the judicial references associated to the case (96% of the cases that compose a cluster bear a judicial reference). Regarding the type of crime, our most frequently observed crime categories are: (1) organized crime, (2) theft, (3) violent theft, (4) burglary, (5) laundering/concealment, (6) sex crimes, (7) assault, (8) threats/false bomb alarm, and (9) arson. Unfortunately, these codes usually cover a large variety of crimes. For example, the 'sex crimes' category covers gross indecency, sexual harassment, prostitution, human trafficking and rape. Similarly, the 'organized crime' category is sometimes used to facilitate the management of criminal affairs by merging several cases into one. Moreover, judicial references received from investigative judges contain no information on the crimes (their nature is therefore considered as 'unknown') but can be assumed to concern 'serious crimes' (i.e., crimes that violate the integrity of the body or lead to a lengthy sentence). The closest data that we have to approximate the location is the judicial district that handles the case, and to which the magistrate belongs. Our dataset is such that we have 28 judicial district categories (including the federal level).

The problem of internal ordering refers to the difficulty of finding reliable and precise temporal information. Regrettably, the closest information that we have on the time that the crime was committed is the year included in the judicial reference file, which corresponds to the time the case was opened by the magistrate. This information was available for most of the cases (n = 17,158, i.e., 96%). In those for which the information was not directly available (n = 729, i.e., 4%), it was necessary to manually extract the temporal information from additional sources.

Other temporal variables that could have been used were: (a) the date an administrative case was created in the NDD, (b) the date of reception of a DNA profile in the NDD department, and (c) the date it was treated in the database (i.e., recorded and/or compared). Although a date seems to be richer information than a year, it may be preferable to use the year of the judicial reference rather than the dates of the operations in the NDD department because these NDD operations are the last steps of the chain. As such, they might have been slowed down by a variety of factors (e.g., delays at the court registries, in the DNA laboratory, in the magistrate's office).

Based on the methodological principles evoked in the previous paragraphs, 7,535 offending trajectories were constructed, implementing operations in R (R Core Team 2016), and using the 'purrr' and 'plyr' packages (Wickham 2011, 2016). All the profiles that are part of the 7,535 individual offenders were found. For each of these profiles, we retrieved its administrative case. Because they have no case information, 2,572 international profiles were filtered out of the dataset. Using this process, we obtained 7,535 trajectories made of 17,887 cases.

What can be learned from DNA profiles: an illustration

An illustration of the offending trajectories is provided in Table 15.1. Each row corresponds to a different individual. The second column corresponds to the highest 'status' achieved by the person: Trace (when the person was never identified[3] and only left traces on crime scenes),

Suspect (when a reference DNA profile was taken of a suspect who has not yet been convicted) and Convicted (when the person has been convicted). The other columns show the crimes within a year from 2005 to 2015. Each cell counts the crime types on the first line and the district types on the second line. For instance, Person 1 who was once identified as a suspect (S), has left DNA profiles in three crimes: a burglary (B) in Bruges (bg) in 2005, a burglary (B) in Liège (li) in 2009 and a burglary (B) in Antwerp (an) in 2015. Person 2, who has been convicted (C), was involved in 22 cases (18 **B**urglaries, 1 **E**vasion, 1 **O**rganized **C**rime, 1 **T**hreat, 1 **V**iolent **T**heft). No crime is registered in the NDD for Person 2 in 2013 and 2014, but the reasons for this can be very diverse (the offender could be incarcerated, he could have been out of the country, he could have committed other offences that do not involve taking DNA traces, he could have experienced a period of 'intermittency' in his criminal behaviour, i.e., a temporary 'pause', e.g., Carlsson 2013). Then, in 2015, a new trace is registered for this offender.

These 12 trajectories have not been chosen arbitrarily; they all belong to the same network of co-offenders, as shown in Figure 15.3 (Jeuniaux, Duboccage et al. 2015). For instance, the DNA profiles of Person 1 and Person 2 were found at the same location (that of a burglary in

Table 15.1 Twelve offending trajectories

Person	Status	2005	2006	2007	2008	2009	2010	2011	2012	2013	2014	2015
1	S	B bg				B li						B an
2	C		4B 3ha tg	7B E 4ha 2li de tu	B OC ha le	VT B le li	2B 2hu	2B 2li	B li			T li
3	T					VT le		OC li				
4	T					B tg	2B 2hu	OC B li ha	2B ha tg			
5	T					B le		B li				
6	T							OC li				
7	C				VT li			OC li		B li		
8	T								B li			
9	T								B li	B li		
10	S											3B 2an tg
11	C									B li		B an
12	C					M br						B an

Note: T = Trace, S = Suspect, C = Convicted, B = Burglary, E = Evasion, OC = Organized Crime, VT = Violent Theft, M = Miscellaneous, T = Threat

Liège in 2009). From this set of offenders, we can readily see that we have a diversity of trajectories in terms of time span, types of crimes, districts and so on.

The (Belgian) offences that compose these trajectories have been handled in a judicial district from 1990 to 2016. Our dataset therefore presents a larger time span (1990–today) than the period during which the NDD has been operational (2002–today).

One element of interest to criminal career research can be inspected relatively easily: the time span of the career as shown by the NDD. For each person, the duration in number of years between the first year a crime was handled and the last year can be calculated (the time range). This shows a minimum of 0 year (i.e., every crime was handled in the same year) and a maximum of 25 years (M = 2.7, Median = 1).

Also relevant for the study of criminal careers is the number of cases one can find in a trajectory. Here it is important to remember that our unit of analysis is the cluster (i.e., the set of DNA profiles that match and are therefore thought to belong to the same individual). Table 15.2 classifies the 7,535 clusters in function of the number of Belgian cases (from 1 to more than 7) and in function of whether the clusters were involved in a match with any of the Prüm partners (the Netherlands, France, Germany, Luxembourg).

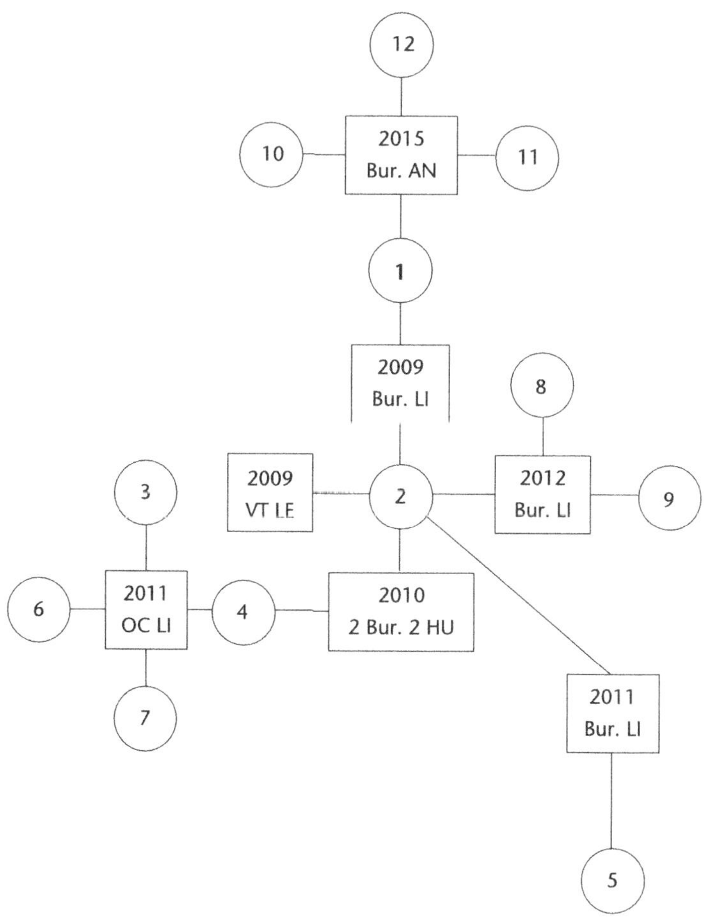

Figure 15.3 A network of co-offenders (circles) involved in the same cases (rectangles)

Table 15.2 Number of clusters in function of Belgian and Prüm cases

Number of Belgian cases	*1*	*2*	*3*	*4*	*5*	*6*	*7*	*> 7*	*TOTAL*
Involving Prüm cases	1,829	361	113	54	29	21	6	32	2,445
Not involving Prüm cases	21	3,207	1,016	425	190	89	47	95	5,090
TOTAL	1,850	3,568	1,129	479	219	110	53	127	7,535

Overall, 2,445 clusters (32%) show offending mobility as revealed through the current state of the Prüm operation (i.e., the number will likely evolve as the number of Prüm partners increases), whereas 5,090 clusters (68%) show no foreign matches. The number of Belgian cases that are found in a cluster ranges from 1 to 62. The most represented number of cases is 2. Of the clusters, 1,850 (25%) have only one Belgian case. The majority of these clusters (1,829; 99% of 1850) involve a Prüm match, whereas the (21) remaining clusters result from a coding error.

In terms of the location of crime, it is also possible to make some observations. Each of the 17,887 cases that composed the trajectories was handled by one of the 28 districts or the federal level (see Table 15.3). Among these districts, one can distinguish on the first line of the table those of the Flemish region and the region of Brussels (BR), and on the fourth line, districts of the Walloon region and the federal level, which represent 57%, 14%, 27% and 1%[4] of the cases respectively.

In terms of the prevalence of different types of crime, this variable is simplified by regrouping violent thefts, assaults, threats/bomb alarms, kidnappings and arsons as 'violence'; theft and shoplifting are regrouped as 'theft'. Half of the cases are composed of burglaries and a quarter by violent acts (see Table 15.4).

Overall, we have shown that we were able to use a clearly delineated procedure to construct trajectories on the basis of forensic DNA data, and that these trajectories are potentially composed

Table 15.3 Frequency and proportion of districts[1] of the 17,887 cases that compose the trajectories

District	*VU*	*IE*	*BG*	*KO*	*GE*	*OU*	*DE*	*AN*	*ME*	*TU*	*LE*	*HA*	*TG*	*BR*
Freq.	87	154	601	461	931	194	1,213	2,994	283	749	471	1,541	597	2,577
Prop.	0.00	0.01	0.03	0.03	0.05	0.01	0.07	0.17	0.02	0.04	0.03	0.09	0.03	0.14
District	TN	MO	CH	NI	NA	DI	HU	LI	VE	EU	MA	NE	AR	FD
Freq.	192	779	1,331	393	330	81	193	1221	120	102	82	62	25	122
Prop.	0.01	0.04	0.07	0.02	0.02	0.00	0.01	0.07	0.01	0.01	0.00	0.00	0.00	0.01

1 The district codes refer to Veurne (VU), Ypres (IE), Bruges (BG), Kortrijk (KO), Ghent (GE), Oudenaarde (OU), Dendermonde (DE), Antwerp (AN), Mechelen (ME), Turnhout (TU), Leuven (LE), Hasselt (HA), Tongeren (TG), Brussels (BR), Tournai (TN), Mons (MO), Charleroi (CH), Nivelles (NI), Namur (NA), Dinant (DI), Huy (HU), Liège (LI), Verviers (VE), Eupen (EU), Marche-en-Famenne (MA), Neufchâteau (NE), Arlon (AR), Federal (FD).

Table 15.4 Frequency and proportion of crime types of the 17,887 cases that compose the trajectories

Crime type	*Burglary*	*Violence*	*Org. crime*	*Sex*	*Unknown*	*Drugs*	*Murder*	*Other*	*Theft*	*TOTAL*
Frequency	9,020	4,523	841	826	688	626	514	452	397	17,887
Proportion	0.50	0.25	0.05	0.05	0.04	0.03	0.03	0.03	0.02	1.00

of crimes and geographical units of a diverse nature, which are spread over a 25-year range. It is therefore clearly possible to envision this data as an indicator of offending trajectories.

Offending patterns (e.g., specialization) can be studied with this data set (although we only have approximations of time, crime type and locations).

Some dimensions of criminal careers are much harder to study based on data from the NDD. The circumstances of the end of the career are hard to study beyond the identification status (trace vs suspect or convicted offender) unless the judicial references contained in the data are used in order to consult the judicial dossiers. Similarly, the onset of the criminal career and its context is hard to study. For one thing, we usually do not have the age of the perpetrator.

A very interesting aspect of the NDD relates to the fact that some of the offenders are known, whereas some others are not yet identified (i.e., they are still unknown). Most offenders are identified (57%): convicted offenders represent 46%, while suspects who, according to our data, have not been convicted, represent 11%. This means all remaining offenders with a criminal career are not yet identified; they represent 43% of the offenders with at least two profiles, which is almost half of all those with an offending trajectory.

This split between identified and unidentified offenders is a unique item in terms of data about criminal careers. Official records only deal with identified offenders. This unique feature of the NDD enables researchers to study the impact of certain factors (e.g., geographical diversity, crime versatility, crime seriousness) on the probability of arrest or identification (as Lammers and others did), and it also allows a comparison between some dimensions of the criminal careers of known versus unknown offenders in the NDD.

Discussion

Where does the above exploration leave us in terms of studying criminal careers when drawing on forensic evidence?

Criminal career research generally draws on official records (arrests, convictions, and so on). Although these are known to be biased by selectivity, the NDD is open to its own selectivity. Furthermore, there are indications that the NDD misses out on many offences that may be represented in official records. A recent analysis of a large cohort (n = 136,530) in the national conviction records shows a frequency that ranges between 1 and 169 (Mine et al. 2015, 41), while the NDD shows a range between 1 and 62. Many convictions never lead to a DNA trace (or another type of forensic trace), which means the NDD, in some sense, is even more selective than other data sources used in the study of criminal careers (and among the official records, it is generally accepted that the higher up the chain, the more selective the data become, which implies that the conviction records are much more selective than are police data). The process leading to a registration of a trace in the NDD suggests that the use of DNA would produce only a highly partial image of criminal careers.

On the positive side, the NDD provides criminal career researchers with a data source that includes both known and yet unidentified offenders. This feature can be capitalized on depending on the type of research question that is asked. It allows researchers to compare the available information in the NDD about known and unknown offenders and, furthermore, it provides them with the opportunity to also compare certain criminal career dimensions as constructed on the basis of official records (arrests, convictions) with criminal career dimensions of unknown offenders. For example, comparisons of police data with data from the NDD will be used in a study of co-offending; we also envisage analyses that compare criminal career patterns and dimensions based on the national conviction records with criminal career dimensions from the NDD.

Conclusions

The concept of criminal career refers to the temporal sequence of crimes committed by the same individual. As the literature shows, it is helpful in answering criminological research questions on patterns in offending trajectories.

Three types of data sources can be used to reconstruct criminal careers: (1) official records (e.g., criminal record of convicted offenders); (2) surveys (e.g., self-report crime surveys); and (3) operational devices (e.g., forensic DNA databases). All these types suffer from some biases. Depending on our research question, it may be good to either draw on forensic evidence (e.g., forensic DNA data) alone, or to mobilize forensic data in comparison to other types of data (e.g., judicial records or judicial dossiers).

We have illustrated that a DNA-based dataset can serve to construct offending trajectories involving a diversity of crimes and places. We know, however, that these trajectories suffer from problems of: (1) unit selection (e.g., our view is biased toward crime involving a specific chain using forensic DNA), (2) unit counting (e.g., the definition of what counted as a crime), (3) unit ordering (e.g., we had only the year the crime was handled by the authorities and not the date the crime was committed), and (4) sequence characterization (e.g., we had relatively poor information on the nature of the crimes and their location).

The use of DNA for the purpose of studying criminal careers may be limited because of the above-mentioned problems. On the other hand, the NDD contains information about unknown offenders, which provides researchers with an opportunity to compare between known and unknown offenders and a number of criminal career dimensions.

In all, it seems safe to conclude at this point that a firm assessment of the use of forensic evidence such as DNA for the study of offending trajectories is not yet possible (further research is needed), but there are positive and negative arguments to be taken into account.

To conclude: the link between forensic data and criminal careers can also be reversed, in that perhaps on the basis of the existing knowledge about criminal careers, questions can be raised about the collection and/or the conservation of forensic evidence. This has not been dealt with in this chapter.

Acknowledgements

Patrick P.J.M.H. Jeuniaux benefited from the financial support of the Internal Security Fund (ISF) of the European Commission for the 'Prüm DNA BE' project (# ISF-P-17-02). Sabine De Moor and Caroline Stappers received financial support from the Belgian Research Action through Interdisciplinary Networks (BRAIN-be) program of the Belgian Science Policy Office (BELSPO) for the 'Be-Gen' project (# BR/132/A4/Be-Gen).

Notes

1 Nationaal Instituut voor Criminalistiek en Criminologie (NICC) / Institut National de Criminalistique et de Criminologie (INCC).

2 Through the application of the Prüm Treaty since 2014, Belgium automatically compares its DNA profiles with those of the Netherlands and France, and since 2016, with Germany and Luxembourg. As per application of the treaty, Belgium will compare its DNA profiles with those of other Prüm countries in the future.

3 At the national level (since we ignored international cases).

4 Rounding errors account for the fact that it does not sum to 100%.

References

Auty, K.M., D.P. Farrington and J.W. Coid. 2015. 'The Validity of Self-Reported Convictions in a Community Sample: Findings from the Cambridge Study in Delinquent Development'. *European Journal of Criminology* 12(5): 562–580. http://doi.org/10.1177/1477370815578198.

Babinski, L.M., C.S. Hartsough and N.M. Lambert. 2001. 'A Comparison of Self-Report of Criminal Involvement and Official Arrest Record'. *Aggressive Behavior* 27 (1): 44–54. http://doi.org/10.1002/1098-2337(20010101/31)27:1<44::AID-AB4>3.0.CO;2-O.

Bernasco, W., M. Lammers and C.P.K. van der Beek. 2015. 'Cross-Border Crime Patterns Unveiled by International Exchange of DNA Profiles'. *Security Journal* 28(4). http://doi.org/10.1057/sj.2015.27.

Biderman, A.D., and A.J. Reiss. 1967. 'On Exploring the "Dark Figure" of Crime'. *The ANNALS of the American Academy of Political and Social Science* 374(1): 1–15. http://doi.org/10.1177/000271626737400102.

Blumstein, A., and J. Cohen. 1987. 'Characterizing Criminal Careers'. *Science* 237: 985–991. http://doi.org/10.1126/science.237.4818.985.

Blumstein, A., J. Cohen and D.P. Farrington. 1988. 'Criminal Career Research: Its Value for Criminology'. *Criminology* 26(1): 1–35.

Blumstein, A., J. Cohen, J.A. Roth and C.A. Visher. 1986. *Criminal Careers and 'Career Criminals'*, vol. 1. Washington, DC: National Academy Press.

Carlsson, C. 2013. 'Processes of Intermittency in Criminal Careers: Notes from a Swedish Study on Life Courses and Crime'. *International Journal of Offender Therapy and Comparative Criminology* 57(8): 913–938. http://doi.org/10.1177/0306624X12443656.

De Castelbajac, M. 2014. 'Brooding over the Dark Figure of Crime: The Home Office and the Cambridge Institute of Criminology in the Run-up to the British Crime Survey'. *British Journal of Criminology* 54(5): 928–945. http://doi.org/10.1093/bjc/azu047.

DeLisi, M., and A.R. Piquero. 2011. 'New Frontiers in Criminal Careers Research, 2000–2011: A State-of-the-Art Review'. *Journal of Criminal Justice* 39: 289–301. http://doi.org/10.1016/j.jcrimjus.2011.05.001.

De Moor, S., T. Vander Beken and S. Van Daele (2016). 'DNA Databases as an Alternative Data Source for Criminological Research'. *European Journal on Criminal Policy and Research*. https://doi.org/10.1007/s10610-016-9327-9.

Farrington, D.P. 2001. *What Has Been Learned from Self-Reports about Criminal Careers and the Causes of Offending?* London: Home Office.

Farrington, D.P., K.M. Auty, J.W. Coid and R.E. Turner. 2013. 'Self-Reported and Official Offending from Age 10 to Age 56'. *European Journal on Criminal Policy and Research* 19(2): 135–151. http://doi.org/10.1007/s10610-012-9195-x.

Farrington, D.P., and M.M. Ttofi. 2014. 'Criminal Careers in Self-Reports Compared with Official Records'. *Criminal Behaviour and Mental Health* 21(1): 225–228. http://doi.org/10.1002/cbm.1932.

Jeuniaux, P.P.J.M.H., L. Duboccage, B. Renard, P. Van Renterghem and V. Vanvooren. 2015. 'Establishing Networks in a Forensic DNA Database to Gain Operational and Strategic Intelligence'. *Security Journal*, 1–19. http://doi.org/10.1057/sj.2015.31.

Jeuniaux, P.P.J.M.H., B. Renard, L. Duboccage, S. Steuve, C. Stappers, I. Gallala and V. Vanvooren. 2015. 'Managing Forensic DNA Records in a Divided World: The Belgian Case'. *Records Management Journal* 25(3): 269–287. http://doi.org/10.1108/RMJ-05-2015-0018.

Kivivuori, J. 2011. *The Discovery of Hidden Crime: Self-Report Delinquency Surveys in Criminal Policy Context*. New York: Oxford University Press.

Lammers, M. 2014. 'Are Arrested and Non-Arrested Serial Offenders Different? A Test of Spatial Offending Patterns Using DNA Found at Crime Scenes'. *Journal of Research in Crime and Delinquency* 51(2): 143–167. http://doi.org/10.1177/0022427813504097.

Lammers, M., and W. Bernasco. 2013. 'Are Mobile Offenders Less Likely to Be Caught? The Influence of the Geographical Dispersion of Serial Offenders' Crime Locations on Their Probability of Arrest'. *European Journal of Criminology* 10(2): 168–186. http://doi.org/10.1177/1477370812464533.

Lammers, M., W. Bernasco and H. Elffers. 2012. 'How Long Do Offenders Escape Arrest? Using DNA Traces to Analyse when Serial Offenders Are Caught'. *Journal of Investigative Psychology and Offender Profiling* 9(1): 13–29. http://doi.org/10.1002/jip.1353.

Laub, J.H., and R.J. Sampson. 2001. 'Understanding Desistance from Crime'. *Crime and Justice* 28: 1–69.

Mazerolle, P. 2014. 'Criminal Careers and Public Policy Responses'. In B. Bruinsma and D. Weisburd, eds., *Encyclopedia of Criminology and Criminal Justice*, 800–807. New York: Springer.

Mine, B., L. Robert and E. Maes. 2015. *Recidive na een rechterlijke beslissing. Nationale cijfers op basis van het Centraal Strafregister / La récidive après une décision judiciaire. Des chiffres nationaux sur la base du Casier judiciaire central* (No. 38). Brussels: Institut National de Criminalistique et de Criminologie.

Paternoster, R. 2014. 'Career Criminals and Criminological Theory'. In G. Bruinsma and D. Weisburn, eds., *Encyclopedia of Criminology and Criminal Justice*, 276–285. New York: Springer.

Piquero, A.R., D.P. Farrington and A. Blumstein. 2003. 'The Criminal Career Paradigm'. In M. Tonry and N. Morris, eds., *Crime and Justice: A Review of Research*, 30: 359–506. Chicago: University of Chicago Press.

R Core Team. 2016. *R: A Language and Environment for Statistical Computing*. Vienna, Austria: R Foundation for Statistical Computing. Retrieved from www.R-project.org.

Renard, B., L. Duboccage, P. Jeuniaux and V. Vanvooren. 2013. 'Les banques nationales de données génétiques en Belgique. Un premier bilan de 10 ans d'activité'. *Revue de Droit Pénal et de Criminologie* 12: 927–961.

Rossy, Q., S. Ioset, D. Dessimoz and O. Ribaux. 2013. 'Integrating Forensic Information in a Crime Intelligence Database'. *Forensic Science International* 230(1–3): 137–146. http://doi.org/10.1016/j.forsciint.2012.10.010.

Skogan, W.G. 1977. 'Dimensions of the Dark Figure of Unreported Crime'. *Crime & Delinquency* 23(1): 41–50. http://doi.org/10.1177/001112877702300104.

Tilley, N., and M. Townsley. 2009. 'Forensic Science in UK Policing: Strategies, Tactics and Effectiveness'. In J. Fraser and R. Williams, eds., *Handbook of Forensic Science*, 359–379. London: Willan Publishing.

Townsley, M., C. Smith and K. Pease. 2005. *Using DNA to Catch Offenders Quicker: Serious Detections Arising from Criminal Justice Samples*. London: Jill Dando Institute of Crime Science, University College London.

Wickham, H. 2011. 'The Split-Apply-Combine Strategy for Data Analysis'. *Journal of Statistical Software* 40(1): 1–29.

Wickham, H. 2016. 'Purrr: Functional Programming Tools'. Retrieved from https://CRAN.R-project.org/package=purrr.

16

The contribution of forensic science to the analysis of crime networks

Quentin Rossy and Carlo Morselli

Introduction

Analysing crime data to detect patterns relies on the ability of practitioners and researchers to deconstruct the problem into simple parts. To do so, networks are commonly used as convenient models. Two methodologies that are based on graph-like models have merged over time: 'link analysis' and 'social network analysis' (SNA). In this chapter, we start with the historical foundations of these approaches, which may be found in computer science, policing, sociology and legal science. As a descriptive model, networks are more often than not used to model criminal networks of offenders, but practices and research have proven that their scope may be broadened. We therefore discuss some ideas and misconceptions about their uses and present some general methodological recommendations. Finally, the contributions of forensic science to reconstructing crime networks are examined in regard to the potential of using traces to infer relationships among actors, the presence of unknown linked entities, and the identification of their characteristics.

The network dimension of crime

Networks as models to describe and analyse crime or deviant activities are based on the root principle that such activities can be modelled by a graph of entities connected by relationships. This model aims to detect, collate and interpret the ties between relevant entities (e.g., persons, events, locations). It supports the reconstruction of a criminal activity that may involve a complex set of individuals and events and the inference of the roles or influences of a network structure to the realization of a criminal activity. Networks, like other models, are used to facilitate the analysis of complex problems. Formalized by Chen (1976), the entity-relationship model offers a unified and natural view of the real world. He defines an entity 'as a "thing" which can be distinctly identified and relationships are associations among entities' (Chen 1976, 10). An entity is thus a thing having a separate and identifiable existence.

This model was published nearly at the same time as Harper and Harris's (1975) paper, which defines 'link analysis' as the core method for criminal intelligence analysis in policing. They attribute the earliest application of the approach—in engineering—to Gilbreth and Gilbreth (1917) (cited in Harper and Harris 1975) and they suggest its application to describe organized crime problems. The link analysis approach is a qualitative method to describe organized crime structures with nodes and edges. In fact, graph-based techniques have been exploited since the nineteenth century to model data gathered during an investigation. They can be found in the work of John Henry Wigmore, whose method inspired the argument diagramming in which nodes represent facts and assumptions linked with causal relationships (Wigmore 1913).

Akin to the link analysis framework is the concept of social network, which, in the social sciences, is defined as 'a set of socially relevant nodes connected by one or more relations' (Marin and Wellman 2011, 11). Individuals and organizations are the most common classes of entities analysed in the social network approach. The concepts of 'nodes', 'actors' or 'entities' are often used as synonyms. Here we use the concept of 'entity' as a distinctly identified part of the reality (e.g., a person, an event or a location) and the notion of 'node' as its representation in the network model. The social network approach aims at modelling and studying patterns of relationships between entities and not only their characteristics. 'The unit of analysis in network analysis is not the individual, but an entity consisting of a collection of individuals and the linkages among them' (Wasserman and Faust 1994, 5). A network, by itself, is thus an entity embedding a set of interconnected entities. But networks are not the same as groups (Marin and Wellman 2011), which are classifications of a particular type of thing in a common set or a particular discrete group membership. The social network approach is thus a particular modelling process where an object of study is defined with an entity-relationship model to describe the social phenomena.

General overviews of social network analysis, such as Marin and Wellman (2011) and Wasserman and Faust (1994) classify the exploitation of the network model in two main categories. For a recent review of the multiple contributions of SNA to criminology, see Bouchard and Malm (2016). On the one hand, a network can be considered as a dependent variable, which may be explained by a theory of causation. On the other hand, it may be considered as the independent variable leading to a particular phenomenon. In this latter scenario, the social network approach is based on the hypothesis that causation is attributable to social structures and not located in the traditional individual attributes that have formed the basis of social science explanatory models. Thus, the roots of criminal activities may be explained by the relationships between social entities (e.g., personal relationships, opportunities or community settings) and not solely by their intrinsic attributes (e.g., gender or age): 'More than a set of methods—it is an orientation toward the understanding of human behaviour that focuses on the importance of social relations and their consequence' (McGloin and Kirk 2010, 210). From a formal perspective, modern social networks find their origins in anthropology and sociology, in particular in the sociometric models pioneered by Jacob L. Moreno and Helen Jennings (Jennings 1943; Moreno 1932 and 1934; see Freeman 2004 for a historical overview of their collaborative work). This approach relies on a network model combined with the use of mathematical measures describing the global structure of the network or the structural importance of its nodes.

In criminology, the network model has been used both to describe (as a dependent variable) and to explain (as an independent variable) crime (Papachristos 2011, 2014). McGloin and Kirk (2010) and Carrington (2011) state that the social network approach is at the crossroads between Sutherland's differential association theory and Hirschi's social control theory. Social networks are seen as a key predicator of crime: 'one of the most robust findings in the field of criminology, namely that the bulk of delinquency is carried out in groups' (McGloin and Kirk 2010, 209). Sutherland (1939) formulated that criminal behaviours, rationalizations and attitudes are learned in the context of overly positive associations with offenders. This was extended into Akers' learning theory (1998); he proposed a social structure model to categorize the factors influencing deviant actions: the social organization or community, the socio-demographic characteristics of individuals and groups, the social disorganization or group conflict and, finally, the social location in groups. It is this latter social structure that is typically modelled by a network approach. Carrington (2011) argues that both Sutherland's differential association theory and Hirschi's social control theory can be interpreted and tested with network models at a micro-level (i.e., the ego network of an individual). Furthermore, the network approach can also be applied to the macro-level of communities or neighbourhoods in relation to social disorganization theory (see Carrington 2011) or even at the country level (see Boivin 2014). A social network approach can also integrate the analysis of individual's attributes, such as age, nationality and gender. One of the main concepts from this perspective is *homophily*, which refers to individuals in the same social network sharing similar demographic characteristics (van Mastrigt and Carrington 2014; McPherson et al. 2001). In addition, Papachristos (2011) links the social network approach to opportunity theories, in the sense that 'everyday life is structured by peer groups and the availability of behavioural options in the group' (117). The assumption is that the network dimension of criminal activities generates opportunities (Morselli 2009). For instance, the social network approach may be combined with a geographical analysis through the analysis of the 'journey to associates' (Malm et al. 2008). Papachristos (2014) promotes the concept of 'social space' to describe how neighbourhoods and communities are more than just geographic concepts but are also related to the network dimension of crime.

As a descriptive model, social networks are more often than not used to model criminal networks of individuals involved in a shared illicit activity. Much research on criminal networks does not focus on the aetiology of crime but rather on the description of the organization of a particular subgroup of individuals. The criminal network as an object of study leads to such questions as how to detect, to describe and to measure the regularities and patterns of social structures. Papachristos (2011) even argues that methods within the social network analysis repertoire could move past the descriptive model to the understanding of the generative processes or aetiology of criminal groups.

Analysing criminal networks

Analysing crime problems by their network dimension is commonly associated with the analysis of organized criminal networks to support criminal investigations that aim at developing disruption strategies (Strang 2014). Indeed, the use of link charts has emerged in criminal intelligence analysis as an investigative tool to structure information gathered during an investigation and to reconstruct the network of organized criminal groups (Harper and Harris 1975). Social network analysis methods have then been proposed to enrich the approach by the use of centrality metrics (Klerks 2001; Sparrow 1991). This has led to a narrow view of the overall scope of approaches. In this section, we discuss some ideas and misconceptions about their uses for both practical and research purposes.

Summarizing network analytic techniques as the description and analysis of complex organized criminal groups is an oversimplification. Indeed, for the last 20 years, many researchers have shown how these techniques can support the analysis of a broader range of crime problems and many lines of questioning. Extant research has shown that co-offending generally involves small groups that are not stable in time, which is contrary to the assumption that criminal groups are more often than not hierarchically structured (Hashimi et al. 2016; Morselli 2009; Reuter 1983). Indeed, the size of a network may be positively associated with the probability of detection. Small, flexible and ephemeral groups may be hypothetically more resilient (Reuter 1983). Research has shown that co-offending groups are not stable and are generally composed of two or three co-offenders (Hashimi et al. 2016). Duijn et al. (2014) show that criminal groups are often not characterized by a stable hierarchical structure but rather by a flexible organization.

The more ways or paths a network has to achieve its goal, the more flexible and resilient it is to law enforcement actions against its actors (Morselli and Roy 2008). The flexibility of a network is related to its self-organizing capacities that result from its creation process. It relies on the development of interactions between the multiple relationships that each actor of the network has (Morselli, 2009). This is the snowball effect described by Kleemans (2007).

It should be noted that the flexibility of a network as a core characteristic of its resilience does not necessarily imply that central actors are absent. Some actors may lead the activities or play a strategic intermediary role between unlinked actors. As key middlemen, known as brokers, they are said to control the flow of information and make others dependent on their activities (Freeman 1977). The key role of brokers has been studied in many areas, such as drug trafficking (Desroches 2005; Natarajan 2006; Pearson and Hobbs 2001; Zaitch 2002), illicit markets (Bruinsma and Bernasco 2004; Morselli and Roy 2008) and human trafficking (Kleemans 2007; Zhang 2008; Zhang and Chin 2002). They may spread the flexibility of the networks by their ability to contact several co-offenders to perform a specific task, thus increasing opportunities. It is worth noting that the key role of an actor may be unrelated to its direct centrality and more related to its functional roles within the criminal activity. The roles of actors are thus a key element in analysing criminal networks, leading to new frameworks for combining social network and script analysis (Bright et al. 2014; Morselli and Roy 2008).

The detection of central actors may serve to disrupt the functioning of a network by neutralizing key actors. But the examination of criminal networks may also aim at analysing the formation, composition and functioning of co-offending groups whether or not they are well structured (McGloin and Nguyen 2014). The focus is placed on the way criminal groups emerged and grew to settle prevention strategies: 'the goal is not to dismantle a network but rather to prevent it from occurring in the first place' (McGloin and Nguyen 2014, 20). Network analytic techniques may thus support the comparison of structures of multiple criminal groups and the analysis of their differences and similarities. They allow the evaluation of the roles of several sources of information to the reconstruction of criminal networks and how these sources influence their perception (Corazza and Esseiva 2013). In policing, they are key technics used to structure the information gathered during an investigation and facilitate the analysis of a case. As an external aid, they support collaborative thinking and support joint decision-making processes (Rossy and Ribaux 2014). Finally, they may also support the evaluation of disruption strategies in regard to their impact on the structure of criminal groups.

Methodological elements

To analyse crime from its network dimension, graph-based techniques are more often than not used to model the problem. They can be classified into two main methodological categories. First, link analysis relies on the drawing of a qualitative graph depicting relationships between several types of entities by using adequate visual properties of nodes and edges (or links). Second, social network analysis uses a simpler visual model of nodes and edges but extends the model with quantitative measures depicting the structure of the global network or the structural features of its nodes. In this section, we present the aims, key concepts and methodological aspects of each.

Link analysis

Link analysis is based on the conception of graph-like charts that aim to describe crime problems with a network model of nodes representing entities of interest such as persons, objects, traces, events or location, and their relationships. Link charts are used in criminal investigations to facilitate the processing of large-scale investigation data. They are commonly used to memorize the collected data and keep an overview of the relevant information. As working memory, they support investigators to remember the elements of the case and facilitate communication within teams or with partners. Even if they are not completely independent of language, link charts are generally well understood in international inquiries. When well designed, they are intuitive and do not require the mastery of complex formalism. In addition, the overview offered by link charts is generally highly appreciated by managers within police and criminal intelligence organizations.

The conception of link charts implies the adherence to some general recommendations. Some are found repeatedly in criminal analysis textbooks (Fedpol 2010; Interpol 1997; UNODC 2002) and the scientific literature (Harper and Harris 1975; Morris 1986; Senator 2005). For instance, 'minimizing edge crossings' and 'favouring orthogonally' to improve the readability of the chart are repeatedly promoted. Global methodology and a review of these recommendations can be found in Rossy and Ribaux (2014) and Rossy (2016).

Traditionally, these graph-like techniques are used for the representation of criminal networks, smuggling of goods, chronologies of events, as well as the visualization of telephone records and financial data. In this context, visualizations are used for many objectives, such as analysing the traces and information gathered, evaluating a cold case, helping along the categorization of a particular offence, facilitating the transmission and receipt of a case or supporting an argument at trial (Rossy and Ribaux 2014). The identification of recurrent forms of usage in regard to repetitive crime and investigative problems has led to the formalization of patterns of visualizations. They are formalized to describe a design framework defined by the problem. Traditional link chart patterns are: (1) the criminal network chart; (2) the chart of illicit trafficking; (3) the event chart; and (4) the chart of a series. The first two support investigations involving the reconstruction of criminal groups. The latter two are intended to support the reconstruction process of complex criminal events whether a single case or a sequence of cases. A complete description of these patterns can be found in Rossy (2016).

The identification of patterns in link charts aims at formalizing adequate visual representations to support decision-making. Without cumulative experience, effort and time may be required to design an effective chart (Innes et al. 2005). Indeed, the design of a link chart is based on the understanding of the problem addressed by the analyst and his or her ability to model it in the form of a network representation (Peterson et al. 2000). The quality of the representation is then dependent on the analyst's ability to identify and classify entities and relationships relevant to the investigation and to distinguish them from those that may be omitted. The design involves both an ability to produce an expressive visual structure and an ability to properly model the situations encountered. Some authors note that a link chart does not solve the problem of information overload (Klerks 2001; Schroeder et al. 2007). Indeed, link charts seem to work well when the number of entities and relationships represented is limited. Moreover, if visualizations provide many benefits, they are not neutral and may induce biases. Designer choices, whether intentional or not, and user-induced effects (e.g., confusion, distraction or misinterpretation) are two frequent causes of bias (Bresciani and Eppler 2009). For instance, the designer may oversimplify the problem and leave aside crucial elements that may lead to ambiguities and interpretation mistakes (Rossy and Ribaux 2012). This kind of bias may feed rhetoric in court.

However, these methods continue to be exploited and seem to respond to concrete needs. They allow for a common support to managing a large amount of heterogeneous data and they facilitate both the analysis and communication of information. The visual language is sufficiently rich and expressive to integrate the diversity of concepts encountered during the analysis of a criminal activity.

Social network analysis

Social network analysis is based on a simpler network model usually consisting of one set of social entities. Usually nodes depict individuals, but they may also represent groups of individuals or moral persons such as companies. Relationships among such actors are then depicted by edges between the nodes. This form of social network is known as a one-mode network. Analyses may also be derived from two-mode network data (i.e., two types of nodes) by extracting relations that consist of co-membership or affiliation to a group or co-attendance to an event. The number of node types represented on a social network is the main feature that distinguishes it from a link chart. More often than not, a one-mode approach is used (Borgatti 2012; Strang 2014). On a link chart, the number of types of entities represented is not limited in the model, but defined by the criminal activity and chosen in consistency with the investigative questions.

The key methodological aspect of social networks is the integration of quantitative measures to depict the structure of the global network or the structural importance of specific nodes. The first category of methods, known as first order metrics, aims to describe the network as a whole. Among others, classical measures are the size of the network, its density, average degree, average shortest path (geodesic) and degree or betweenness centralization. The size of a network is calculated in terms of the number of nodes or links. The network density is the ratio between actual connections between nodes to all potential connections. A network containing all possible links is called a clique. The average degree is the mean of the number of links per node, and the average geodesic describes how far apart any two given nodes are (i.e., the average number of intermediates between two nodes). Degree and betweenness centralization describe the amount of variation in degree and betweenness scores for each node of the network (see below). These four calculations are often used to compare the value of a specific node to the average value of all nodes in the whole network. They are based on metrics that aim to describe the centrality of the nodes within a network. Such calculations are known as second order metrics or 'centrality measures'. Classical measures are degree, closeness, betweenness and eigenvector centralities. Additional indicators have been developed and classified into three types of measures: local, distance and feedback (Brandes and Erlebach 2005).[1]

Since centrality may come in many forms, the centrality metrics aim at distinguishing them. Degree (i.e., the number of direct links with other nodes) and closeness (i.e., the shortest distance between a particular node and all other nodes) centrality measures aim to detect whether one individual could be central because he or she has many contacts. Others may have few contacts, but remain central because they link unconnected entities. The betweenness measure (i.e., the number of times a node lies on the shortest path between two other nodes) and eigenvector measure (i.e., the degree to which an individual is connected to other highly connected individuals) aim to detect these intermediaries or related roles. The interpretation of the metrics is an unresolved problem. Sparrow (1991) argued that it is a sign of strength, whereas Peterson (1994) sees a high degree of centrality as a vulnerability (see Morselli 2010 for an assessment within crime contexts). But no matter how they are interpreted, centrality measures allow discrimination of nodes and the detection of particular nodes that may have specific or abnormal activity within the network. They allow a quantitative description that may support the examination of the evolution of the network and the comparison of multiple networks. More specifically, social networks support: (1) the detection of central individuals or subgroups in a criminal network; (2) the identification of their interactions; (3) the description of the structure of the network; (4) the evaluation of the impact of removing an individual from the network; and, finally, (5) the analysis of a network's information flows (Morselli et al. 2013). Researchers, however, have to be cautious of the limitations of the approach. Indeed, the reconstruction of co-offending networks often fails to integrate the social environment of offenders and relies on abilities to detect crimes. The perception of the networks is highly influenced by the efforts taken to reconstruct them (Bouchard and Malm 2016). As described below, these challenges are common to both methods.

Common challenges of conception

The conception process of both link charts and social network graphs relies on key considerations. The first is known as the boundary specification problem (Laumann et al. 1992). Whatever the problem being addressed, it is necessary to realize that the information gathered and its network model may be incomplete and reflect only one part of the whole picture. Analysing a whole network requires one to consider all connected nodes. Such an analysis is based on the assumption that the knowledge gathered is sufficient to describe the network as a whole. This is often not the case, and the classical way to address this problem is to clearly specify its delimitation. One way is to analyse an egocentric network dataset that focuses on the nodes surrounding one node known as the ego. Alternatively, a set of preset nodes may be selected. For instance, this is the case when an investigator analyses the telephone record data of the suspects in an investigation. However, even if several nodes are used as ego, this conception process leads to a bias. Indeed, the ego will naturally be central. This process is typical during investigations (Sparrow 1991). Laumann et al. (1992) identify three approaches to addressing this boundary specification problem: (1) considering those entities that are members of a known group, such as the members of an organization; (2) defining the population by limiting the entities to those involved in an event or a series of events; and (3) selecting the entities based on a particular type of relationship. The conception process must thus be documented and the incompleteness in data should be well documented. Relevant entities and relationships must be selectively chosen, leaving out the rest. The definition and the selection of the relevant entities rely on a clear definition of the aims of the analysis and the decisions it has to support.

The second consideration to address is how to handle uncertainties. They must be clearly identified and expressed in the model. Uncertainty can take several forms in a network. In particular, it may be unclear whether two entities are distinct. One physical person may, for instance, have multiple aliases not identified as related to the same entity. A link between two entities may also be uncertain. On a link chart, it is common to distinguish unconfirmed links by dashed lines. Uncertainties may also be handled with probabilities attached to the links and integrated in centrality measures as well as with simulation-based methods (Adar and Re 2007; Svenson 2008). Moreover, a distinction must be made between facts and hypotheses. This distinction is at the core of the investigation and the research processes, which aim at identifying the causes (i.e., the hypotheses) of the observed effects (i.e., the facts).

Finally, a key element of the conception is to clearly define the nature of the entities and the relationships involved (Rossy and Ribaux 2014). Indeed, a network model aims at analysing the relationships among entities, while also understanding their nature and roles, in order to reconstruct the network. Consequently, the nature and characteristics of the relationships must be described as well as their frequency and uncertainty. Relations may be observed or measured, binary or valued. They may also be directed or undirected. The type of relation may be directly defined by its nature, such as the membership to a group that is undirected or a sale of goods that is directed. However, the definition of the relationships may also imply making a decision in regard to the available data (Marin and Wellman 2011). For instance, Borgatti et al. (2009) identify four main categories of relations: similarities (e.g., a shared attribute), social relations (e.g., affective ties, friendships), interactions (e.g., participation in an event) and flows (e.g., an exchange or transfer between nodes). Since network analytical techniques aim at analysing the relationships between the entities, the data source underlying their detection and the formalism used to describe them should be well documented.

The role of forensic science: traces in the reconstruction of networks

In this section, we discuss the roles of traces in reconstructing criminal activities within a network model of crime where they can take the form of relationships or entities. On the one hand, and as Locard's principle of exchange states, traces can be used to infer links between entities of interest such as individuals, locations and events. On the other hand, they may be used to infer the presence of a particular entity, such as a person or an object, based on Kirk's principle of individualization; to infer the presence of a set of entities or to provide information about the nature of the entity of interest through its identification (i.e., the definition of its class).

Locard's principle of exchange defines the trace as the result of a transfer during a particular abnormal activity (i.e., a crime or a deviant or illicit activity). In regard to the entity-relationship model, a trace can be considered as an entity. It has its own distinctive existence, for example, a bloodstain or a shoemark. The trace as an entity is an observable and collectable pattern, signal or material that has its own existence and results from an activity of interest in a particular environment.

Of particular interest to the reconstruction of a criminal network is the fact that a trace is also the sign of the presence of one or more related entities in the network. Even if the identity of the source of the trace is unknown, the trace's presence is the sign of the activity of one or more individuals. For instance, DNA profiles extracted from biological traces may be used to infer the presence of an offender. A network of offenders can thus combine both known and unknown persons based on the traces they left during crimes. As Kirk's principle states, forensic science relies on the process of individualization that aims to infer the unique source (i.e., a person, an object or a material) of a detected trace (Kirk 1963; Margot 2011). The process relies on the detection of characteristics within the trace, which lead to the discrimination of a particular entity among all the other possible sources. For instance, event A is committed by offender A and crime B by offender B. Both are linked by the same DNA profile, which does not belong to A or B. In such a case, a network of three offenders can be inferred: A is linked to an unknown offender, which is linked to B. Whether or not the source of the trace is known, its existence may be the sign of the presence of a related, distinctly identified person. This unknown entity may be defined as a 'virtual entity' or more specifically as a 'virtual person' in the case of a DNA profile. A virtual entity is an abstract entity (i.e., a node in a network model) with a unique identity that may be related to one or more physical or digital entities (Jaquet-Chiffelle et al. 2008, 2009). For instance, the DNA profile of a trace is the identity of a virtual person that may be a unique individual or twins. A broad variety of traces can be used to infer the presence of virtual entities or, more specifically, virtual persons, in networks even if their roles are not identified. For instance, if two drug seizures are linked by forensic profiling, one may infer a common activity of an individual (or a group of individuals) that can be modelled and integrated in the network as an unidentified virtual entity (Corazza and Esseiva 2013). Such hypotheses can then be evaluated in regard to other sources of information collected during the investigation. In a network model of a criminal activity, one trace can thus be used to infer the presence of one or more virtual entities, which may be related to a specific physical entity or to several.

Traces can also be used to infer some specific characteristics of an unknown entity or offender. A trace can indeed be used to define the class of an entity. For instance, the gender of an offender can be detected from a biological trace, or an unknown powder may become an identified illicit drug. This is the process known as the identification of an entity. A trace can thus be used in a network as a partial identifier (i.e., an identity-related information) (Jaquet-Chiffelle et al. 2008). In this case, the trace is not the sign of the presence of a specific, fully identified entity but of a 'frame' of entities. The concept of frame defined by Kind (1987, 1994) referred to the set of persons of interest or entities of interest during an investigation. More broadly defined, it is the set of entities that matches the identity-related information.

A trace can also be interpreted as a tie between involved entities, commonly the source entity that produces it and the substrate entity where it was left during the event. Traces can link involved entities in both directions, as the principle of exchange states. For instance, a stain mark resulting from an assault can link a particular individual to the victim. But a trace as a tie may also link multiple entities, such as an email involving more than two email addresses that may be linked to several individuals. A stain mark containing a mixture of several DNA profiles can be associated with two or more individuals. In a network model of criminal activity, one trace can thus be used to infer one or more relationships among entities. The trace as a relationship is an observable and collectable tie, resulting from an activity of interest in a particular environment, between two or more entities.

A trace can thus link many types of entities, but the reconstruction of criminal networks aims at the identification of links between individuals. In these regards, traces may be used as direct links when the source of the trace is a person, or as indirect links when the source is an object. The relationship may also involve several types of entities such as a link between an individual and an event or a link to a location. Such links are of particular interest in reconstructing a two-mode network or a link chart of the criminal activity. Traces as a relationship can thus be classified according to the types of entities involved:

(1) A relationship between individuals: a stain mark of an offender found on a victim or a mixture of DNA profiles found at the crime scene linking multiple offenders.
(2) A relationship through objects: the trace is a sign of a transaction such as a telephone call, an email or bank transfer that is commonly used by criminal intelligence analysts to reconstruct networks of offenders. The trace is the result of an activity involving several types of entities such as mobile phones, bank accounts or computers. To infer a link between offenders, their relationships to the objects used should be evaluated.
(3) A relationship to an event: the trace is a sign of an activity such as gunshot residues resulting from the use of a firearm or glass fragments resulting from a glass breakage. Situating traces in time is a key aspect to inferring a link between a relevant entity and a particular event. Such links may be reconstructed by the use of direct markers of time (such as a digital record), ageing techniques or by reconstructing chronologies (Weyermann and Ribaux 2012).
(4) A relationship to a location: the trace is a sign of the presence of the offender such as stain marks, fingerprints or shoemarks detected at a specific location. Traces linked to the location such as soil, fibre or glass microtraces may also be recovered on a suspect. Records of digital traces are also used to link an individual to a location with geocoded databases (e.g., the geocoded cell of a mobile phone call, the record of a GPS signal or a geocoded IP address).

A single trace can thus be considered as a sign of a relationship between two or more entities of interest in a network model. But the comparison of two or more traces detected on several events can also serve the detection of multiple forms of relationships among events. This forensic link is defined as 'a relationship established between forensic science entities sharing similar features that stems from the hypothesis of a common cause' (Baechler et al. 2015, 186). The common cause is the most plausible explanation of the observed similarity (Cleland 2013). It is often a unique source entity such as an individual or an object or a similarity of actions such as a modus operandi reconstructed by the observation of traces (Baechler et al. 2015). Forensic links can be classified according to the nature of the inference involved. Several hypotheses about the common cause may indeed be inferred (for more details, see Ribaux et al. 2006). If two biological traces share the same DNA profile, one may infer a unique person as the source of both traces. In this case, traces may link a distinctly identified entity such as a person or an object. The link may also be less specific. For instance, if two shoemarks shared the same pattern, one may infer the presence of a frame of entities (i.e., the same type of objects). The detection of forensic links is at the core of the forensic intelligence process, which covers a broad range of exploitation of forensic science in policing (see Ribaux and Caneppele, 'Forensic intelligence', in this volume). The use of forensic case data to reconstruct criminal networks is one form of exploitation of the informative value of traces in the field of knowledge known as forensic intelligence (Ribaux 2014; Ribaux and Talbot Wright 2014).

Traces can thus be integrated in a network model of criminal activities as relationships between entities of interest or to infer the presence of one or more entities from the profile of the trace itself. They may also serve the identification of the type of an entity. When multiple traces are considered, a forensic link between two or more events may be inferred. It takes the form of a virtual entity describing a common source. The profile of the trace defines the identity of the virtual entity, which may be linked to one physical or digital entity of the real world or a frame of entities (see Table 16.1 for a summary).

Table 16.1 The roles of forensic case data in a network model of criminal activities

Network model		*Physical/digital world*	*Examples*
A trace to infer the presence of one or more virtual entities	A virtual entity*	– An object or a person – A set of objects/persons sharing the same virtual identity	*A fingerprint of a person* *A DNA profile of twins, an email or an IP address*
	Multiple virtual entities	– A set of distinctly identified objects or persons	*A DNA mixture*
	An identity-related information of a virtual entity	– A frame of objects or persons – A modus operandi of an event	*A partial DNA profile, a shoemark's pattern* *A drug synthesis method, a website conception*
A trace to infer relationships among virtual entities	A relationship** between individuals	– A direct link between two or more persons	*A stain mark of an offender found on a victim, a DNA mixture*
	An indirect relationship through objects	– An indirect link between two or more persons through the use of objects	*A telephone call, an email, a bank transfer*
	A relationship to an event	– A link between an object/person and an event	*A gunshot residue, some glass fragments, a time stamp of a file*
	A relationship to a location	– A link between an object/person and a location	*A soil trace, a GSP record*
Two or more traces to infer the presence of one or more virtual entities	A same virtual entity	– An object or a person as a source entity	*A same DNA profile, a same shoe or tire mark*
	A same identity-related information of a virtual entity	– A frame of objects or persons – A modus operandi of an event	*The model of an object* *A drug synthesis method, a website conception*

* *In a network model, a virtual entity refers to a node.*

** *In a network model, a relationship refers to an edge between two nodes or multiple edges between more than two nodes.*

Conclusion

To conclude, decades of research have demonstrated the potential of the network perspective to analyse crime phenomena, and thousands of intelligence analysts are using link analysis and SNA methods, all around the globe, to manage the flow of information they must handle in real cases and to infer the activities of offenders. The entity-relationship model seems to complete and complement the geospatial and temporal dimensions of analysis of crime and supports both qualitative and quantitative research. Nevertheless, analysts and researchers should be cautious about the pitfalls and limitations of these approaches. These limitations are promoted by 'what you see is what you get' technologies, which hide challenges and methodological rules.

The growth of (digital) data collated during an analysis raises the temptation to jump to the use of the technical/technological, whereas the first step of any analysis is the careful evaluation of the objectives and the evaluation of the quality of the information at hand. This is one of the root principles of any scientific inquiry and this is where the trace may play a critical role. We have shown in this chapter how traces—whether they are physical or digital—as the most direct remnant of any criminal activity can be used to reconstruct criminal networks. Both link analysis and social network analysis approaches constitute a promising venture for forensic scientists and criminologists to collaborate around a shared model that supports the analysis and the integration of multiple sources of information to detect patterns in crime data.

Note

1 For more details about the centrality measures, see Bonacich 1987; Borgatti 2005; Brandes and Erlebach 2005; Freeman 1979 and Wasserman and Faust 1994.

References

Adar, E., and C. Re. 2007. 'Managing Uncertainty in Social Networks'. *IEEE Data Engineering Bulletin* 30(2): 15–22.

Akers, R.L. 1998. *Social Learning and Social Structure: A General Theory of Crime and Deviance*. Boston: Northeastern University Press.

Baechler, S., M. Morelato, O. Ribaux, A. Beavis, M. Tahtouh, K.P. Kirkbride, P. Esseiva, P. Margot and C. Roux. 2015. 'Forensic Intelligence Framework. Part II: Study of the Main Generic Building Blocks and Challenges through the Examples of Illicit Drugs and False Identity Documents Monitoring'. *Forensic Science International* 250(May): 44–52.

Boivin, R. 2014. 'Macrosocial Network Analysis: The Case of Transnational Drug Trafficking'. In J.A. Masys, ed., *Networks and Network Analysis for Defence and Security*, 49–61. New York: Springer.

Bonacich, P. 1987. 'Power and Centrality: A Family of Measures'. *American Journal of Sociology* 92(5): 1170–1182.

Borgatti, S.P. 2005. 'Centrality and Network Flow'. *Social Networks* 27(1): 55–71.

Borgatti, S.P. 2012. 'Two-Mode Concepts in Social Network Analysis'. In A.R. Meyers, ed., *Computational Complexity: Theory, Techniques, and Applications*, 2912–2924. New York: Springer.

Borgatti, S.P., A. Mehra, D.J. Brass and G. Labianca. 2009. 'Network Analysis in the Social Sciences'. *Science* 323(5916): 892–895.

Bouchard, M., and A. Malm. 2016. *Social Network Analysis and Its Contribution to Research on Crime and Criminal Justice*. Oxford Handbooks Online. www.oxfordhandbooks.com/view/10.1093/oxfordhb/9780199935383.001.0001/oxfordhb-9780199935383-e-21.

Brandes, U., and T. Erlebach. 2005. *Network Analysis*. Berlin: Springer Heidelberg.

Bresciani, S., and E. Eppler. 2009. 'The Risks of Visualization: A Classification of Disadvantages Associated with Graphic Representations of Information'. In P.J. Schulz, U. Hartung and S. Keller, eds., *Identität Und Vielfalt Der Kommunikations-Wissenschaft*. Konstanz, Germany: UVK Verlagsgesellschaft mbH.

Bright, D.A., C. Greenhill, M. Reynolds, A. Ritter and C. Morselli. 2014. 'The Use of Actor-Level Attributes and Centrality Measures to Identify Key Actors: A Case Study of an Australian Drug Trafficking Network'. *Journal of Contemporary Criminal Justice* 31(3): 262–278.

Bruinsma, G., and W. Bernasco. 2004. 'Criminal Groups and Transnational Illegal Markets'. *Crime, Law and Social Change* 41(1): 79–94.

Carrington, P.J. 2011. 'Crime and Social Network Analysis'. In J. Scott and P.J. Carrington, eds., *The SAGE Handbook of Social Network Analysis*, 236–255. Thousand Oaks, CA: SAGE Publications Ltd.

Chen, P.P.-S. 1976. 'The Entity–Relationship Model: Toward a Unified View of Data'. *ACM Transactions on Database Systems* 1(1): 9–36.

Cleland, C.E. 2013. 'Common Cause Explanation and the Search for a Smoking Gun'. *Geological Society of America Special Papers* 502: 1–9.

Corazza, D., and P. Esseiva. 2013. 'L'apport de la trace matérielle dans l'enquête criminelle: évaluation de la contribution des liens chimiques issus du profilage de produits stupéfiants par l'analyse des réseaux sociaux'. *Revue internationale de criminologie et de police technique et scientifique* 66(3): 341–363.

Desroches, F.J. 2005. *The Crime That Pays: Drug Trafficking and Organized Crime in Canada*. Toronto: Canadian Scholars' Press.

Duijn, P.A., V. Kashirin and P.M. Sloot. 2014. 'The Relative Ineffectiveness of Criminal Network Disruption'. *Scientific Reports* 4: 1–15.

Fedpol. 2010. *Manuel d'analyse criminelle opérationnelle*. Suisse: office fédéral de la police.

Freeman, L.C. 1977. 'A Set of Measures of Centrality Based on Betweenness'. *Sociometry* 40(1): 35–41.

Freeman, L.C. 1979. 'Centrality in Social Networks: Conceptual Clarification'. *Social Networks* 1(3): 215–239.

Freeman, L.C. 2004. *The Development of Social Network Analysis: A Study in the Sociology of Science*. North Charleston, SC: Booksurge Publishing.

Harper, W.R., and D.H. Harris. 1975. 'The Application of Link Analysis to Police Intelligence'. *Human Factors* 17(2): 157–164.

Hashimi, S., M, Bouchard, C. Morselli and M. Ouellet. 2016. 'A Method to Detect Criminal Organizations from Police Data'. *Methodological Innovations* 9: 1–14.

Innes, M., N. Fielding and N. Cope. 2005. 'The Appliance of Science? The Theory and Practice of Crime Intelligence Analysis'. *British Journal of Criminology* 45(1): 39–57.

Interpol. 1997. *Guide sur l'analyse criminelle*. 2nd ed. Lyon : Interpol.

Jaquet-Chiffelle, D.-O., B. Anrig, E. Benoist, R. Haenni, M. Hildebrandt, E. Kosta and K. Lefever. 2008. *FIDIS Deliverable D2.13: Virtual Persons and Identities*. www.fidis.net/deliverables.

Jaquet-Chiffelle, D.-O., E. Benoist, R. Haenni, F. Wenger and H. Zwingelberg. 2009. 'Virtual Persons and Identities'. In K. Rannenberg, D. Royer and A. Deuker, eds., *The Future of Identity in the Information Society: Challenges and Opportunities*, 75–122. Springer-Verlag Berlin Heidelberg.

Jennings, H.H. 1943. *Leadership and Isolation: A Study of Personality in Inter-Personal Relations*. New York: Longmans, Green, and Company.

Kind, S.S. 1987. *The Scientific Investigation of Crime*. Harrogate: Forensic Science Services Ltd.

Kind, S.S. 1994. 'Crime Investigation and the Criminal Trial: A Three Chapter Paradigm of Evidence'. *Journal of the Forensic Science Society* 34(3): 155–164.

Kirk, P.L. 1963. 'Criminalistics—a New and Independent Discipline Evolves from Modern Techniques and New Concepts of Individualization'. *Science* 140: 367–370.

Kleemans, E.R. 2007. 'Organized Crime, Transit Crime, and Racketeering'. *Crime and Justice* 35(1): 163–215.

Klerks, P. 2001. 'The Network Paradigm Applied to Criminal Organizations: Theoretical Nitpicking or a Relevant Doctrine for Investigators? Recent Developments in the Netherlands'. *Connections* 24(3): 53–65.

Laumann, E.O., P.V. Marsden and D. Prensky. 1992. 'The Boundary Specification Problem in Network Analysis'. In L.C. Freeman, D.R. White and A.K. Romney, eds., *Research Methods in Social Network Analysis*, 61–87. Piscataway, NJ: Transaction Publishers.

Malm, A.E., J.B. Kinney and N.R. Pollard. 2008. 'Social Network and Distance Correlates of Criminal Associates Involved in Illicit Drug Production'. *Security Journal* 21(1–2): 77–94.

Margot, P. 2011. 'Forensic Science on Trial—What Is the Law of the Land?' *Australian Journal of Forensic Sciences* 43(2–3): 89–103.

Marin, A., and B. Wellman. 2011. 'Social Network Analysis: An Introduction'. In J. Scott and P.J. Carrington, eds., *The SAGE Handbook of Social Network Analysis*, 11–25. Thousand Oks, CA: SAGE Publications Ltd.

McGloin, J.M., and D.S. Kirk. 2010. 'Social Network Analysis'. In A.R. Piquero and R. Weisburd, eds., *Handbook of Quantitative Criminology*, 209–224. New York: Springer.

McGloin, J.M., and H. Nguyen. 2014. 'The Importance of Studying Co-Offending Networks for Criminological Theory and Policy'. In C. Morselli, ed., *Crime and Networks*, 13–27. New York: Routledge.

McPherson, M., L. Smith-Lovin and J.M. Cook. 2001. 'Birds of a Feather: Homophily in Social Networks'. *Annual Review of Sociology* 27: 415–444.

Moreno, J.L. 1932. *Application of the Group Method to Classification*. New York: National Committee on Prisons and Prison Labor.

Moreno, J.L. 1934. *Who Shall Survive? A New Approach to the Problems of Human Interrelations*. Washington, DC: Nervous and Mental Disease Publishing Company.

Morris, J. 1986. *Crime Analysis Charting*. Loomis: Palmer Press.

Morselli, C. 2009. *Inside Criminal Networks*. New York: Springer.

Morselli, C. 2010. 'Assessing Vulnerable and Strategic Positions in a Criminal Network'. *Journal of Contemporary Criminal Justice* 26(4): 382–392.

Morselli, C., V.H. Masias, F. Crespo and S. Laengle. 2013. 'Predicting Sentencing Outcomes with Centrality Measures'. *Security Informatics* 2(1): 1–9.

Morselli, C., and J. Roy. 2008. 'Brokerage Qualifications in Ringing Operations'. *Criminology* 46(1): 71–98.

Natarajan, M. 2006. 'Understanding the Structure of a Large Heroin Distribution Network: A Quantitative Analysis of Qualitative Data'. *Journal of Quantitative Criminology* 22(2): 171–192.

Papachristos, A.V. 2011. 'The Coming of a Networked Criminology?' *Advances in Criminological Theory* 17: 101–140.

Papachristos, A.V. 2014. 'The Network Structure of Crime'. *Sociology Compass* 8(4): 347–357.

Pearson, G., and D. Hobbs. 2001. *Middle Market Drug Distribution*. London: Home Office.

Peterson, M.B. 1994. *Applications in Criminal Analysis: A Sourcebook*. Westport: Praeger.

Peterson, M.B., B. Morehouse and E. Wright. 2000. *Intelligence 2000: Revising the Basic Elements*. Lawrenceville: Law Enforcement Intelligence Unit and International Association of Law Enforcement Intelligence Analysts.

Reuter, P. 1983. *Disorganized Crime: The Economics of the Visible Hand*. Cambridge, MA: MIT Press.

Ribaux, O. 2014. *Police scientifique. Le renseignement par la trace*. Lausanne: Presses polytechniques et universitaires romandes.

Ribaux, O., and B. Talbot Wright. 2014. 'Expanding Forensic Science through Forensic Intelligence'. *Science & Justice* 54(6): 494–501.

Ribaux, O., S.J.J. Walsh and P. Margot. 2006. 'The Contribution of Forensic Science to Crime Analysis and Investigation: Forensic Intelligence'. *Forensic Science International* 156(2–3): 171–181.

Rossy, Q. 2016. 'La visualisation relationnelle au service de l'enquête'. In R. Boivin and C. Morselli, eds., *Les réseaux criminels*, 17–39. Montréal: Les Presses de l'Université de Montréal.

Rossy, Q., and O. Ribaux. 2012. 'La conception de schémas relationnels en analyse criminelle: au-delà de la maîtrise des outils'. *Revue internationale de criminologie et de police technique et scientifique* 65(3): 345–362.

Rossy, Q., and O. Ribaux. 2014. 'A Collaborative Approach for Incorporating Forensic Case Data into Crime Investigation Using Criminal Intelligence Analysis and Visualisation'. *Science & Justice* 54(2): 146–53.

Schroeder, J., J. Xu, H. Chen and M. Chau. 2007. 'Automated Criminal Link Analysis Based on Domain Knowledge'. *Journal of the American Society for Information Science and Technology* 58(6): 842–855.

Senator, T.E. 2005. 'Link Mining Applications: Progress and Challenges'. *SIGKDD Explorations* 7(2): 76–83.

Sparrow, M.K. 1991. 'The Application of Network Analysis to Criminal Intelligence: An Assessment of the Prospects'. *Social Networks* 13(3): 251–274.

Strang, S.J. 2014. 'Network Analysis in Criminal Intelligence'. In J.A. Masys, ed., *Networks and Network Analysis for Defence and Security*, 1–26. New York: Springer.

Sutherland, E.H. 1939. *Principles of Criminology*. 3d ed. Philadelphia: Lippincott.

Svenson, P. 2008. 'Social Network Analysis of Uncertain Networks'. *Proceedings of the 2nd Skövde Workshop on Information Fusion Topics*, 1–3. University of Skövde, Sweden.

UNODC. 2002. *Criminal Intelligence Training: Manual for Analysts*. Vienna: United Nations Office on Drugs and Crime.

van Mastrigt, S.B., and P. Carrington. 2014. 'Sex and Age Homophily in Co-Offending Networks'. In C. Morselli, ed., *Crime and Networks*, 28–51. New York: Routledge.

Wasserman, S., and K. Faust. 1994. *Social Network Analysis*. Cambridge: Cambridge University Press.

Weyermann, C., and O. Ribaux. 2012. 'Situating Forensic Traces in Time'. *Science and Justice* 52(2): 68–75.

Wigmore, J.H. 1913. *The Principles of Judicial Proof as Given by Logic, Psychology, and General Experience, and Illustrated in Judicial Trials*. Boston: Little, Brown, and Company.

Zaitch, D. 2002. *Trafficking Cocaine: Colombian Drug Entrepreneurs in the Netherlands*. The Hague: Springer.

Zhang, S. 2008. *Chinese Human Smuggling Organizations: Families, Social Networks, and Cultural Imperatives*. Stanford: Stanford University Press.

Zhang, S., and K.L. Chin. 2002. 'Enter the Dragon: Inside Chinese Human Smuggling Operations'. *Criminology* 40(4): 737–768.

17

The forensic science of place

Rémi Boivin

Identifying high-risk places

The geography of crime (also known as spatial criminology) has been a sub-field in criminology for some time. In the nineteenth century, Quételet and Guerry compared relatively large-scale court statistics (cities or judiciary districts) to identify high-risk areas. At the beginning of the twentieth century, research conducted at the School of Chicago and led by Burgess, Shaw and McKay focused on smaller urban areas that they defined as 'neighbourhoods'; their work confirmed that crime in the city was not evenly dispersed across time and space. More recent work has validated this observation and further explained crime concentration. Research focused on areas, situations and contexts—as opposed to individual characteristics—reached an important new stage with the recent development of 'the criminology of place' (Weisburd et al. 2012).

Thus, one basic observation supports all the work on the geography of crime: crime is concentrated in space. This observation has been generalized as the 'law of concentration at places' (Weisburd 2015; Weisburd and Telep 2014) or the '80–20 rule' (Clarke and Eck 2005) since many empirical studies have found that approximately 80 percent of crimes are concentrated among 20 percent of offenders, victims or places. Since the 1980s, many researchers have explored the idea of hot spots of crime, and their analyses have had clear benefits for crime prevention (see Weisburd [2015] for a recent review of this body of work). Different types of crimes have been analysed at various (or even multiple) levels of aggregation, in different cultural contexts (e.g., Australia: Livingston 2008; Britain: Johnson 2014; Canada: Andresen and Malleson 2013; Felson and Boivin 2015; Cape Verde: Petrosino and Pace 2015; Japan: Takagi and Kawachi 2014; the Netherlands: Bruinsma et al. 2013; the United States: Sherman et al. 1989; Braga and Bond 2008; Weisburd et al. 2012). Even today, work on the concentration of crime forms an important part of recently published work in criminology (e.g., Bones and Hope 2015; Shiode et al. 2015).

Virtually all studies of crime concentration rely on the most basic source for information about criminal activity: police records. For example, Sherman et al. (1989) geocoded more than 300,000 calls for service received by the Minneapolis Police Department in a year, while Felson and Boivin (2015) analysed the location of 115,000 crimes recorded by the police of a large Canadian city for a similar period. A clear advantage of this type of data is its systematic compilation: call information is routinely logged to allow quick and appropriate response by police officers, while crimes are documented for many purposes (e.g., statistical reports, staffing distribution, insurance claims). The existence of a well-known 'dark figure' in studies of crime should, however, be mentioned here. Official police records make it possible to study only infractions that were detected, reported to the police and recorded by them; police records thus capture the result of a selection process that might bias attempts to provide an overview of criminal activity (MacDonald 2002).

Measuring routine activities

Despite their unrivalled advantages, police records provide relatively little information about each incident, which is why some researchers complement this data with information from other sources. Perhaps more important, researchers have recently come to the conclusion that official data (e.g., from censuses) largely fails to adequately measure the elements involved in routine activity, a concept often used to explain crime concentration. According to theories of routine activity, crime occurs where criminal opportunities arise, i.e., where likely offenders meet suitable targets in the absence of capable guardianship (Cohen and Felson 1979). The relationship between crime and population size is one of the few accepted 'facts' in criminology (e.g., Siegel 2003): crime is more frequent in more populated areas, a statement confirmed by most cross-sectional research (Ousey 2000). Population flows are crucial: individuals are potential offenders, targets/victims and guardians, so the number of people in a given area increases the potential both for crime and for its prevention (Felson and Eckert 2015).

In empirical studies of social phenomena, the population data used is usually residential population—the number of individuals residing in households in a given territory—in part because of the relative ease with which such data can be obtained: there are numerous sources for information on the number of individuals living in defined areas, starting with the national censuses conducted regularly by virtually all nations. However, understanding routine activity requires precise measures of presence and, consequently, of population movements. Work by Brantingham and Brantingham (1993) emphasizes concepts such as nodes, paths and direction to conclude that offenders should be assumed to be mobile, not sedentary (see also Frank et al. 2012). Studies of crime mobility triangles analyse relations between crime location, offender's residence and victim's residence (for a review, see Bernasco and Elffers 2010), and Rengert (2004) noted that three basic elements of a journey-to-crime are of interest to criminologists: the starting point, the distance travelled by an offender from origin to destination and the direction the offender moves in. However, despite Boggs's and Gibbs's and Erickson's early warnings (Boggs 1965; Gibbs and Erickson 1976), researchers have only recently begun to provide evidence that challenges the use of residential population size in analysing crime rates. Recent studies have increasingly been interested in the ambient population as well in order to look at the total population present in a spatial unit, regardless of where individuals live (Andresen 2006, 2007; Andresen and Jenion 2010; Boivin 2013; Foote 2015; Rotolo and Tittle 2006). Andresen (2006), for instance, finds that, at census tract level, residential-based crime rates do not successfully predict whether the population is at risk for criminal victimization.

These findings suggest that alternative sources of data are needed. The ambient population has been measured through direct estimations using satellite imagery (e.g., Andresen 2006) and through indirect 'proxies', such as the number of workers who indicate they work in a particular area (e.g., Boivin 2013), activity in a large stadium (Kurland et al. 2014) in an area, etc. Recent technological progress has allowed researchers to consider signs of human activity based on global positioning systems. Two studies are particularly useful to illustrate the potential of this fast-evolving source of data. The first, by Traunmueller et al. (2014), links crime counts in the area of Greater London (UK) with mobile telecommunication data from one major mobile phone provider. The authors were provided aggregated data containing more than 12 million footfall count entries over the course of three weeks and were able to locate people by mapping their presence in small grid cells drawn on a map. Interestingly, this data can be broken down by gender, type (residents, visitors, workers) and age group. They found that, as expected, age diversity was related to levels of crime (a higher presence of young people was correlated with higher crime rates), while a higher ratio of visitors was linked to lower crime activity, and gender was not related to crime.

The second study, by Malleson and Andresen (2015), used messages from mobile devices (such as smart phones) posted to Twitter in Leeds., England, to measure the population at risk of violent crime. Twitter has a unique feature that is particularly useful for researchers in urban dynamics: a significant number of messages are associated with GPS coordinates, which makes it possible to identify the location from which a message was sent and, in turn, to estimate how many people are present at a given place at a given time. In their study, Malleson and Andresen analysed almost 2 million messages that, in addition to GPS coordinates, contained 'information regarding the user account, the text itself, and the time of the message' (114). They found that the Leeds city centre was relatively safe when the ratio of amount of criminal activity to estimated ambient population was calculated, despite a large volume of violent criminal events. They also found high rates of crime related to ambient population levels for a small number of deprived neighbourhoods very close to the city centre that are usually neglected by observers because of their relatively low volume of crime events. It remains unclear, however, if Twitter data provides an accurate estimation of ambient population or captures only a portion of this population, namely young adults active on social media. In a more recent study, Malleson and Andresen (2016) found that mobile telephone activity and workday population estimates from the census were highly correlated, suggesting that they capture a similar population, but that Twitter data was comparatively poorly correlated with other population measures, whether for ambient or residential population. Future work may be able to use this type of data to understand motivations of users and try to relate the content of their messages to the frequency and type of criminal activity at specific places.

Linking places

A growing number of studies are also attempting to link events based on common elements. Grouping crime events involves identifying events that can be attributed to a common offender or group of offenders, which is very useful in police investigations (Porter 2016). For instance, pooling information about different crime events might facilitate identification of offenders and allow for a more precise evaluation of future risks (Bernasco and Nieuwbeerta 2005). And if the offender has already been identified, being able to link crimes helps strengthen the case against serial offenders and provide valuable information in legal proceedings (Grubin et al. 2001).

For these reasons, crime linkage systems have been implemented in many countries to support police investigations. For example, police in Canada use the Violent Crime Linkage Analysis System (ViCLAS), in which arresting officers are asked 156 questions related to victim, offender, and offence information (Bennell et al. 2012). This system makes it possible to search the database thus created for various aspects of an offender's modus operandi (the set of behaviours that allow an offender to successfully carry out a crime), behavioural signature (distinctive behaviours not necessarily linked to the successful completion of a crime) and other situational characteristics (e.g., crime location). Recent technological advances mean that forensic data can act as a supplement to behavioural and situational similarities and can arguably provide more robust linkages (Albertetti et al. 2013; Porter 2016; Rossy et al. 2013).

More relevant to this chapter, linking crimes committed at different locations makes it possible to use sophisticated investigative tools such as geographical profiling. This set of techniques is used to identify areas where a serial offender is likely to have an anchor point (e.g., home) and thus facilitate apprehension (Rossmo 2000). Geographical profiling produces 'probability maps' based on multiple crime locations and is especially useful when the offender is a 'local hunter' or marauder rather than a commuter who resides outside the criminal domain (although this characteristic is, of course, seldom known before the crimes are solved) (Hammond 2013; Snook et al. 2005).

But crime linkage can also be useful in better understanding target selection. Criminal target choice has been described as a multi-staged process in which the offender first selects a suitable area and then chooses a specific target (Bernasco and Block 2009). Three categories of predictors of offender location choice have been distinguished: (1) difference in reward, (2) difference in effort, and (3) difference in risk (Townsley et al. 2015). Difference in reward is measured by indicators of target availability and area affluence: for example, areas of commercial land use (especially areas containing shopping centres) in Burnaby, British Columbia, had considerably higher assault and motor vehicle theft rates than residential areas, suggesting a direct link between some activities and crime (Kinney et al. 2008). Difference in effort includes various aspects of target vulnerability, such as characteristics of the urban 'mosaic' (i.e., the presence of major roads) that facilitate the movement of offenders and thus increase the probability of crime (Bernasco and Block 2011; Stucky and Ottensmann 2009). Finally, various indicators have been found to measure difference in risk between areas. For example, Bernasco (2010) found that offenders who commit robberies, residential burglaries, thefts from vehicles and assaults are more likely to target areas in which they had formerly resided than similar areas where they had never lived. These results strongly support the crime pattern theory put forward by Brantingham and Brantingham (1993), which emphasizes that offenders usually act within their awareness space—the perimeter that includes their activity nodes (e.g., work, home) and the routes between them.

In both cases—criminal investigations and understanding target choice—a key requirement is that crimes can be shown to be linked. For example, Rossmo (2005) suggests that a minimum of five crimes is needed for detection of a stable pattern. Researchers from the École des sciences criminelles (Université de Lausanne) have developed expertise in crime linkage through forensic information and have suggested sophisticated methods for linking crimes more systematically on the basis of forensic similarities. An interesting feature of their work is that 'civilian' crime analysts could use the proposed methods and thus help reduce the workload of police investigators. For example, CriLiM methodology is a form of computational forensics that operates as an exploratory method to relate events, offenders, victims and places (Albertetti et al. 2013). To test their method, Albertetti et al. analysed 2,320 cleared crimes involving residential burglaries conducted by single offenders in the Canton de Vaud (Switzerland). The links between these cases were already known, which made it possible to test whether the method was effective in detecting crime series. They were able to connect about 40 percent of cases exclusively on the basis of various types of indicators. The CriLiM methodology is thus a valuable addition to traditional investigative techniques.

In order to rank the importance of various traces in the forensic analysis of crimes, Rossy et al. (2013) compared the contribution of three types of traces (shoe prints, DNA and images such as CCTV footage) to the detection of different types of crime series. While they found that situational information about crimes was the most useful element in investigations, 29.7 percent of all events in their sample could be linked through forensic information only, although only 8.1 percent of events already linked could be confirmed by forensic information. In other words, they found that forensic information was useful in detecting new series or adding events to known crime series, but had a limited contribution as a way to confirm existing series. They also confirmed that, as expected, DNA was an important indicator in crime linkage: when the same DNA is found at two separate crime scenes, these two places can be related with high confidence, at least as compared to other indicators. They also note that images were increasingly being used to link crimes and suggest that the increasing availability of visual evidence made possible by technological advances means that images should continue to be an important kind of trace.

Finally, crime linkage methods, as well as forensic intelligence, can be used for public health purposes. Morelato et al. (2014) describe how they used gas chromatography-mass spectrometry (chemical profiling) to link seizures of MDMA in Australia, based on patterns of impurities that indicated that samples had a common origin. MDMA is an excellent candidate for such an analysis because it is rarely 'cut' after production (Maxwell 2005). When the same drug was seized in two or more places, common impurities indicated that it had been produced in the same lab and thus was somehow connected. This information is crucial if, for example, a batch is contaminated or a major allergen has been added. When related to the location of seizures, linked samples help track the distribution of drugs and prevent the spread of their distribution, decreasing public health issues. Morelato et al. (2014) found a range of impurities, from organic compounds to aluminium, lithium and zinc, and used their findings to highlight unique 'signatures'. Their analysis is also telling about drug markets: they found that only half the seizures linked by other means (e.g., a logo) were also linked by chemical profile, suggesting that retail sellers get their supply from various sources and consequently cannot guarantee the quality and content of the MDMA they sell. More important, they found that using a single analytical technique was sufficient to link seizures based on chemical profiles (thus reducing time and costs required to obtain accurate and precise results), but suggest that non-chemical tools (e.g., physical, investigative) should be used as well.

Conclusion

The criminology of place is the most recent version of the important literature on spatial variations of crime. Coincidentally, as many contributions in the current volume demonstrate, forensic science has reached a point where it can contribute to our understanding of crime in addition to its important contribution to investigations and prosecutions. This chapter reviewed some of the ways in which forensics has been used by researchers to understand spatial variations and suggests how this literature should be expanded. The main limitation is that these fields require different sets of analytical skills and, for the moment, remain largely separate. Spatial criminology is becoming more and more sophisticated as it borrows theoretical concepts from sociology and methods from geography; forensic science researchers need qualifications in a diversity of 'hard sciences', such as biology, physics and toxicology. However intelligent and interested researchers in these different areas may be, it can be difficult for them to understand both approaches, which is arguably why so few studies benefit from both perspectives. As commonplace as it may sound, studies of the forensics of place thus require multidisciplinary research teams. To be sure, some efforts are being made in this direction but, as history tells us, combining social science and natural science to understand a common phenomenon—here, criminal activity—requires time, work and commitment.

References

Albertetti, F., P. Cotofrei, L. Grossrieder, O. Ribaux and K. Stoffel. 2013. 'The CriLiM Methodology: Crime Linkage with a Fuzzy MCDM Approach'. *European Intelligence and Security Informatics Conference*, 12–14 August 2013, Uppsala, Sweden, 67–74.

Andresen, M.A. 2006. 'Crime Measures and the Spatial Analysis of Criminal Activity'. *British Journal of Criminology* 46(2): 258–285.
Andresen, M.A. 2007. 'Location Quotients, Ambient Populations, and the Spatial Analysis of Crime in Vancouver, Canada'. *Environmental Planning* 39(10): 2423–2444.
Andresen, M.A., and G.W. Jenion. 2010. 'Ambient Populations and the Calculation of Crime Rates and Risk'. *Security Journal* 23(2): 114–133.
Andresen, M.A., and N. Malleson. 2013. 'Crime Seasonality and Its Variations Across Space'. *Applied Geography* 43: 25–35.
Bennell, C., B. Snook, S. MacDonald, J.C. House and P.J. Taylor. 2012. 'Computerized Crime Linkage Systems: A Critical Review and Research Agenda'. *Criminal Justice and Behavior* 39(5): 620–634.
Bernasco, W. 2010. 'A Sentimental Journey to Crime: Effects of Residential History on Crime Location Choice'. *Criminology* 48(2): 389–416.
Bernasco, W., and R. Block. 2009. 'Where Offenders Choose to Attack: A Discrete Choice Model of Robberies in Chicago'. *Criminology* 47(1): 93–130.
Bernasco, W., and R. Block. 2011. 'Robberies in Chicago: A Block-Level Analysis of the Influence of Crime Generators, Crime Attractors and Offender Anchor Points'. *Journal of Research in Crime and Delinquency* 48(1): 33–57.
Bernasco, W., and H. Elffers. 2010. 'Statistical Analysis of Spatial Crime Data'. In A.R. Piquero and D. Weisburd, eds., 699–724. *Handbook of Quantitative Criminology*. New York: Springer.
Bernasco, W., and P. Nieuwbeerta. 2005. 'How Do Residential Burglars Select Target Areas? A New Approach to the Analysis of Criminal Location Choice'. *British Journal of Criminology* 44(3): 296–315.
Boggs, S.L. 1965. 'Urban Crime Patterns'. *American Sociological Review* 30(6): 899–908.
Boivin, R. 2013. 'On the Use of Crime Rates'. *Canadian Journal of Criminology and Criminal Justice* 55(2): 263–277.
Bones, P.D.C., and T.L. Hope. 2015. 'Broken Neighborhoods: A Hierarchical Spatial Analysis of Assault and Disability Concentration in Washington, DC'. *Journal of Quantitative Criminology* 31(2): 311–329.
Braga, A.A., and B.J. Bond. 2008. 'Policing Crime and Disorder Hot Spots: A Randomized Controlled Trial'. *Criminology* 46(3): 577–607.
Brantingham, P. J., and P.L. Brantingham. 1993. *Environment, Routine, and Situation: Toward a Pattern Theory of Crime*. New Brunswick, NJ: Transaction Publishers.
Bruinsma, G.J.N., L.J.R. Pauwels, F.M. Weerman and W. Bernasco. 2013. 'Social Disorganization, Social Capital, Collective Efficacy and the Spatial Distribution of Crime and Offenders: An Empirical Test of Six Neighborhood Models for a Dutch City'. *British Journal of Criminology* 53(3): 942–963.
Clarke, R.V., and J. Eck. 2005. *Crime Analysis for Problem Solvers in 60 Small Steps*. Washington, DC: Office of Community Oriented Policing Services, United States Department of Justice.
Cohen, L.E., and M. Felson. 1979. 'Social Change and Crime Rate Trends: A Routine Activity Approach'. *American Sociological Review* 44(4): 588–608.
Felson, M., and R. Boivin. 2015. 'Daily Crime Flows within a City'. *Crime Science* 4(31).
Felson, M., and M. Eckert. 2015. *Crime and Everyday Life*, 5th ed. Thousand Oaks, CA: Sage.
Foote, A. 2015. 'Decomposing the Effect of Crime on Population Changes'. *Demography* 52(2): 705–728.
Frank, R., M.A. Andresen and P.L. Brantingham. 2012. 'Criminal Directionality and the Structure of Urban Form'. *Journal of Environmental Psychology* 32(1): 37–42.
Gibbs, J.P., and M.L. Erickson. 1976. 'Crime Rates of American Cities in an Ecological Context'. *American Journal of Sociology* 82(3): 605–620.
Grubin, D., P. Kelly and C. Brunsdon. 2001. *Linking Serious Sexual Assaults through Behaviour*. London: Home Office.
Hammond, L. 2013. 'Geographical Profiling in a Novel Context: Prioritising the Search for New Zealand Sex Offenders'. *Psychology, Crime and Law* 20(4): 358–371.
Johnson, S.D. 2014. 'How Do Offenders Choose Where to Offend? Perspectives from Animal Foraging'. *Legal and Criminological Psychology* 19(2): 193–210.
Kinney, J.B., P.L. Brantingham, K. Wuschke, M.G. Kirk and P.J. Brantingham. 2008. 'Crime Attractors, Generator and Detractors: Land Use and Urban Crime Opportunities'. *Built Environment* 34(1): 62–74.
Kurland, J., S.D. Johnson and N. Tilley. 2014. 'Offenses around Stadiums: A Natural Experiment on Crime Attraction and Generation'. *Journal of Research in Crime and Delinquency* 51(1): 5–28.
Livingston, M. 2008. 'Alcohol Outlet Density and Assault: A Spatial Analysis'. *Addiction* 103(4): 619–628.
MacDonald, Z. 2002. 'Official Crime Statistics: Their Use and Interpretation'. *The Economic Journal* 112(477), F85–F106.

Malleson, N., and M.A. Andresen. 2015. 'Spatio-Temporal Crime Hotspots and the Ambient Population'. *Crime Science* 4, DOI: 10.1186/s40163-015-0023-8.

Malleson, N., and M.A. Andresen. 2016. 'Exploring the Impact of Ambient Population Measures on London Crime Hotspots'. *Journal of Criminal Justice* 46: 52–63.

Maxwell, J.C. 2005. 'Party Drugs: Properties, Prevalence, Patterns, and Problems'. *Substance Use & Misuse* 40(9–10): 1203–1240.

Morelato, M., A. Beavis, M. Tahtouh, O. Ribaux, P. Kirkbride and C. Roux. 2014. 'The Use of Organic and Inorganic Impurities Found in MDMA Police Seizures in a Drug Intelligence Perspective'. *Science and Justice* 54(1): 32–41.

National Institute of Justice. 2016. *Forensic Sciences*. Research portfolio presented online at http://nij.gov/topics/forensics/Pages/welcome.aspx, accessed 23 November 2016.

Ousey, G.C. 2000. 'Explaining Regional and Urban Variation in Crime: A Review of Research'. In G. LaFree, ed. *Criminal Justice 2000: The Nature of Crime: Continuity and Change*, 1: 261–308. Washington, DC: National Institute of Justice.

Petrosino C., and J. Pace. 2015. 'Social Cohesion, Collective Efficacy, and the Response of a Cape Verdean Community to Hate Crime: Learning a New Reality'. *American Behavioral Scientist*, published online before print, DOI: 10.1177/0002764215588818.

Porter, M.D. 2016. 'A Statistical Approach to Crime Linkage'. *The American Statistician* 70(2): 515–530.

Rengert, G.F. 2004. 'The Journey to Crime'. In G. Bruinsma, H. Ellfers and J. de Keijser, eds., *Punishment, Places and Perpetrators: Developments in Criminology and Criminal Justice Research*, 169–197. Portland, OR: Willan Publishing.

Rossmo, D.K. 2000. *Geographic Profiling*. Boca Raton, FL: CRC Press.

Rossmo, D.K. 2005. 'Geographic Heuristics or Shortcuts to Failure? Response to Snook et al.' *Applied Cognitive Psychology* 19(5): 651–654.

Rossy, Q., S. Ioset, D. Dessimoz and O. Ribaux. 2013. 'Integrating Forensic Information in a Crime Intelligence Database'. *Forensic Science International* 230(1–3): 137–146.

Rotolo, T., and C.R. Tittle. 2006. 'Population Size, Change, and Crime in U.S. Cities'. *Journal of Quantitative Criminology* 22(4): 341–367.

Sherman, L.W., P.R. Gartin and M.E. Buerger. 1989. 'Hot Spots of Predatory Crime: Routine Activities and the Criminology of Place'. *Criminology* 27(1): 27–56.

Shiode, S., N. Shiode, R. Block and C.R. Block. 2015. 'Space-Time Characteristics of Micro-Scale Crime Occurrences: An Application of a Network-Based Space-Time Search Window Technique for Crime Incidents in Chicago'. *International Journal of Geographical Information Science* 29(5): 697–719.

Siegel, L.J. 2003. *Criminology*. Belmont, CA: Wadsworth/Thomson Learning.

Snook, B., P.J. Taylor, and C. Bennell. 2005. 'Shortcuts to Geographic Profiling Success: A Reply to Rossmo (2005)'. *Applied Cognitive Psychology* 19(5): 655–661.

Stucky, T.D., and J.R. Ottensmann. 2009. 'Land Use and Violent Crime' *Criminology* 47(4): 1223–1264.

Takagi, D., and I. Kawachi. 2014. 'Neighborhood Social Heterogeneity and Crime Victimization in Japan: Moderating Effects of Social Networks'. *Asian Journal of Criminology* 9(4): 271–284.

Tilley, N., and A. Ford. 1996. *Forensic Science and Crime Investigation*. Crime Detection and Prevention Series, Paper 73. London: Home Office.

Townsley, M., D. Birks, S. Ruiter, W. Bernasco and G. White. 2015. 'Target Selection Models with Preference Variation between Offenders'. *Journal of Quantitative Criminology*, first online, DOI: 10.1007/s10940-015-9264-7.

Traunmueller, M., G. Quattrone and L. Capra. 2014. 'Mining Mobile Phone Data to Investigate Crime Theories at Scale'. In L.M. Aiello and D. McFarland, eds., *Social Informatics*, 396–411. New York: Springer.

Weisburd, D. 2015. 'The Law of Crime Concentration and the Criminology of Place'. *Criminology* 53(2): 133–157.

Weisburd, D., E.R. Groff and S.-M. Yang. 2012. *The Criminology of Place: Street Segments and Our Understanding of the Crime Problem*. Oxford: Oxford University Press.

Weisburd, D., and C.W. Telep. 2014. 'Hot Spots Policing: What We Know and What We Need to Know'. *Journal of Contemporary Criminal Justice* 30(2): 200–220.

18

Exploratory Spatial Data Analysis Methodologies (ESDA)

How they can be used to analyse forensic case data

Simon Baechler and Stefano Caneppele

Introduction

In the last 40 years, the development of new methodologies and technology has fostered a wider and more intense use of geography, and more recently of geographic information systems (GIS), to support data analysis, a development that has proven helpful to various disciplines. Coming from exploratory data methodologies (EDA) (Tukey 1977), exploratory spatial data methodologies (ESDA) have benefited from a growing quantity of georeferenced data generated by systems, people and things. ESDA examines the spatial distribution of a phenomenon to recognize spatial outliers, discover spatial association in attributes, identify clusters of events, suggest spatial heterogeneity, and recognize spatial trends (Anselin 1994; Bailey and Gatrell 1995; Groff et al. 2009; Messner et al. 1999). Like EDA, ESDA methodologies focus on data and their exploration/visualization in order to find patterns and models of interest.

Criminology, along with many other disciplines, has realized the great potential of ESDA methodologies to explore data and study crime. In this perspective, various crime data, including forensic case data such as biological evidence, shoemarks, illicit drugs or dispersed human remains, can be gathered and processed. This chapter describes the characteristics of ESDA methodologies and shows how they have already been used in relation to forensic case data of different types. In conclusion, the authors discuss why and how spatial (and time) analysis of forensic case data may foster an original dimension to the study of crime, address future developments and emphasize the need to bridge different disciplines in that endeavour.

ESDA methodologies: origins and developments

There is little doubt that ESDA originates from exploratory data analysis as originally presented by Tukey (1977). In particular, EDA and ESDA try to answer similar concerns. Interestingly, Tukey used the example of the criminal justice system to better explain the role of EDA: 'The processes of criminal justice are clearly divided between the search for evidence—in Anglo-Saxon lands the responsibility of the police and other investigative organisations—and the evaluation of evidence's strength—a matter for juries and judges. In data analysis a similar distinction is helpful.

Exploratory data analysis is detective in character. Confirmatory data analysis is judicial or quasi-judicial in character' (Tukey 1977, 2–3). Therefore, ESDA methodologies have been developed to detect what is spatially relevant. They differ to some extent from EDA methodologies, however, since the techniques used are different (Symanzik 2014).

What should ESDA detect? In a nutshell, spatial autocorrelation (or spatial association) (Anselin 1998). Spatial autocorrelation recalls the first law of geography, which states that everything is related to everything else, but near things are more related than distant things (Tobler 1970, 236). In practice, the exploration aims at locating non-random clusters of cases and/or at identifying possible correlations among different spatial variables. In this sense, exploratory analysis is a preparatory stage for confirmatory analysis, which tests the robustness of the formulated hypothesis. This paradigm stood in contrast to the classical data analysis approach (analysis comes from a model) but it is mainstream in spatial analysis. Several reasons support this direction. First, our knowledge about spatial analysis and its methodologies is relatively recent. Exploration is more appropriate for a better understanding of the unknown. Second, the size, number and type of the data sources under analysis are constantly growing. Often analysts have to select among different sources. Under these circumstances, exploration allows them make choices more quickly and therefore at lower costs. Last but not least, GIS and software have become more user-friendly, inexpensive and easily accessible. Computer graphics and visualization techniques are today necessary tools for up-to-date spatial research and a growing community continues to develop ever more performing software and tools. This paves the way to a larger audience that can engage in exploratory analysis without particular expertise in ESDA methodologies. Accessibility and usability have been the key to success of ESDA approaches, but vulgarization may have risks. The most common risk lies in the routinization and standardization, with users employing default programme settings without questioning their appropriateness (Grubesic 2006).

ESDA deals with spatial data that can be grouped into four main types (Symanzik 2014, 66–67): (1) point patterns, which indicate a specific location with X and Y coordinates (crime locations, car accidents, police stations, etc.); (2) lattice data (also known as area, aeral or grid data), which indicates data grouped by geographic area both as an administrative datum (e.g., country, jurisdiction or other administrative boundaries) and as non-administrative datum; (3) geostatistical data, which are continuous data such as temperature or precipitation measurements; and 4) origin-destination flow data, also called link or spatial interaction data, measured between a pair of point locations or a pair of areas (e.g., distance to crime is the distance calculated between the offender residence and the crime location/s). In this chapter, only the first two types are discussed

ESDA techniques may vary according to the types of dataset, but some techniques are versatile. A first group of simple techniques focuses on data visualization. For lattice data (e.g., choropleth maps), software tools may link geovisualizations (choropleth maps, box map, cartograms) to EDA visualizations (e.g., strip charts, box plot, histograms, density plot, parallel coordinate plot, scatter plot) (Anselin 1994) and similar combinations can be used for points pattern data (Bivand 2010). Since the 1990s, brushing and linking functions have been developed to increase interactivity and to maximize data exploration (Anselin 1994). A second group of techniques focuses on detecting concentrations. For example, global and local Moran's I statistic allow testing for clustering in a geodataset and testing where clusters are locally (Anselin 1995). Nearest neighbour analysis (NNA) and nearest neighbour hierarchical clustering (NNH) perform the same function for point pattern data, although there are other popular techniques, such as kernel density estimation (Levine 2006).[1] These techniques have been used with longitudinal analysis in order to detect crime trends/patterns, and to understand whether places, like humans, may have a criminal career (Weisburd et al. 2004). In a nutshell, more and more criminologists have used ESDA techniques to visualize crime data and to detect crime concentration both with lattice and point pattern data

(Anselin et al. 2000), with a methodological reflexion on what is a crime concentration (hot spot) and how it can be detected (see, for example, Weisburd et al. 2009). They concluded that 'place matters' (Weisburd et al. 2016), even for preventing/reducing crime in practice. Specifically, cluster/hot spot analysis contributed to reshaping some police tactics (Sherman and Weisburd 1995; Braga et al. 2014), and it has paved the way to approaches such as geographic profiling (Rossmo 2000), geographic risk assessment (see, for example, Kennedy et al. 2011) and crime prediction modelling (also called predictive policing) (Ratcliffe 2013, 2016).

This chapter supports the idea that ESDA fits well with forensic science. They both share the same exploratory perspective in which data/traces have priority. Their analysis/visualization allows hypotheses to be formulated and tested further. Criminology and forensic science can, then, mutually benefit from an ESDA approach. However, the integration of forensic case data with spatial and temporal dimensions is not as straightforward as one might at first think. Weyermann and Ribaux described the various and complex aspects related to situating forensic traces in time (Weyermann and Ribaux 2012). A similar effort remains to be done to situate traces in space, since the articulation of forensic case data and the question 'Where?' may be understood in very different ways.

ESDA methodologies and forensic case data: scope, state of the art and recent applications

The combination of forensic science with the spatial dimension may be viewed from several perspectives.[2] This chapter addresses a perspective oriented toward criminological interest in which the projection of forensic case data into spatial and temporal dimensions aims to explore and analyse crime phenomena and crime series. In that perspective, a specific strength of forensic case data is to draw links between different and possibly distant crimes on a reliable and measurable basis (Milne 2012; Ribaux et al. 2003; Ribaux and Margot 1999, 2003; Rossy et al. 2013). Indeed, a piece of forensic evidence found on a first crime scene sharing a profile similar to another piece of evidence found on a second crime scene enables investigators and analysts to infer with confidence that these two crimes were committed by a common offender, making him a serial offender. Such forensic links hold whether or not the offender is known, providing a unique perception of unidentified serial offenders, and also offering a supplemental source of criminological data on identified offenders. Forensic links between offences and alternative data (location, time, type of crime, target, loot, modus operandi, etc.) should be integrated to provide an original and comprehensive spatiotemporal analysis of crime. The following sections provide examples using forensic case data of different types.

Biological evidence—DNA

The contribution of biological evidence, in particular DNA, to crime investigation and crime intelligence is now widespread and well known. DNA evidence (biological fluid stains such as blood, saliva or semen, or contact and touch DNA traces) is indeed routinely collected on serious crimes as well as volume crimes (Bond and Hammond 2008; Buckleton et al. 2004; Walsh et al. 2002). Beyond these common practices, DNA matches between crime scene traces, or between crime scene traces and persons, may also be meaningful in the study of spatiotemporal crime patterns, the mobility of offenders or criminal careers (Ribaux, Baylon, Roux et al. 2010). In 2000, Wiles and Costello worked on a data extract from the Forensic Science Service DNA database to assess what they call 'offender movement', thus opening this innovative perspective. These authors described the movement of an offender leaving his DNA at different crime scenes through discrete spatio-jurisdictional categories (administrative datum), ranging from 'no movement' (50 percent of DNA matches were found between crime scenes managed by the same police territorial unit) to movement between non-adjoining police forces' jurisdictions (7 percent of DNA matches). Interestingly, spatial movement patterns highlighted by DNA confirmed findings based on alternative and more conventional data sources (police recorded crime data and offenders interviews). Offenders' mobility, mostly burglars in this study, in the subject areas in England were found to be essentially limited to police force jurisdiction boundaries (Wiles and Costello, 2000).

In a recent series of papers, Lammers, Bernasco and their colleagues used data of the Dutch national DNA database to study and compare the characteristics of identified versus unidentified serial offenders, as well as arrested versus non-arrested serial offenders (Bernasco et al. 2016; Lammers, 2014; Lammers and Bernasco 2013; Lammers et al. 2012). In a first paper, using a dataset of 14,135 crimes committed by 4,414 offenders, these researchers studied whether and to what extent the mobility of serial offenders (reflected by the geographical dispersion of crime locations linked by a common DNA profile) influences their probability of arrest. Geographical dispersion was measured by three discrete spatio-jurisdictional indicators, namely, the number of police regions in which serial offenders who had left their DNA have committed their crime, the spatiotemporal ordering (i.e., number of times the current crime has been committed in a different region from the previous crime) and the distance (i.e., number of borders between the regions in which crimes are committed by taking the shortest possible route). Based on these measurements, the authors assert that 'offenders with a more geographically dispersed pattern of crimes have a smaller probability of getting arrested than offenders who commit geographically clustered crime series' (Lammers and Bernasco 2013, 182). The probability of arrest decreases as the number of police regions in which the offender commits his crime increases, and it also decreases as the number of times an offender commits the current crime in a different region increases. However, the number of borders crossed between police regions seems to have no influence on the probability of arrest (Lammers and Bernasco 2013).

In a second paper, based on a dataset of 5,392 crimes committed by 1,861 offenders, Lammers investigated spatial offending patterns using a quantitative and continuous spatial measurement: the mean intercrime distance between crime locations linked by a common DNA profile (in kilometres). Findings of this second study contrasted with those found using the previous discrete spatio-jurisdictional indicators, since no significant differences were found between the mean intercrime distance associated to arrested and to non-arrested offenders, both means being of about 30 km (standard deviation of about 45 km; medians between 7 and 8.5 km). The authors conclude from these results that arrest data appear to be less selective than sometimes expected by criminologists. Furthermore, the mean intercrime distance did not seem to influence the duration between committing the crimes and arrest (Lammers 2014).

In a third paper, Bernasco and his colleagues studied cross-border offending patterns thanks to DNA matches highlighted through the systematic exchange of DNA profiles between the Netherlands and 18 other European countries participating in the Treaty of Prüm. Due to data limitations, the geographical location of crimes (mainly burglaries and vehicle crimes) from which 79,171 DNA traces were collected also had to be restricted to a discrete spatio-jurisdictional categorization across the 25 Dutch police regions. Chloropleth maps were used to compare results in different regions. The study shows that DNA profiles associated to cross-border crime series concern 4 percent (about 3,300) of all the DNA traces recorded in the Dutch database. Of these 3,300 DNA traces, 86 percent connect two countries, 12 percent three and the rest four to six countries. Most cross-border offenders active in the Netherlands appear to be also active in Germany, since 50 percent of cross-border DNA links match traces collected in these countries. Cross-border DNA profiles are mainly found in the southeast part of the Netherlands, which borders highly populated regions in neighbouring countries. The authors observe different results depending on the countries and regions considered, and conclude that cross-border crime globally consists of mixtures of local and non-local offending patterns. Interestingly, cross-border offending patterns associated with volume crime and serious crime did not show any systematic difference (Bernasco et al. 2016).

In an innovative piece of research, Jeuniaux and his colleagues studied co-offending patterns through an extract of the Belgian national DNA database covering 81,968 DNA profiles collected in 61,143 cases (the majority being burglaries and robberies). Co-offenders and potential members of an organized crime group were inferred when the DNA profiles of different offenders were found jointly at a given crime scene. Such relationships enabled the authors to build 445 'DNA-based networks of individuals' (Jeuniaux et al. 2016). Among other analyses, the networks were studied from a geographical perspective, but cases' location had to be limited to a discrete spatio-jurisdictional categorization (i.e., the judicial district handling the case out of the 27 districts in Belgium). Networks appear to concern a mean number of judicial districts of 2.76, with a minimum of 1 and a maximum of 23 districts. Only a third of networks are homogeneous in terms of the district concerned. Networks that concern more than one district tend to concentrate around specific regions of the country like the north of Belgium or the Brussels district. This research provides relevant insights about geographical extent and mobility of connected criminals and criminal networks.

Shoemarks, toolmarks, glovemarks and images

Authors in Great Britain and Switzerland were the first to report in literature that integrating systematic comparisons of shoemarks, toolmarks or glovemarks found at crime scenes with spatio-temporal information analysis may efficiently support the investigation of crime series and the detection of crime problems (Birkett 1989; Milne 2001; Ribaux et al. 2003; Ribaux et al. 2006; Ribaux and Margot 1999). In his book *Forensic Intelligence*, Milne reports that the Metropolitan Police Service in London uses software called 'Interactive Offender Profiling System' (IOPs), developed in partnership with the University of Liverpool, that performs smallest-space analysis. It integrates and correlates 'crime, forensics, location, time, and other intelligence' to locate anchor points of offenders and reveal offending patterns and helps to figure out crime series geographically (Milne 2012, 65). As an example, Milne mentions that the geographical distribution of comparable bolt cutter marks left on broken locks on outbuildings in specific boroughs of London helped to highlight and target a crime problem. In another example, the spatiotemporal analysis of recurrent Reebok 49 shoemarks collected on several burglaries indicated the activity of a mobile serial offender who was hypothesised not to be living in the targeted neighbourhood, but to arrive there through a specific metro station. In another situation, forensic case data enabled the identification of an offender in one case that belonged to a large series of burglaries. The subsequent mapping of crime locations revealed that this offender lived in the centre of the geographical cluster of cases, which supported his involvement in committing the whole series of burglaries.

In order to highlight trends and identify potential crime series, the computerized shoemark database in Great Britain (SICAR) enables the monitoring of the frequency of shoemark patterns in specified geographical areas and between certain dates (Milne 2012). In a similar perspective, Ribaux and his colleagues proposed a two-step crime analysis method to reveal hotspots and crime series that combines forensic databases with a crime mapping system and cumulative temporal diagrams: step 1 'provide[s] promising set of cases from extraordinary concentrations of crime identified based on common general characteristics of shoemarks, toolmarks and/or glovemarks', and step 2 conducts to 'further scrutinise and combine with other types of data in order to find links or allow assumptions about the existence of a crime series' (Ribaux et al. 2003, 2006, 175).

Rossy and his colleagues describe the use of a regional crime intelligence database in Switzerland that fully integrates forensic links (based on comparisons of shoemarks, DNA and images) with situational information (spatiotemporal, loot, modus operandi, type of event, stolen and recovered vehicles) in order to interpret the crime environment for investigation and mainly intelligence purposes (Rossy et al. 2013). The combination of forensic case data with spatial and temporal dimensions is viewed as critical and the authors observe that 'more often than not, links detected with forensic case data would not be detected with situational information [only]' (Rossy et al. 2013, 145). Interestingly, situational links as well as forensic links of different types reveal crime relationships at different geographical and time scales. For instance, about 85 percent of links based on situational information connect cases that happened within the same jurisdiction and within a period of less than five weeks, whereas about 60 percent of shoemarks, DNA and images links connect cases at the regional level. The authors suggest that such regional crime intelligence databases will serve in the future as an original source of data for criminological research, in particular the study of the mobility and polymorphism of offenders.

Geographic profiling, while far from being recent (Kind 1987), is also an interesting spatiotemporal crime analysis method 'that uses the locations of a connected series of crime to determine the most probable area of offender residence' (Rossmo 2000, 1). Geographic profiling can leverage forensic case data, but to our knowledge no dedicated method or systematic study has yet been published in that regard. The potential of geographic profiling based on forensic findings will thus be illustrated here using an example drawn from the professional experience of one of the authors. Several burglaries occurred in shooting ranges and other premises of a given region over a period of several months. These burglaries could be reliably linked thanks to a recurrent group of shoemark patterns, indicating the series was caused by a cohesive group of offenders. Despite finding fingerprints, DNA profiles and shoemarks of good quality at the different crime scenes, police were unable to identify the offenders. That led to the hypothesis that the offenders were unknown from police records, probably rather young and, looking at the series' spatiotemporal profile, probably living in the region. Surveillance operations on possible future targets proved unsuccessful, and it was decided to perform geographic profiling using burglary locations (restricted to cases linked by forensic evidence to enhance accuracy). The centre of gravity or centroid of the series fell close to a road about a kilometre away from a village. Surveillance of that road led to a young man driving back to his house late at night who appeared to be wearing a pair of shoes that matched one of the shoemark patterns collected on the burglaries. That 'hit' enabled the subsequent identification of the whole group of offenders.

Prior to performing geographic profiling, forensic case data is pivotal to weighting the strength of the association between each case and the series, and also to excluding cases with too limited a probability of association. This increases the accuracy of geographic profiling, as shown in the investigation of a serial rapist and murderer in Las Vegas, where cases connected to the series thanks to DNA and fingerprints were given higher weights (Canter et al. 2000). To erroneously include one or several cases in a series based on flawed forensic evidence or a lack thereof may significantly bias geographic profiling (Ruffell and McKinley 2008).

The above examples present methods and practices that are more and more widespread among forensic, investigation and crime intelligence services. Their implementation calls for the development of robust methodologies and ever-evolving tools that efficiently combine spatial and temporal dimensions. Rossy provides guidance in that regard and has proposed an innovative software (using a python plugin of Quantum GIS) that divides 'temporal views with an appropriate use of colours corresponding to defined geographical areas shown on a map' (Rossy 2013, 34). However, unlike the criminology-oriented studies conducted on DNA mentioned above, the treatment of shoemarks, toolmarks, glovemarks and images remains essentially limited to tactical and operational police-oriented applications. As will be discussed in the conclusion, the strategic and criminological potential associated with spatiotemporally analysing forensic case data is presently overlooked. Methods used to solve crime series and to provide crime intelligence would certainly also prove useful in providing relevant insights at a higher level of generality.

Miscellaneous forensic case data

The reasoning process and methods illustrated for DNA, shoemarks, toolmarks, glovemarks and images can be transposed to forensic case data of any kind. However, some types of data provide specific opportunities. Digital traces such as mobile phone or GPS records lend themselves very well to spatiotemporal analyses and to geographical information systems (GIS). They are regularly used to test hypotheses about a suspect's location, her journey or habits, and they daily assist investigators in linking suspects to crimes geographically, temporally and relationally (Birrer and Terrettaz-Zufferey 2008; Rossy 2013). Rossy reports how the selection of phone calls at specific time periods and the plotting of their spatial positions using the above-mentioned software enables the location of a suspect's residence (Rossy 2013). As was observed above concerning shoemarks and other traces, the spatiotemporal analysis of global system for mobile communication (GSM) and GPS data is now essentially limited to a tactical and investigative focus. However, as demonstrated by Deville in the field of human geography, mobile phone data has great potential for unveiling hidden patterns and could provide a relevant pathway to study crime (Deville et al. 2014).

In the field of environmental crime and pollution, spatial analysis methods and GIS have been used to investigate the presence, flow paths and spatial distributions of illicit drugs contaminants in a Spanish natural park (Pascual Aguilar et al. 2014). The authors combined social and environmental data (population distribution pattern, locations of sewage plants and irrigation systems) with the spatial location of 16 water samples that had been chemically analysed to reveal the presence of 14 different drugs.

Manhein and his colleagues used spatial analysis methods and GIS to study whether specific geographical patterns exist in the dispersal of human and skeletal remains (Manhein et al. 2006). Using a set of 36 cases in Louisiana, they did not find any pattern that would make it possible to predict the location of dumped and scattered human remains. They note, however, a significant relationship between the shortest distance human remains had been scattered and the post-mortem time interval.

GIS also proves useful in the field of forensic drug intelligence. The Metropolitan Police Service in London uses the IOPs software mentioned above to 'relate the closeness of dealer arrests to scientific links and their journey to crime and distil, from a vast amount of data, manageable numbers of persons for further research in the telecommunications, financial, surveillance, or other areas' (Milne 2012, 215). Times, locations, drug type, forensic profile and wrappings type are correlated 'to reveal the extent and development of drug dealing and to study the whole drug problem as a commodity market' (Milne 2012, 216). Milne reports a market profile analysis about the illegal production of cannabis in England and Wales supported by forensic links established between illegal cannabis factories. That analysis made it possible to map and better understand the trafficking structure at the national level, and assisted in uncovering the criminal network financing the production (Milne 2012). Forensic links based on chemical analyses of cocaine and heroin seizures as well as cutting patterns can be compared over time and space to provide insights into drug markets, their structure, extent and dynamics, to highlight similar or different trends in various areas, as well as to study the lifespan of drug batches entering the market (Broséus et al. 2015; Broséus, Baechler et al. 2016; Broséus, Gentile and Esseiva 2016).

In a similar way, forensic examinations and comparisons of false identity documents provide objective knowledge of how such crime markets extend over space and jurisdictions. Besides confirming and quantifying the cross-jurisdiction and cross-border nature of crime markets related to forged documents (depending on the type of document, between 22 and 73 percent of forensic links and classes are transjurisdictional or transnational), forensic intelligence provides information on the duration of prolific forgers' activities and indicates how the quality of forged documents evolves over time. Plotting in time and space the seizures of false identity documents according to their type and manufacturing method reveals relevant patterns such as modus operandi, concentration or displacement (Baechler and Margot 2016).

Conclusion and further developments

The projection of forensic case data in spatial and temporal dimensions is still in its early stages. The initiatives, methods and examples mentioned in this chapter have to be viewed as a first approach that would certainly benefit from a more extended use of ESDA methodologies. At present, the potential contribution to forensic criminology is overlooked. The problem is twofold: on the one hand, among the many uses of GIS and spatiotemporal analyses to study crime, very few leverage forensic case data. On the other, most applications and developments that consider forensic case data are targeted to support investigative and crime intelligence efforts. That situation may be explained by the existence of gaps between different scientific and professional communities, such as crime scene officers, laboratory scientists, crime analysts, criminologists and specialists in spatiotemporal analysis and GIS applications. Hopefully, more and more initiatives in line with this book will help to address the issue.

We argue that access to forensic databases should be made easier for criminologists, and at the same time, criminologists and forensic scientists should be made more aware of the potential and limits of using forensic case data in support of criminological studies. Forensic scientists need to pay attention to geotagging their data and findings more systematically, since this is not happening now. Even if their primary focus is, of course, on processing evidence, the lack of spatiotemporal information and contextualization limits the exploration and analyses that can be conducted afterward, as illustrated in several examples provided in this chapter where location had to be restricted to discrete spatio-jurisdictional categories (administrative datum). Spatiotemporal data needs to be properly recorded within the metadata of forensic evidence, and standards must be set up and followed in order to minimize inaccuracies and errors (Miranda et al. 2012).

Even with its advantages and the unique perception of unidentified offenders and crime series it provides, forensic case data is, of course, not a perfect indicator. Primarily, its availability and representativeness have some limitations, since forensic evidence is not systematically collected on every crime due to various strategies and resources across organizations, but also because some crime types lend themselves better than others to collecting traces (Rossy et al. 2013). This explains, for instance, why many of the studies mentioned considered mainly property crimes such as burglaries, robberies and vehicle crimes. These limitations may, of course, affect the resulting spatiotemporal patterns of crime. A promising solution to overcoming this is to integrate forensic case data of different types such as shoemarks, DNA, images and digital traces, and combine them with alternative crime data. Finally, it must also be borne in mind that forensic links come with a degree of uncertainty, which can however be assessed and measured.

Concerning further developments, a stronger integration between forensic case data and spatiotemporal analysis would pave the way to broadening the range of research areas. For instance, forensic links derived from ballistics comparisons could be used to study gang territories and understand their dynamics (Gagliardi 2009, 2010). Forensically comparing and situating in time and space seizures conducted abroad, at border points and within the country could provide an understanding of the structure, flows and pathways of different criminal trades, such as illicit drugs, false identity documents and counterfeit goods. The growing digital dimension of society and crime generates new issues but also new forensic case data (extracted from social networks or the Darknet, for instance) that provide original spatiotemporal data relevant to crime. In these endeavours, data mining techniques will naturally gain in importance (Albertetti et al. 2016; Grossrieder et al. 2013, 2016; Grossrieder and Ribaux 2017).

We view as very promising the support that forensic case data could provide to comparative criminology studies. Indeed, forensic information has the advantage of being measurable and objective, it can be fairly easily schematized, and forensic methods are, to a certain extent, more comparable across jurisdictions and countries than other crime data or police practices. For example, offenders' mobility in the Netherlands revealed by DNA could be compared to the mobility of criminals in other countries by replicating the method using respective national DNA databases, or even at a European level (Bernasco et al. 2016). Beyond DNA, any forensic case data could serve as a basis for comparison between crime phenomena in different areas.

Current projects also imagine the relationship between forensic case data and spatiotemporal analyses the other way round. Such analyses and GIS could provide real-time information to the crime scene investigator as to which traces have been collected at other crime scenes in the vicinity of the current case. Such an approach would foster not only a more efficient and intelligence-led crime scene processing but also facilitate the early detection of crime series and crime problems (Ribaux, Baylon, Lock et al. 2010; Ribaux, Baylon, Roux et al. 2010).

Notes

1 For an in-depth discussion about ESDA techniques, see Bivand 2010 and Symanzik 2014.

2 Some forensic methods are dedicated to revealing the geographical origin of a given piece of evidence, such as genetic analysis to infer bio-geographic ancestry of a DNA stain (Phillips 2015), the use of chemical analyses such as IRMS (Gentile et al. 2011; McLean et al. 2014) or methods to locate where a picture was taken (Saurer et al. 2016). Other methods are developed to spatially situate a point of interest, such as finding a pollution source (Estoppey et al. 2015; Pascual Aguilar et al. 2014), locating hidden items or dead bodies using geoscience techniques (Ruffell and McKinley 2008, 2014), inferring the home location of an offender using GSM data (Birrer and Terrettaz-Zufferey 2008; Rossy 2013) or finding out which sensors within large and complex video surveillance networks have filmed sequences of a crime event (Codreanu et al. 2015). Another understanding lies in the challenge of situating and illustrating faithfully and efficiently where pieces of evidence have been found at the crime scene (Milliet et al. 2015; Ruffell and McKinley 2014; Schmitz et al. 2013; Walter and Schultz 2013). In support of death investigations, studies assess the spatiotemporal variability of necrophagous insects (Hwang and Turner 2005; Moretti and Godoy 2013). Other authors discuss how the location and living place of a suspect should be interpreted when assessing the strength of forensic evidence (K.A.J. Walsh et al. 1994).

References

Albertetti, F., L. Grossrieder, O. Ribaux and K. Stoffel. 2016. 'Change Points Detection in Crime-Related Time Series: An On-Line Fuzzy Approach Based on a Shape Space Representation'. *Applied Soft Computing* 40(C): 441–454.

Anselin, L. 1994. 'Exploratory Spatial Data Analysis and Geographic Information Systems'. In *New Tools for Spatial Analysis*, Proceedings of Workshop, Lisbon, 18–20 November 1993, 45–54. Luxembourg: Eurostat.

Anselin, L. 1995. 'Local Indicators of Spatial Association—LISA'. *Geographical Analysis* 27(2): 93–115. https://doi.org/10.1111/j.1538-4632.1995.tb00338.x.

Anselin, L. 1998. 'Exploratory Spatial Data Analysis in a Geocomputational Environment'. Conference on Geocomputation 1998, Bristol. www.ibrarian.net/navon/paper/EXPLORATORY_SPATIAL_DATA_ANALYSIS_IN_A.pdf?paperid=9844009.

Anselin, L., J. Cohen, D. Cook, W. Gorr and G. Tita. 2000. 'Spatial Analyses of Crime'. In D. Duffie, ed., *Criminal Justice: Measurement and Analysis of Crime and Justice*, vol. 4, 213–262. Washington, DC: National Institute of Justice.

Baechler, S., and P. Margot. 2016. 'Understanding Crime and Fostering Security Using Forensic Science: The Example of Turning False Identity Documents into Forensic Intelligence. *Security Journal*. https://doi.org/10.1057/sj.2015.26.

Bailey, T.C., and A.C. Gatrell. 1995. *Interactive Spatial Data Analysis*. Harlow: Longman.

Bernasco, W., M. Lammers and K. van der Beek. 2016. 'Cross-Border Crime Patterns Unveiled by Exchange of DNA Profiles in the European Union'. *Security Journal* 29(4): 640–660. https://doi.org/10.1057/sj.2015.27.

Birkett, J. 1989. 'Scientific Scene Linking'. *Journal of the Forensic Science Society* 29(4): 271–284.

Birrer, S., and A.-L. Terrettaz-Zufferey. 2008. 'Croisement spatial et temporel de données issues d'activités délictueuses et d'appareils permettant une géolocalisation. L'apport de la théorie des graphes dans l'automatisation de la comparaison entre des données personnelles issues de téléphones mobiles'. *Revue internationale de criminologie et de police technique et scientifique* 61(4): 481–500.

Bivand, R. 2010. 'Exploratory Spatial Data Analysis'. In M.M. Fischer, ed., *Handbook of Applied Spatial Analysis—Software Tools*, 219–254. New York: Springer International Publishing. www.springer.com/us/book/9783642036460.

Bond, J.W., and C. Hammond. 2008. 'The Value of DNA Material Recovered from Crime Scenes'. *Journal of Forensic Sciences* 53(4): 797–801. https://doi.org/10.1111/j.1556-4029.2008.00746.x.

Braga, A.A., A.V. Papachristos and D.M. Hureau. 2014. 'The Effects of Hot Spots Policing on Crime: An Updated Systematic Review and Meta-Analysis'. *Justice Quarterly* 31(4): 633–663. https://doi.org/10.1080/07418825.2012.673632.

Broséus, J., S. Baechler, N. Gentile and P. Esseiva. 2016. 'Chemical Profiling: A Tool to Decipher the Structure and Organisation of Illicit Drug Markets. An 8-Year Study in Western Switzerland'. *Forensic Science International* 266(September): 18–28. https://doi.org/10.1016/j.forsciint.2016.04.008.

Broséus, J., N. Gentile, F. Bonadio Pont, J.M. Garcia Gongora, L. Gasté and P. Esseiva. 2015. 'Qualitative, Quantitative and Temporal Study of Cutting Agents for Cocaine and Heroin over 9 Years'. *Forensic Science International* 257(December): 307–313. https://doi.org/10.1016/j.forsciint.2015.09.014.

Broséus, J., N. Gentile and P. Esseiva. 2016. 'The Cutting of Cocaine and Heroin: A Critical Review'. *Forensic Science International* 262(February): 73–83. https://doi.org/10.1016/j.forsciint.2016.02.033.

Buckleton, J., C.M. Triggs and S.J. Walsh. 2004. *Forensic DNA Interpretation*. Boca Raton: CRC Press.

Canter, D., T. Coffey, M. Huntley and C. Missen. 2000. 'Predicting Serial Killers' Home Base Using a Decision Support System'. *Journal of Quantitative Criminology* 16(4): 457–478.

Codreanu, D., A. Peninou and F. Sedes. 2015. 'Video Spatio-Temporal Filtering Based on Cameras and Target Objects Trajectories—Videosurveillance Forensic Framework'. In 10th International Conference on Availability, Reliability and Security (ARES) Proceedings, 611–617. https://doi.org/10.1109/ARES.2015.102.

Deville, P., C. Linard, S. Martin, M. Gilbert, F.R. Stevens, A.E. Gaughan, … A.J. Tatem. 2014. 'Dynamic Population Mapping Using Mobile Phone Data'. *Proceedings of the National Academy of Sciences* 111(45): 15888–15893. https://doi.org/10.1073/pnas.1408439111.

Estoppey, N., J. Omlin, A. Schopfer, P. Esseiva, E.L.M. Vermeirssen, O. Delémont and L.F. De Alencastro. 2015. 'Low Density Polyethylene (LDPE) Passive Samplers for the Investigation of Polychlorinated Biphenyl (PCB) Point Sources in Rivers'. *Chemosphere* 118(1): 268–276. https://doi.org/10.1016/j.chemosphere.2014.09.032.

Gagliardi, P. 2009. 'Helping Police Link More Crimes, Guns, and Suspects Using Regional Processing Protocols'. *Forensic Science Policy & Management: An International Journal* 1(1): 43–48.

Gagliardi, P. 2010. *The 13 Critical Tasks: An Inside-Out Approach to Solving More Gun Crime*. Cote St. Luc: Forensic Technology WAI Inc.

Gentile, N., L. Besson, D. Pazos, O. Delémont and P. Esseiva. 2011. 'On the Use of IRMS in Forensic Science: Proposals for a Methodological Approach'. *Forensic Science International* 212(1–3): 260–271. https://doi.org/10.1016/j.forsciint.2011.07.003.

Groff, E., D. Weisburd and N.A. Morris. 2009. 'Where the Action Is at Places: Examining Spatio-Temporal Patterns of Juvenile Crime at Places Using Trajectory Analysis and GIS'. In D. Weisburd, W. Bernasco and G. Bruinsma, eds., *Putting Crime in Its Place: Units of Analysis in Geographic Criminology*, 61–86. New York: Springer International Publishing. http://link.springer.com/chapter/10.1007/978-0-387-09688-9_3.

Grossrieder, L., F. Albertetti, K. Stoffel and O. Ribaux. 2013. 'Des données aux conaissances, un chemin difficile: réflexions sur la place du data mining en analyse criminelle'. *Revue internationale de criminologie et de police technique et scientifique* 66(1): 99–116.

Grossrieder, L., F. Albertetti, K. Stoffel and O. Ribaux. 2016. 'From Traces to Knowledge: Towards a Computational Forensic Criminology?' Proceedings of the 2016 ANZSOC Conference. www.anzsoc.com/1988.

Grossrieder, L., and O. Ribaux. 2017. 'Towards Forensic Whistleblowing? From Traces to Intelligence' *Policing: A Journal of Policy and Practice*. https://doi.org/10.1093/police/pax039

Grubesic, A. 2006. 'On the Application of Fuzzy Clustering for Crime Hot Spot Detection'. *Journal of Quantitative Criminology* 22(1). https://doi.org/10.1007/s10940-005-9003-6.

Hwang, C., and B.D. Turner. 2005. 'Spatial and Temporal Variability of Necrophagous Diptera from Urban to Rural Areas'. *Medical and Veterinary Entomology* 19(4): 379–391. https://doi.org/10.1111/j.1365-2915.2005.00583.x.

Jeuniaux, P., L. Duboccage, B. Renard, P.V. Renterghem and V. Vanvooren. 2016. 'Establishing Networks in a Forensic DNA Database to Gain Operational and Strategic Intelligence'. *Security Journal* 29(4): 584–602. https://doi.org/10.1057/sj.2015.31.

Kennedy, L.W., J.M. Caplan and E. Piza. 2011. 'Risk Clusters, Hotspots, and Spatial Intelligence: Risk Terrain Modeling as an Algorithm for Police Resource Allocation Strategies'. *Journal of Quantitative Criminology* 27(3): 339–362. https://doi.org/10.1007/s10940-010-9126-2.

Kind, S.S. 1987. 'Navigational Ideas and the Yorkshire Ripper Investigation'. *Journal of Navigation* 40(3): 385–393.

Lammers, M. 2014. 'Are Arrested and Non-Arrested Serial Offenders Different? A Test of Spatial Offending Patterns Using DNA Found at Crime Scenes'. *Journal of Research in Crime and Delinquency* 51(2): 143–167. https://doi.org/10.1177/0022427813504097.

Lammers, M., and W. Bernasco. 2013. 'Are Mobile Offenders Less Likely to Be Caught? The Influence of the Geographical Dispersion of Serial Offenders' Crime Locations on Their Probability of Arrest'. *European Journal of Criminology* 10(2): 168–186. https://doi.org/10.1177/1477370812464533.

Lammers, M., W. Bernasco and H. Elffers. 2012. 'How Long Do Offenders Escape Arrest? Using DNA Traces to Analyse When Serial Offenders Are Caught'. *Journal of Investigative Psychology and Offender Profiling* 9(1): 13–29. https://doi.org/10.1002/jip.1353.

Levine, N. 2006. 'Crime Mapping and the Crimestat Program'. *Geographical Analysis* 38(1): 41–56. https://doi.org/10.1111/j.0016-7363.2005.00673.x.

Manhein, M.H., G.A. Listi and M. Leitner. 2006. 'The Application of Geographic Information Systems and Spatial Analysis to Assess Dumped and Subsequently Scattered Human Remains'. *Journal of Forensic Sciences* 51(3): 469–474. https://doi.org/10.1111/j.1556-4029.2006.00108.x.

McLean, S.J., H. Ikegaya, P.J. Saukko, H.Y. Zheng, K. Itoh and S. Fushiki. 2014. 'The Utilization of Stable Isotope Analysis for the Estimation of the Geographic Origins of Unidentified Cadavers'. *Forensic Science International* 245(December): 45–50. https://doi.org/10.1016/j.forsciint.2014.10.011.

Messner, S.F., L. Anselin, R.D. Baller, D.F. Hawkins, G. Deane and S.E. Tolnay. 1999. 'The Spatial Patterning of County Homicide Rates: An Application of Exploratory Spatial Data Analysis'. *Journal of Quantitative Criminology* 15(4): 423–450. https://doi.org/10.1023/A:1007544208712.

Milliet, Q., O. Delémont, E. Sapin and P. Margot. 2015. 'A Methodology to Event Reconstruction from Trace Images'. *Science & Justice* 55(2): 107–117. https://doi.org/10.1016/j.scijus.2015.02.001.

Milne, R. 2001. 'Operation Bigfoot—a Volume Crime Data Project'. *Science & Justice* 41(3): 215–217.

Milne, R. 2012. *Forensic Intelligence*. Boca Raton: CRC Press.

Miranda, D., D. Russo and R. a. L. Alves. 2012. 'Upgrading to Postgis 2.0 in the Brazilian Federal Police Forensics GIS'. *International Archives of the Photogrammetry, Remote Sensing and Spatial Information Sciences* (ISPRS), vol. 39–B4, 371–374. https://doi.org/10.5194/isprsarchives-XXXIX-B4-371-2012.

Moretti, T.D.C., and W.A.C. Godoy. 2013. 'Spatio-Temporal Dynamics and Preference for Type of Bait in Necrophagous Insects, Particularly Native and Introduced Blow Flies (Diptera: Calliphoridae)'. *Journal of Medical Entomology* 50(2): 415–424. https://doi.org/10.4172/2157-7145.1000147.

Pascual Aguilar, J.A., V. Andreu, P. Vázquez and Y. Picó. 2014. 'Presence and Spatial Distribution of Emerging Contaminants (Drugs of Abuse) in Protected Agroecological Systems (L'Albufera de Valencia Coastal Wetland, Spain)'. *Environmental Earth Sciences* 71(1): 31–37. https://doi.org/10.1007/s12665-013-2688-1.

Phillips, C. 2015. 'Forensic Genetic Analysis of Bio-Geographical Ancestry'. *Forensic Science International: Genetics* 18(May): 49–65. https://doi.org/10.1016/j.fsigen.2015.05.012.

Ratcliffe, J. 2013. 'What Is the Future… of Predictive Policing?' *Practice* 6(2): 151–166.

Ratcliffe, J. 2016. *Intelligence-Led Policing*. 2nd ed.. London; New York: Routledge.

Ribaux, O., A. Baylon, E. Lock, O. Delémont, C. Roux, C. Zingg and P. Margot. 2010. 'Intelligence-Led Crime Scene Processing. Part II: Intelligence and Crime Scene Examination'. *Forensic Science International* 199(1–3): 63–71.

Ribaux, O., A. Baylon, C. Roux, O. Delémont, E. Lock, C. Zingg and P. Margot. 2010. 'Intelligence-Led Crime Scene Processing. Part I: Forensic Intelligence'. *Forensic Science International* 195(1–3): 10–16.

Ribaux, O., A. Girod, S.J. Walsh, P. Margot, S. Mizrahi and V. Clivaz. 2003. 'Forensic Intelligence and Crime Analysis'. *Law, Probability and Risk* 2(1): 47–60.

Ribaux, O., and P. Margot. 1999. 'Inference Structures for Crime Analysis and Intelligence: The Example of Burglary Using Forensic Science Data'. *Forensic Science International* 100(3): 193–210.

Ribaux, O., and P. Margot. 2003. 'Case Based Reasoning in Criminal Intelligence Using Forensic Case Data'. *Science & Justice* 43(3): 135–143.

Ribaux, O., S.J. Walsh and P. Margot. 2006. 'The Contribution of Forensic Science to Crime Analysis and Investigation: Forensic Intelligence'. *Forensic Science International* 156(2–3): 171–181.

Rossmo, D.K. 2000. *Geographic Profiling*. Boca Raton: CRC Press.

Rossy, Q. 2013. 'Spatiotemporal Analysis of Forensic Case Data: A Visualisation Approach'. *Bulletin de la Société Géographique de Liège* 60(1): 33–43.

Rossy, Q., S. Ioset, D. Dessimoz and O. Ribaux. 2013. 'Integrating Forensic Information in a Crime Intelligence Database'. *Forensic Science International* 230(1–3): 137–146.

Ruffell, A., and J. McKinley. 2008. *Geoforensics*. Chichester, UK: John Wiley & Sons.

Ruffell, A., and J. McKinley. 2014. 'Forensic Geomorphology'. *Geomorphology* 206(February): 14–22. https://doi.org/10.1016/j.geomorph.2013.12.020.

Saurer, O., G. Baatz, K. Köser, L. Ladický and M. Pollefeys. 2016. 'Image Based Geo-Localization in the Alps'. *International Journal of Computer Vision* 116(3): 213–225. https://doi.org/10.1007/s11263-015-0830-0.

Schmitz, P., C. Eloff, R. Talmakkies, C. Linnen and R. Lourens. 2013. 'Forensic Mapping in South Africa: Four Examples'. *Cartography and Geographic Information Science* 40(3): 238–247. https://doi.org/10.1080/15230406.2013.800273.

Sherman, L.W., and D. Weisburd. 1995. 'General Deterrent Effects of Police Patrol in Crime "Hot Spots": A Randomized, Controlled Trial'. *Justice Quarterly* 12(4): 625–648. https://doi.org/10.1080/07418829500096221.

Symanzik, J. 2014. 'Exploratory Spatial Data Analysis'. In M.M. Fischer and P. Nijkamp, eds., *Handbook of Regional Science*, 1295–1310. Berlin, Heidelberg: Springer Berlin Heidelberg. http://link.springer.com/10.1007/978-3-642-23430-9_76.

Tobler, W.R. 1970. 'A Computer Movie Simulating Urban Growth in the Detroit Region'. *Economic Geography* 46(June): 234–240. https://doi.org/10.2307/143141.

Tukey, J.W. 1977. *Exploratory Data Analysis*. 1st ed. Reading, MA: Pearson.

Walsh, K.A.J., J.S. Buckleton and C.M. Triggs. 1994. 'Assessing Prior Probabilities Considering Geography'. *Journal of the Forensic Science Society* 34(1): 47–51. https://doi.org/10.1016/S0015-7368(94)72882-6.

Walsh, S.J., D.S. Moss, C. Kliem and G.M. Vintiner. 2002. 'The Collation of Forensic DNA Case Data into a Multi-Dimensional Intelligence Database'. *Science & Justice* 42(4): 205–214. https://doi.org/10.1016/S1355-0306(02)71830-3.

Walter, B.S., and J.J. Schultz. 2013. 'Mapping Simulated Scenes with Skeletal Remains Using Differential GPS in Open Environments: An Assessment of Accuracy and Practicality'. *Forensic Science International* 228(1–3): e33–e46. https://doi.org/10.1016/j.forsciint.2013.02.027.

Weisburd, D., W. Bernasco and G.J.N. Bruinsma, eds. 2009. *Putting Crime in Its Place*. New York: Springer New York. http://link.springer.com/10.1007/978-0-387-09688-9.

Weisburd, D., J.E. Eck, A.A. Braga, C.W. Telep, B. Cave, K. Bowers, … S.-M. Yang. 2016. *Place Matters: Criminology for the Twenty-First Century*. Cambridge: Cambridge University Press. http://ebooks.cambridge.org/ref/id/CBO9781139342087.

Weisburd, D., C. Lum and S.-M. Yang. 2004. *The Criminal Careers of Places: A Longitudinal Study*. Rockville, MD: National Institute of Justice, US Department of Justice.

Weyermann, C., and O. Ribaux. 2012. 'Situating Forensic Traces in Time'. *Science & Justice* 52(2): 68–75. https://doi.org/10.1016/j.scijus.2011.09.003.

Wiles, P., and A. Costello. 2000. *The 'Road to Nowhere': The Evidence for Travelling Criminals*. London: Home Office Research Study.

19

Data mining in criminology and forensic science

Jean-Pierre Guay and Francis Fortin

Introduction

Whether we observe it or not, we are living in an increasingly data-driven world. Technological advancements and breakthroughs are occurring at an exponential rate, and these have invariably led to an accumulation of all types of information (Witten, Frank, Hall and Pal 2017). Throughout the day, our electronic devices store astronomical amounts of data. These devices may store numerical traces on our movements, actions, and conversations. In addition to a surplus of traditional data on the activity of humans, data are also available from a variety of sources, such as telephone conversations, text messages, images, videos, biometric processes, and geolocation. Data are also increasingly unstructured, and therefore more difficult to process using traditional research strategies. As technology allows for an accumulation of data, there is an increasing demand for appropriate analytical approaches to process large datasets. In many cases, traditional analytical strategies and models derived from statistics may not be sufficient to extract meaning from these datasets. Data mining strategies remain the most adapted to this context and may be the most suitable approach when looking to extract meaning from increasingly common, large and complex datasets.

In criminology and forensic science, data is at the heart of the research process (Ribaux et al. 2016). Data constitutes the core material for reconstructing how offences and crimes unfold. Without detailed and informed data analysis, professionals cannot go beyond mere conjectures. The analytical strategy to assess this type of data must thus be adapted to the complexity of the situation. Data mining presents a method to resolve analytical problems faced by professionals in forensic science and empirical criminology.

What is data mining?

Data mining is part of a broader approach to knowledge development (i.e., Knowledge Discovery) (Fayyad, Piatetsky-Shapiro and Smyth 1996), in which data are collected, stored, organized, and then selected. Data mining captures the research step when data are being analysed to discern patterns that give information about underlying processes. Data mining can be described as the process by which information is extracted from large datasets (Hand et al. 2001) and as 'the process of exploring and analyzing large quantities of data through automated and semi-automated processes with the aim of discovering patterns and rules' (Berry and Linoff 1999, 7).

What types of data mining exist? Supervised and unsupervised learning

There is a general tendency to classify data mining into two major categories: supervised and unsupervised learning (Cherkassy and Mulier 2007). Supervised learning models (or predictive models) aim to identify patterns in the data associated with a target variable, or dependent variable. For instance, identifying the criteria associated with increased recidivism (a classification exercise), the amount of fraud claimed, or the estimated duration of a hostage taking (a prediction exercise) are all questions related to supervised learning. In contrast, unsupervised learning models have no variables to predict and aim to find recurring patterns in datasets. Tasks such as identifying aberrant banking activities or the user-profiles of child pornography are all matters of unsupervised learning.

What are the uses of data mining?

Classification

Classification is a supervised data mining exercise (Sumathi and Sivanandam 2006). The objective is to determine, on the basis of the available data, whether a unit belongs to one category or another. There are numerous examples of classification: determining which individual is most likely to re-offend, which transaction has the highest probability of being fraudulent, or which site of an incident or transaction will most likely be selected, are all examples of classification. Many analytical strategies and data mining techniques have been designed to identify which class a unit belongs to. Two of the most commonly used approaches are classification trees and artificial neural networks. These models aim to identify and formalize classification rules that are useful for new cases. These rules are derived from the analysis of large datasets and may be used by professionals to anticipate new events and thus better prepare for them.

Estimation and prediction

Whereas classification exercises are concerned with classifying units into discrete categories (nominal variables), estimation and prediction aim to determine the values of continuous variables (Larose and Larose 2014). They therefore aim to estimate an expected value for each unit. The exercise of predicting a continuous value is similar to the exercise of estimating that value. The primary difference stems from the fact that the prediction exercise aims to estimate a future value. Data mining techniques therefore offer more flexible alternatives to traditional regression strategies.

Clustering

The aim of clustering is to classify units into homogeneous groups, often called types, profiles, or clusters. It aims to segment or partition large sets of units (Han and Kamber 2006; Tan et al. 2005). In contrast to classification approaches, clustering is not intended to classify units into predefined groups (e.g., recidivists vs non-recidivists) but rather to form subgroups of similar entities that share a number of characteristics or attributes, and that are notably distinguishable from other entities (Zhang and Zhou 2004). Clustering is often a preliminary step when analyzing data, a step that makes it possible to organize large datasets into classes of defined profiles, which are easier to understand.

Affinity grouping

The objective of affinity grouping is to identify which things go together. A classic example of affinity grouping is the grocery basket case. In this case, affinity grouping has been used as a strategy to identify which products are frequently purchased at the same time, such as milk, diapers, and beer. In criminology, affinity grouping strategies may be used to identify which types of drugs are more likely to be trafficked together.

The most commonly used methods

There currently exist multiple methods to solve the various problems of classification, regression, clustering, and affinity grouping. Among the most common methods are classification and regression trees, artificial neural networks, ensemble methods, cluster analysis, and text mining.

Classification and regression trees

Classification and regression trees (CART) were developed by Leo Breiman and colleagues in the 1980s. They were quickly adopted because of their simplicity and the fact that they perform well in a wide variety of situations (Shmueli et al. 2007).

Classification trees make it possible to design a series of intelligible decision rules. The principle behind classification trees is recursive partitioning. Recursive partitioning proceeds by sequentially dividing a multidimensional universe into groups of the most similar possible units with respect to a criterion. At the beginning, all units belong to a single group. Partitioning then identifies variables that will classify units into subgroups that are as similar as possible. In criminology, classification trees may be used in a variety of cases, for example, to identify groups of people who, with respect to their age, have different rates of recidivism. Using a large sample of offenders, the first step would be to compare individuals who are 18 with those who are 19 and older in terms of their recidivism rate. Then, the 18- and 19-year-olds would be compared to those 20 and older, with this process recursively occurring until all possible combinations have been exhausted. The division that offers the greatest purity will be retained. The principle behind recursive partitioning is to divide the dimensional space into non-overlapping multidimensional space.

In a classification tree, the ultimate objective is to determine a combination of predictors that reduces heterogeneity to its maximum. A pure zone (or combination of predictors) is therefore a zone in which all units take on the same value of the dependent variable. Several measures of impurity are commonly used, such as the GINI index or entropy (Patel and Upadhyay 2012).

When classification trees are used, it is possible with a high number of combinations of predictors to perfectly model the link between the set of predictors and the output. In other words, it is possible to propose a tree that reproduces the full set of possible combinations of the predictors. This scenario is referred to as a 'fully-grown tree'. This tree would be free of prediction errors, but would be entirely contingent on the data for which it was developed, and the generalizability of the results to other contexts or datasets would be low. This raises the issue of overfitting. There are two strategies commonly used to reduce overfitting: determining a stopping rule and pruning. In the case of determining the maximum size of the tree (stopping method), it is possible to determine a priori the maximum number of levels, or the maximum number of splits or the minimum size of the units in each of the nodes (thus in the terminal partitioning). Chi-square Automatic Interaction Detector (CHAID) is a method that uses the chi-square independence test (in the case of classification trees) and the t-test (in the case of regression trees) to determine the utility of a variable in reducing the impurity.

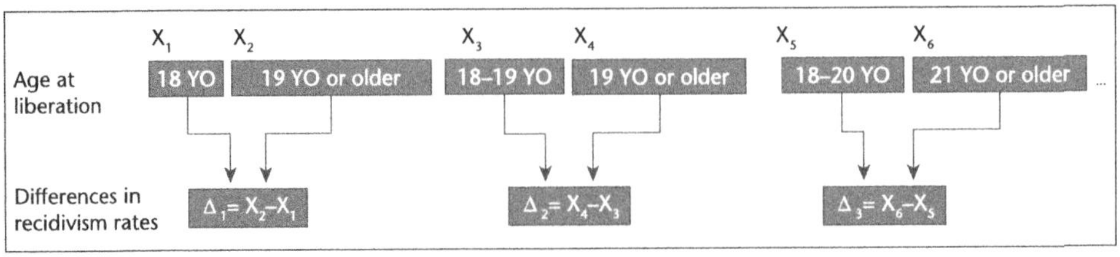

Figure 19.1 The principle behind recursive partitioning

The pruning method proceeds differently. After extending the possibilities of the tree to its maximum, it proceeds to prune the least relevant branches, often those with little input, containing few observations, probably the fruit of the specificity of the learning sample. Pruning is therefore a strategy that aims to find a balance between the size of the tree (its complexity) and its precision.

CART models offer many advantages (Lewis 2000; Roiger and Geatz 2003). First, they allow a large number of different predictors to be processed simultaneously and identify the most important ones. It is not uncommon to process several hundred variables simultaneously. Second, they offer the possibility of processing variables of any type simultaneously and allow for different types of distributions, whether normal or not. They are not constrained by different assumptions. Third, the results are presented in the form of decision trees that are relatively easy to interpret. Fourth, CART models can process datasets with missing data. Missing data can even be considered as values in and of themselves. CART models may also attempt to detect 'surrogate' variables to estimate missing variables. Fifth, CART models may be useful for detecting more complex interaction effects than traditional techniques (such as regression or ANOVA models).

CART models also have important limitations. First, they remain relatively uncommon as compared to traditional techniques such as regression models. Second, they may lead analysts to overfit data, potentially leading to beliefs in high accuracy. It therefore becomes essential to strongly emphasize pruning procedures and rules. The CART model is a step function and not a continuous score; consequently, if the retained model using several variables, even several hundred variables, contains only ten terminal nodes, it can take on only ten different values.

Artificial neural networks

Artificial neural networks (ANNs) comprise a large family of methods inspired by the functioning of the human brain. They were primarily developed in the 1940s by a psychiatrist, Warren McCulloch, and a mathematician, Walter Pitts (1943). Although ANNs are among the most commonly used algorithms, they also appear among the least understood. Some suggest that the use of the brain metaphor and associated jargon has complicated the ease of understanding (Berry and Linoff 1999). While neurons in the brain receive and accumulate electrical pulses from other neurons to which they are connected, ANNs receive and accumulate information from independent variables. As information accumulates, the network attains or does not attain a threshold. Once this threshold is attained, similar to the neuron that accumulates biochemical or bioelectric energy, the network propagates this information. The activation thresholds of ANNs follow different functions, linear in the case of continuous outputs, and logistic in the case of binary outputs.

The innovative nature of ANNs lies in the structure of information processing. The arrays are arranged in a structure in which each of the artificial neurons is connected to several other neurons, which act as output, which can also act as inputs for the following neurons. It is for this reason that Haykin (1999) defines ANNs as a 'massively parallel distributed processor made up

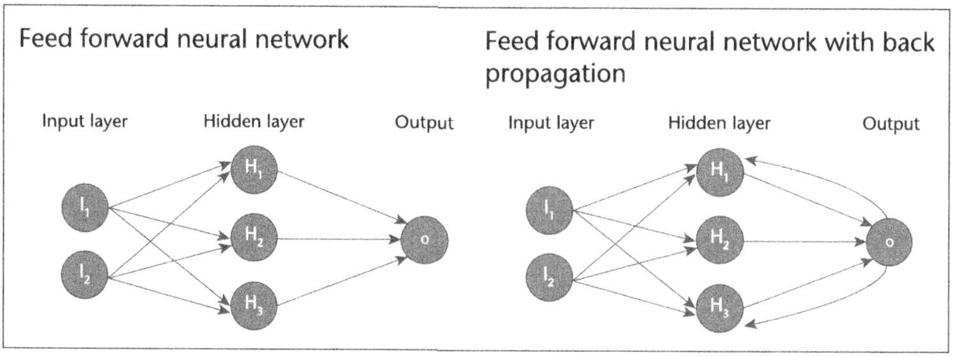

Figure 19.2 Examples of artificial neural network structures

of simple processing units, which has a natural propensity for storing experiential knowledge and making it available for use' (24). It resembles the human brain in two respects: (1) knowledge is acquired from the environment through the network through a learning process, and (2) the strength of interneuronal connections (synaptic weights) is used to store knowledge (Haykin 1999). With ANNs, it is possible to configure a series of weighting parameters to simulate learning. Among the most common are backpropagation (Figure 19.2 above), a process by which the weights are readjusted according to the size of the error.

ANNs are composed of many interconnected elements (here the neurons), and are designed to solve problems. The neurons are linked to one another by weighted interconnections. Each input unit is linked to the output by a weight, or a mathematical transformation of a weight. The neuron treats numerical information using a function. If it meets a certain number of criteria, that is, if the trigger threshold is reached, the neuron is activated and the output information is propagated to the next output or neuron.

The main strength of ANNs is to extract and detect patterns of information far too complex for human beings and even too complex for other data analysis techniques. They offer many advantages, such as allowing modelling of complex and nonlinear relationships (Hornik et al. 1989; White 1989), and recourse to multiple learning algorithms. The processed data can be nominal or continuous. In addition, given the increasing accessibility of software, artificial neural networks are relatively simple to perform, and require less intensive statistical training than traditional models.

ANNs are used for many purposes, both for classification and prediction tasks (Warner and Misra 1996), and can also address unsupervised learning problems. However, ANNs also have a number of limitations. Among the most frequently mentioned is that they constitute a 'black box technique' (Guerriere and Detsky 1991), highlighting the challenges of deriving causal interpretations of the relationships identified (Tu 1996). While a model developer is able to determine the strongest predictors in classical models such as regression models, these cannot be easily determined with an ANN, since it can contain a number of unimportant predictors, and no well-established criteria exist for interpreting the weights in a connection weight matrix (Tu 1996). They can also be computationally intensive.

Different variations of ensemble methods

While supervised learning algorithms, such as CART models or ANNs, produce only one prediction, it is possible to combine the different predictions using several iterations or combinations of these methods. Ensemble methods (Dietterich 1997), or meta-algorithms, primarily aim to combine different methods of predictive modeling. Generally, these techniques make it possible to achieve greater prediction accuracy. The principle is that of a 'vote'. Given that each of the variants of the trees gives a prediction, the combination of all these predictions constitutes the final estimate. Ensemble methods can be employed through numerous different approaches (Berk 2004). Among the most commonly used are bagging, boosting, and random forests.

Bagging, also referred to as bootstrap aggregating (Breiman 1996), consists of repeatedly selecting a number of samples and creating the same number of non-pruned trees. Each dataset makes it possible to resample the same unit more than once, which means that the size of each of the samples is the same as the original set. For each exercise, each of the algorithms gets a 'vote'. The final decision depends on the overall vote of the different models. In contrast, boosting (Freund and Schapire 1996) is an iterative process that allows the weight of the different subsets of training data to vary so that more effort will be dedicated to the classification of units that are difficult to classify. Lastly, ensemble methods that rely on a random forest approach use a large number of different trees, hence the name (Breiman 1999). Each generated tree is composed of binary decisions, and the vote of all the different trees will be the final prediction.

Ensemble methods combine classifiers in order to achieve a better prediction than each of the classifiers taken separately (Rokach 2010). Despite their popularity, ensemble methods have certain limitations (Rokach and Maimon 2015). For example, it is sometimes assumed that a large set of contributive inputs can be reduced to a small number of features; there are several different strategies of ensemble methods, not all of which will improve prediction; and ensemble methods can be extensive in terms of computing resources.

Cluster analysis

Clustering strategies belong to the family of unsupervised learning. The aim of clustering is to organize the units into different coherent sets that capture meaning in the data (Everitt et al. 2011). It therefore aims to create subgroups whose units share common or similar properties, and that are distinguished from other sets of units. They aim to discover patterns of association between units on the basis of several variables, and estimate how similar the units to be classified are. The term 'distance' is often used to describe the similarity between units. The distance should be small for units of the same subgroup or class (a cluster), and large for units of different subgroups.

However, clustering methods do not guarantee that the groupings make sense. It is up to the researcher to interpret the coherence of the proposed groupings, which is why the validity of clustering methods is generally difficult to evaluate (Everitt et al. 2011).

If clustering allows for the identification of patterns of similar responses, it also allows for focusing on patterns of dissimilar responses. For example, it is possible to identify behaviours that are significantly different from the common patterns (i.e., outliers). This feature has commonly been used to detect, for example, patterns of unexpected behaviour, sometimes characteristic of problematic behaviours, such as fraud in banking data, or intrusions into computer systems.

At the core of clustering techniques is the notion of proximity between units. To determine whether two units belong to the same class, it is necessary to estimate how similar they are. Clustering techniques use measures of distances to estimate similarity between units. It is in part the nature of the data that will determine the method most appropriate for measuring the extent to which units are similar.

Clustering methods are relatively numerous and can be broadly divided into two approaches: hierarchical and non-hierarchical. In hierarchical methods, units that are similar are grouped sequentially or agglomeratively. Each unit is considered a cluster and agglomerated to the most similar unit. The units are clustered to the point where they all belong to the same cluster. It is up to the researcher to stop the agglomeration process at a point considered to be optimal. The process may also be divisive, with the starting point of all units belonging to the same group, and subgroups are gradually created on the basis of measures of similarities. Non-hierarchical methods proceed differently. These are prototype-based clustering techniques. These methods, of which the most commonly used are the K-means methods, first define a desired number of clusters and place an initial point in a multidimensional universe. Each unit is then assigned to the centre of its closest cluster, and the centroid is recalculated. The distances between each of the points and the new centroid are recalculated. The process ends when the centroids are stable.

In sum, there exist a large number of clustering techniques, and all of them can generate slightly different cluster solutions. The challenge when it comes to clustering is validating the clustering solution. Many strategies have been put forward to test the validity of the cluster through the testing of homogeneity of the dataset, the use of validation indexes, the evaluation of stability of clustering solutions, and data visualization (Hennig et al. 2016).

Text mining

In an era where tremendous amounts of textual content are shared every day through social media, the need to develop a way to extract knowledge from these sources has become increasingly important. Such texts are expressions of natural language that cannot be easily understood by computers unless they can be appropriately represented and characterized (Milić-Frayling 2005). Text-mining techniques have therefore been developed to recover knowledge from textual databases (Feldman and Dagan 1995). Like data mining in general, their focus is on locating and extracting interesting and non-trivial patterns, but they can also be used to obtain knowledge from unstructured text documents (Tan 1999). In that context, high-quality results are defined by a combination of relevance, novelty, and degree of interest (Han et al. 2012).

Text mining typically involves the linguistic and statistical processing of documents. Linguistics has been investigating ways to characterize and explain language outputs, particularly conversations and writings (Milić-Frayling 2005). Studying the linguistic structures by which people communicate has led to the creation of tools that characterize language (e.g., see Wordnet initiative) and act as a set of rules. While text mining can be performed by the computer without human input (unsupervised), researchers have suggested that integrating knowledge from a specific field may improve the parsing methods as well as the learning and the mining efficiency and the quality of the model (Tan 1999). Text mining is therefore considered to be a multidisciplinary field that involves 'information retrieval, text analysis, information extraction, clustering, categorization, visualization, database technology, machine learning, and data mining' (Tan 1999, 65).

Tasks related to text mining include categorization, clustering, concept and entity extraction, entity-relation modeling, taxonomies, sentiment analysis, and document summarization (Feldman and Sanger 2007). Text clustering requires a pre-processing phase that removes any non-textual information, such as HTML tags and punctuation as well as stop words (such as 'I', 'to', etc.) from the list of terms. The resulting series of terms are typically reduced to their bases by applying a stemming algorithm (Beil et al. 2002), usually the vector-space model. In this model, each term in a text document is represented by a frequency vector. These vectors are then used to perform clustering algorithms such as K-means or K-medoid algorithms. Using term similarity measures, the K-means bisecting algorithm separates the clusters into groups of 2 until the desired number of clusters is obtained (see Steinbach et al. 2000). These tools have also led to new fields of study, such as opinion mining, which are useful for vendors (e.g., feedback from customers), citizens (e.g., summaries of peers' product evaluations), and government (analysis of opinions) (Breck and Cardie 2017).

Researchers are beginning to investigate social media, not only to understand how these technologies are involved in crimes but also to see how deviants share information and how understanding these methods can help in legal processes ranging from detection to prosecution. The Twitter platform allows programmers access to all public content shared in a given period, both text and metadata such as user details and data that accompanies the post (geolocation information, language, reply/retweet, etc.) (see Twitter 2016). This access allows anyone with minimal programming skills to locate particular tweets based on a specific query involving already-formatted fields: text of the tweet, favourite number, in response to another tweet, device used to tweet, screen name, number of retweets, and geolocation information.

Twitter is known for its lack of strict rules, the ability to keep posters anonymous, access to a wide audience, and the efficient and fast dissemination of information characteristic of social media platforms (Weimann 2015). Researchers have argued that Twitter has therefore become 'a widely used and popular technology for radicalized groups like ISIS proponents to spread their real-time messages around the world' (Ghajar-Khosravi et al. 2016, 79).

Law enforcement agencies are also interested in analysing the crime environment on social media. Carter (2009), looking at how open source intelligence can be a valuable and important tool for policing, found that it is particularly useful in investigating several specific categories of crime. Among these are crimes committed by groups or individuals who may constitute a threat because of their extremist ideology and support for or promotion of violence (Carter 2009). The purpose of such groups or individuals is tied to the sharing of beliefs, goals, and even plans of action.

A systematic literature review of online data-mining technology intended for use in law enforcement (Edwards et al. 2015) found that researchers have identified natural language processing (NLP) as one of the most important data mining techniques. Natural language processing is defined as 'a theoretically motivated range of computational techniques for analyzing and representing naturally occurring texts at one or more levels of linguistic analysis for achieving human-like language processing for a range of tasks or applications' (Liddy 2001, 2126). Many studies used NLP in combination with machine learning techniques and classifiers such as SVMs and Naives Bayes. Text and data mining techniques have been used on Twitter data for a wide range of purposes, such as detection of public safety incidents (Marivate and Moiloa 2016), crisis analysis (Spielhofer et al. 2016; Subba and Bui 2017), analysing hate/terrorist/threat discourse (Sobkowicz and Sobkowicz 2010; Banday et al. 2011), or to analyse user demographics (Mislove et al. 2011) and group users geographically according to their shared content (Compton et al. 2014) .

Data mining and law enforcement examples

In this section two examples of data-mining techniques that can be used to address forensic-related problems are presented. The first presents a technique that helps investigators classify spam messages into particular campaigns for investigative purposes, while the second presents a case study related to the analysis of published content online.

Example 1: data mining example in cybercrime (spam analysis)

Data mining techniques have been used to solve problems for law enforcement agencies—in this case, how to aggregate spam messages to determine which messages belong to a specific campaign (Dinh et al. 2015) so that senders can be investigated. A spam campaign is a group of messages that are sent for a specific purpose and can be assumed to be sent by a common entity (person or company).

The initial step in the research was to dissect the spam messages to extract their characteristics, making it possible to collect all the embedded technical information, such as the IP address of the sender and the destination fields, as well as all related characteristics such as technical responsibility for the IP address. These characteristics were then stored in a database for analysis. The method for detecting spam campaigns was based on the Frequent Pattern Tree (FP-Tree) algorithm (Han et al. 2000, 2004). The premise of the study was that the more frequent a characteristic is, the more it will be shared between similar spam messages. The construction of a tree using the FP-Tree algorithm makes it possible to group the spam into campaigns according to shared characteristics. In addition, obfuscated characteristics are naturally discovered in the FP-Tree and this discovery makes it possible to explain the strategies of the spammers. At the end of the process, a tree was obtained in which each node represents a characteristic extracted from spam. Looking at the tree revealed messages that have some common characteristics shared by a part of the path to the root (the root being the most important characteristic). This approach is very effective and reveals the common elements of campaign messages and the characteristics that are obfuscated by spammers.

Example 2: extremists and YouTube comments

This study was aimed at assisting law enforcement agencies in locating hate or radicalization videos on YouTube (Sureka et al. 2010). The basic premise was that people who comment on extremist videos are of particular interest to law enforcement agencies. Researchers studied the comments of 3,037 unique users who commented on 75 extremist videos. The comments of the 12 candidates who posted the highest number of comments were analyzed (2,200 words). First, Linguistic Inquiry and Word Count (LIWC) was performed. The results showed a high frequency of religious and swear words. Researchers also used Latent Dirichlet Allocation (LDA) to discover the topics discussed and better understand the posts. They then generated three categories: theme 1 contained words such as military, *dosti*, succeed, *jang*, *allaho*, *akabar*, while theme 2 contained terms related to sexuality or that were derogatory. Theme 3 involved terrorism and war. Finally, the authors focused their attention on social network analysis (SNA) indicators available on YouTube (friends, subscriptions, favourite and related videos). With these indicators, their system was able to identify 98 users (true positive) as suspicious with an average precision of 88 percent in two iterations. The approach made it possible to effectively locate hate videos.

Conclusion

This chapter has presented an overview of data mining methods and possible applications in forensic science. This overview has described the different approaches to supervised and unsupervised learning, as well as the main uses of data mining techniques, and presented the most commonly used techniques, as well as possible applications in the fields of criminology and forensic science, highlighting the numerous benefits of integrating data mining techniques into forensic activities (Beebe and Clark 2006). First, data mining techniques significantly reduce data processing time. These gains are related both to the duration of operations and to the costs associated with the use of professional time. Professionals can dedicate their energies to the processing of aberrant units or processing errors rather than to encoding or classification. Second, the algorithms allow for increases in the precision of the different classification and estimation exercises, allowing for increases in model optimization. Lastly, the different algorithms can reduce costs significantly. Repetitive and technical tasks formerly performed by humans can be executed by different algorithms in a fraction of the time.

For now, the nature of the operations performed by data mining algorithms is still limited. This has to do, at least in part, with the type of data recognized and processed. Formerly reserved for encoded data, such as data previously formatted in databases and computer files, the different algorithms are able to process more complex unencoded data. Computer systems offer more and more possibilities for extraction, encoding, and preliminary processing, tasks that were initially left to humans. Whereas previously an analyst had to be used to encode images, the various algorithms are increasingly automating such tasks. It is only a matter of time before this task can be mastered, even on complex objects (containing several sources), such as video or multimedia content from the web.

Data-rich, but still knowledge poor

The field of data mining is filled with classical examples of the need to involve humans in extracting meaning from large datasets. The most commonly reported is undoubtedly that of the analysis of the grocery baskets where there was a statistical association between the time of the week, the sale of beer, and the sale of diapers. This association was quickly interpreted as the fact that young men who become fathers are tempted to continue drinking beer despite their new life, and that it would be desirable to activate this association by bringing the two products into stores.

Although methods are progressing rapidly, knowledge development is not proceeding at the same rate. Many will say that we are data-rich, but knowledge poor (Domingos 2007). In areas such as forensic science, analyses need to be enhanced with contextual elements that facilitate understanding. Data patterns are only a coalescence of information, as long as the analyst, researcher, or decision-maker has not integrated it into a wider set of knowledge. The place of the human being is therefore crucial in the extraction of the meaning of the results obtained from analysis resulting from data mining: the latter makes it possible to fill in the gap that separates the results of the analysis and the actions that can be taken (Domingos 2007). To transform the data into knowledge and then into action, it must be inserted into a wider framework.

Several examples support the relevance of a vision that uses forensic science to go beyond specific situations, as is often the case in court cases, and applies findings more generally to whole phenomena, or modus operandi. These new ways of approaching phenomena offer an innovative angle from which to appropriate criminological knowledge. The traditional view of forensic science, which is limited to a legal approach, does not adequately reflect the reality as seen in a broader enforcement context. According to Ribaux et al. (2010), traces can be used in a wide variety of information management processes that support decision-making in many situations at all stages of policing. According to these scholars, the literature on criminalistics focuses on the best methods for making accusations and avoiding procedural flaws in investigative files, but often neglects the informational value of traces. Since numerical traces make up a large part of the investigation files, transformations from survey methods to more efficient methods such as data mining are inevitable. Forensic science, like criminology, must pursue the development of knowledge both from a methodological perspective and that of theoretical integration if it wishes to become knowledge rich.

References

Banday, M.T., J.A. Qadri, T. Jan and N. Shah. 2011. 'Detecting Threat E-mails Using a Bayesian Approach'. *International Journal of Secure Digital Information Age* 1(2): 103–113.

Beebe, N., and J. Clark. 2006. 'Dealing with Terabyte Data Sets in Digital Investigations'. *Advances in Digital Forensics: IFIP International Conference on Digital Forensics* 194, 1–14. http://doi.org/10.1007/0-387-31163-7_1.

Beil, F., M. Ester and X. Xu. 2002. 'Frequent Term-Based Text Clustering'. The Eighth ACM SIGKDD International Conference, 436–442. New York: ACM. http://doi.org/10.1145/775047.775110.

Berk, R.A. 2004. 'An Introduction to Ensemble Methods for Data Analysis'. *Sociological Methods & Research* 34(3): 263–295. DOI: 10.1177/0049124105283119.

Berry, M., and G. Linoff. (1999). *Mastering Data Mining: The Art and Science of Customer Relationship Management*. New York: John Wiley & Sons.

Breck, E., and C. Cardie. 2017. 'Opinion Mining and Sentiment Analysis'. In R. Mitkov, ed., *Oxford Handbook of Computational Linguistics*, 2nd ed., 1–31. Oxford: Oxford University Press. http://doi.org/10.1093/oxfordhb/9780199573691.013.43.

Breiman, L. 1996. 'Bagging Predictors'. *Machine Learning* 26(2): 123–140.

Breiman, L. 1999 'Using Adaptive Bagging to Debias Regressions'. Technical Report 547, Statistics Department. Berkeley: University of California, Berkeley.

Breiman, L., J. H. Friedman, R. Olshen and C. J. Stone. 1984. *Classification and Regression Trees*. Monterey, CA: Wadsworth.

Carter, D.L. 2009. *Law Enforcement Intelligence: A Guide for State, Local, and Tribal Law Enforcement Agencies*, 2nd ed. Washington, DC: US Department of Justice, Office of Community Oriented Policing Services.

Chen, H., W. Chung, J.J. Xu, G. Wang, Y. Qin and M. Chau. 2004. 'Crime Data Mining: A General Framework and Some Examples'. *Computer* 37(4): 50–56.

Cherkassy, V., and F. Mulier. 2007. *Learning from Data: Concepts, Theory, and Methods*. Hoboken: John Wiley and Sons.

Compton, R., D. Jurgens and D. Allen. 2014. 'Geotagging One Hundred Million Twitter Accounts with Total Variation Minimization'. IEEE International Conference on Big Data, Washington, DC.

Dietterich, T.G. 1997. 'Machine Learning: Four Current Directions'. *AI Magazine* 18(4): 97–136

Dinh, S., T. Azeb, F. Fortin, D. Mouheb and M. Debbabi. 2015. 'Spam Campaign Detection, Analysis, and Investigation'. *Digital Investigation* 12, Supplement 1(0): S12–S21.

Domingos, P. 2007. 'Toward Knowledge-Rich Data Mining'. *Data Mining and Knowledge Discovery* 15(1): 21–28.

Edwards, M., A. Rashid and P. Rayson. 2015. 'A Systematic Survey of Online Data Mining Technology Intended for Law Enforcement'. *ACM Computing Surveys* 48(1). http://doi.org/10.1145/2811403.

Everitt, S., S. Landau, M. Leese and D. Stahl. 2011. *Cluster Analysis*, 5th ed. New York: John Wiley and Sons.

Fayyad, U., G. Piatetsky-Shapiro and P. Smyth. 1996. 'From Data Mining to Knowledge Discovery: An Overview'. In U. Fayyad, G. Piatetsky-Shapiro, P. Smyth, and R. Uthurusamy, eds., *Advances in Knowledge Discovery and Data Mining*, 1–36. Cambridge, MA: MIT Press.

Feldman, R., and I. Dagan. 1995. 'Knowledge Discovery in Textual Databases (KDT)'. In Proceedings of the First International Conference on Knowledge Discovery and Data Mining (KDD–95), Montreal, Canada, 20–21 August, 112–117. AAAI Press.

Feldman, R., and J. Sanger. 2007. *The Text Mining Handbook*. Cambridge: Cambridge University Press.

Freund, Y., and R.E. Schapire. 1996. 'Experiments with a New Boosting Algorithm'. In *Machine Learning: Proceedings of the Thirteenth International Conference*, 148–156.

Ghajar-Khosravi, S., P. Kwantes, N. Derbentseva and L. Huey. 2016. 'Quantifying Salient Concepts Discussed in Social Media Content: A Case Study Using Twitter Content Written by Radicalized Youth'. *Journal of Terrorism Research* 7(2): 79–90. http://doi.org/10.15664/jtr.1241.

Guerriere, M.R.J., and A.S. Detsky. 1991. 'Neural Networks: What Are They?' *Annals of Internal Medicine* 115(11): 906–07.

Han, J., and M. Kamber. 2006. *Data Mining: Concepts and Techniques*. 2nd ed. Burlington, MA: Morgan Kaufmann Publishers.

Han, J., M. Kamber and J. Pei. 2012. *Data Mining Concepts and Techniques*. 3rd ed. Burlington, MA: Morgan Kaufmann Publishers.

Han, J., J. Pei and Y. Yin. 2000. 'Mining Frequent Patterns without Candidate Generation'. *ACM Sigmod Record* 29(2): 1–12.

Han, J., J. Pei, Y. Yin and R. Mao. 2004. 'Mining Frequent Patterns without Candidate Generation: A Frequent-Pattern Tree Approach'. *Data Mining and Knowledge Discovery* 8(1): 53–87.

Hand, D., H. Mannila and P. Smith. 2001. *Principles of Data Mining*. Cambridge, MA: MIT Press.

Haykin, S.S. 1999. *Neural Networks: A Comprehensive Foundation*. Upper Saddle River, NJ: Prentice Hall.

Hennig, C., M. Meila, F. Murtagh and R. Rocci. 2016. *Handbook of Cluster Analysis*. Boca Raton: CRC Press.

Hornik, K., M. Stinchcombe and H. White. 1989. 'Multilayer Feed Forward Networks Are Universal Approximators'. *Neural Networks* 2(5): 359–366.

Larose, D.T., and C.D. Larose. 2014. *Discovering Knowledge in Data: An Introduction to Data Mining*. Hoboken: John Wiley & Sons.

Lewis, R.J. 2000. 'An Introduction to Classification and Regression Tree (CART) Analysis'. Presentation at the 2000 Annual Meeting of the Society for Academic Emergency Medicine in San Francisco, CA.

Liddy, E.D. 2001. 'Natural Language Processing'. In M.J. Bates and M.N. Maack, eds., *Encyclopedia of Library and Information Science*, 2nd ed. New York: Marcel Decker, Inc.

Marivate, V., and P. Moiloa. 2016. 'Catching Crime: Detection of Public Safety Incidents Using Social Media'. Pattern Recognition Association of South Africa and Robotics and Mechatronics International Conference (PRASA-RobMech), 2016.

McCulloch, W.S., and W. Pitts. 1943. 'A Logical Calculus of the Ideas Immanent in Nervous Activity'. *Bulletin of Mathematical Biophysics* 5 (1943): 115–133.

Milić-Frayling, N. 2005. 'Text Processing and Information Retrieval'. In A. Zanasi, ed., *Text Mining and Its Applications to Intelligence, CRM and Knowledge Management*, 1–45. Southhampton, UK: WIT Press. http://doi.org/10.2495/978-1-85312-995-7/01.

Mislove, A., S. Lehmann, Y.Y. Ahn and J.P. Onnela. 2011. 'Understanding the Demographics of Twitter Users'. Proceedings of the Fifth International AAAI Conference on Weblogs and Social Media.

Patel, N., and S. Upadhyay. 2012. 'Study of Various Decision Tree Pruning Methods with Their Empirical Comparison in WEKA'. *International Journal of Computer Applications* 60(12): 20–25.

Ribaux, O., A. Baylon, C. Roux, O. Delémont, E. Lock, C. Zingg and P. Margot. 2010. 'Intelligence-Led Crime Scene Processing. Part I: Forensic Intelligence'. *Forensic Science International* 195(1–3): 10–16. http://doi.org/10.1016/j.forsciint.2009.10.027.

Ribaux, O., F. Crispino, O. Délémont and C. Roux. 2016. 'The Progressive Opening of Forensic Science toward Criminological Concerns', *Security Journal* 29(4): 543–560. http://doi.org/10.1057/sj.2015.29.

Roiger, R.J., and W.M. Geatz. 2003. *Data Mining: A Tutorial-Based Primer*. Boston: Addison Wesley.

Rokach, L. 2010. 'Ensemble-Based Classifiers'. *Artificial Intelligence Review* 33(1): 1–39.

Rokach, L., and O. Maimon. 2015. *Data Mining with Decision Trees: Theory and Applications*, 2nd ed. Singapore: World Scientific Publishing.

Shmueli, G., N.R. Patel and P.C. Bruce. 2007. 'Data Mining for Business Intelligence: Concepts, Techniques, and Applications in Microsoft Office Excel with XLMiner'. *International Statistical Review* 75(2): 127–278. doi:10.1111/j.1751-5823.2007.00015_9.x.

Sobkowicz, P., and A. Sobkowicz. 2010. 'Dynamics of Hate Based Internet User Networks'. *The European Physical Journal B-Condensed Matter and Complex Systems* 73(4): 633–643.

Spielhofer, T., R. Greenlaw and D. Markham. 2016. 'Data Mining Twitter during the UK Floods: Investigating the Potential Use of Social Media in Emergency Management'. Third International Conference on Information and Communication Technologies for Disaster Management (ICT-DM), 1–6.

Steinbach, M., G. Karypis and V. Kumar. 2000. 'A Comparison of Document Clustering Techniques'. KDD Workshop on Text Mining, Sixth ACM SIGKDD International Conference on Knowledge Discovery and Data Mining, 20–23 August, Boston, MA.

Subba, R., and T. Bui. 2017. 'Online Convergence Behavior, Social Media Communications and Crisis Response: An Empirical Study of the 2015 Nepal Earthquake Police Twitter Project'. Proceedings of the 50th Hawaii International Conference on System Sciences.

Sumathi, S., and S.N. Sivanandam. 2006. *Introduction to Data Mining and Its Applications*. Berlin: Springer.

Sureka, A., P. Kumaraguru, A. Goyal and S. Chhabra. 2010. 'Mining YouTube to Discover Extremist Videos, Users and Hidden Communities'. In P.J. Cheng, M.Y. Kan, W. Lam and P. Nakov, eds., *Information Retrieval Technology Asia Information Retrieval Symposium*, 13–24. Springer Berlin Heidelberg.

Tan, A.H. 1999. 'Text Mining: The State of the Art and the Challenges'. Proceedings of the PAKDD 1999 Workshop on Knowledge Discovery from Advanced Databases, 65–70.

Tan, P., M. Steinbach and V. Kumar. 2005. *Introduction to Data Mining*. 1st ed. Boston: Addison Wesley Longman Publishing Co., Inc.

Twitter 2016. Best practices—Twitter Developers. https://dev.twitter.com/basics.

Tu, J.V. 1996. 'Advantages and Disadvantages of Using Artificial Neural Networks versus Logistic Regression for Predicting Medical Outcomes'. *Journal of Clinical Epidemiology* 49(11): 1225–1231.

Warner, B., and M. Misra. 1996. 'Understanding Neural Networks as Statistical Tools'. *The American Statistician* 50(4): 284–293.

Weimann, G. 2015. *Terrorism in Cyberspace: The Next Generation*. New York: Columbia University Press.

White H. 1989. 'Learning in Artificial Neural Networks: A Statistical Perspective'. *Neural Computation* 1(4): 425–464.

Witten, I., E. Frank, M. Hall and C. Pal. 2017. *Data Mining: Practical Machine Learning Tools and Techniques*, 4th ed. New York: Morgan Kaufmann.

Zhang, D., and L. Zhou. 2004. 'Discovering Golden Nuggets: Data Mining in Financial Application', *IEEE Transactions on Systems, Man and Cybernetics* 34(4): 513–522.

20

Online crime monitoring

David Décary-Hétu

Traces and offenders on the Internet

Online communities have been using computers and networking equipment since the 1970s. At first, the communities were mainly geared toward academic and military applications and allowed for the rapid dissemination of information (Salus and Vinton 1995). Access to online networks was restricted to a select few, given the scarcity of computer resources. As technology democratized in the 1980s, new types of communities emerged. These communities were much more open, in many cases granting access to anyone and everyone. They took on the forms of virtual bulletin boards (Aboba 1993; Parks and Floyd 1996) and allowed participants to phone in to remote computers to leave messages for one another and to exchange files. The networks that hosted these first-generation online communities were very slow compared to today's standards. Their speed was limited by the phone lines and modems they used, which were at first limited to 56 kpbs, about 0.1 percent of the speed of an average modern Internet connection (Speedtest 2016). These networks also had very limited concurrent connections, since each user needed to have an open phone line to connect to. Finally, the networks were expensive since some had subscriptions costs and were in different locales from their users who consequently had to pay long-distance charges for the duration of their call. These limits helped to push online community participants in the 1990s to a new type of network, the Internet. The Internet promised higher speeds, a greater number of concurrent connections on a single system and no long-distance charge when connecting to systems anywhere in the world.

Internet communities quickly grew in size and have taken many forms that can generally be classified into one of four groups. Discussion forums (Guzdial and Turns 2000) are asynchronous communication platforms akin to the old virtual bulletin boards. Users leave messages for each other and can exchange files. The forums keep a history of their participants' activities, which can be analyzed at a later date. Chat rooms (Décary-Hétu et al. 2014; Reid 1991) are similar to discussion forums in that they allow their participants to exchange messages and files but offer only synchronous communications. These communications are usually not stored, which means that participants who are away when a message is broadcast are unlikely to be able to read it later. Blogs (Boulos et al. 2006) are websites where authorized users can post messages. Other participants can comment on this information but are usually not able to post new information. Finally, online markets (Turban et al. 2009) are virtual marketplaces where one or more vendors can put up products and services for sale. Potential customers can compare ads and then select the product that best fits their need and the vendor with the most trustworthy history. Amazon and eBay are two examples of successful online markets that have endured the test of time.

Online communities make it easy for individuals to network with one another and to buy and sell products and services. The technologies they use are in many cases free and easy to learn, meaning that everyone can adapt them to their needs. It is therefore not surprising that past research has provided many examples of how all of the online communities' platforms, going back to the 1980s, were at some point adopted by offenders. Virtual bulletin board systems were very popular with phone phreaks who sought to manipulate the telephone networks and play tricks on one another (Meyer 1989). They were also an essential part of the intellectual property fraud community that sought to illegally share proprietary content such as movies and software for free (Tickle 1994). Later on, chat rooms were used extensively to share once again intellectual property such as music and movies (Cooper and Harrison 2001; Honick 2005). Many cases were also reported where chat rooms were used to buy and sell personal and financial information as well as malware (Benjamin et al. 2015; Franklin et al. 2007; McCarty 2003). Discussion forums were also used as online illicit markets where offenders could post ads for the illicit goods and services for sale and receive inquiries from potential customers (Décary-Hétu and Laferrière 2015). More recently, second-generation online illicit markets named cryptomarkets have appeared and offer the ability to buy and sell illicit goods and services with a high level of impunity (Martin 2014). These cryptomarkets take advantage of the Tor network, a subset of the Internet where the IP address of users and websites (their unique identifier online) is obfuscated using a series of anonymous relays. Tracking their connection and location is therefore very difficult. Cryptomarkets also make use of virtual currencies like bitcoin, which allow for instantaneous, international and anonymous transactions where all the parties involved are known only by a unique identifier that is hard to associate with a real identity.

The Internet and its online communities have provided offenders with many new opportunities and benefits. First, they have created new and international convergence settings where offenders can meet and share information (Soudijn and Zegers 2012). These have exposed offenders to the best practices of their peers and helped them to maximize their benefits while limiting their risks. The Internet, through its multiple online communities, also allowed for the creation of online markets which facilitate the sale of illicit goods and services (Décary-Hétu 2013). Cryptomarkets alone are believed to be facilitating the sale of hundreds of millions in US dollars of illicit goods and services per year and have shown just how big the underground economy has become (Soska and Christin 2015). The adaptation of offenders to the Internet may at first be seen as a challenge for regulators and law enforcement agencies. This chapter argues, however, that it also represents an opportunity for researchers who study offenders.

Indeed, no matter which community offenders are involved in, it is very likely that their activities will leave traces that can be collected at a later time. Most communities keep logs of their participants' activities for quality of service purposes or to ensure that they can deliver the service they promised. Discussion forums, for example, need to keep a copy of all of their members' messages if they are to provide them with a history of the forum activities. Additional information about members is also routinely collected. Discussion forums will often log the IP addresses of their members so that they can more effectively block the members who have been banned from the forum. Third parties also collect much of the information available in online communities. The Internet Archive (Internet Archive 2017) crawls the entire Internet, seeking to preserve a historical copy of its content. Doing so, it visits online communities that bring together offenders, and traces of their activities can therefore be collected there. The cache of web pages stored by the Google search engine provides an alternative means of accessing traces left by offenders online.

The aim of this chapter is to explore the research opportunities afforded by the Internet. To do so, this chapter will describe both the indirect and direct monitoring techniques used to monitor the traces offenders leave online. It will then provide examples of how these traces were used to better understand three types of offenders: those involved in prostitution, in financial fraud or in drug dealing. This chapter will conclude with a discussion of the challenges of collecting and analyzing traces online and the future developments we should expect from this field of research.

Indirect and direct online monitoring of traces on the Internet

To take advantage of the traces left online by offenders, indirect and direct monitoring techniques can be used. Indirect monitoring refers to the use of leaked documents posted on the Internet. While there are many reasons why documents may leak online (e.g., a non-secure server allowing Google to index confidential information), the most interesting leaks have so far been a result of the fierce competition between online offenders. Offenders may compete with each other online to prove their worth to others, for revenge and, perhaps more importantly, to take down competitors. Offenders who run online markets earn a commission on the sales that their platform facilitates (Christin 2013). They may also collect membership fees (Yip et al. 2013), a per-listing fee (Hutchings and Holt 2014) or fees for other services such as escrow services (Holt 2013). As such, offenders may have a vested interest in driving the sale of illicit goods and services toward their platform to increase their commissions. One way to achieve this is to destroy competitors' reputations by hacking them and distributing the confidential information of their communities' participants online (Poulsen 2012). Such actions have led to the publication of backups of databases of online forums and customers lists that contain a wide array of information on offenders (Motoyama et al. 2011). These leaks can contain gigabytes of information and include public and private messages, email addresses, IP addresses and passwords. In other cases, offenders use a more targeted attack, also called doxing, which is the act of divulging the identity of an individual online (Leong and Morando 2015). The information leaked in those cases is much smaller but may provide very detailed reports on the characteristics and identity of offenders.

Indirect monitoring is time sensitive. Leaks are often short-lived and posted on websites that may not remain online for long. It is therefore difficult to find files that were leaked years or even months in the past. Constantly monitoring the Internet for leaks is therefore essential to collecting traces on offenders. Researchers should build online sentinel software that looks for keywords in online forums, specialized blogs and social media networks. Further information could also be gleaned from security podcasts, which often review important leaks. Indirect monitoring can be used to extract information from third parties that collect data on the Internet in general. Search engines and the Internet Archive, for example, constantly crawl the open Internet, looking for content to index and store. Such repositories can be used to extract information from offenders without ever getting in direct contact with them. This approach has the added benefit of stealth and limiting the exposure of researchers. There have been cases when online offenders have sought to strike back at researchers who published too much information about them (Krebs 2016), and adding this layer of abstraction between the researcher and the offenders may help to protect the former from retaliation (see Barratt and Maddox [2016] for further discussion on this topic).

Rather than wait and hope to find interesting leaks, researchers can adopt a more proactive stance and monitor the online activities of offenders themselves (Décary-Hétu and Aldridge 2015). The technology used to conduct such monitoring will vary depending on the platforms that need to be monitored. Chat rooms have been monitored in the past using automated systems but have proven to be challenging (Décary-Hétu et al. 2014), since the most interesting discussions and activities happen in password-protected chat rooms. Many chat rooms also tend to ban users who do not actively participate in the activities of the community either by posting messages or buying and selling goods and services. This active participation is often prohibited by ethics review, and the obstacles to maintaining a stealth presence on chat rooms may explain the scant research that has been published using chat rooms as data sources. Much more research has used the mirroring technique, which uses a software package to collect web pages (Aldridge and Décary-Hétu 2016; Chen 2011; Soska and Christin 2015; Westlake et al. 2012). The software is a two-stage process that starts with a crawler robot that connects to a server and downloads a web page. Once downloaded, the robot stores the web page for later and extracts from it all of the hyperlinks. It then requests each hyperlink, looking for more links to put in its download queue. This process is repeated iteratively until the download queue is empty. At that point, the software switches to its scraper robot, which goes through each of the downloaded pages, looking for specific information.[1] Researchers have to teach the scraper robot what to look for and to store the information it has extracted in structured databases. The speed at which information can be collected will vary depending on the available resources, but a simple crawler robot can easily download hundreds of pages per minute.

A small portion of the Internet is indexed by search engines and easily reachable, simply by tapping a URL in a browser (Bindal and Muktawat 2010). Most crawlers share the same limit and are unable to reach the deep web and darknet. The deep web is the part of the Internet that is protected by access control systems. It includes, for example, the salary information of companies, information deemed confidential. Some of the deep net can be accessed by registering accounts on websites and then passing the credentials to the crawler so that it can index the content protected by the login page. However, this requires a more sophisticated crawler that may be more difficult to design. Many login forms are also protected by CAPTCHAs and questions that are difficult to answer via automated crawlers. These can, however, be bypassed through the use of grey market commercial services that employ thousands of humans paid a few pennies to solve the CAPTCHAs and the questions (Petsas et al. 2015). The darknet is a subset of the deep web and refers to the section of the Internet that requires that all communications be encrypted. The darknet is most commonly known for hosting the Tor network but also encompasses other networks such as the I2P network and the Freenet network (Conrad and Shirazi 2014). Crawlers can be configured to index the content of websites hosted on the darknet relatively easily, but discovering websites to crawl may be more difficult. Mainstream search engines have mostly stayed away from the darknet websites for now and some queries that take advantage of the TOR2WEB bridge to the Tor network may return some results by using search terms like 'site:onion.link illicit content'. Some Tor-specific search engines can also be found, but their reliability is still mostly unknown. Researchers will therefore need to build a list of websites without much help from traditional search tools and look at discussion forums, blogs and social network posts.

Social networks like Facebook, Twitter, Instagram and Snapchat are also themselves very rich sources of data for researchers and need be indexed actively, as leaks are few and far between. With its 1.6 billion users (Adler 2016), Facebook is without contest the largest social network service, and Americans spend on average five hours a week on social networks in general (Mosendz 2017). Given the proportion of the world population that uses social networks, it is to be expected that offenders will also use social networks, to target victims and to post messages about themselves. Social networks have become very adept at detecting crawlers and blocking them from indexing their content. They do, however, offer access to their data servers through their application programming interfaces (APIs). APIs are formalized rules that guide how researchers can access information from social networks (Graham 2008). They commonly limit what information can be collected and the number of requests that can be made on a daily or hourly basis. Some social networks like Twitter are known for their very open APIs, while others like Instagram impose very strict limits on what can be collected through their APIs as well as who is able to access them. Many social networks are open to commercial contracts where researchers can negotiate for an enhanced access to the social networks data in exchange for money or other compensation.

The direct monitoring of offenders online requires a level of computer technical skills that most researchers outside the computer science world are unlikely to have. Many commercial services have been launched to help these researchers—although they mostly focus on corporate customers—to actively monitor online activities (see, for example, Import.io [2017]; Scraping Hub [2017]) and Web Scraper [2017]). These commercial services are costly and will still require that the researchers invest serious resources into the cleaning and formatting of the data they collect.

Exploiting traces collected on the Internet

Given the costs of hiring commercial services to actively monitor offenders online, researchers may also resort to collecting their data by hand, building their databases one web page at a time. This is the technique that Holt and his team (Blevins and Holt 2009; Holt and Blevins 2007; Holt et al. 2008, 2014) opted to use when monitoring the online activities of sex workers and their johns. Most work focusing on prostitution had up to then used police data and interviews to understand the motivation, practices and business of prostitution. There are well-known limits to using police data, since they are severely affected by the dark figure of crimes, an issue even more prevalent with consensual offences (MacDonald 2002). Interviews are for their part likely to be limited in size and scope and are therefore unlikely to provide a generalized understanding of prostitution. Turning to the online monitoring of offenders allows for access to untainted data, since johns and sex workers communicating online are unlikely to change how they talk and behave based on the remote possibility that their messages may at some point be used as research material. Of course, not all actors involved in prostitution will use the Internet to communicate, but given the pervasiveness of computer-mediated communications in everyday lives, it is likely that a fair share of actors will at some point be caught in online monitoring of their activities. Using this monitoring, Holt found that discussion forums actually played an important role in finding sex workers through their online ads and references from other johns. These johns used argot to communicate with one another, which created a somewhat hermetic community around them, insulating them from unknown actors and, to a certain extent, law enforcement officers. Risk management is a big concern for johns given the reputational—and criminal—risks associated with hiring sex workers. Many online discussions would deal with the regulating operations of law enforcement agencies and the identification of fake ads trying to lure johns to law enforcement officers posing as sex workers. Online monitoring gave Holt and his team a view into the adaptation of johns and the techniques they used to displace their activities and reduce their risks. These techniques also applied to sex workers themselves, who sometimes opted to steal from and assault their clients.

Dubrawski et al. (2015) have suggested that it is possible to monitor sex workers online and that this monitoring can generate interesting results. Dubrawski et al. collected massive numbers of sex workers' online ads and identified predictors of listings that could feature trafficked women. Contact information of sex workers can also be used to build networks of providers of sex services online, leading to better intelligence about the state of the industry. Alvari et al.

(2016) and Nagpal et al. (2016) also provide support for using machine learning to identify sex workers' ads potentially linked to human trafficking, although all research stops short of actually contacting the sex workers to confirm whether or not they are victims of human trafficking. This represents an interesting vector for forensic science to identify ads of interest and for criminologists to build on this research to find research subjects.

An important perk of using the online monitoring of offenders is that researchers can glean a direct understanding of offenders from the point of view of offenders themselves. This was the case for sex workers and it is also the case for financial fraud. Financial fraudsters are still using physical means such as mail theft to steal credit cards and make purchases in stores that are later resold on the Internet (Peretti 2008). Fraudsters have also, however, moved to the Internet to steal financial information (Décary-Hétu and Leppänen 2013). This can be achieved through a number of means including hacking payment processing systems and luring unsuspecting users to fake websites that steal their bank credentials (Gomzin 2014; James 2005). Offenders involved in the theft of financial information are in large part unwilling or unable to monetize this information and instead opt to sell the information to other fraudsters who have mastered the art of monetizing stolen financial information. This can be achieved by printing fake credit cards and making in-store purchases, which are later refunded for cash or more commonly resold online (Meijerink 2013). Another technique used is to make online purchases and once again have the goods resold online (Hutchings and Holt 2014). To bring these two types of financial fraudsters together, online markets were launched, first on discussion forums and in chat rooms and later on cryptomarkets. Past research has shown that very large communities with thousands of financial fraudsters could be found online (Motoyama et al. 2011). They are hosted on online markets that facilitate the sale of financial information and its subsequent monetization, first by matching vendors and customers, and second by sharing the best practices developed by offenders. Fraudsters looking to buy financial information can look at the past history of vendors, including the feedback from past customers, to determine the trustworthiness of vendors (Yip et al. 2013). Prices can also be easily compared to find the right product at the right price. There appear to be very large quantities of financial information for sale on online markets and its price appears to be low, with the price of a single credit card number at less than $10. Some researchers believe that these large quantities of financial information are finding buyers and that the impact of financial fraudsters on the financial system is significant (Holt et al. 2016). Others have argued that the low price for the financial information is indicative of its low value and that much of the information available on online markets is either fake—and therefore of no value—or never sold (Herley and Florêncio 2010). The impact of financial fraud would therefore be much lower.

Large-scale datasets have also been collected on a new and innovative use of online markets to sell illicit drugs (Aldridge and Décary-Hétu 2016; Soska and Christin 2015). These sales are mostly concentrated on cryptomarkets where dealers put up listings for specific amounts of drugs. Customers can once again study the history of dealers and compare prices (Martin 2014). The drugs are shipped stealthily through the mail to the customer, who is unlikely to be arrested as long as she purchases from dealers who are located in the same country as she is. Parcel inspections are indeed unlikely when the parcel does not cross national borders. Many researchers have sought to understand the displacement of drug dealing from the physical to the virtual world by monitoring the online activities of drug dealers and drug users. Their research has indicated that the size and scope of cryptomarkets has vastly increased over the past few years, with annual sales ranging now in the hundreds of millions of dollars (Soska and Christin 2015). Cryptomarkets now facilitate the sale of hundreds of types of drugs with dozens of countries being involved in their sale (Kruithof et al. 2016). Major Western countries like the United States of America, the United Kingdom and the Netherlands are major suppliers of drugs online.

While most listings are intended either for drug users or social suppliers, many listings are also geared toward other drug dealers who may be looking to source their stock online. Aldridge and Décary-Hétu (2016) found that such dealers generated a significant portion of revenues and that cryptomarkets were to some extent business-to-business platforms. The direct online monitoring of offenders has therefore allowed researchers to understand the size and scope of online drug dealing. It has also allowed for the understanding of the impact of police operations on drug markets (Décary-Hétu and Giommoni 2016; Van Buskirk et al. 2017). In line with past research on traditional drug markets, cryptomarket research found that the police operations had little impact on the drug dealing activities and that targeting the cryptomarkets themselves without making dealer arrests simply disrupted the dealers' activities for a limited period of time. While not surprising, the results based on cryptomarket data offers a much more conclusive picture of the impact of police operations by analyzing all of the drug market activities rather than a subset generated through select interviews of drug dealers and drug users. There are, finally, many more examples of physical and digital traces that can be collected on cryptomarkets (see Rossy and Décary-Hétu, chapter 21, this volume). These include using the PGP keys of vendors to link their accounts together across cryptomarkets and the analysis of physical drugs bought on cryptomarkets.

Challenges and future developments

Forensic science focuses on the study of traces that are generated through criminal activities. The online monitoring of offenders, both indirect and direct, offers arguably one of the most interesting opportunities for criminologists and forensic scientists to collaborate with one another. Forensic scientists are increasingly developing their expertise in the collection and analysis of digital traces. These traces can either be artefacts of a user on a desktop computer or traces left by offenders on the Internet. With their hard science background, forensic scientists have already developed some of the skills and methodology necessary for the collection of online traces. Criminologists, on the other end, have developed methods and research design to understand offending behaviour even when very limited data were available. This was the case for sex worker research that had to be based on interviews and police data reports. Through online monitoring, criminologists are likely to gain a much deeper insight into offending trajectories including who offenders are, how they become offenders, how they operate and how they desist from crime. Using data collected by forensic scientists, criminologists may be able to answer—or shine a new light on—questions that have plagued criminology for quite some time.

A major challenge for forensic scientists and criminologists will be to find a way to manage the massive amount of traces that offenders generate every day. On cryptomarkets alone, thousands of offenders offer hundreds of thousands of products and services on a daily basis (Kruithof et al. 2016). These generate thousands of sales every day. Collecting and managing this information will require important investments in computer equipment but also the development of optimizing strategies to store and search all of this information. Another concern is with the validity of the data that is collected. It is easy, for example, for cryptomarket administrators to generate fake reviews to make potential customers believe that their cryptomarket is very active when that is not the case. Researchers who use the feedback as proxies for the level of activity of cryptomarkets may falsely claim that a cryptomarket is gaining traction when, in fact, the activity is only a mirage designed by the cryptomarket administrators. Much effort will also need to be invested in the cleaning, structuring and validation of the data as debates have already started about the validity of certain data collection efforts (Munksgaard et al. 2016).

One strategy to validate information may be to use a small data approach rather than a big data approach. The online monitoring of offenders can generate very rich datasets where offenders post long and detailed messages about their experience. By concentrating on more qualitative analyses, researchers are likely to be better able to detect suspect postings and to discard them from their research. They are also more likely to derive generalizable results through effective sampling of the massive amount of information that is collected. Big data quantitative analyses will of course be needed, if only to measure the size and scope of the online offending communities. But the focus of research should perhaps stay on small and more detailed analyses rather than bulk analyses.

Another challenge for researchers will be to gain access to the deep web and darknet. Much of the Internet's information is located in the deep web and darknet and these have remained largely untouched by researchers so far. Netnographies (Kozinets 2010)—ethnographies that use the Internet—can help researchers gain acceptance within offenders' communities and thereafter access more private sections. But these actions will take time and only deliver results in the long term. Ethics review boards strictly control how information can be collected online, and the hacking of closed communities is still rightly out of reach of researchers. As such, researchers should be cautious when seeking to publish generalizable results. It is also very likely that more professional offenders are communicating with each other over private channels that are difficult for researchers to monitor. The offenders that are commonly included in studies may therefore be considered amateurs rather than established professional offenders.

Social networks sites like Facebook and Snapchat will also represent a major challenge for researchers. While many of them offer access to their data through APIs, some do not, and others limit the speed at which information can be gathered. It would be interesting, for example, to evaluate the risk of identity theft of citizens in a given country by downloading, for all of the citizens, the available personal identifiable information they have posted on social networks. Such an experiment would likely require that millions of requests be made to a social networks' API and, with the current rate limiting of APIs, this data collection could take decades to complete. As individuals move more and more of their life online (and to social networks), gaining access to social networks will be a challenge that researchers need to address. At this point, examples of collaboration between researchers and social network sites are rare.

Moving forward, researchers will need to address the representativeness of online offenders. This chapter argues that crime is transitioning more and more to the Internet but such crime will likely never replace crime in the physical world. Indeed, some forms of violence, for example, can only occur in the physical world. Still, online harassers and threat makers do use the Internet, and thus some broad knowledge about violence could still be gleaned through the online monitoring of offenders. To what extent this knowledge would apply to offline offenders is still unknown, however. Exploring this question should be included in future research designs.

A non-exhaustive study of the programs of major forensic and criminological association conferences shows that the online monitoring of offenders is still a data collection method that is seldom used in either discipline. This chapter has highlighted the potential of this method using three case studies where the online monitoring of offenders led to interesting and innovative research. The lack of enthusiasm for the online monitoring of offenders could be explained by the computer skills that are needed to build data collection infrastructures. These often require large investments in economic and human resources to design, launch and run. Commercial services are available to help those that lack the proper computer skills, but their existence is still a well-kept secret in the research field. Researchers may also lack the background necessary to formulate problems and to evaluate the quality of the propositions of commercial services. The aim of this chapter has been to provide an overview of how online monitoring of offenders could be achieved and to demonstrate its ability to push back the limits both of forensic science and criminology. As the Internet becomes more and more ingrained in all our lives, the online monitoring of offenders is likely to become an essential part of both forensic science and criminology.

Note

1 Some software scrape the content at the same time as it is downloaded. Whether the scraping work happens later or not does not impact the speed of the data collection.

References

Aboba, B. 1993. *The Online User's Encyclopedia: Bulletin Boards and Beyond*. Boston: Addison-Wesley.

Adler, E. 2016. 'Social Media Engagement: The Surprising Facts about How Much Time People Spend on the Major Social Networks'. *Business Insider*. www.businessinsider.com/social-media-engagement-statistics-2013-12.

Aldridge, J., and D. Décary-Hétu. 2016. 'Hidden Wholesale: The Drug Diffusing Capacity of Online Drug Cryptomarkets'. *International Journal of Drug Policy* 35(September): 7–15.

Alvari, H., P. Shakarian and J.K. Snyder. 2016. 'A Non-Parametric Learning Approach to Identify Online Human Trafficking'. In 2016 IEEE Conference on Intelligence and Security Informatics (ISI), Tucson, AZ: 133–138.

Barratt, M.J., and A. Maddox. 2016. 'Active Engagement with Stigmatised Communities through Digital Ethnography'. *Qualitative Research* 16(6): 701–719.

Benjamin, V., W. Li, T. Holt and H. Chen. 2015. 'Exploring Threats and Vulnerabilities in Hacker Web: Forums, IRC and Carding Shops'. Paper presented at the Intelligence and Security Informatics (ISI), 2015 IEEE International Conference, Baltimore, MD.

Bindal, S., and H.S. Muktawat. 2010. *Deep Web*. Online: www.researchgate.net/publication/261773660_Deep_Web.

Blevins, K.R., and T.J. Holt. 2009. 'Examining the Virtual Subculture of Johns'. *Journal of Contemporary Ethnography* 38(5): 619–648.

Boulos, M.N.K., I. Maramba and S. Wheeler. 2006. 'Wikis, Blogs and Podcasts: A New Generation of Web-Based Tools for Virtual Collaborative Clinical Practice and Education'. *BMC Medical Education* 6(1): 41.

Chen, H. 2011. *Dark Web: Exploring and Data Mining the Dark Side of the Web*. Vol. 30. New York: Springer Science & Business Media.

Christin, N. 2013. 'Traveling the Silk Road: A Measurement Analysis of a Large Anonymous Online Marketplace'. Paper presented at the Proceedings of the 22nd International Conference on the World Wide Web, Rio de Janeiro.

Conrad, B., and F. Shirazi. 2014. 'A Survey on Tor and I2P'. Paper presented at the Ninth International Conference on Internet Monitoring and Protection (ICIMP2014), Paris.

Cooper, J., and D.M. Harrison. 2001. 'The Social Organization of Audio Piracy on the Internet'. *Media, Culture & Society* 23(1): 71–89.

Décary-Hétu, D. 2013. 'Le capital virtuel: entre compétition, survie et réputation'. PhD Diss., Université de Montréal.

Décary-Hétu, D., and J. Aldridge. 2015. 'Sifting through the Net: Monitoring of Online Offenders by Researchers'. *European Review of Organised Crime* 2(2): 122–141.

Décary-Hétu, D., B. Dupont and F. Fortin. 2014. 'Policing the Hackers by Hacking Them: Studying Online Deviants in IRC Chat Rooms'. In A.J. Masys, ed., *Networks and Network Analysis for Defence and Security*, 63–82. New York: Springer.

Décary-Hétu, D., and L. Giommoni. 2016. 'Do Police Crackdowns Disrupt Drug Cryptomarkets? A Longitudinal Analysis of the Effects of Operation Ononymous'. *Crime, Law and Social Change* 67(1): 55–75.

Décary-Hétu, D., and D. Laferrière. 2015. 'Discrediting Vendors in Online Criminal Markets: Disrupting Criminal Networks'. In A. Malm and G. Bichler, eds., *Disrupting Criminal Networks: Network Analysis in Crime Prevention*, 129–152. Boulder: Lynne Reinner.

Décary-Hétu, D., and A. Leppänen. 2013. 'Criminals and Signals: An Assessment of Criminal Performance in the Carding Underworld'. *Security Journal* 29(3): 442–460.

Dubrawski, A., K. Miller and M. Barnes. 2015. 'Leveraging Publicly Available Data to Discern Patterns of Human-Trafficking Activity'. *Journal of Human Trafficking* 1(1): 65–85.

Franklin, J., A. Perrig, V. Paxson and S. Savage. 2007. 'An Inquiry into the Nature and Causes of the Wealth of Internet Miscreants'. Paper presented at the ACM Conference on Computer and Communications Security, Chicago.

Gomzin, S. 2014. *Hacking Point of Sale: Payment Application Secrets, Threats, and Solutions*. Indianapolis: John Wiley & Sons.

Graham, W. 2008. *Facebook API Developers Guide*. New York: Infobase Publishing.

Guzdial, M., and J. Turns. 2000. 'Effective Discussion through a Computer-Mediated Anchored Forum'. *The Journal of the Learning Sciences* 9(4): 437–469.

Herley, C., and D. Florêncio. 2010. 'Nobody Sells Gold for the Price of Silver: Dishonesty, Uncertainty and the Underground Economy'. In T. Moore, D. Pym and C. Ioannidis, eds., *Economics of Information Security and Privacy*, 33–53. New York: Springer.

Holt, T.J. 2013. 'Exploring the Social Organisation and Structure of Stolen Data Markets'. *Global Crime* 14(2–3): 155–174.

Holt, T.J., and K.R. Blevins. 2007. 'Examining Sex Work from the Client's Perspective: Assessing Johns Using On-Line Data'. *Deviant Behavior* 28(4): 333–354.

Holt, T.J., K.R. Blevins and J.B. Kuhns. 2008. 'Examining the Displacement Practices of Johns with On-Line Data'. *Journal of Criminal Justice* 36(6): 522–528.

Holt, T.J., K.R. Blevins, and J.B. Kuhns. 2014. 'Examining Diffusion and Arrest Avoidance Practices among Johns'. *Crime & Delinquency* 60(2): 261-283.

Holt, T.J., O. Smirnova and Y.-T. Chua. 2016. *Data Thieves in Action: Examining the International Market for Stolen Personal Information*. New York: Springer.

Honick, R. 2005. *Software Piracy Exposed*. Sebastopol, CA: Syngress.

Hutchings, A. and T.J. Holt. 2014. 'A Crime Script Analysis of the Online Stolen Data Market'. *British Journal of Criminology* 55(3): 596–614.

Import.io. 2017. Import.io. www.import.io/.

Internet Archive. 2017. Wayback Machine. https://archive.org/web/.

James, L. 2005. *Phishing Exposed*. Sebastopol, CA: Syngress.

Kozinets, R.V. 2010. *Netnography: Doing Ethnographic Research Online*. London: Sage Publications.

Krebs, B. 2016. 'Mir Islam—the Guy the Govt Says Swatted My Home—to Be Sentenced June 22'. https://krebsonsecurity.com/2016/06/mir-islam-the-guy-the-govt-says-swatted-my-home-to-be-sentenced-june-22/.

Kruithof, K., J. Aldridge, D. Décary-Hétu, M. Sim, E. Dujso and S. Hoorens. 2016. *Internet-Facilitated Drugs Trade: An Analysis of the Size, Scope and the Role of the Netherlands*. Cambridge: Rand Corporation.

Leong, N., and J. Morando. 2015. 'Communication in Cyberspace'. *North Carolina Law Review* 94(1): 105–159.

MacDonald, Z. 2002. 'Official Crime Statistics: Their Use and Interpretation'. *The Economic Journal* 112(477): F85–F106

Martin, J. 2014. 'Lost on the Silk Road: Online Drug Distribution and the "Cryptomarket."' *Criminology and Criminal Justice* 14(3): 351–367.

McCarty, B. 2003. 'Automated Identity Theft'. *IEEE Security & Privacy* 99(5): 89–92.

Meijerink, T.J. 2013. 'Carding: Crime Prevention Analysis'. PhD. diss., University of Twente, The Netherlands.

Meyer, G.R. 1989. 'The Social Organization of the Computer Underground'. MA thesis, Northern Illinois University, DeKalb..

Mosendz, P. 2017. 'Middle-Aged Americans Beat Millennials in Time Spent on Social Media'. *Bloomberg*. www.bloomberg.com/news/articles/2017-01-25/middle-aged-americans-beat-millennials-in-time-spent-on-social-media.

Motoyama, M., D. McCoy, K. Levchenko, S. Savage and G.M. Voelker. 2011. 'An Analysis of Underground Forums'. Paper presented at the Proceedings of the 2011 ACM SIGCOMM Conference on Internet Measurement, Berlin.

Munksgaard, R., J. Demant and G. Branwen. 2016. 'A Replication and Methodological Critique of the Study "Evaluating Drug Trafficking on the Tor Network"'. *International Journal of Drug Policy* 35: 92–96.

Nagpal, C., K. Miller, B. Boeking and A. Dubrawski. 2016. 'An EntityResolution Approach to Isolate Instances of Human Trafficking Online'. *arXiv preprint arXiv*:1509.06659.

Parks, M.R., and K. Floyd. 1996. 'Making Friends in Cyberspace'. *Journal of Communication* 46(1): 80–97.

Peretti, K.K. 2008. 'Data Breaches: What the Underground World of Carding Reveals'. *Santa Clara High Technology Law Journal* 25(2): 375–413.

Petsas, T., G. Tsirantonakis, E. Athanasopoulos and S. Ioannidis. 2015. 'Two-Factor Authentication: Is the World Ready?: Quantifying 2FA Adoption'. Paper presented at the Proceedings of the Eighth European Workshop on System Security, Bordeaux.

Poulsen, K. 2012. *Kingpin: How One Hacker Took Over the Billion-Dollar Cybercrime Underground*. New York: Random House Digital, Inc.

Reid, E. 1991. 'Electropolis: Communication and Community on Internet Relay Chat'. PhD diss., University of Melbourne.

Salus, P.H., and G. Vinton. 1995. *Casting the Net: From ARPANET to Internet and Beyond*. Boston: Addison-Wesley Longman Publishing Co., Inc.

Scraping Hub. 2017. Scraping Hub. https://scrapinghub.com/.

Soska, K., and N. Christin. 2015. 'Measuring the Longitudinal Evolution of the Online Anonymous Marketplace Ecosystem'. Paper presented at the USENIX Security Conference, Washington, DC.

Soudijn, M.R., and B.C.T. Zegers. 2012. 'Cybercrime and Virtual Offender Convergence Settings'. *Trends in Organized Crime* 15(2–3): 111–129.

Speedtest. 2016. Speedtest® Market Report. www.speedtest.net/reports/united-states/.

Tickle, K. 1994. 'The Vicarious Liability of Electronic Bulletin Board Operators for the Copyright Infringement Occuring on Their Bulletin Boards'. *Iowa Law Review* 80(2): 391–418.

Turban, E., J.K. Lee, D. King, T.P. Liang and D. Turban. 2009. *Electronic Commerce 2010*. Upper Saddle River, NJ: Prentice Hall Press.

Van Buskirk, J., R. Bruno, T. Dobbins, C. Breen, L. Burns, S. Naicker and A. Roxburgh. 2017. 'The Recovery of Online Drug Markets Following Law Enforcement and Other Disruptions'. *Drug and Alcohol Dependence* 173: 159–162.

Web Scraper. 2017. Web Scraper. http://webscraper.io/.

Westlake, B., M. Bouchard and R. Frank. 2012. 'Comparing Methods for Detecting Child Exploitation Content Online'. Paper presented at the Intelligence and Security Informatics Conference (EISIC), Odense, Denmark.

Yip, M., C. Webber and N. Shadbolt. 2013. 'Trust among Cybercriminals? Carding Forums, Uncertainty and Implications for Policing'. *Policing and Society* 23(4): 516–539.

21

Internet traces and the analysis of online illicit markets

Quentin Rossy and David Décary-Hétu

From behaviour crime systems to virtual convergence settings

Aristotle is believed to be the first to have said that 'man is by nature a social animal' (Vinciarelli et al. 2012). The social nature of all things related to humanity has unsurprisingly also been identified and studied in much of the past research on crime. Sutherland (1947), for example, through his differential association theory, argued that crime is a behaviour that is learned through contact with others. Repeated and intimate contact with offending others may turn certain individuals into offenders through exposure to unfavourable definitions of laws and social norms. Other researchers have since followed in Sutherland's footsteps (Bandura 1971; Akers et al. 1979) and offered a revised social learning theory that focuses on learning behaviours from others through contact with them but also through observation and reinforcements and punishments.

A perhaps even more important contribution of Sutherland to criminology comes from his behaviour crime systems theory, which focuses on the macro interactions of offenders (Tremblay 2010). Sutherland (1947) argues that offenders should be categorized, for research purposes, in very small but homogeneous sociological units called behaviour crime systems. These systems are built around a very specific type of offence such as confidence fraud or theft. The legal definitions of offences are of no use to Sutherland as they are broad and encompass many types of offenders. Indeed, kidnappers can target their victims for political gains, money or even revenge in the case of intra-family kidnappings. These different motivations can be found in kidnappers of different types who have very little in common. Sutherland (1947) surmises that to understand crime, it is necessary to drill down to the core of each type of offence and study the offenders who are involved in it as a unit. These offenders likely share with each other a group way of life, motivations, tools and techniques. They also likely share a sense of belonging with their peers as well as many rationalizations. Of the utmost importance to participants in behaviour crime systems are their 'convergence settings' (Felson 2003) where they can meet and debate the best offending practices for maximizing benefits and minimizing risks. Traditionally, these convergence settings were often local bars and resorts attended by offenders and their social relations.

Behaviour crime system theory, although understudied (Tremblay 2010), makes a significant contribution to the field of criminology and crime sciences in general by highlighting the presence and the need for convergence settings. In our modern connected world, these convergence settings have moved on past local bars and resorts and are now hosted on the

Internet (Soudijn and Zegers 2012). These now virtual settings were at first meeting spaces like newsgroups and bulletin board systems (BBS) where offenders could meet and share information and electronic tools (Meyer 1989). Their functionalities were very limited, allowing only for the sending of public and private messages and the sharing of computer files. As computer-mediated communications evolved, so did the convergence settings, which moved from newsgroups and BBS to the open World Wide Web. Convergence settings have evolved toward synchronous communication channels hosted in online chat rooms that have the benefit of not storing any messages for later review. All participants have to be online at the time of broadcast to capture messages (Décary-Hétu et al. 2014). They've also evolved toward asynchronous communication channels hosted on online forums where participants can build personal profiles and interact with others both publicly and privately (Holt 2007). Both synchronous and asynchronous communications also integrate the ability to share files.

The size and scope of virtual convergence settings are believed to vary greatly from a single-digit number of participants for private and exclusive settings to hundreds of thousands of participants for the largest, public settings. Participants will take on many roles and normally follow the Internet 1 percent rule (van Mierlo 2014). This rule states that about 90 percent of participants will only view content while about 9 percent will very occasionally edit or create content and about 1 percent will be responsible for the bulk of content creation.

Online illicit markets as virtual convergence settings

In addition to helping offenders share their best practices, tools and techniques, virtual convergence settings have over the past decades slid toward becoming online commodity markets (Holt and Lampke 2010; Motoyama et al. 2011; Décary-Hétu and Leppänen 2016). These online illicit markets allow offenders to buy and sell illicit goods and services rather than share them for free. Buyers and sellers can put up listings for what they are looking to buy, rent or sell along with a description and a price. These listings can be browsed and out-of-band channels can be used to negotiate a price. Online illicit markets were at first specialized in virtual goods and services, mostly financial fraud, intellectual property fraud and computer fraud (Kruithof et al. 2016). These had the benefit of being virtual, meaning that offenders did not have to commit at any point in time to a connection with the physical world. More recently, online illicit markets have grown to encompass the sale of physical goods, which are shipped through the mail (Christin 2013). Offenders have become quite skilled at hiding their products in innocuous packages that can evade inspections by law enforcement and mail services (Rhumorbarbe et al. 2016; Aldridge and Askew 2017).

Online illicit markets can be classified in two groups: dedicated websites and online communities. The former includes online shops created and hosted by sellers. Most of the dedicated websites, which are mainly oriented to the sale of counterfeit goods and pharmacy, are organized in 'affiliate programs', where affiliate websites advertise and redirect the client to a main shopping website that provides products (Levchenko et al. 2011; Kanich et al. 2011). Online communities are shared settings where sellers may integrate their shops or their listings within a predefined marketplace that may be known to support legal trade (e.g., eBay) or to be focused on the trade of illicit goods and services (e.g., cryptomarkets on Tor). The annual sales facilitated by cryptomarkets, a small subset of all online illicit markets, are believed to be in the range of hundreds of millions of US dollars per year (Soska and Christin 2015; Kruithof et al. 2016). Online communities that host the sale of illicit goods and services also include crowdfunding services, which have been used to promote the development of goods that will never be produced (Fredman 2015). Promoters may also present their product as innovative and new but in reality, their product may simply be already available counterfeit goods that are produced and sold after the crowdfunding campaign. Peer-to-peer applications are another setting used by sellers of illicit goods and services. OpenBazaar,[1] for instance, is a peer-to-peer bitcoin marketplace where illicit trade seems to have emerged.[2] Illicit markets are also moving to mobile applications such as Wish where counterfeit goods are plentiful, and to anonymous messaging applications like Whisper. As far as we know, no dedicated illicit shop application is available on mobile devices, apart from the misuse of applications dedicated to the selling of medical marijuana (e.g., Nestdrop).

To help buyers evaluate the trustworthiness of sellers, review sites have been launched so that buyers can share experiences and rate sellers. These sites take on the form of dedicated websites such as blogs or of online communities (e.g., boards and forums). Instant messages on a direct peer-to-peer app such as Skype or asynchronous messaging applications such as Whatsapp or emails may also be used. The sustained analysis of review convergence settings may feed qualitative research (Van Hout and Hearne 2017) and the reconstruction of social networks of actors involved in online illicit markets (Décary-Hétu and Laferrière 2015). Review sites can also feed intelligence-led screening strategies to detect new online illicit markets (Pineau et al. 2016).

In synergy with the trends affecting licit businesses, illicit markets have been transformed by their online setting, which impacts the promotion strategies, the sales process, the sharing of feedback and the communications between buyers and sellers (Holt et al. 2016). To reach potential customers, sellers tend to use one of two techniques. They may first try to impose themselves into their potential customers' online space. This can be achieved through the use of massive or targeted email campaigns (Levchenko et al. 2011) or by taking advantage of online advertisement (ads) services (Li et al. 2012). An alternative is to wait until potential customers actively search for illicit products and end up on the sellers' page. Global search engines (e.g., Google, Bing, Yandex, Baidu) are obviously excellent tools for sellers looking to get noticed and these search engines can be manipulated through search-redirection attacks. Also known as 'cloaking', this attack changes search results or the action that is taken once a link is clicked in a search engine (Leontiadis et al. 2011). Private and localized search engines integrated in online communities may also be used by sellers to get noticed. This has led to the emergence of a fraudulent accounts market where accounts are sold to promote scams, phishing and other illicit markets (Thomas et al. 2013). Other online communities, such as classified advertisements websites, are also important promotion convergence settings for illicit markets (see the example of trafficking in human beings [THB] described below).

In some cases, the same virtual convergence setting can host multiple sections that serve to promote, sell and review sellers (see Table 21.1). Facebook pages can be used as a promotion means to redirect customers to a dedicated sale website, as a direct online storefront that advertises products for sale and as a review site through dedicated groups. Cryptomarkets may contain a forum to facilitate discussions and integrate a review system to rate sellers. Moreover, if emails are more often than not used to redirect the target to a website, they may also lead to a direct communication and a sale.

Internet traces to apprehend online illicit markets

Online illicit markets have attracted a lot of attention from researchers since they provide a vast and fertile ground from which to collect data on offenders (see Décary-Hétu, 'Online crime monitoring' in this volume). This data is collected through online monitoring that acquires digital (i.e., computer) traces that are available on the Internet. As defined by Margot (see Margot, 'Traceology, the bedrock of forensic science and its associated semantics' in this volume),

Table 21.1 Virtual convergence settings used to support online illicit markets

Virtual convergence settings	*Promotion*	*Selling*	*Review*
Dedicated websites	Global search engine's indexing and ads Thematic websites	Shops	Thematic websites Blogs
Online communities	Internal indexing and ads Classified ads websites	Shops Marketplaces Classified ads Crowdfunding projects	Forums
Peer-to-peer / Mobile applications	Ads	Marketplaces Messaging apps	Instant messages
Emails	Spams	Direct selling	Direct communications

a trace is the fundamental and most direct remnant of a criminal activity. In this context, a criminal activity has to be understood in its broadest sense to include litigious and security issues that cause harms. Jaquet-Chiffelle (personal communication) further defines a trace as a subsequently observable modification (e.g., an adjunction, a transformation or a suppression) resulting from an (crime) event. Digital traces can be considered a subtype of traces that may be collected on all kinds of electronic systems, including computers but also devices like mobile phones (Casey 2011, 7).

The digital forensic field encompasses all forms of digital traces related to criminal activities. It focuses much of its efforts on digital traces that can be directly collected by physically accessing a device. Digital traces can also, however, be accessed from virtual environments that are remote to the forensic scientist (i.e., the Internet and most frequently in the web). These digital traces are called Internet traces to express their specificity. Internet traces are the remnants of a criminal activity that leads to a modification, subsequently observable through the Internet. Internet traces pose a challenge to forensic scientists because they only allow the observation and copying of digital traces, never their collection. Indeed, only private access to the file system allows the extraction (or copy) of the specimen physically present on the remote computer. Collecting traces requires a physical access to its source (a computer system) that can be thousands of kilometres away. Aside from hindering the possibility of collecting the traces, the Internet as an indirection between the forensic scientist and the digital trace creates transformations that may be assimilated to an observation effect. Indeed, forensic scientists may use different software to collect Internet traces and these variations may render Internet content in different ways or, even worse, may not render some of the content at all. In some cases, the website programmer himself may choose to change the content depending on the tool used to access it or the visitor's location.[3] Combined, these challenges demonstrate the need to fully understand the implications of using Internet traces for research purposes.

The next section introduces the discussion of the roles of Internet traces in reconstructing the illicit activities of online sellers. It starts with the importance of trust in illicit markets and how this may lead to a new form of traceability of offenders based on the way they manage their identities. It then addresses the question of the reconstruction of networks of offenders and networks of markets based on the detection of forensic links (see Ribaux and Caneppele, 'Forensic intelligence' in this volume) inferred from Internet traces. Finally, the current state of research on how the Internet has impacted trafficking in human beings is presented as a special case of illicit markets where the 'products' sold are not goods, but human beings' services.

Trust in online markets: impact on the traceability of seller identities

Online illicit markets pose a series of logistical and security challenges to their participants. The first challenge relates to trust and the detection of participants who act opportunistically when entering into contact with others (Wehinger 2011). Given the relative anonymity that the Internet affords, it can be difficult for participants to evaluate the trustworthiness of others and to identity undercover agents posing as drug dealers or fraudsters exploiting the market to steal money or data from other participants. To address this challenge, offenders have built online personas around a vanity name (Décary-Hétu and Eudes 2015). These personas have a history that is stored online publicly so that others can go through it and evaluate its experience and past realizations. Building a trustworthy online persona is, however, not enough, since trusted vendors face the very real risk of identity theft. Indeed, other vendors may take advantage of the reputation of an alias and use it on other online illicit markets. More structured tools have also been created to manage reputation including automated feedback systems, which log feedback following transactions between participants. Participants can use these systems to shame others who have acted opportunistically and drive participants to sellers who have delivered on their word in the past. Participants also rely on higher authorities, namely market administrators who are tasked with the social regulation of the markets (Holt and Lampke 2010). These administrators vet new participants, test the products and services they have for sale and hold payments in escrow until a transaction is completed. While administrators may strive to limit opportunistic behaviour among their market participants, many markets appear to be 'lemon markets' where so many sellers are acting opportunistically that it becomes difficult for reliable sellers to sell their goods and services at a decent price. These sellers are forced to sell at a lower price, matching that of disreputable sellers. This creates tension in online illicit markets, which are prone to conflicts.

Another challenge for market participants revolves around their need for anonymity. Participants need to communicate with each other in a secure fashion and have adopted encryption protocols like PGP to protect against eavesdropping (Soska and Christin 2015; Broséus et al. 2016b) and as an authentication means to avoid identity theft. Connections between the markets and their participants are also increasingly encrypted, and the use of the Tor network facilitates the use of encryption to obfuscate both the participants' location and the location of the servers hosting the illicit markets. The payment methods for goods and services sold in online illicit markets were for a long time either money transfers using private companies like Western Union, or virtual currencies like Liberty Reserve. More recently, the creation of cryptocurrencies, which are based on cryptography (e.g., the Bitcoin) rather than trust, has removed the need for third parties to manage the currency.

Reconstructing the market structure using Internet traces

Offenders leave many Internet traces, either through their promotion and sales activity or through their efforts to remain anonymous. This has created new opportunities to observe traces of offenders that can be used to link virtual identities together, identify and gather intelligence on new and unknown offenders, find the physical location of offenders and estimate the size and scope of their activities. The acquisition of Internet traces in order to reconstruct the market structure and, in particular, networks of offenders, differs between dedicated websites and online communities. In online communities, offenders take advantage of settings created by third parties that might be criminal or not. They post information and leave traces in web pages' content but do not handle the creation and management of the website, whereas the creation of a dedicated website requires instrumental precondition and preparation during which offenders may leave other kinds of traces (e.g., when registering a domain name or hosting the website). These traces are dependent on the infrastructure and the protocols used on the Internet. We thus refer to them as protocol traces.

To detect links between virtual identities in online communities, communications (public and private messages) and transactions data (feedback) have been used as the fundamental pieces of information for analysis. Past research on communications has shown that online illicit markets are often decentralized settings where few key players can be identified (Décary-Hétu et al. 2012). The networks are far from dense and are structured around cliques. They bring together large numbers of loosely connected actors.

In addition to linking offenders together, Internet traces can be used to link dedicated websites that facilitate the sale of illicit goods and services. Relationships between websites can be detected using unique identifiers located in the source code of websites. Google Analytics identifiers, for example, have been used to connect online illicit markets to each other (Pazos et al. 2013) and to deanonymize up to a certain point the actors who run these markets.[4] The analytics software requires that the website owner insert his unique identifier in his code and if that trace is found on multiple websites, these websites are likely controlled or at least managed by the same group of actors. Secure socket shell (SSH) certificates are also highly valuable to infer links among websites, and in some cases, they may deanonymize hidden services hosted on servers containing websites available through the 'surface web'.[5] These certificates are bound to a single identity and can therefore be used to link websites together.

Internet traces can also be used to identify links based on technical traces created by the many protocols used to communicate through the Internet (i.e., protocol traces). Online illicit markets are hosted on web servers and must use the domain name system (DNS) to translate their domain name (e.g., evilmarket.com) to an IP address that computers can understand. This requires that market administrators register their domain names with legitimate companies called registrars. This registration process leaves digital traces in publicly available databases known as WHOIS records databases. Contact information of the registrant (i.e., a name, a physical address or an email) can be mined on these databases. Although this data can be spoofed or anonymized, it may help in the detection of relationships between domain names acquired by the same offenders. Because DNS records store the IP address of each domain name, it is also possible to look for websites hosted on the same IP address as online illicit markets and to create ties between all the websites hosted on the same IP address. Researchers or investigators have, however, to be cautious when interpreting such links, since several computers may share the same IP address at the same time because their hosting service may use carrier-grade network address translation (CGN) to overcome the limits of the IPv4.[6] Software like Maltego[7] have been devised to automate as much as possible the analysis of the infrastructure used by offenders to lift their anonymity by collecting connection logs and contact information.

The collection of HTTP traffic headers can be used to detect the type of server being run, the version of the operating system it runs and other discriminant traces like cookies. At the application level, each choice made by the designer of a website leaves traces. Of particular interest is the integration of other services such as anonymization services (e.g., Cloudflare) and content delivery networks where offenders have to register an account and potentially divulge information about themselves. This can help build a technological profile (i.e., a 'web app fingerprint'[8]) of offenders' infrastructure that can support the detection of their activities. Finally, a completely unexplored field of study is the exploitation of clock skews to infer links between web servers. Each clock of a computer has deficiencies that may lead to temporal shifts due to imperfections in the cheap quartz they use. If these clock skews are not enough discriminant to lead to an individualization, they may, nevertheless, complete the profile of a website infrastructure to infer or revise links (Polcák and Franková 2015). These traces are of particular interest, since they are, as far as we know, the only Internet traces (i.e., timestamps of several protocols) resulting from a purely physical process.[9]

Whether they operate on dedicated websites or in online communities, offenders also routinely leak information about themselves through their social interactions and allow for the gathering of intelligence about them. Mining the content of their websites and their public posts has proven extremely valuable. Past research has identified email addresses and other personal information of offenders that have helped lift the veil of anonymity surrounding them. The case of the Silk Road administrator, the first cryptomarket launched in 2011, is particularly interesting. Its administrator appears to have posted on a forum a message asking for help to design his cryptomarket using his personal email address (Paul 2015). This supposedly led to his identification and subsequent arrest. In addition to an email address, phone numbers, Skype aliases, PGP keys and Bitcoin Wallet IDs are all traces that can be used to link together the activity of multiple online personas (see, for instance, Broséus et al. 2016b).

The content of messages has also been mined for stylometry analysis to connect different online personas together. These studies have shown that many offenders used multiple nicknames but that their writing styles could leak information about their identity. A forensic analysis of the passwords used by offenders has similarly found connections between sets of offenders who used the same password to identify themselves in online illicit markets (Décary-Hétu and Eudes 2015). On dedicated websites, a content comparison may also help to infer links between markets. Two approaches may be used. First, textual or multimedia content can be extracted and compared with hashes, for example. Second, traffic analysis can be used to define a profile of a web page content that can be compared to other web pages (Hintz 2002). This process may for instance support the comparison of the index page of websites. It may also support the detection of changes. Indeed, modifications are of high value to monitor online markets. On the one hand, they allow the detection of new activities and trends. On the other hand, a concomitant change can be the sign of the activity of a same offender. These kinds of coordinated modifications may be directly visible in the content of the web page (e.g., an offer or contact information modification) or more subtly, as in a technological choice modification. The same inference is done by comparing newsletters that offenders make available on selling websites. Indeed, a relationship can be detected when the same news is simultaneously received from two apparently distinct websites.

Evaluating the validity and the strength of a relationship inferred on the basis of Internet traces is challenging. Indeed, this forensic process relies on the evaluation of the probability of a common source (e.g., a same person, a same object) or a common cause (i.e., the criminal activity). This analogical reasoning is uncertain by nature and requires controlled conditions (i.e., situations where the common source or cause is known to be true) to estimate a probabilistic value to the link. Nevertheless, as noted by Morelato and colleagues (2014, 184), 'the analyses conducted in an intelligence perspective are different from those conducted in the probative (traditional) process since what is sought is the proximity between two objects rather than the discrimination between objects'. Thus, if all Internet traces described above may be used to infer a common cause or activity, they may also be compared with each other to evaluate their validity or strengthen the hypotheses. Another approach is to combine Internet and physical traces (see below).

Identifying offenders' physical location is a key challenge with online illicit markets. Indeed, the market structure may greatly vary across countries (Broséus et al. 2016a; Broséus et al. 2017). Many Internet traces are linked to physical locations and their combination may lead to the localization of offenders: (1) IP addresses checked against geoip databases such as Maxmind; (2) area code extracted from phone numbers (although international call forwarding may be detected); (3) ccTLD and WHOIS information obtained from a URL; (4) a geotag in the metadata of an image; (5) the time zone of a timestamp; and (6) finally, text content and language can also be an indicator.

The estimation of illicit order volumes is also challenging but some research has suggested inference techniques based on test purchases and online store order numbering, or based on opportunistic server log data access (Kanich et al. 2011; McCoy et al. 2012). A small subset of research has also sought to follow the money, a key endeavour of offline money laundering and drug dealing investigations. Sellers posting their Western Union client number or their Liberty Reserve identification number could indeed be tracked across markets or identified if they tried to create a new seller account after being banned for abusing other offenders. Cryptocurrencies now afford opportunities for even better tracking of offenders, since most cryptocurrency transactions are posted publicly on the Internet in public ledgers which can be data mined and analysed. These ledgers have been used to evaluate the size and scope of cryptomarkets and to characterize ransomware campaigns, the type of malware attack that encrypts files on computers and then asks for a ransom to provide the decryption key. Specialized software like BitCluster offers a free and open-source tool to monitor the flows of cryptocurrencies like bitcoin (Lavoie and Décary-Hétu 2016).

Trafficking in human beings: the case of sexual exploitation

Information technologies have facilitated the rise of new forms of human trafficking. In this section, we focus on sexual exploitation, which can be defined as obtaining services of a sexual nature through the use of force, threat, deception or coercion.[10] Sexual exploitation is the most frequently identified form of human trafficking. Past research indicates that the Internet can serve as an enabler of sexual exploitation and thus warrants further attention (Walby et al. 2016). Indeed, many virtual convergence settings are used by the actors in this market to either recruit victims or sell sexual services. In addition, the Internet is also being used to communicate with clients, to gather information on available services and even to provide reviews of escort services by the clients (Kunze 2010; Sarkar 2015).

To recruit victims, online advertisements are: (a) placed on classified advertisements sites, (b) placed on dedicated thematic websites of au pairs, international marriage or dating agencies, (c) shared through direct contacts in chat rooms or social networking services; or (d) sent by unsolicited emails (Europol 2014; Tidwell 2016; Sykiotou 2007; Watson et al. 2015). Victims may be attracted by job opportunities such as waitressing, childcare, dancing or modelling (Logan et al. 2009; McAlister 2014; Dixon 2013; Nazemi 2011; Sykiotou 2007). The extent to which the Internet is used and how effective it is in recruiting victims remains unclear. Indeed, in many cases of sex trafficking in Europe, the Internet does not seem to be used to recruit victims but rather as a facilitator to advertisements for the selling of services (Sykiotou 2007).

The Internet is an excellent medium to match sexually exploited individuals with clients using online illicit markets. Much of the traditional street prostitution trade appears to have moved online in favour of Internet-enabled indoor and hidden forms of prostitution (Farley et al. 2013). The Internet appears to have had the greatest impact on communications between sellers and buyers. Traffickers are using many types of websites to advertise including classified advertisement websites, social networking websites, chat rooms and dedicated escort websites. More recently, mobile applications are also used to assist customers to locate nearby sex services (Finn and Stalans 2016). More often than not, traffickers use legitimate services to promote their activities by hiding them as massage or 'dating' services (Heil and Nichols 2014). The detection of sex trafficking activities managed by organized crime groups (OCG) through the analysis of publicly available advertisements is thus the main challenge. Indeed, dedicated methodologies have to be settled to distinguish OCGs' advertisements from posters who are selling their own independent services (Konrad et al. 2017; Farley et al. 2013; Heil and Nichols 2014). Several approaches have been proposed and tested on American online services such as Craigslist and Backpage, to name two. The methodologies are based on the detection of: (a) occurrences of terms of interest compiled through interviews with law-enforcement investigators, (b) language patterns such as the use of the third person or plural pronouns, (c) keywords related to a child (e.g., 'candy', 'fresh', 'new to the game', 'doll', 'daddy's girl'), (d) countries of interest, (e) multiple victims advertised, (f) age and weight as a sign of a child, (g) references to escort websites or spa massage therapy, (h) images, and finally (i) contact information (Kennedy 2012; Wang et al. 2012; Silva et al. 2014; Heil and Nichols 2014; Nichols and Heil 2015; Dubrawski et al. 2015; Nagpal et al. 2016; Alvari et al. 2016; Finn and Stalans 2016).

The detection of specific traces allows the reconstruction of networks of advertisements, which may be linked to OCGs. Contact information (e.g., phone numbers, emails, URLs, social media handles) is of particular interest in inferring the activity of a same group of offenders. Language homologies, similarities in content, as well as locations and displacement patterns can also help to bridge gaps between groups (Latonero et al. 2012; Dubrawski et al. 2015; Nagpal et al. 2016; Alvari et al. 2016; Konrad et al. 2017). Spatial analysis of advertisements may also serve the detection of sex tours that may be the sign of exploitation (Hughes 2014). However, only a few online advertisements are currently accurately classified as linked to trafficking (Dubrawski et al. 2015; Alvari et al. 2016).

Peppet (2012) argues that the Internet has provided a new means for both clients and prostitutes to sort through and review each other and thus to reduce harms and the spread of diseases. Independent prostitutes may reach a huge number of customers and screen them on the web (e.g., by emails, online blacklists and identity verification services) to reduce risks of violence and disease. However, this may be true only if they are not coerced (Cunningham and Kendall 2013). Interactive review sites and escort websites allow clients to talk about and rate prostitutes online (Peppet 2012). This may inherently degrade women and creates an added stressor for prostitutes and a new way of exerting pressure for traffickers (Cunningham and Kendall 2013).

Since offenders leave Internet traces that can support law enforcement investigations, the development of accurate methodologies to detect the activities of OCGs during the online advertising process (for both recruitment and selling of services) is promoted as a key leverage that can lead to proactive actions (Europol 2016). Benefits include the ability to detect suspicious activities and 'hot spots' to start undercover operations and criminal investigations (Mitchell and Boyd 2014). Overall, the key issues are: (a) the identification and protection of victims, (b) the development of a shared methodology to gather and interpret Internet traces, (c) the development of methodologies and technologies for detecting traffickers, and (d) the use of the Internet to disseminate and raise public awareness about THB and the danger of online recruitments (Walby et al. 2016).

Toward the integration of Internet and physical traces to reconstruct illicit trafficking

A rarely explored trend in research on online illicit markets is the collection and analysis of physical traces. The online activities of illicit markets' offenders are indeed only a part of the whole illicit trafficking process (see Figure 21.1). Even if each stage of the process may happen

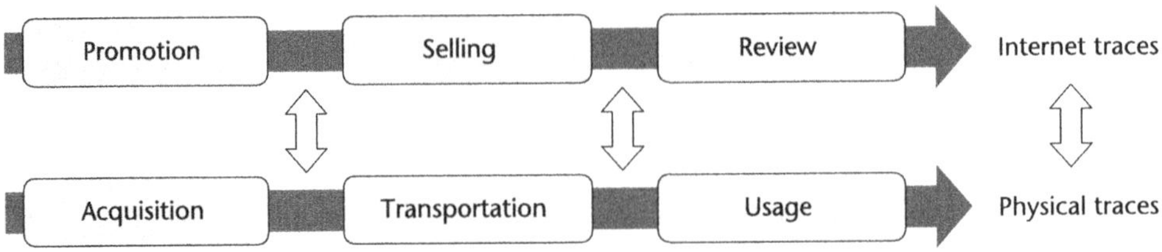

Figure 21.1 Integration of Internet and physical traces to apprehend the full process of illicit goods trafficking

in the physical world, we focus our discussion on the relationships between situations where promotion, selling and review steps happen online and physical goods such as illicit drugs or counterfeiting goods are trafficked. Indeed, when digital goods are the object of the traffic, all the stages may happen online. The promotion, selling and review stages have already been discussed earlier in this chapter. The term 'acquisition' is chosen because 'manufacturing' only applies to physical goods, although illicit trafficking may concern stolen goods as well as the trafficking of human beings. In the former case, 'acquisition' means 'theft' and it corresponds to the 'recruitment phase' in the latter.

The integration of Internet traces with physical traces can take many forms. It may first help to better understand the structure of a market (i.e., the number of actors and their relationships) at each stage of the trafficking process, whether it takes place online and/or in the physical world. Ultimately it aims to compare the findings at each stage to reconstruct the whole structure. Such a combination of information may lead to the evaluation of the volume of sales, their temporal trends, the number of actors, their location and their relationships all along the process. Moreover, comparisons lead to the evaluation of the validity, significance and pertinence of each source of information and may help to interpret the findings.

The physical and/or chemical analyses of products bought in online markets or seized by law enforcement agencies are the first pathway to achieve integration. These products can be bought by law enforcement or interested groups like industry lobby groups seeking to help protect their members and researchers. For the last group, this may raise ethical considerations, since purchasing illicit goods is illegal (McCoy et al. 2012). Further ethical considerations are raised, since making purchases finances organized crime, which could lead to the victimization of certain individuals. Such cases are, therefore, few and far between. An innovative approach to skirt the ethical conundrums is to ask offenders themselves to provide researchers with samples. This is what Dr X has achieved with his drug-testing lab in Spain (Caudevilla et al. 2016). Offenders pay 50 euros to get a drug sample analyzed, and the report Dr X and his team generate can even help improve the public health of drug users, as they can make sure that the drugs they are using are not dangerous.

In some case, researchers have managed to purchase illicit drugs such as cocaine, cannabis and GBH (Pazos et al. 2013; Rhumorbarbe et al. 2016). These purchases led to analyses of the chemical composition of the products and to the evaluation of the purity of their active ingredients as well as the detection of forensic links between purchases. The chemical composition (i.e., purity, cutting agents) of cocaine purchased online was similar to specimens confiscated in the streets, but a lower purity than claimed was observed (Rhumorbarbe et al. 2016). Packaging and concealment techniques described by sellers (in their online listings) appear to be accurate in regard to received products. Thus, a more systematic analysis of online description may lead to interesting new knowledge (Aldridge and Askew 2017). From the few studies that have performed online purchases, global outcomes may be outlined: (1) the forensic analysis of products bought online allows the evaluation of the relevance and, in some cases, the accuracy of digital data collected on the website (Rhumorbarbe et al. 2016); (2) the analysis of transportation traces such as delivery notes, tracking information and packaging may confirm the country of origin; (3) links detected between websites may be compared to physical and/or chemical links detected by the forensic analysis of products to better understand the market structure at each step (Pazos et al. 2013; Broséus et al. 2016a); and (4) financial traces may be analysed and order numbering used to evaluate sales' volumes (Levchenko et al. 2011; McCoy et al. 2012).

Another promising integration between Internet and physical traces is the comparison of online selling and review settings with the analysis of wastewater. On the one hand, identifying the most discussed substances in online forums (see, for instance, Pineau et al. 2016) or sold online (see, for instance, McCoy et al. 2012) may help target the strategy of wastewater analysis. On the other hand, the comparison of online and physical indicators may lead to a more accurate evaluation of the prevalence and detection of new trends of consumption (for a more detailed discussion, see Esseiva et al., 'Evaluating the consumption of illicit drugs via wastewater analysis' in this volume).

Conclusion

This chapter has reflected on the use of Internet traces either on their own or in combination with physical traces. Through this discussion, we highlighted the numerous challenges that offenders face when buying and selling illicit goods and services online as well as the challenges researchers are likely to face when collecting Internet traces.

In order to maximize the research potential of Internet traces, collaboration between forensic scientists, criminologists and even computer scientists will be essential. The acquisition of this particular type of digital trace requires the use of adequate methodologies and technical tools. Criminologists and most forensic scientists are not trained in the use of these tools and will need each other and/or the help of computer scientists to determine appropriate approaches and integrate them into their data collection processes. Given the specificity of Internet traces, it is essential that researchers who take advantage of them are aware of their limits in order not to overstate their meaning. And as explained earlier, the software used to collect web pages may transform their content and not collect parts of the page in many cases. Researchers or investigators must therefore be very careful when they analyze Internet traces. The forensic scientists who have the necessary skills to collect Internet traces and physical traces may not be familiar enough with the context of online illicit markets and the networks of offenders who populate them. They may therefore be able to gather traces but have more difficulty giving them some context and understanding how they fit in the overall markets. Such lack of knowledge may even prevent them from detecting or using relevant traces. Herein lies a dual relationship between forensic science and criminology.

The study of online illicit markets is therefore an excellent example of how combining physical and Internet traces can help both disciplines to better understand offenders. This collaboration will become ever more important as more and more offenders shift their activities to the Internet either in the 'surface web' or the 'dark web'. Their activities will likely become stealthier over this transition and a precise understanding of who the actors are and how they network with each other will be needed. It appears that the rate of criminal innovation is constantly increasing and the collaboration between forensic scientists and criminologists will be one important strategy in keeping up with offenders who work in teams that benefit from the specialization of their members.

Notes

1 https://openbazaar.org/.
2 www.financemagnates.com/cryptocurrency/education-centre/went-shopping-drugs-fake-ids-guns-using-bitcoin-openbazaar/.
3 See geopeeker.com and insert a well-known url such as www.ubs.com or more interesting: www.timescopy.cn.
4 Several online databases are available to search links with Google Analytics identifiers: http://sameid.net, http://spyonweb.com, www.shodan.io or http://nerdydata.com.
5 For instance, see the online databases of www.shodan.io or https://censys.io.
6 This situation may occur in the specific case of a dynamic addressing of the IP address.
7 www.paterva.com.
8 See, for instance, http://wappalyzer.com.
9 Although we can speculate that the accelerometer and the gyroscope of a mobile device may also produce or impact digital traces, they might unlikely be Internet traces.
10 www.ohchr.org/EN/ProfessionalInterest/Pages/ProtocolTraffickingInPersons.aspx.

References

Akers, R.L., M.D. Krohn, L. Lanza-Kaduce and M. Radosevich. 1979. 'Social Learning and Deviant Behavior: A Specific Test of a General Theory'. *American Sociological Review* 44(4): 636–655.

Aldridge, J., and R. Askew. 2017. 'Delivery Dilemmas: How Drug Cryptomarket Users Identify and Seek to Reduce Their Risk of Detection by Law Enforcement'. *International Journal of Drug Policy* 41: 101–109.

Alvari, H., P. Shakarian and J.K. Snyder. 2016. 'A Non-Parametric Learning Approach to Identify Online Human Trafficking'. IEEE Conference on Intelligence and Security Informatics: Cyber Security and Big Data (ISI): 133–138.

Bandura, A. 1971. *Social Learning Theory*. New York: General Learning Press.

Broséus J., S. Baechler, N. Gentile, and P. Esseiva. 2016a. 'Chemical Profiling: A Tool to Decipher the Structure and Organisation of Illicit Drugs Markets: An 8-Year Study in Western Switzerland'. *Forensic Science International* 266(September): 18–28.

Broséus J., D. Rhumorbarbe, C. Mireault, V. Ouellette, F. Crispino and D. Décary-Hétu. 2016b. 'Studying Illicit Drug Trafficking on Darknet Markets: Structure and Organisation from a Canadian Perspective'. *Forensic Science International* 264: 7–14.

Broséus, J., D. Rhumorbarbe, M. Morelato, L. Staehli and Q. Rossy. 2017. 'A Geographical Analysis of Trafficking on a Popular Darknet Market'. *Forensic Science International*, submitted.

Casey, E. 2011. *Digital Evidence and Computer Crime: Forensic Science, Computers, and the Internet*. Waltham, MA: Academic Press.

Caudevilla, F., M. Ventura, I. Fornís, M.J. Barratt, C. Vidal, P. Quintana, A. Muñoz and N. Calzada. 2016. 'Results of an International Drug Testing Service for Cryptomarket Users'. *International Journal of Drug Policy* 35: 38–41.

Christin, N. 2013. 'Traveling the Silk Road: A Measurement Analysis of a Large Anonymous Online Marketplace'. Proceedings of the 22nd International Conference on World Wide Web, Rio de Janeiro.

Cunningham, S., and T. Kendall. 2013. 'Prostitution 3.0: A Comment'. *Iowa Law Review Bulletin* 98: 131–141.

Décary-Hétu, D., B. Dupont and F. Fortin. 2014. 'Policing the Hackers by Hacking Them: Studying Online Deviants in IRC Chat Rooms'. In A.J. Masys, ed., *Networks and Network Analysis for Defence and Security*, 63–82. New York: Springer.

Décary-Hétu, D., and M. Eudes. 2015. 'Partenariats criminels au sein d'un forum de carding: alliés, rivaux ou escrocs? Étude de l'utilisation d'identités virtuelles multiples'. *Revue internationale de criminologie et de police technique scientifique* 68(3): 299–314.

Décary-Hétu, D., and D. Laferrière. 2015. 'Discrediting Vendors in Online Criminal Markets'. In A. Malm and G. Bichler, *Disrupting Criminal Networks: Network Analysis in Crime Prevention*, 129–152. Boulder: Lynne Rienner.

Décary-Hétu, D., and A. Leppänen. 2016. 'Criminals and Signals: An Assessment of Criminal Performance in the Carding Underworld'. *Security Journal* 29(3): 442–460.

Décary-Hétu, D., C. Morselli and S. Leman-Langlois. 2012. 'Welcome to the Scene: A Study of Social Organization and Recognition among Warez Hackers'. *Journal of Research in Crime and Delinquency* 49(3): 359–382.

Dixon, H. 2013. 'Human Trafficking and the Internet (and Other Technologies, Too)'. *Judges Journal* 52(1): 36–39.

Dubrawski, A., K, Miller and M. Barnes. 2015. 'Leveraging Publicly Available Data to Discern Patterns of Human-Trafficking Activity'. *Journal of Human Trafficking* 1(1): 65–85.

Europol. 2016. *Situation Report: Trafficking in Human Beings in the EU*. The Hague: Europol.

Europol. 2014. *Trafficking in Human Beings and the Internet*. The Hague: Europol, Intelligence Notification 15/2014.

Farley, M., K. Franzblau and M. Kennedy. 2013. 'Online Prostitution and Trafficking'. *Albany Law Review* 77(3): 1039–1094.

Felson, M. 2003. 'The Process of Co-Offending'. In M.J. Smith and D.B. Cornish, eds., *Theory for Practice in Situational Crime Prevention* 16, 149–168. Devon: Willan Publishing.

Finn, M.A., and L.J. Stalans. 2016. 'How Targeted Enforcement Shapes Marketing Decisions of Pimps: Evidence of Displacement and Innovation'. *Victims & Offenders* 11(4): 578–599.

Fredman, C. 2015. 'Fund Me or Fraud Me? Crowdfunding Scams Are on the Rise'. Online www.consumerreports.org/cro/money/crowdfunding-scam.

Heil, E., and A. Nichols. 2014. 'Hot Spot Trafficking: A Theoretical Discussion of the Potential Problems Associated with Targeted Policing and the Eradication of Sex Trafficking in the United States'. *Contemporary Justice Review* 17(4): 421–433.

Hintz, A. 2002. 'Fingerprinting Websites Using Traffic Analysis'. In *International Workshop on Privacy Enhancing Technologies*, 171–178. New York: Springer Berlin Heidelberg.

Holt, T.J. 2007. 'Subcultural Evolution? Examining the Influence of On- and Off-Line Experiences on Deviant Subcultures'. *Deviant Behavior* 28(2): 171–198.

Holt, T.J., and E. Lampke. 2010. 'Exploring Stolen Data Markets Online: Products and Market Forces'. *Criminal Justice Studies* 23(1): 33–50.

Holt, T.J., O. Smirnova, and Y.T. Chua. 2016. 'Data Thieves in Action: Examining the International Market for Stolen Personal Information'. New York: Palgrave Macmillan.

Hughes, D.M. 2014. 'Trafficking in Human Beings in the European Union: Gender, Sexual Exploitation, and Digital Communication Technologies'. *SAGE Open* 4(4): 1–8.

Kanich, C., N. Weaver, D. McCoy, T. Halvorson, C. Kreibich, K. Levchenko, V. Paxson, G.M. Voelker and S. Savage. 2011. 'Show Me the Money: Characterizing Spam-Advertised Revenue'. Proceedings of the USENIX Security Symposium, San Francisco, 5–15.

Kennedy, E. 2012. 'Predictive Patterns of Sex Trafficking Online'. Honours thesis, Carnegie Mellon University, Pittsburgh. http://repository.cmu.edu/hsshonors/155/.

Konrad, R., A.C. Trapp, T.M. Palmbach and J.S. Blom. 2017. 'Overcoming Human Trafficking via Operations Research and Analytics: Opportunities for Methods, Models, and Applications'. *European Journal of Operational Research* 259(2): 733–745.

Kruithof, K., J. Aldridge, D. Décary-Hétu, M. Sim, E. Dujso and D. Hoorens. 2016. *Internet-Facilitated Drugs Trade: An Analysis of the Size, Scope and the Role of the Netherlands*. RAND Corporation, Santa Monica, CA, and Cambridge, UK. www.rand.org/pubs/research_reports/RR1607.html.

Kunze, E.I. 2010. 'Sex Trafficking via the Internet: How International Agreements Address the Problem and Fail to Go Far Enough'. *Journal of High Technology Law* 10(2): 241–289.

Latonero, M., J. Musto, Z. Boyd, E. Boyle, A. Bissel, K. Gibson and J. Kim. 2012. *The Rise of Mobile and the Diffusion of Technology-Facilitated Trafficking*. Research Series on Technology and Human Trafficking. http://technologyandtrafficking.usc.edu/files/2012/11/Tech_Trafficking_2012_SUMMARY.pdf.

Lavoie, M., and D. Décary-Hétu. 2016. 'De-Anonymizing Bitcoin One Transaction at a Time'. https://livestream.com/internetsociety2/hopeconf/videos/130587981.

Leontiadis, N., T. Moore and N. Christin. 2011. 'Measuring and Analyzing Search-Redirection Attacks in the Illicit Online Prescription Drug Trade'. Proceedings of the USENIX Security Symposium, San Francisco, 1–17.

Levchenko, K., A. Pitsillidis, N. Chachra, B. Enright, M. Félegyházi, C. Grier, T. Halvorson, C. Kanich ... and S. Savage. 2011. 'Click Trajectories: End-to-End Analysis of the Spam Value Chain'. 2011 IEEE Symposium on Security and Privacy. Oakland, CA (SP): 431–446.

Li, Z., K. Zhang, Y. Xie, F. Yu and X. Wang. 2012. 'Knowing Your Enemy: Understanding and Detecting Malicious Web Advertising'. Proceedings of the 2012 ACM Conference on Computer and Communications Security, 674–686.

Logan, T.K., R. Walker and G. Hunt. 2009. 'Understanding Human Trafficking in the United States'. *Trauma, Violence & Abuse* 10(1): 3–30.

McAlister, R. 2014. 'Webscraping as an Investigation Tool to Identify Potential Human Trafficking Operations in Romania'. Proceedings of the ACM Web Science Conference (WebSci '15), 2. New York: ACM.

McCoy, D., A. Pitsillidis, G. Jordan, N. Weaver, C. Kreibich, B. Krebs, M. Voelker, S. Savage and K. Levchenko. 2012. 'Pharmaleaks: Understanding the Business of Online Pharmaceutical Affiliate Programs'. Proceedings of the 21st USENIX Conference on Security Symposium, Bellevue, WA.

Meyer, G.R. 1989. 'The Social Organization of the Computer Underground'. MSc thesis, Northern Illinois University.

Mitchell, K.J., and D. Boyd. 2014. 'Understanding the Role of Technology in the Commercial Sexual Exploitation of Children: The Perspective of Law Enforcement'. Durham, NH: Crimes Against Children Research Center, University of New Hampshire. http://scholars.unh.edu/ccrc/37/.

Morelato, M., S. Baechler, O. Ribaux, A. Beavis, M. Tahtouh, P. Kirkbride, C. Roux and P. Margot. 2014. 'Forensic Intelligence Framework. Part I: Induction of a Transversal Model by Comparing Illicit Drugs and False Identity Documents Monitoring'. *Forensic Science International* 236(March): 181–190.

Motoyama, M., D. McCoy, K. Levchenko, S. Savage and G.M. Voelker. 2011. 'An Analysis of Underground Forums'. Proceedings of the 2011 ACM SIGCOMM Conference on Internet Measurement, Berlin, Germany, 71–80.

Nagpal, C., K. Miller, B. Boecking and A. Dubrawski. 2016. 'An Entity Resolution Approach to Isolate Instances of Human Trafficking Online'. arXiv preprint arXiv:1509.06659.

Nazemi, N. 2011. 'Role of Internet in Human Trafficking'. *Indian Journal of Social Development* 11(2): 517–540.

Nichols, A.J., and E.C. Heil. 2015. 'Challenges to Identifying and Prosecuting Sex Trafficking Cases in the Midwest United States'. *Feminist Criminology* 10(1): 7–35.

Paul, K. 2015. 'How Silk Road's Founder Could Have Avoided Getting Busted'. Online: https://motherboard.vice.com/en_us/article/the-five-hidden-service-commandments.

Pazos D., P. Giannasi, Q. Rossy and P. Esseiva. 2013. 'Combining Internet Monitoring Processes, Packaging and Isotopic Analyses to Determine the Market Structure: Example of Gamma Butyrolactone'. *Forensic Science International* 230(1–3): 29–36.

Peppet, S.R. 2012. 'Prostitution 3.0'. *Iowa Law Review* 98: 1989–2060.

Pineau, T., A. Schopfer, L. Grossrieder, J. Broséus, P. Esseiva and Q. Rossy. 2016. 'The Study of Doping Market: How to Produce Intelligence from Internet Forums'. *Forensic Science International* 268(November): 103–115.

Polcák, L., and B. Franková. 2015. 'Clock-Skew-Based Computer Identification: Traps and Pitfalls'. *Journal of Universal Computer Science* 21(9): 1210–1233.

Rhumorbarbe D., L. Staehli, J. Broséus, Q. Rossy and P. Esseiva. 2016. 'Buying Drugs on a Darknet Market: A Better Deal? Studying the Online Illicit Drug Market through the Analysis of Digital, Physical and Chemical Data'. *Forensic Science International* 267(October): 173–182.

Sarkar, S. 2015. 'Use of Technology in Human Trafficking Networks and Sexual Exploitation: A Cross-Sectional Multi-Country Study'. *Transnational Social Review* 5(1): 55–68.

Silva, D.R., A. Philpot, A. Sundararajan, N.M. Bryan and E. Hovy. 2014. 'Data Integration from Open Internet Sources and Network Detection to Combat Underage Sex Trafficking'. Proceedings of the 15th Annual International Conference on Digital Government Research—dg.o '14, Aguascalientes, Mexico, 86–90.

Soska, K., and N. Christin. 2015. 'Measuring the Longitudinal Evolution of the Online Anonymous Marketplace Ecosystem'. Proceedings of the 24th USENIX Security Symposium, Washington, DC, 33–48.

Soudijn, M.R., and B.C.T. Zegers. 2012. 'Cybercrime and Virtual Offender Convergence Settings'. *Trends in Organized Crime* 15(2–3): 111–129.

Sutherland, E.H. 1947. *Principles of Criminology*. 4th ed. Chicago: J.B. Lippincott Co.

Sykiotou, A.P. 2007. *Trafficking in Human Beings: Internet Recruitment*. Directorate General of Human Rights and Legal Affairs, Council of Europe, Strasbourg. https://ec.europa.eu/anti-trafficking/publications/trafficking-human-beings-internet-recruitment-misuse-internet-recruitment-victims_en.

Thomas, K., D. McCoy, C. Grier, A. Kolcz and V. Paxson. 2013. 'Trafficking Fraudulent Accounts: The Role of the Underground Market in Twitter Spam and Abuse'. Proceedings of the 22nd USENIX Security Symposium 13: 195–210.

Tidwell, R. 2016. 'Caught in the Web: The Importance of Ethical Computing Illustrated via an Exploration of the Online Recruitment of Women and Girls into Sex Trafficking'. Honors Senior thesis, Western Oregon University. http://digitalcommons.wou.edu/honors_theses/111/.

Tremblay, P. 2010. *Le délinquant idéal. Performance, discipline, solidarité.* Montréal: Liber.

Van Hout, M.C, and E. Hearne. 2017. 'New Psychoactive Substances (NPS) on Cryptomarket Fora: An Exploratory Study of Characteristics of Forum Activity between NPS Buyers and Vendors'. *International Journal of Drug Policy* 40: 102–110.

van Mierlo, T. 2014. 'The 1% Rule in Four Digital Health Social Networks: An Observational Study'. *Journal of Medical Internet Research* 16(2): e33.

Vinciarelli, A., M. Pantic, D. Heylen, C. Pelachaud, I. Poggi, F. D'Errico and M. Schroeder. 2012. 'Bridging the Gap between Social Animal and Unsocial Machine: A Survey of Social Signal Processing'. IEEE Transactions on Affective Computing 3(1): 69–87.

Walby, S., J. Towers, B.J. Francis, K. Shire, L. Kelly, B. Apitzsch, J.E. Armstrong, S. Balderston, A.R. Fish, C. Hardaker, S. Kirby, C.A. May-Chahal and C.E. Palmer. 2016. *Study on Comprehensive Policy Review of Anti-Trafficking Projects Funded by the European Commission.* HOME/2014/ISFP/PR/THBX/0052. http://eprints.lancs.ac.uk/82220/.

Wang, H., C. Cai, A. Philpot, M. Latonero, E.H. Hovy and D. Metzler. 2012. 'Data Integration from Open Internet Sources to Combat Sex Trafficking of Minors'. Proceedings of the 13th Annual International Conference on Digital Government Research: 246–252.

Watson, H., A. Donovan and J. Muraszkiewicz. 2015. 'Role of Technology in Human Trafficking'. http://trace-project.eu.

Wehinger, F. 2011. 'The Dark Net: Self-Regulation Dynamics of Illegal Online Markets for Identities and Related Services'. European Intelligence and Security Informatics Conference (EISIC), Athens, 209–213.

A bright road ahead for forensic science and criminology

David Décary-Hétu, Quentin Rossy, Olivier Delémont and Massimiliano Mulone

The *Handbook of Forensic Intelligence and Criminology* has showcased some of the most up-to-date research in forensic science and criminology from researchers in Europe, North America and Oceania. Through its three sections, it sought to explain how crime—the common social phenomenon that unites both disciplines—has developed into the problem it is today, how it impacts society and how social controls, both formal and informal, are reacting to (and in some cases seeking to prevent) it.

In the introduction, we explained that forensic scientists and criminologists had up to now few opportunities to collaborate with each other. This schism in the study of crime was due in large part to the different paradigms of forensic science and criminology, the former focusing on 'hard' sciences while the latter focuses on 'soft' sciences. The difference in focus leads to different research questions, research design and methodologies used to answer these questions. Another differentiation point between the two disciplines is their respective apparent aims. Over the last decades, forensic science moved more and more towards a technically focused science aiming to support law enforcement and tribunals in the conduct of their activities. Criminology has a more distant approach to crime detection and, while it does contribute to the justice system and law enforcement activities, many of its contributions aim at understanding and explaining crime and its related actors in multiple prisms. Forensic science and criminology may have appeared to be two completely different disciplines that are difficult to reconcile, but this handbook is one among many efforts to prove this wrong and to search for bridges between the two disciplines.

The most salient bridge is to recognize and capitalize on traces, both material and digital, as the most direct remnant of criminal activities. The handbook has enumerated many of the traces that forensic scientists collect over the course of their work. Perhaps the best known, fingermarks, foot marks, DNA and images and videos are all routinely collected on crime scenes. Crime is, however, constantly evolving and this leads to new types of traces. Technological development has led to the integration of computer systems into a wide range of everyday objects, such as our phones, cars, doorbells and stereos, to name the most common, creating a proliferation of possible traces witnessing criminal activities. Material and digital traces are thus combining at 'traditional' crime scenes. Moreover, this development has transformed many of our routine activities, which have moved from the physical environment to a virtual one, known as the Internet, created by the interconnection of these devices and the 'personal' computers that extend our cognitive abilities. Letters and payments have been almost completely digitalized. Goods and memories are following the same path (e.g., family albums, wallets, archives). Personal and professional meetings happen online; so do (or soon will) games, teaching, voting and more broadly, shopping. Crime has thus followed these new opportunities and moved online. This transformation, which occurred in the last two decades, is driving an almost 'natural' reunification of the disciplines studying crime because of the necessity of reinventing their methods and models. Both communities now have a unique opportunity to join in a collaborative approach that would capitalize on their epistemological differences.

Material and digital traces are aggregated in massive databases managed at the local, regional, national and even international level by, for example, the Prüm Convention, Europol or Interpol. These databases can contain millions of traces collected over a number of years. These traces constitute a unique source of information on offenders but also have some limitations. Considering the complexity associated with the commission of a criminal activity and the expansion of traces' typologies, it is hardly conceivable that an offender can take all precautions to avoid the generation of not just one but multiple traces witnessing his presence or actions. However, there are several reasons why none of these traces may be in position to deliver their information. They may disappear, be contaminated, not be searched for, not be detected, not be collected, etc. Moreover, because traces are produced by any action, and not only the litigious one that occurred at the scene of a crime, forensic scientists are faced with the problem of distinguishing pertinent traces—needles—in the haystack of traces. This is why criminologists need to maintain their approaches to crimes and still innovate in the definition of adequate indicators. The comparison of traces with interviews, as well as official and private data, may lead to more complete models and cross-evaluation.

Another challenge is that some traces may be associated with the identity of a specific individual while others are not. Trace databases provide an image of the offences and co-offending patterns of offences on a given territory although only from a limited perspective. Indeed, there is an asymmetry of occurrence in databases: several offences are not even processed for traces collection, so they will never appear in such databases. On the contrary, a tiny portion of others will involve a large quantity of traces and drain the available resources. This is the case with very serious crimes, such as violent homicides, that are fertile in trace production, and are intensively investigated, resulting in a massive collection of traces. Trace databases may also be very fragmented and more often than not limited by artificial jurisdictional borders. Each law enforcement agency is likely to manage its own databases and to protect this information for security and privacy reasons. Each database will therefore be a partial representation of all crimes that occurred in a certain region. This situation, mainly driven by legal constraints, is sometimes further accentuated by backlogs or a narrow view of the role of traces in policing.

The fragmented and partial nature of forensic traces databases is problematic for criminologists who do research. Without a known, quantifiable population, all criminological analyses are likely to have an unknown error margin that reduces their value. However, efforts are increasing to cross-check databases at both national and international levels for both practical and academic purposes. Despite providing an incomplete and imperfect perspective, forensic traces databases open new opportunities for criminological research that would not otherwise be available. A good example of this is how unknown offenders can be tracked through the traces they leave on crime scenes. The offenders, even if their identity is unknown, can be traced over time, and places and criminological theories of how crime is displaced can be tested through these forensic traces databases. A similar approach can be used to detect co-offending patterns. These databases offer insights into a type of offender criminologists have always found difficult to investigate: the unidentified and unarrested offender. Much of the criminologist's research has been based on official police and justice system data which is biased by the arrest and conviction rates. Some have argued that official data target only the 'bad' offenders, those with fewer skills. Forensic traces databases open a new field of investigation that allows for the study of offenders who are not part of official records and who may also be unwilling to answer questions about their past criminal activities.

Of course, to take advantage of forensic traces databases, criminologists will first need to become acquainted with forensic science and the collection and management of traces. Criminologists are indeed unlikely to be aware of the range of available databases and the opportunities they provide. They are also unlikely to be aware of the benefits and limits of the traces that are collected, analysed and stored. These parameters are very important, since they will impact the discussion of results and the intelligence that can be generated from them. Forensic traces databases could be used to generate new knowledge about crime but also to validate or overturn past findings. Theories about co-offending patterns, for example, could be studied by focusing on crime scenes where traces left by multiple offenders were detected. Researchers could then determine if, as many believed, more experienced offenders (that have been leaving traces on crime scenes for an extended period of time) are indeed collaborating with younger offenders (who have yet to leave a trace on a crime scene). In the digital world, the identification of patterns will be of even more importance given the wealth of traces that is likely to be collected. A single online discussion forum can generate millions of interactions among its members and mapping the structure of the network can become a very difficult problem to solve.

This brings us to a new challenge. While databases of physical traces are perhaps the most commonly used by forensic scientists and criminologists, there is no doubt that in the coming years individuals will generate many more traces through their use of electronic systems. The shift in size and scope of traces collected from the physical to the virtual environment is inevitable. This shift will provide much information for certain types of crimes that are centred around new technologies. These include of course cybercrime-related offences but also financial crimes that take advantage of electronic payments and virtual currencies. Databases articulated around digital traces will also generate new insights into more traditional forms of offences as offenders are likely to brag or discuss their offences, which were committed offline (e.g., sexual assault). Traces of their communications could be gleaned to build a case against them but also to better understand what led to the assault, how it happened and how the offender rationalized his/her actions afterward. Some types of offences that were difficult to monitor before the Internet are also likely to be more easily detected and tracked. In the case of harassment, for example, detecting and gathering evidence on this type of abuse was difficult in the past. With online social media and other communications platforms, it is now much easier to collect traces of harassment and to understand the evolution of a victimization over time. This is also true for violent interactions with law enforcement (either from or against), which can now be filmed using cell phones from multiple perspectives. While testimonies used to be the only material by which to judge an event, it is now much easier to have access to pictures and videos that complement what was said by the actors and the witnesses.

Digital traces offer forensic scientists and criminologists the opportunity to collaborate on more levels than ever before. Given the technical skills and experience needed to collect physical traces, criminologists would be limited in the help they could provide in gathering and analysing such traces. In the virtual environment, however, the tools to collect traces are more generally available, and the technical skills needed to collect them may be easier to learn given the vast number of online tutorials. Still, forensic scientists are likely to be doing the bulk of traces collection and analysis given their expertise in this field. Forensic scientists, relying on a computer and natural scientific background, are closer to the engineers who design the digital traces systems and are therefore more likely than criminologists to transition toward the collection of digital traces. Still, the move to digital traces provides an interesting opportunity for researchers from both fields to collaborate. Indeed, criminologists are used to making sense of large ensembles of data and have developed methodologies to extract trends. They have also developed many theories that provide the hypotheses that will be tested using digital traces.

Forensic scientists seek to collect and analyse traces but also to individualize the traces they collect, that is, to assign a trace to an individual, a place or an object. Forensic scientists will, for example, try to determine who left a footmark on a crime scene or whether a bullet was shot using a specific gun. In the case that such an individualization is not possible, forensic scientists will strive to assign a trace to a broader yet still somewhat specific identified frame of entities. A partial DNA profile may be limited to a few siblings and a bullet may be traced back to a specific brand of gun rather than one gun in particular. Through this identification and classification process, forensic scientists are seeking to recognize things or classes of things. Whereas less discriminant than other characteristics, this information may lead to the identification of similarities and trends among criminal activities. Criminologists have a vast experience in this area and could help forensic scientists to take advantage of the traces they collect. Criminologists have indeed been mining official databases ever since they were created and have developed methodologies to identify significant trends. Their work with databases is perhaps more visible in life-course criminology, which seeks to build pathways of crime from its start to desistance. Forensic scientists and criminologists will need to work hand in hand to build efficient tools and methodologies to take advantage of these very rich sources of data. On the one hand, forensic scientists use traces to distinguish and identify classes of things. On the other hand, criminologists are used to distinguishing and identifying ideal types of individuals and behaviours, as well as types of crime opportunities. They may share a general approach to crime that relies on traces and the recognition of the multiple identities of things, persons or activities. Such an approach is problem-based by nature. It is where both forensic science and criminology may find their distinct identity from other sciences whether they are natural, social, information or hard sciences. Crimes and others forms of harmful activities are at the core of their concerns.

Criminologists have much to learn from their forensic science counterparts. They also have much to offer. While forensic scientists have been trying to understand offenders through the traces they generate, criminologists have been in direct contact with offenders for over a century. Sutherland was famous for hosting dinners with thieves and other offenders and even chronicled the life of a professional thief. His practice set the tone for other criminologists to source their information directly from the offenders themselves rather than from proxies like law enforcement case files. Criminologists have been able to generate highly precise information about how offenders operate, and this information would be of great use to forensic scientists. For example, many interviews have been conducted with burglars who explain each decision they make when doing burglaries. These insights would be very helpful for forensic scientists looking for traces. They could limit their action to the places where burglars are most likely to leave traces and intensify their search for traces in those areas. For forensic scientists to collect traces, they must be able to 'invent traces', i.e., infer from their understanding of the situation and their technical knowledge that a trace could exist at a certain place and be able to detect and collect it. Criminologists will play a key part in generating new insights about where to look for traces—even though that may be an unintended consequence of their research.

Criminologists can also contribute to forensic science through their study of the organizations in which forensic scientists work. There is an extensive tradition in criminology that seeks to understand how and why law enforcement agencies operate and what the best practices are when it comes to managing law enforcement investigations. Criminologists have developed many metrics that question how resources should be invested and when. An increase, for example, in the intensity of patrols may not generate an increase in the feeling of security of citizens, but a very targeted approach to patrols on crime hot spots may be much more efficient. Since it may be difficult for forensic scientists who work inside law enforcement organizations to evaluate their own, criminologists can serve as a trusted third party that can evaluate the efficiency and operations of law enforcement agencies. Criminologists have also traditionally sought to understand how other actors that generate security, such as private security firms, play a role in investigations. Criminologists have developed the nodal governance of security and have studied how this distribution of roles and responsibilities may impact the work of law enforcement agencies. Forensic scientists have been questioned about their efficiency and about whether their work really needs to be integrated into the investigative units or if outside labs could also be used to do exactly the same work. Through their analyses, criminologists can generate insights into the most efficient way to organize forensic work.

Given all the potential benefits of helping forensic scientists and criminologists to work together, we believe that efforts in this direction that build on this handbook will be of the utmost importance in the prevention and regulation of offences and offenders. Since forensic scientists and criminologists speak in many cases very different languages, it will be essential to create fora (in its etymological sense) where attention is given to the languages used so that all may feel included. These fora should include publications but also conferences, workshops and even collaboration initiatives between universities and departments. The Université de Montréal and the Université de Lausanne have a long tradition of interdisciplinary theory and practice that has now been extended in continuous exchanges of students and professors, keeping the communication going between forensic scientists and the criminologists. We believe this leads to fruitful outcomes.

The next step is perhaps to foster crossover from both disciplines. Forensic science departments could hire criminologists as faculty members to provide a different point of view on the traces they collect and analyse. Criminology departments could take advantage of forensic scientists' expertise to foster their research and help them navigate the numerous forensic trace databases that are currently being used. This model could extend beyond the academic world to also include law enforcement agencies. Already, many agencies have research labs where criminologists analyse official police data and forensic labs where police evidence is processed. There are very weak ties between these institutions and each could greatly benefit from the other's experience.

Forensic science and criminology both have a rich and long experience in the study of crime. While the two were mostly disconnected during the twentieth century, the increased sharing of knowledge and the advent of digital traces opens up new opportunities for these disciplines to collaborate. This handbook is but one example of what can be achieved when forensic scientists and criminologists collaborate. We look forward to the creation of more hybrid departments—like the one at the Université de Lausanne—to help bring both disciplines into the twenty-first century.

Index

Made in the USA
Las Vegas, NV
20 April 2026

45642809R00164